Preparation for Crisis

Preparation for Crisis: Adult Education 1945-80

D. Ben Rees

G.W. & A. Hesketh, Ormskirk & Northridge

First published 1982 by G.W. & A. Hesketh, P.O. Box 8, Aughton Street, Ormskirk, Lancashire L39 5HH, Great Britain and of 18765 Tuba Street, Northridge, California 91324, U.S.A.

Copyright © D. Ben Rees, 1981.
Design by G.W. & A. Hesketh, Ormskirk, L39 5HH.
Photosetting & Origination by Lloyd Williams, 22 Union Street, Southport.
Printed in Great Britain by A. Wheaton & Co. Ltd., Hennock Road, Exeter, EX2 8RP.

ISBN 0 905777 15 8 Paperback.

Presented in memory of
the late J.R. Ryno and Dr. Montague
Solomon, MB, CHB, MRCGP, DPH: two
loyal students in my WEA classes
at the Royal Institution,
Liverpool (1975 - 1981)

Contents

Preface and Acknowledgements

In a study which encompasses so many movements in the education of adults in England and Wales one accumulates a large number of debts and I have in the course of the book and in the bibliography mentioned those individuals who on behalf of the movements have been so helpful to my inquiries.

I owe a particular debt. to Professor Dr. Loraine Baric and her Department in the University of Salford whose stimulation and care ensured that four years of collecting, collating and writing the material ended in a PhD thesis and in this book. I am also grateful to Mr. Ken Roberts of the University of Liverpool for his comments after reading the thesis. I should say also that this study was accepted for the PhD degree in the University of Salford but that a great deal has been added to the thesis since its acceptance in December 1979, and that it was re-arranged for publication as a book in the summer of 1980.

I was most fortunate in being able to use the library facilities of the Universities of Liverpool and Salford and in particular I owe a great debt to Mr. Peter Rowley, Librarian of the Department of Extension Studies at the University of Liverpool. His kindness and knowledge of the literature of adult education is immense and I was able to make use of his bibliographical lists.

I have also made use of the William Brown Central Library, Liverpool, as well as the National Library of Wales at Aberystwyth. I have received material on adult education from Jean-Pierre Titz, Division for Out-of-School Education, Council of Europe, Strasbourg, Hywel Ceri Jones of the Adult Education Department of the EEC at Brussels, as well as from the European Centre for Leisure and Education, Prague, Czechoslovakia, and from the principals of Adult Education Centres, who belong to many of the Universities in England. Mr. J.W. Saunders of the Leeds Adult Education Centre in Middlesbrough is a good example from among those who responded to my letter sent in July 1980. I was unable to make use of all the material received but I hope to have an opportunity of writing on other issues that are relevant to the education of adults.

Very sincere thanks are due also to Professor Gwyn Williams of Trefenter, Ceredigion, Dyfed, who was kind enough to read the final draft of the thesis and J.P.M. Millar who had been the General Secretary of the NCLC read Chapter 3 in the first draft; to Mrs. Sheila Ward for her expert typing and to Dr. Gordon Hesketh of G.W. & A. Hesketh of Ormskirk for his care for this publication. Lastly, I am indebted to my wife in innumerable ways but especially for her enthusiasm for the project and her support throughout the preparation and the writing of this book.

D. Ben Rees, Liverpool

1
Trends and Topics in Adult Education

In this book we are concerned to indicate how adult education (which means the formal provision) and the education of adults (which means the informal provision) in England and Wales in the post-War period (1945-1980) increased its scope and yet to a great extent due to economic, political and sociological factors never assisted the millions of people that the Adult Education Movements (in particular the Workers Educational Association) intended to educate. The book is concerned with the theoretical and philosophical ideas of the adult educators and how these concepts have rarely been modified by facts. Adult education policies have been based on theoretical concepts and very little has been learnt from the actual situation. Education was still in the post-War period as Robert Hutchins, Head of the Centre for the Study of Democratic Institutions in Santa Barbara, California wrote in *The Learning Society*, the privilege of the few. He wrote:

> The mind of the slum child, unless he is removed from the slum long before he goes to school, will show the effects of the slum as long as he lives. His family and his neighbourhood decisively mould the child before the school has a chance. (Hutchins, 1968, p.15)

Adult education has to contend also with the environment of family, community, mores, media, advertising, propaganda, in short with the culture of society. Statistics in every country including the Soviet Union and the United States of America show the same pattern; the social or economic class or level of one's parents determines one's educational chances. "Those who have passed with the least shock into the system go farthest in it" (Hutchins, 1968, p.17). Similar results have been produced in Britain as one finds in the book *Social Mobility* edited by D.V. Glass in 1954. It showed then that the type and level of education depended very heavily upon the social status as measured in terms of occupation of the subjects' fathers. We also found in our study that so often the type and level of education one receives as a child influences his subsequent attitude towards education as an adult. He cannot escape from his early educational experience. This point will appear again in the course of the book.

But it is imperative now to be reminded that in our period (1945-1980) England and Wales witnessed a growth in adult education provision. A.H. Halsey has shown how in the years between 1945 and 1967 adult education was providing more classes and gaining more students. Table I is the evidence.

Year	No. of Classes	Registered Students
1945-6	5,050	99,333
1951	8,090	162,850
1961	8,288	164,148
1967	10,615	236,330

Table 1.1

1

In Table I there is no mention of vocational or residential courses. Halsey has also broken down the type of courses and the number of women and men taking the courses of adult education provided by responsible bodies.

Type of Courses	1951		1961		1967	
	M	W	M	W	M	W
Literature & Language	7,277	13,526	6,852	13,315	9,799	19,233
History	11,829	14,183	9,798	15,341	18,415	28,414
Geography	2,022	1,943	1,318	1,557	2,199	2,617
Social Studies	23,473	20,241	15,214	14,328	27,564	17,571
Natural Sciences & Mathematics	7,946	5,626	8,588	7,522	14,437	11,849
Music and Visual arts	9,553	15,561	10,019	19,908	12,556	25,972
Philosophy & Psychology	5,811	8,110	4,425	5,286	5,240	8,834
Other	8,236	7,513	13,369	17,308	14,735	16,895
Total	76,147	86,703	69,583	94,565	104,945	131,385

Table 1.2

These figures exclude students on residential courses, and the Literature and Language Courses include English, ancient, modern, and Welsh Language, Literature and Culture. History includes historical subjects and Archaeology. Social Studies includes political science, economics, industrial organisation and sociology. Natural Science includes physics and biological science and mathematics. Unclassified includes International and Commonwealth Affairs, Religion, Law and unclassified subjects. These figures also do not include the informal education that is carried out through voluntary organisations, clubs, societies, television, the printed word, nor does it include the work of the local education authorities which could boast in 1961 that not less than one million people were engaged in adult education in formal classes (Jessup, 1961, p.3).

All this was part of the silent revolution unleashed by the Second World War and the 1944 Education Act. Opportunities for both full time and part-time study for adults improved but as it turned out only temporarily. The Emergency Training Scheme for Teachers and the second chance higher education of all kinds were offered to returning service-men whose careers had been suspended by the War. The decision by the Labour Government in 1947 to offer State Scholarships for a small number of adult students was part of this new mood of sympathy towards adult education. For an unprecedented few years institutions of higher education enrolled a substantial number who had left school at fourteen. These temporary training schemes set precedents and patterns of attainment which were taken as evidence of the capabilities of adult students. The boom did not last but it did create a greater public awareness of

2

the need for adult education. It was assumed also that an increase in facilities for adult students would bring in more working class adults, in fact, there was no evidence for this assumption (Hopper and Osborn, 1975, p.43). To the contrary, all available evidence suggested that most of these adults came from the lower middle social class and not from the working class. It was also very evident in the next decade - the affluent fifties - that the Welfare State had not succeeded in eliminating inequalities in society, that the class system still existed, and that education including adult education had not provided equal opportunities for all. At the same time ordinary people saw their environment often being vandalised by large scale development, which, in some cities like Liverpool, has been nothing short of a serious disaster. The ways in which the clearance programmes were executed have produced an environment that has no resemblance in social terms to what existed before. It is often stated that old communities of great cultural strength have been destroyed and it is important to avoid being romantic about what has gone. While sociologists in England and Wales do not lament the passing of overcrowded houses with no bathroom, they feel sympathy for people who lamented in the sixties in our urban areas at the passing of communal solidarity. The clearances in the cities of England and Wales stacked people vertically when they had been accustomed to living horizontally and people were moved arbitrarily so that old social networks based on the family and the local meeting places (chapel, church, pub and the local shop) were disrupted. Education reports in the sixties - Crowther, Newsom, Plowden (Central Advisory Council for Education 1960, 1963, 1967) all saw the disadvantages of working class children within the educational system. The fifties and the sixties also saw the growth of pressure groups to alleviate the problems of the working classes and the disadvantaged within the working class, such as the Child Poverty Action Group, but as Tom Lovett pointed out in his pioneering study *Adult Education Community Development and the Working Class* (1975) adult education agencies such as the Workers' Educational Association was not to be found actively engaged in the forefront of this process of local self-help and dynamic community action.

Adult education it seemed had lost its enthusiastic message in the great depression as understood by R.H. Tawney and John Stocks, Vice-Chancellor of Liverpool University, who died in 1937 as he was fulfilling a Workers' Educational Association speaking engagement at Swansea (Stocks, 1970, p.163). The WEA had, in fact, moved increasingly towards the typical image of a middle class voluntary organisation, seeking a broad educational role, and though it had a special interest in the educationally underprivileged it was to a large extent unable to cope with the needs of the under privileged. Ernest Green, the General Secretary of the WEA had looked at the problem of the educationally underprivileged in the fifties. Of nearly two thousand people who participated in two questionnaires that he devised only eleven described themselves as unskilled workers (Green, 1955, p.42). At WEA conferences attempts were made to remove the offending word 'Workers' from the title of the association, a title which was called outmoded and thereby presenting a public image which was associated with the Labour Movement. This was inevitable, for within the Labour Party itself there was the same controversy. Shortly after the Labour Party's defeat in the 1955 General Election, Hugh Gaitskill, the leader, voiced the party's need to restate its aims in phrases designed to impress the rising generation (Brand, 1965, p.284). The adverse trend which was repeated in the 1959 General Election was in Hugh Gaitskill's view rooted in economic and social factors. His message had an impact within the WEA as he was a former full time WEA Tutor/Organiser. Gaitskill argued that there were fewer manual workers and more clerical, administrative and technical ones; the typical factory worker was more likely to be a skilled man in a new modern plant than an underpaid cotton operative in a dark, obsolete cotton mill. Class lines were becoming blurred. Workers were better paid, many of these people were buying homes and cars; some paid income tax and they considered themselves middle class. Anthony Crosland wrote a Fabian pamphlet in 1960, *Can Labour Win?*, in which he stated that younger voters reacted strongly against Labour's class image (Crosland, 1960, p.4). Geoffrey Rhodes who had fought two General Elections for the Labour Party agreed as he met people with an identical background to himself who would not vote Labour. "These people were young professionals with parents of largely working class background" (Rhodes, 1962, p.12). Surveys indicated that children of Labour fathers were more apt to go over to the other Party than were those of Conservative ones (Epstein, 1962, pp.136-50). Woodrow Wyatt, the Labour MP for Bosworth, went as far as to say after the Orpington Liberal by-election victory that the General Election of 1964 was going to be decided by the young, skilled white-collared who rejected Toryism and cloth-cap Labour. Wyatt favoured an electoral agreement between Labour and the Liberals *(Observer,* 18th March, 1962).

The middle class image was not only evident in the WEA but was vociferous within the political party of workers, the Labour Party. The WEA was attacked also for serving the interests of no more than 0.2% of the adult population. It was a low percentage for an organisation that claimed to 'satisfy the demands of workers for education'. To make matters worse many of its so-called students according to John Lowe knew "nothing about the aims of the Association, its organisation, history and traditions" (Lowe, 1970, p.120). This situation in time angered some of the WEA staff-tutors and this is clearly seen in the written work of Tom Lovett who was seconded by the Workers Educational Association in 1969 to join the Liverpool Educational Priority Area Project. Lovett, who had worked as a fitter and bus conductor in his native city of Belfast before he left to study at the age of 27 in Ruskin College, Oxford, does not mince his words about the WEA

Aside from its Trade Union work, the WEA is just as far removed from the working class and their problems as any other educational organisation and suffers from the same defects. The WEA seeks to 'have its cake and eat it' to be a general provider and have a special responsibility towards the 'educationally deprived' the phrases themselves are indicative of the clouded mirror through which the working class is viewed.   (Lovett, 1975, p.12).

4

Lovett saw adult education as an agent of social change and was very much influenced by the Brazilian educator, Paulo Freire and author of *Pedagogy of the Oppressed* published in New York in 1970. This attitude is sometimes called new leftism. Adult education should not help people they maintain to accept and adapt to society, but should help them to shape their society to human needs. Adult education must help individuals to grasp the idea and translate it into practice.

"School and university prepare people for existing society. Adult education prepares people to change society" (Simpson, 1972, p.155). To Paulo Freire, like Ivan Illich, schools are instruments of social control and both emphasise the impossibility of a neutral education. Freire states:

It means that no matter if we are conscious or not as educators, our praxis is either for the liberation of men - their humanisation, or for their domestication - their domination.
(Freire, 1970, p.7).

Lovett felt that this liberation, the humanisation was a possibility for the working class if adult education really involved itself, and especially if it took up the challenge.

Radical adult education for the working class is not a dream or a hope; it is a real possibility. It will require new methods and approaches allied with a radical educational and social philosophy. Above all, however, it requires dedication and a sense of realistic idealism.
(Lovett, 1975, p.153).

He came to this conclusion after being involved among working class people in the inner city area of Liverpool, in his research and development in the field of working class education. The results of his study reinforced what was known before to a large extent namely that, traditional education has failed amongst the working class long before the adult education stage and largely for the same reasons. The work of Basil Bernstein on language and class has stressed the cultural gap that does exist. But so often the resources and the initiative is lacking on behalf of the adult education movements, and more important adult education policies are rarely modified by facts. This is the key to the situation.

In my experience also, one of the neglected areas for adult education is the housing estates and the new towns. The WEA in Liverpool asked me one summer to deliver six lectures to young mothers in the new town of Skelmersdale. It was an unusual experience for the young mothers who attended with their children were interested but totally ignorant in the subject, which was Current Affairs. They had no idea who their Member of Parliament was. To the question 'How do you vote at General Elections?' the answer came - 'Labour - like the fellow!' They never watched the television news but after a few weeks attendance at the WEA classes they admitted that they were showing an interest in what was happening in the political arena of the world. These young mothers and one unemployed father who was very knowledgeable in left wing politics were literally being starved of education. At the end of this session I wrote to the Lancashire and West Cheshire WEA District Office a report and asked them to repeat the experiment. To my knowledge this was not done.

5

There is no doubt that new towns and housing estates provide a fertile field for all forms of adult education, and especially, as Sewell Harris emphasised, for "informal and exploratory adult education" (Harris, 1954, p.31). One of the best known adult education efforts on a large housing estate took place in the seventies at Leigh Park, an overspill housing estate for Portsmouth. It is important to refer to it as it re-emphasises our central thesis of the difficulty of adult education to discard its long cherished philosophies in favour of new and more relevant concepts. The results have been collated and written by Paul Fordham, Geoff Poulton, Lawrence Randle of the Department of Adult Education at the University of Southampton in *Learning Networks in Adult Education: Non formal Education on a Housing Estate* (1979). They chose to work in Leigh Park because it seemed typical of those areas in England and Wales where neither professional adult education organisers nor the voluntary enthusiasts of WEA branches had made any effective impact because of their difficulty in accepting new concepts. The whole project is very relevant therefore, as it was in the first place strongly influenced by the work of Tom Lovett and Keith Jackson in Liverpool. The members chosen to work in Leigh Park also got very involved in the community projects (that is, holiday play scheme, community newspaper and other experiments) and the whole educational process was geared to the well being of the whole community. This report suggested that:

> if adult educational resources are to be utilised by a wider section of the population, then they must be relevant, easily accessible and free from ideological constraints.
>
> (Fordham, Poulton, Randle, 1979, p.229)

They also stated their belief that the growth of adult education within an area should be ecological. It begins, in other words, where people are, and assists their intellectual, social, psychological, cultural and political growth by using their own environment as a basis for development. But even these researchers found that the people who boarded the adult education train, as they put it, were people who had in the first place self confidence and a great deal of experience of the educational process.

> The results of our survey showed that people from the estate who attended adult education classes tended to be those who had higher-status jobs, better formal educational attainment and were mobile. We suggest that this group generally had a more enhanced self-concept and probably felt that they had more control over their own lives. We further suggest that these students' experience in attending adult classes may have helped to increase their self-concept. In other words, once the educational train has been boarded, it can contribute to the individual status of the passengers and possibly increase their degree of power in making life choices. The problem for potential passengers lies in gaining sufficient confidence to board the train. (Fordham, Poulton, Randle, 1979, p.235).

Women have been persuaded to "board the train" because the curriculum is of interest to them and especially when it is relevant to their homes. As an educationalist explained:

> The most popular technical subject for women in community centres has probably been dressmaking, often with a teacher supplied by the local education authority.
>
> (Harris, 1954, p.30).

6

This happened in the period under consideration.

In 1938 men outnumbered the women in the adult classes and the trend was not reversed until 1967 when women students in adult education classes outnumbered men by nearly 30,000. Women tend on the whole to be more interested in Arts subjects and in Music while men prefer the Social Studies, though the pattern of interests changes a great deal over the years. The only exception seems to have been in the adult education of the Co-operative Movement, and it was claimed that more women at the beginning of the post-War period belonged to this adult educational agency than any other (Lewis, 1947, p.134). The basis of this work was done in the weekly Co-operative Women's guilds, but this situation did change as part of the liberation of women in British Society. Jennifer Rogers made a forceful point when she coined the phrase of 'captive wives' and the appeal of adult education. "Articles" she writes "now commonly appear in women's magazines round about September, extolling the benefit of adult education and urging women to undertake a class to stimulate their minds" (Roger, 1971, p.15).

But these points are to some extent supported in the research carried out in 1965 by Sally Pickering, who was then the Vice-Principal of the James Graham College at Leeds. She gave out a questionnaire and 89 mature women who were students at the college responded. Eighty-eight had gained a great deal, and the reasons given were as follows: Stimulating contacts (73 people); wider interests (61 people); awareness of previously unrecognised abilities (49 people); reawakened academic interests (28 people). The real test of further education is the continued interest of the student and this can best be measured by the numbers studying for further qualifications or for pleasure. Out of the hundred and seven mature women candidates trained as teachers between 1959 and 1963, nearly 77 per cent were teaching full time and a further seven per cent part time (Pickering, 1966, pp. 17-19). It is a remarkable figure compared with the wastage of the 18-21 level at conventional colleges and universities. It indicates that mature women were highly motivated in their educational studies. There is no doubt that student wastage in further education colleges and technical colleges is a huge and daunting problem. Britain, however, has a better record as far as higher education is concerned than most countries.

In Australian universities the wastage rate of 30-40 per cent was stable for most of our period, at least from 1950 to 1970 (Miller, 1970, pp.20-21).

Another trend that is noticeable in our book is that a large number of groups have a great deal done for them in adult education but in a most haphazard manner, and again with very little having been learnt from the actual situation when preparing for adult education provision. In the course of the book we will look at these groups, often ethnic minorities, and sometimes outsiders, like the gypsies, and though all these groups belong to the working class, the provision is again haphazard and depends upon the motivation of a few dedicated educators. The same difficulties are encountered among these groups who are often called disadvantaged groups as encountered by the adult education movements - that the more initial education one has received the more education one desires. This can be documented by looking at adult education in prisons. Very little provision was made for prisoners until 1923, but in 1945 the Durham Local Education Authority decided to adopt the prison at Durham as an evening institute and by the end of the year a full programme was in operation with classes ranging from economics for the men and mothercraft and music for the women. A Prison Education Advisory Committee, of which Sir Lionel Fox was the Chairman, took notice of the pioneering work in Durham and recommended in 1947 an extension of the scheme. Legal provision was made by the Education (Miscellaneous Provisions) Act 1948, and Local Authorities became responsible for all the prisons and borstals in their areas. In 1948, 600 weekly classes were provided for men, 100 for women, and by 1961 some 3,000 classes were held weekly (Nicholson, 1967, pp.83-90).

In a study of adult education among prisoners, W. Forster found that the educational experience can change attitudes and make the prisoner alienated from the prison, and if the adult prisoner comes from a poor educational background, then it can alienate him from his family and the social background that he came from. Education can make a working class prisoner feel alienated. One inmate with a middle class background confessed to Forster that his studies for an Open University degree is ". . . an expression of an alienation I already felt. I applied so that for just a few hours a week I could get away from the obscenities, the prison gossip, the scheming. A lot of us are alienated before we start this sort of thing".

The second manifestation of alienation was in the experience of those prisoners who spoke about their pre-sentence background. There seems to be some evidence for claiming that the experience of higher education makes the family relationship even more difficult. Letters suddenly seemed 'to say nothing' and in some cases inmates suddenly became critical of the spelling and syntax of letters from home (Forster, n.d., p.24). It is significant also that some of the prison inmates visited by W. Forster, of the Department of Adult Education in the University of Leicester, were intelligent enough to admit that in the curriculum there were two subjects which were 'dangerous subjects', namely Sociology and Psychology. It was felt by the prisoners that to study subjects which force you to examine your own 'deviant' personalities in such detail makes the educated inmate critically aware of his own or her immediate environment. This can be a most disconcerting experience (Forster, n.d., p.25).

Another important step that took place in the post-war period was the establishment by Reading Local Authority of an adult education centre called Katesgrove House for deprived people. It was opened in September 1970 and it faced the multiple problems of an urban area namely poverty, poor housing, poor health, large families and social and educational disadvantages. The first initial class at the Katesgrove House Centre was in homemaking and the adults were also encouraged to discuss together in an informal situation when carrying out the washing up. In this way a community was built up at the Katesgrove House. The adult education centre, however, was faced with problems of accommodation and with their motivating philosophy. There was no room to expand at Katesgrove House and this severely limited the educational work. The teachers, like their colleagues everywhere, wanted to see results (Legge, 1975, p.381), but they had to learn at Reading to approach the undertaking among the disadvantaged adults in terms of the clients' needs and the resources available. This is a lesson that most adult educators have to learn in working class communities, and is another example to support our argument that concepts are rarely modified by facts in adult education.

Working class communities suffer the lack of facilities due to the lack of leadership. In communities where there are middle class activists then there is a better chance. Most pressure groups like Shelter find themselves in the same situation as the WEA - depending upon middle class activists. A study of a Berkshire village which had 2,100 inhabitants in the middle of the nineteen sixties found the existence of three groups. Group A 'the gentry' was composed of the professionally upper middle class, Group B included most of the newcomers to the village and they were mostly ex-grammar school pupils with a few University graduates (Still, 1966, p.20). Group C was composed of skilled and unskilled manual workers. Just under a quarter of all the villagers belonged to one or more of the village organisations. There were two hundred committee places filled by 69 from Group A, 76 from Group B and 55 from Group C. But the most striking finding was that between 1957 and 1965 there was a decline of involvement of 9.5 per cent for Group A, an increase of 14 per cent for Group B and a decline of 4.5 per cent from Group C which indicated quite clearly that the middle class had taken over the organisational and cultural activities of the Berkshire village. The same pattern was to be repeated many times over in other villages and towns; in adult education centres as well as in adult education classes. Elizabeth Still's heading of 'The Middle Class takes over' summed up in a nutshell the situation as far as adult education was concerned. This only reinforces the standpoint of the radical adult educationists that adult education has great potentiality and that the failure to deliver an effective adult education service to the disadvantaged, to the working class, is a reflection of the unequal distribution of resources generally throughout British society.

The third main strand in our introductory argument is that adult education suffered throughout this period due to lack of financial resources. Though George Tomlinson, the Labour Minister of Education in the Attlee Administration, had a great deal of sympathy with adult education, in the early fifties the Conservative Minister of Education, Miss Florence Horsburgh, planned to cut in 1953 the grant for adult education, including the WEA, by ten per cent. It appears that due to pressure from the educational agencies the Prime Minister, Sir Winston Churchill, personally intervened with the result that the grant was not cut. But it was not until the mid-fifties that educational expenditure was assumed to be an economic investment. David Eccles proved a very fine Conservative Minister of Education between 1954 and 1957 and again between 1959 and 1962, and so did Edward Boyle, and the Labour Minister of Education, Anthony Crosland. All three listened to the pleadings of educational pressure groups and were sensitive to the writings of educationalists. Crosland and Boyle would not contemplate any major educational change or innovation without at least consulting Sir William Alexander, Secretary to the Association of Education Committees. But many of those involved in adult education were dissatisfied with the situation and Harold Clay, a WEA stalwart, expressed this in 1958 when he claimed that the Government had a "grudging and discouraging attitude to adult education" and that this was true of the post-war period except for the "mid nineteen-forties" (Clay, 1958, p.543). It is very difficult to disprove this contention for it seems that the adult education organisations were not able to persuade succesive governments to invest in adult education to the extent that it needed, and to be able to fully document this aspect one would need access to cabinet papers. But at least we know that the education of adults was not even given the same priority as the other aspects of the educational system, and that the responsible bodies thereby suffered.

We can also take the evidence of adult educationists who had to deal with the Ministry of Education. John Lowe noted that in 1967 a deputation from the National Institute of Adult Education in England and Wales was received by the Minister of Education. They drew attention to the crucial importance of adult education, deplored the inadequacy of State Aid, and urged the Labour Government to behave more generously. The Minister replied that he saw no evidence of a great demand for adult education and that even if such a demand were shown to exist, it did not follow that the public purse should find the money to satisfy it. The Minister of Education also asked for some evidence to be produced. It was futile for the deputation to assert that the evidence was staring him in the face, that the importance of lifelong learning was universally acknowledged and that a great deal of literature had been produced especially on the continent of Europe, for the Minister of Education in 1967 wanted to see tangible proof of the alleged demand and the work of collating the evidence had not been done then. John Lowe sounds the warning to adult education agencies that it is essential, when soliciting Government support or grant-awarding trusts for financial support, to have made a thorough and statistical plea. In other words it is essential to produce documentary evidence for the Ministry of Education (Lowe, 1971, p.79). One can surmise that it was this which was often missing in the deputations and pleas on behalf of adult education in the post-war era.

Another area of adult education that was hardly discussed in the post-war period (1945-80) was the adult student wastage. To an adult education tutor (part time or full time) with the WEA there is a great relief at the end of the first class of the session when enough students have turned up to pay their fees and enrol as members. The requirements are fair. For a twelve week class it is expected that twelve adults will register and in my experience, as a part time WEA tutor for fifteen years, there is a great deal of elasticity. If only ten adults turn up for a twelve week course then the go ahead is usually given to the WEA. Let us take an hypothetical case of a ten week WEA class and that at the first meeting ten members turn up to register. It is very unlikely that during or at the end of the ten weeks course the ten paid up members will attend every class or indeed survive the term. When asking WEA students for their experience, and even asking those who have left certain classes, one is faced with a number of factors. An obvious factor is that of change of circumstances, moving to another job or domestic illness or problems. But one can also suggest two other factors - dissatisfaction with the class itself due to dull presentation by the WEA or adult education tutor or dissatisfaction with other members of the class. Those two factors are valid ones according to a survey carried out at the City Literary Institute in London in 1967 (Jones and Glynn, 1967, pp.139-149). How one is to overcome this should be the concern of all adult education practitioners, and a number of suggestions can be put forward. The teacher's role is extremely important throughout the educational system, and this is true in the education of adult students in higher education as well as mature students in the university extra-mural, LEA or other WEA classes. This demands counselling, approachability and friendliness. Jennifer Rogers put it well when discussing counselling:

> All counselling must guarantee confidentiality, and the counsellor must be prepared to accept his client totally for what he is.   (Rogers, 1971, p.36).

Enid Hutchinson made the same plea earlier in an important article in *Adult Education* in May 1969. The tutor-counsellor, as he was designated in the seventies by the Open University, has encouraged the adult student, for he has often the capability to complete succesfully his studies. A.H. Iliffe found in 1969 at the University of Keele that students aged up to forty and even fifty years of age did as well as school leavers. In the traditional universities counselling is being accepted and this was the main plea of G.W. Miller in a very detailed analysis of student wastage published in 1970. G.W. Miller found a number of university lecturers who did not appear to welcome questions and some students were too diffident in asking them (Miller, 1970, p.160). He felt that counselling is needed for potential university students before entering a university and that it should take place in the sixth form of secondary schools. There is no doubt that adult education suffers due to the experience of people at the secondary stage, and this is a barrier to access for some individuals. Some people were unable in the post-war period to cope with their early compulsory education and the consequences have pursued them into adulthood limiting their desire to seek and their capacity to perceive further educational opportunities. To other adults the system appears to retain the learning barriers they previously found insuperable and, regardless of a desire to improve their knowledge or broaden their skills, they continue to shy away from the educational process. Motivation appears to be inhibited by fear of the

11

same failure experienced in the primary and secondary educational system.

More and more educationalists came to accept the need for a new approach to the education of adults in the post-war period but it was not possible to overcome the conservatism of adult educationists. We will look in Chapter 2 at the different theories, Lifelong Learning, Continuing Education, Permanent Education and Recurrent Education. But all these theorists would agree with one of the findings of the Parliamentary Commission of the Commonwealth of Australia in their Report (Volume i) of April 1974 on *Technical and Further Education in Australia*

> ... Formal schooling alone to the age of 15 or 16 is unlikely to educate a person for a lifetime, especially as the pace of technological and social change appears to be increasing and affecting the nature and structure of occupations. (Canberra, 1975, p. XXIV).

The demand for education throughout life was proclaimed by few philosophers of adult education in the post-war period, not only because of changes in technologies and social organisation but also because people were becoming increasingly aware of the practical advantages that the individual received in respect of employment and livelihood.

The concept of the learning society was a concept that one came across in some educational writings at the end of the second World War like the writings of Sir Richard Livingstone. It was also the concept that we found at the end of our period in 1980. But this time it was becoming much more fashionable to discuss the concept of the learning society especially with the advent and success of the Open University. The vision was held by a few academics of a society where lifelong continuing education is the norm, where both education and work are so organised as to permit people of all ages to transfer as their needs require between one and the other, where education is measured in terms of fully developed people rather than by formal evidence of the acquisition of knowledge, where the educational system emphasises learning rather than teaching and produces self motivated people equipped with the basic skill of learning, where enthusiasm for learning is kindled and not extinguished by an education that many felt to be irrelevant, and where the gap between the educated who became more educated and the uneducated who have not acquired the skills of learning is reduced. Different educational systems will remain but barriers between them will be abolished, as will the barriers between formal and non-formal education. It envisages not equal treatment for everyone, within the existing system where merit is a criterion and a password, but the provision for each individual of a suitable education at an appropriate place and time. Continuing education, permanent education, recurrent education, all become a necessity to enable the individual to cope with a rate of change in modern society. Change whether technological or social is continually opening up new directions. It is envisaged in these philosophies that there should be ample educational opportunities for those who desire to repair, as often as necessary, insufficiencies of their initial education. They should also be able to add to, or replenish, their education. Where and when the replenishment takes place should be a matter for the individual. All that the adult educational system should do is to try and ensure that there is an opportunity available. This would have far reaching consequences if it was accepted but the signs were not at all hopeful due to practical and economic difficulties that England and Wales would see these concepts being put into practice.

Many educationists still thought at the end of the seventies that recurrent education and other allied philosophies were thought of as a part-time study - in the student's own time or partly in the employers' own time. But one will see in the course of this book that some adults will best be served by returning full-time to formal teaching institutions for a period. This would require much more flexibility of working time than British industry has known in the post-war period. But one cannot envisage continuing education being successful without the flexibility of working life and flexibility of approach by adult educational agencies. Many European countries took this seriously in the seventies. Substantial numbers of West German workers are entitled to recurrent paid leave for civic and general as well as vocational education. The French Law of the 16th of July 1971 on continuous vocational training within the framework of recurrent education, the first general national legislation of this kind in any Western country. Belgium and Luxembourg both passed laws on paid educational leave in 1973. In Sweden the least educated have tended to use traditional forms of recurrent education least, and the Swedish bill pin-pointed this group as the one to which priority should be given (Fogarty, 1975, p.110). In England and Wales we lagged far behind and this book will indicate our efforts, our provision and our haphazard, diversified approach as an industrialised nation to the world of adult education. But the main theme that will come out of our study is that in this period the old concepts of liberal adult education and workers education were still being pursued by adult educational agencies and how these concepts should have been either discarded or modified in face of new technological or social changes. Those adults who needed more adult education were still outside the system while those who had good schooling and college education were being catered for. It is basically an account of how the middle classes took over adult education, and how adult educational concepts were not adapted to the actual situation. It is fair to point out that this happened also in all kinds of organisations including the Labour Party that represented the working class in Parliament. In the 1959 General Election of its 621 candidates 129 were sponsored by Trade Unions but the great majority were such middle-class men as educators, lawyers, and journalists (Brand, 1965, p.285). The experience of education at an advanced stage seems to be a key factor. Even the students who fail in higher education carry on with education. Many of them as we find out in Michael Kendall's study are successful and do succeed in practising what is often envisaged in the concept of recurrent education. Michael Kendall of the Research Unit for Student Problems decided to survey two groups of students, a four year entry to the University College, London (1948-51) and a three year entry to the

University of Liverpool (1947-49). Postal questionnaires were sent out to nearly 1,400 students in 1962 and the overall response was about 50 per cent. The main finding of this survey was that a majority of the men made some attempt to gain a higher qualification. Most were successful and half of the remainder were still studying by the time of completing their questionnaire (Kendall, 1964, p.406). This is borne out more than once in the course of our study.

2
Defining the Theme

1 The philosophical argument

Adult education has suffered throughout its history from a lack of a concise definition. It is a tremendous, complicated story with a large number of philosophers propounding their different theories. Our task is to unfold aspects of adult education in England and Wales over a period of thirty-five years in the context of the concepts that were important in adult education and those who had written about adult education theories such as Continuing Education.

The period between 1945 and 1980 saw an unprecedented growth in the formal provision of adult education as well as in the informal education that is associated in the main with the mass media. Our interest is to map the course and to detect the influences that were at work. We are conscious of the immense field, and that we can only refer briefly to all of the movements involved in the adult education process. The growth in all aspects of education has been immense as W. Kenneth Richmond rightly points out at the beginning of the seventies:

> So far as education is concerned, the past quarter of a century (1945-1970) has been a period
> of unprecedented growth and expansion. (Richmond, 1972, p.2).

While the growth has been immense the philosophical thinking behind adult education has been varied, sporadic and very uneven. Economic, political and sociological factors have been responsible for the trends and growth in adult education as the theories of adult educators. Some would argue that the educators have lagged behind and sounded a very unclear and uncertain note, but this criticism is not wholly substantiated, as we intend to point in this detailed evaluation.

The greatest difficulty is that of defining adult education. At the beginning of our period C.R. Morris could say dogmatically:

> I make no apology, when speaking of the aims of adult education, in talking about
> education in the highest kind - education in the sense in which the great philosophers and the
> great educators have talked about it. I believe that adult education is either that or nothing.
> (Morris, 1945, p.88).

Long before the end of our period, however, John Lowe argued that adult education was an "unhappy term" and one has to agree with him (Lowe, 1970, p.25). Adult education did not seem to motivate working class people who were largely untouched by the provisions prepared for them by the responsible bodies, and these bodies were also unable to take advantage of a new era. While it is impossible to describe the work carried out by the WEA; university extramural departments; trade union movement; local education authorities without using the words adult education, we propose to mention briefly what one can call the education of adults, which takes into account the haphazard provision that is provided by voluntary agencies of all kinds as well as the educational provision of the mass media, through television, radio, newspapers, magazines and books.

But long before 1980 other educational concepts were attached to adult education, philosophical concepts of adult education that had been formulated and put into practice in a number of nations. England and Wales were dragging behind and unwilling in the main to accept even the adult philosophical jargon. Permanent education sounded too formal in English usage besides being an uncomfortable reminder that the term is of French invention. Recurrent education and lifelong learning were also terms accepted by some adult educationists and not by others. Continuous education seemed to be the term most widely accepted for it was a concept that had been written upon by a few in Britain since the Second World War. The philosopher who was responsible for this more than anybody else was Sir Richard Winn Livingstone (1880-1960) whose books are extremely important in the British context and some of his ideas were accepted. Livingstone received his inspiration and gained his model from the continent of Europe. To Sir Richard W. Livingstone adult education was the important stage in the educational system. The philosophers of education had largely devoted their energies to the education of the child and had forgotten Frederick Denison Maurice's point in the nineteenth century that adult education should precede all other branches of education. The efforts in the middle ages and the early universities to F.D. Maurice were all preoccupied with the education of adults and firmly entrenched in the belief that this was their mission.

Sir Richard Livingstone was concerned with a large number of important concepts. He felt that education had not been neglected but that the schools in the main were ignoring an educational principle which could be rectified in the education of adults. As this point is valid in the philosophy of lifelong education one can quote what Livingstone wrote in his classic *The Future in Education:*

> That almost any subject is studied with much more interest and intelligence by those who know something of its subject-matter than by those who do not; and, conversely, that it is not profitable to study theory without some practical experience of the facts to which it relates. (Livingstone, 1941, p.6).

To Livingstone as a scholar immersed in the classics there were many subjects (such as politics and ethics) which could only be taught in adult education. Sir Richard Livingstone was in favour of raising the school leaving age which at that time was fourteen. It meant "intellectual death" (Livingstone, 1941, p.4). He also criticised the schools for providing for the minority who attended universities and to him the future pattern should include   a. raising school leaving age   b. secondary education to all and   c. to strive for the education of the masses of the nation.

Livingstone's blueprint was continuing education, and he specially commended the example of the Danish Folk High School or as he called it the Danish People's High School, where adults attended during the winter months, and young women during the summer months. Livingstone expands:

> It has reached the very classes for which we have done little or nothing. It has taught them to care for subjects like history and literature which seem remote from the man in the street. It has transformed the country economically, given it a spiritual unity, and produced perhaps the only educated democracy in the world. (Livingstone, 1941, p.44).

The Danish People's High School was unique. It was a force quite unlike anything in Britain and the only comparable institutions were the residential adult colleges such as Coleg Harlech in Wales and Woodbrooke College in England. Britain during the Second World War had nine residential colleges in a country of forty-four and a half million, while Denmark had fifty-seven for a population of three and a half million.

Livingstone saw the success of the People's High School in the light of continuing education. It was fundamentally a school for adults. Secondly the movement in Denmark emphasised residential life. The summer schools were important where adults lived together for three to five months wholly steeped in the atmosphere of education. Danish adult education was essentially social. R.W. Livingstone stresses this:

> I do not think that we shall succeed in developing adult education unless we make it more social. (Livingstone, 1941, p.52).

Livingstone's dream was the development of residential colleges which he called the "Oxford and Cambridge of the poor man". He doubted if any voluntary nation-wide system of adult education was possible without residential education, and due to these powerful arguments there arose as we will see a general movement after the end of the second world war towards the establishment of residential colleges. By 1948 there were already more than a dozen in England and twenty years later there were around thirty colleges available for short-term residential adult education. Livingstone thirdly saw the Danish Model as a moral and spiritual force. He said:

> Their aim was not to impart knowledge but to awake intelligence and idealism. (Livingstone, 1941, p.56).

The People's High School movement had influenced Denmark in three ways:

i   individual
ii   economic
iii political

But Livingstone had to admit that the People's High School movement had made little progress in the towns and only ten per cent of the students came from the urban areas. Britain after all was an industrialised country and R.W. Livingstone does not deal in sufficient depth with the need to reach the adults who lived in urban areas; a deficiency that adult education agencies were

17

unable to tackle because of their inability to adopt the newer ideas that Livingstone in particular touched upon.

Sir Richard W. Livingstone is very important in the history of adult education in England and Wales as it was he above all who introduced the concept of life-long education to Britain. We shall see how this concept was largely ignored for a long time but that does not diminish his importance as a philosopher of adult education and it reinforces our central thesis. Livingstone believed that the time spent at school was normally wasted in the case of most children if the object of all the effort was to learn, that is acquiring knowledge.

> The main object of school is acquiring good habits - the habits and virtues necessary for living life well. *(Livingstone, 1954, p.6)*.

The majority of teachers and educational policy teachers chose to ignore the important argument of Livingstone at the Second Vaughan Memorial Lecture delivered at Doncaster in 1954. This is understandable in many ways for the twentieth century was to be the century of the child. The century of the school-child we may call it with greater accuracy but it is hotly argued by many if the schools have successfully integrated these children into adult society. It seems in this study that Britain had no alternative in 1980 but of merging the school educational system with the concept propounded thirty years earlier by Sir R.W. Livingstone. But there were no actual indications that this was going to happen from central or local government or from the syllabuses of the responsible bodies. Studies that were conducted in different parts of Europe in the seventies reiterated the arguments of Sir R.W. Livingstone. The place of the school has to be considered in the concept of continuing education, for after all the schools provide the basic education for most adults. Primary education has never been looked upon as an integrative factor but as an end in itself. To many adults their future attitude towards education is based on their happy or unhappy memories of primary and secondary schools. Sir R.W. Livingstone argued for the setting up of citizen centres for adult education and not to try and use the school premises for adult education work:

> Schools are built and equipped for children. They do not offer a suitable environment for the individual and social development of adults (Livingstone, 1943, p.3)

He was willing for the use of school halls and gymnasiums, but goes on to warn of the danger that was totally ignored in the provision of adult education by the local education authorities:

> But total, or even large, reliance upon schools for the purposes of adult education would invite the ruin of the scheme. (Livingstone, 1943, p.9).

Livingstone saw the proposed citizen centres for adult education in the light of the educational work of the settlements movement, which again owed so much to the ideas of F.D. Maurice and the christian socialist movement. The educational settlements saw their task in integrating the individual with society, and to do this, one needed living and learning. But a common hearth was essential which had lecture room, discussion rooms, library, canteen and if possible concert halls and theatres. A warden was also an asset. The writers of the pamphlet pointed out that the proposed adult centres would have no stereotyped system and they should not be too large. A centre to cater for seven to eight hundred adults would be ideal.

The pamphlet *Citizen Centres for Adult Education* spelt out that once the process had begun it "must be both continuous and progressive" *(Citizen Centres for Adult Education,* 1943, p.3). One of the fundamental points that needs to be stressed in adult education was respect for the adult learner. The war-time development of adult education in the army taught an invaluable lesson to adult tutors and education. The scheme known as ABCA (Army Bureau of Current Affairs) was based not on a teaching method but on a discussional technique.

The important pamphlet that Sir R.W. Livingstone had written a foreword to emphasise that the interests of adults are different and cannot be treated in the same way as the interests of children. The whole scheme which was launched in 1943 was ignored completely by the local and national government. It seems to us at the end of the period - in the eighties - that if the educational scheme first propounded in 1943 had been put into operation the adult education scene would have been transformed.

They envisaged a building which would have been in a convenient place for the area. It would have been an attractive building and the local education authority and the Voluntary Bodies (aided from the Board of Education) would be responsible for the Centre. The authors of the report make an important point when they claim that

> English education has too long suffered from the fact that the Board of Education is almost entirely preoccupied with administration; the mistake must not be repeated when adult education is put on to a truly national basis.
> *(Citizen Centres for Adult Education,* 1943, p.21)

The report envisaged a centre for every 70,000 in the urban areas, and one per 10,000 in the rural areas, and this would mean between 500 and 1,000 centres.

Sir R.W. Livingstone was a classicist who drew his inspiration from the ancient world of Greece. Its philosophy and Plato in particular gave him the ideas of continuing education. To Livingstone Plato was the parent of adult education (Livingstone, 1944, p.7). Plato did not hold the view that education could be completed at school or at university. To him the ruling class could only reach the climax of their education at the age of fifty and even then continued to divide their lives between action and thought, the world and the study. Livingstone also received inspiration from one of the foremost of the English poets John Milton (1608-1674) and a voracious student, who traced the initial cause of his blindness to his having, from his twelfth year, rarely quitted his books before midnight. In 1644 Milton published one of his best known pamphlets *Of Education,* where he gave a large place to all kinds of science as well as the ancient classics. Milton was Platonic - "to know God aright and out of that knowledge to love him, to imitate him, to be like him, by possessing our souls of true virtue" (Livingstone, 1944, p.12). Milton and Matthew Arnold agreed with Plato's definition of education as "training to goodness". Livingstone felt that the English type of education lacked the breadth of the Platonic ideal of continuing education:

> We go about education in the English fashion, meeting immediate needs, feeling our way, unguided by any very exact aim; like some low, though efficient, type of organism, which adapts itself subconsciously to its immediate surroundings.   (Livingstone, 1944, p.13).

Livingstone felt that there were a number of people who were responsible for driving "our ships out of its course". The first culprit was the French-Swiss moralist Jean Jacques Rousseau (1712-1778) who wrote *Emile,* which has often been called the charter of childhood. Rousseau stressed the importance of helping children to grow and develop naturally and he started a revolution in educational theory. Livingstone also placed blame on twentieth century psychology and American pragmatism, meaning no doubt on the last score the educational writings of one of Rousseau's illustrious followers, John Dewey (1859-1952). The basic weakness of Rousseau and his followers was that the theory started with the child and not with the adult.

Livingstone could discern three other influences which had affected education. There was the accumulation of knowledge, the need to earn a living and the development of science and technology. All this in his opinion tended to give a special direction to education. But like a good Platonist he returns to the master who had advanced views on the role of adult education and maintains that no one can deny the words of Plato - "The noblest of all studies is what man is and how he should live" (Livingstone, 1944, pp.26-27).

Livingstone's diagnosis was far-reaching and in the British context he was the pioneer of the concept of continuing education. His life and work refutes W. Kenneth Richmond's unfair criticism of the period 1945-70 as an "age of big ideas and little men" (Richmond, 1972, p.4).

Sir Richard W. Livingstone embodied also other aspects of the philosophy of adult education as we shall presently see as we take a broad look at the various philosophical standpoints that have belonged to the education of adults in England and Wales in the years between 1945 and 1980.

I   The Christian Spiritual Approach

. This approach has in the past had many philosophers. Albert Mansbridge was inspired to start the Workers Educational Association by the spiritual values of education rather than any feeling of class solidarity. His main supporters were all similarly inspired, and a good example would be the Anglican Church leader William Temple, who for a short time during the Second World War occupied the ancient see of Canterbury. Bishop J.W.C. Wand summed up the late Archbishop William Temple's adult education message in a public lecture delivered at King's College, London, in 1958 by saying:

> To him his work with the WEA was not just another job; it was not even just an outlet for a laudable desire to help his fellow-men or to spread the light of learning. It was a genuine expression of his religion, and he thought of it in religious terms. WEA itself was a kind of sacrament in which the organisation was the outward sign, and the inward grace was the pursuit of knowledge and brotherhood. (Wand, 1958, p.36).

A great number of movements which provided education for adults' organisations have a Christian base (that is, the Young Men's Christian Association and the Young Womens' Christian Association) or belong to the Christian denominations. The important and valuable educational work of the Sisters of Notre Dame has not changed since the early nineteenth century because every sister of the Order agrees with the Blessed Julie Billiart's definition of adult education in 1815:

> There can be no true education which is not wholly directed to man's last end and that in the present order of providence . . . there can be no ideally perfect education which is not Christian education. (Linscott, 1960, p.294)

The adult educationist who embodied this approach more than anyone else in the post-war period was Sir Richard Winn Livingstone whom we have already studied in relationship to his pioneering work on the need for continuing education, as outlined in the classic, *The Future in Education.* Fifty thousand copies were sold and as the *Times Education Supplement* rightly pointed out in 1941 it "may well re-orient all our thought". Livingstone felt that adult education should be an inspiring force like the Danish People's High School founded in 1844 with a strong and passionate spiritual emphasis.

Sir Richard W. Livingstone has had his disciples and to some extent the work of the Christian Churches is an assertion of the need to give adults spiritual guidance. Theological education is an important part of higher education in England and Wales and theological colleges have always had mature students among its candidates for the Christian Ministry. Many of the theological college staff are very involved in adult education and this is specially true in the Welsh context. Principal Rev. Dr. Pennar Davies of the Swansea (Welsh Congregationalist) Memorial College and his counterpart at the Aberystwyth United Theological College (Presbyterian Church of Wales) Principal Rve. S.I. Enoch in the sixties were every winter tutors for the University Extra-Mural Departments. The individual Christian denominations have always given a great deal of emphasis on educating its members and a continuing on going process is being undertaken throughout the year in the most active churches, especially in urban areas. The Sunday School movement in Wales has always catered for adults and the annual Sunday School Summer School at Aberystwyth attracts young people as well as adults of all ages. It all indicates that the Christian Spiritualist approach has still a great deal to offer in the education of adults.

II   The vocational approach in adult education

The role of vocational education has been regarded as part of the adult education scene since man began to see that training, information and knowledge is essential to cope with new discoveries and technologies. But in the post-war period a new trend appeared, and that was the emphases within the traditional responsible bodies for adult education to provide the skills and the information needed by adults to enrich their lives and to cope with their environment. Even within the Extra-Mural Departments or Adult Education Departments (which had for decades been catering for liberal adult education) this new trend of providing technological expertise for adults was very evident. This will be looked at again in our chapter on adult education in the seventies but it is sufficient at this stage to state that this trend was worrying some adult educationists while for others it was a trend that had to be welcomed and even extended. It seems that adults wanted vocational training and to possess certificates, diplomas and even as the Open University has demonstrated, degrees. A well-known adult educationist - Allaway who supported this trend wrote of the value of certificate courses:

> There is a greater keeness and enthusiasm amongst those preparing for awards than amongst other students. This is not to say that the condition of non-certificate courses is unsatisfactory but rather than in Certificate Courses it is really excellent
>
> (Allaway, 1967, p.46).

The outcome of this trend was to some a 'Diploma Disease' to borrow Ronald Dore's title of a book published in 1976. It also meant to these same people that the process of schooling becomes preoccupied with passing examinations in order to gain paper qualifications which becomes progressively devalued as competition for top jobs in the labour market intensified. In this process John Dewey's concept of education as "all one with living" virtually disappears.

By the end of our period, a university had been established and had operated for a decade, namely the Open University, which provided courses for a sizeable section who felt the need for vocational training. A few adult educationists, like Dr. W.E. Styler of the University of Hull, felt that the 'part-time degree' was the missing element in adult education (Simpson, 1972, p.106). Adult educationists agencies are slow to respond as a rule as we maintain in this book and this was the case with regard to innovations. The development of vocational adult education lacked its philosophers, but its methods and training in skills were needed for the workers' interest in education of the kind which promotes and involves rapidity of reaction to stimuli, sensitivity, and creativity (Simpson, 1972, p.111). Adult education was to be relevant, realistic and practical, and from this came the demand for career orientated adult education, and a willingness to respond to it from some of the adult education organisations.

III   The ideal of liberal education

The history of adult education in England and Wales had largely of necessity been a history of liberal adult education. A contemporary adult educationist puts it well:

> It is not by chance that the liberal tradition is associated with the cause of adult education for adults come for education precisely in order to be freed from the ignorance in which primary and even secondary education has left them.   (Barratt-Brown, 1972, p.140).

Amongst the many recommendations of the Smith Report of 1919 were the following:

> That the provision of a liberal education for adults should be regarded by universities as a normal and necessary part of their functions.

The growth of the University extra-mural departments and the W.E.A. in the inter-war years was largely carried out as providers of liberal adult education. Some commentators even claimed that the movement in the direction of democracy in England and Wales in the first half of the twentieth century had been smooth and peaceful due largely to developments in adult education (Robinson, 1955, pp.101-110).

What is a liberal adult education? Sir Richard Winn Livingstone wrote extensively and gave the background from Greek literature. "To understand it", he said, "we must imagine ourselves in the Greek world where the great distinction was between free men and slaves, and a liberal education was the education fitted to a free citizen" (Livingstone, 1945, p.68). The free man was to be a complete man and the only way possible for a breadwinner to become a complete man was for him to receive the knowledge necessary for living as well as the chance to develop his gifts and faculties of human nature. Man had a two-fold task in life: to earn a living and to be a man. Education had to recognise this and help each man to achieve his goal, of what a man ought to be. Sir Richard Livingstone defined liberal adult education in a nutshell:

> That was the meaning of a liberal education, and that is the aim - the making of men; and clearly it is different from a technical education which simply enables us to earn our bread, but does not make us complete human beings.   (Livingstone, 1945, p.69).

Livingstone realises that the phrase 'complete human beings' needs a further definition, and as a classicial scholar he finds his support in the Greek heritage. The Greek stressed that human beings have bodies, minds and characters and that each part has to be trained so as to 'excel'. Livingstone goes on to state:

> This trinity of body, mind and character in man: man's aim, besides earning his living, is to make the most of all three, to have as good a mind, body and character as possible; and a liberal education, a free man's education, is to help him to do this; not because a sound body, mind and character help to success, or even because they help to happiness, but because they are good things in themselves, and because what is good is worth-while, simply because it is good. So we get that clear and important distinction between technical education which aims at earning a living or making money or at some narrowly, practical skill, and the free man's character which aims at producing as perfect and complete a human being as may be.   (Livingstone, 1945, pp.69-70).

Livingstone then analyses the content of liberal education - the study of the material universe is a necessity and so is the study of man as a sentient, thinking and spiritual being. Great emphasis is placed on the sciences as well as on literature and history.

On the practical side one is faced with the tremendous amount of liberal adult education that was witnessed in the period between 1945 and 1970, and one particular aspect was the encouragement given to the Arts. The Council for the encouragement of Music and the Arts was set up in 1939 to raise public morale in the provinces and to re-deploy the orchestras and theatre companies which had been temporarily ousted from London. So effectively did it function that the Labour Government decided to make it a permanent organisation under the name of the Arts Council. W.E. Williams, who was a key figure in the growth of the Arts Council, stressed that the duty of the movement to take literature and culture to the people, and also to safeguard the professional standards before every other consideration. He added, "it is no good subsidising mediocrity" (W.E. Williams, 1963, p.25). But W.E. Williams had to admit in the sixties that the local authorities could not invest more in culture because the financial restrictions are always in the background.

The ideal of liberal education permeated the thought and action of the WEA from its inception at the beginning of the twentieth century. Max Adler regarded the "rise of the working class in Britain" as part of a "silent revolution", and his over-optimistic picture of the ordinary man and woman who were to be served by the WEA has a grain of truth in its generalisation:

> More and more working class people will be given the mental tools of discovering the spiritual inheritance of the nation and of mankind. Many of them exchange already beer for books, and dogs for concerts. Thus, the defence of the middle class status in the field of culture is being undermined all the time. (Adler, 1949, p.150).

The WEA, however, prided itself in the work it achieved on behalf of the working class and a product of the Lancashire working class, George Tomlinson, expressed the philosophy of liberal adult education admirably as Minister of Education in a House of Commons' debate on the 31st July 1947:

> I want the factory worker to be interested in literature, music and the arts. I want a scheme of education embracing technical and other spheres which will give the person engaged in industry an opportunity for utilising such knowledge for his own advancement.

Tomlinson added a warning that would have been echoed by R.H. Tawney, G.H. Douglas Cole and every adult educationist imbued with the liberal adult education philosophy:

> For I hold the view that just as the individual dies when he ceases to learn, so does the nation.

Our discussion on liberal education would not be complete without mentioning one of the four classic documents of English adult education, *Learning and Working* by Frederick Denison Maurice. Maurice's immediate concern in the writing and delivery, in 1854, of the six lectures which constitute the main part of the book was to gain support for the proposal of himself and some of his friends to establish a workingmen's college in London. But he asks questions which still in our period have not been fully answered.

Maurice pleaded for 'liberal' education for workers, but it was his conviction that the material for this education is to be found in daily experience and everyday work. Time and time again F.D. Maurice reverted to this theme in *Learning and Working,* and all that he had to say about it became very relevant in our generation: the question of the relation between study and work, 'liberal' and 'vocational' adult education. In the twentieth century the WEA and the university extra-mural departments devoted their resources almost exclusively to promoting 'the liberal education of adults', largely in consequence of grant regulations of the Board and Ministry of Education and at the end of our period the Department of Education and Science, which restricted the use of grants to this work. Maurice would not have agreed with this for his book *Learning and Working,* is a plea for an association of vocational and liberal education. He was as interested in vocational as in liberal education. But in the post-war period this standpoint was not accepted and those extra-mural departments who provided training courses and vocational studies were frowned upon and a considerable amount of controversy was provoked in adult education journals. It is another example of our main thesis - how some educational concepts (in particular liberal education) dictated the course of events in the adult education world, while other concepts (continuing education) which had developed to meet the social changes were not acceptable to Government or responsible bodies.

IV   Social Adult Education

Leisure has increased since 1945 to all workers in England and Wales though it is a well-known fact that an increasing number of people used their leisure to work overtime in the sixties and seventies and also imitated the american practice of having a second job. So the so-called 'problem of leisure' is certainly not the problem of people kicking their heels on street corners. For leisure has taken over to a large extent the hallowed place given at one time to work. The 'Socialist Gospel of Work' preached by the early Independent Labour Party is no longer attractive to the rank and file in the trade union movement who realise that boredom and monotony can only be satisfied by a substantial pay packet at the end of the working week.

The majority of workers are not expected to respond to their task in a creative manner as in the days of the craftsman or to show imaginative skill. The decline in work satisfaction has gone hand in hand with a general disappearance of what has been called the protestant ethic, whereby, in a sense, leisure was regarded as merely what was left over after a satisfying day's work which could easily have started at 6.00 a.m. and finished at 6.00 p.m. It was a licensed relaxation from the purposefulness which had been manifested in the everday work task. Indeed the populist movements which won greater leisure for the masses were never sure or certain what this would entail in the long run.

25

Karl Marx thought it would be "the space for human development", while Proudhon prophesied that it would be used "for free composition and popular astronomy".

The truth is that the new leisure has evolved an entirely new pattern, and given a new dimension to the education of adults. The home has become a centre of educational activity, and courses which assist in any way the home life have become extremely popular. Affluence has been of great impetus in this, as it opened up possibilities of courses which taught people how to do things for themselves. Home decoration, the use of new hand power tools, or of new materials and pigments - foam-rubber, polystyrene, fur-fibre and fibre glass, the maintenance of the family car or cars, these are a few of the numerous courses that have been introduced in local education evening institutes and in the curriculum of adult education centres.

Changes in the social class structure have also contributed, since allied with the subjects mentioned already there are many others which are useful in the search for social prestige, and in climbing the social ladder. The voluntary organisations like the Women's Institutes and the Townswomen's Guilds have come into their own in this way, with courses and demonstration in fashion designs, the making of clothes and the appreciation of style. Even Christian Churches have taken on occasionally the same popular arrangement as shown by the secular movements. Courses in flower arranging, in elegant speech, public speaking, etiquette have all been in the calendar of events of many of the organisations which fulfil social education among adults.

The affluence of the post-war period has meant also that the well-established voluntary movements like the Women's Institutes have been joined by other voluntary movements which have come into being to fulfil a specific purpose. The post-war period has witnessed a spectacular rise in these clubs, such as yachting clubs, stamp-collecting clubs, bridge clubs, local history societies, folklore societies and societies which cater for wild life, travelling, riding skiing, small boat sailing, the collection of antique procelain, silver or furniture, coin collecting, knowledge of flora and fauna, and an unending list. The occult became in the late sixties a subject on the WEA syllabuses in centres like Liverpool and London.

What are our assessment and valuation of the social education that has so far been listed? Is it more than snobbery or social rat-racing? Or are we in adult education waking up to the fact that every activity that enriches an individual or his family is a worth-while experiment? What are the places of other informal agencies in this social education, such as the flourishing women's magazines, and indeed what is the influence of the government in its policies which have a bearing on social education? A campaign launched by the Government on health education or on saving energy is part of a campaign to educate adults. How are the influences evaluated?

One must also ask what are the motives that bring people to a movement or organisation that caters for people's needs. It can be argued that whatever the motives are an informed, dedicated educator can make the class or tutorial a vehicle of true education.

One cannot but point again to the influence of Sir Richard Livingstone on the concept of social adult education. It was he who gave the Women's Institute Movement the necessary intellectual confidence to embark on their most adventurous step of establishing a residential college for its members. Sir Richard Livingstone was recognised as the intellectual mentor by being invited by the National Federation of Women's Institutes in 1948 to open the residential college, known as Denman College.

Sir Richard Livingstone at the opening service reiterated succinctly what has become the philosophy of social adult education. Livingstone said that the business of education was to help people to do the things they wanted to do, but could not without help:

> Read books, enjoy music and art, grow flowers and vegetables, decorate a house, do needlework, bring up children, understand engines or the stars, and much else.
> (Kay, 1970, p.48).

He continued:

> Many people do not, or cannot, learn at school. Anyhow, we discover new interests and needs in later life and want help to pursue them.
> (Kay, 1970, p.48).

This idealism was put into practice at Denman College and throughout the country in the post-war period. Amongst the practical courses and academic courses immediately instituted at Denman College in 1949 for the ordinary members ('A' Courses) one gets an idea of the usual syllabuses of social adult education: Catering, Home Management, Gardening, Fruit Preservation, Soft Toy Making, Smocking, and Nature Lovers' Courses. Academic courses included, Books and Music, The Victorian Age, and Feeding the Hungry People (Kay, 1970, p.55). Many adult educationists were slow to make use of this new development for a long time, and the bulk of the work was left to the voluntary organisations and then the local education authorities.

V   New concepts of Adult Education

We have already seen how some adult education philosophers like Sir Richard Winn Livingstone were writing during the second world war on the need for a new approach to the education of adults in Britain. His plea and plans were listened to by many but in the main they were discarded. The new concepts which became known in the sixties and seventies were usually the result of experiments in other countries and as Richard Livingstone was inspired by Denmark it seems that in Britain educationists were also inspired by american adult education philosophers like Cyril O. Houle, canadian adult education philosophers (For example, J.R. Kidd) and french adult education philosophers (for example, Paul Lengrand).

But there are sociological and cultural reasons why a new concept of adult education was needed in the context of the United Kingdom. Society was undergoing a fundamental change and the needs of individuals were also different to that of their fathers or grandfathers.

British society was no more a static hierarchical society. It was a changing society which received different labels. It was called the mass society; the post industrial society; the informed society, the consumer society, the functional society. Each label was relevant. But it also received another label, the learning society. This label deserves some attention for it emphasised the right to education arising out of democratic ideas. "Education came to be regarded as a necessity to the state because it seemed to be the path to prosperity and power" (Hutchins, 1968, p.5). The problem confronted educators - how to educate everybody.

> For centuries, the west believed that the attempt to educate everybody must end in the education of nobody; the task would be so great and the differences in ability so confusing that the dilution or dissolution of any intelligible program was inevitable.
>
> (Hutchins, 1968, p.11).

But this resulted in the belief that all men are educable but some are given better opportunities than others due to their social rank, or their ability to pay, or due to the place where you live. It was realised also in Britain that some countries were much more successful than others in the task of educating the educable. It seemed that the Communist countries and in particular Russia and China were very successful. The Russian experience had knocked on the head the notion that only a few can understand difficult subjects. This was true also in China as the 'Red' Dean of Canterbury, Dr. Hewlett Johnson was very fond of reminding the British public. But in Britain the idea was still around that only the few could be educated, and education was still the privilege of the few. Environment was a very powerful and influential factor.

But there was blame also on the initial education in the schools of England and Wales. Studies of streamed children in English primary schools showed not only that more middle class children were put in the highest stream than were entitled to - but also that working class children in a low stream were actually duller at the age of eleven than when their parents handed them over at the age of five (Jackson, 1964, pp.144-45). Education has to contend with society and its cultural aspects as well as with the social and economic class of one's family.

This situation led a number of education philosophers to question the traditional curriculum of primary schools and also secondary schools and even question the institution of schools. This response was well expressed by Ivan Illich whom we have already met and who wrote in the late sixties a great deal about the ills of formal education and argued that there was a fundamental difference between genuine education (learning that is primary self-directed and continual) and schooling (a system of certification and classification). Illich could not see the requirement of educational institutions for learning. After all learning is so deeply ingrained in man that it is almost involuntary. This argument of Illich is extreme but his standpoint has great relevance for adult education. The traditional pattern of adult education can often be off putting and a barrier for genuine learning and in the experience of some people too inflexible. Informal education has to be regarded as an important strand in the education of adults and we accept this as having the utmost relevance. Certain work experiences can be exceedingly relevant educationally, travel and reading on one's own can obviously be likewise; various kinds of leisure-time activities - attending concerts, visiting art galleries are surely as educationally beneficial says Rodney T. Hartnett as certain "courses in art appreciation" (Hartnett, 1972, p.22). Peter J. Harvey argued in a study of a Workingman's Club in Lancashire that the experience on a committee and in the in-club educational processes (the micro-perspective) may be more important than the formal Club Institute Union provision. He argued that the type of activity fulfilled both the need for social relationship and for self-realisation. Adult education now takes on a new dimension:

> When mankind watches a landing on the moon, the educative impact of this experience transcends all traditional forms of adult education. (Cassirer, 1970, p.38)

Adult education was then compelled to break out of the narrow confines of institutional education in many parts of the world, and in particular in the Third World countries and some of the non-aligned nations. The Brasilian adult educator, Paulo Freire, influenced Latin American thinking on literacy and rural education programs. His psychosocial method was used in Chile and his advice to adult educator tutors was applicable wherever they were. Freire saw the task of the tutor as the Christian Church had seen in the past the task of its priests, clergy and ministers:

> You need to love. You must be convinced that the fundamental efforts of education is the liberation of man, and never his 'domestication'. (Freire, 1971, p.61)

Adult education in a traditional sense can hardly function without a tutor, but the advice of Freire is not often heard:

> It is important, indeed indispensable, that you be convinced that each meeting with your group will leave both you and its members enriched. (Freire, 1971, p.62)

But in Yugoslavia a revolution has taken place in social, economic and in the education of adults during the period under our consideration. Adult education became a social necessity. A network of Workers' Universities were established throughout Yugoslavia. Marxist leaders felt the need for education and adult education came to be identified as one of the central activities of Yugoslav society. At the same time there was a growing demand for an education of a general cultural nature - such as history and literature - that would satisfy the individual. Education centres for adults were organised in industry and Yugoslavia became the first country in the world to have statutory guarantees of a right to adult or permanent education (Krajne, 1971, p.56).

29

Yugoslavia paved the way for the acceptance of permanent education in other countries, in east european countries as well as in western europe. In 1970 the Federal Republic of Germany adopted *Gesamtplan* based on a principle - the establishment of a fourth level of education the first three being primary, secondary and higher education. But it is questionable whether Federal Republic of Germany have really understood the ideas of continuing education as propounded for example by Dr. J. R. Kidd of Canada and Cyril O. Houle from the United States of America. Dr. J. R. Kidd is a household figure in the adult education world, and his whole emphasis is to see the relationship between the development of the faculties of the mind and the good of society as well as the enrichment of the individual. Dr. Kidd sees the concept of education permanent as a concept that will bring about sweeping changes, it is another world for life-long education:

> Continuous learning is a concept; it is an attitude, it is a totality; it is not a segment or a special field or division of education. Continuous learning is not a new concept. It is an old as the race, but it never was taken seriously until the present. (Kidd, 1969, pp.10-11)

J. R. Kidd sees continuing education working in a perpendicular and a horizontal dimension. It is learning continuing throughout the entire life-span as well as learning penetrating into every discipline and into every form of intellectual and spiritual activity known to man.

Dr. J. R. Kidd realises also that adults have a capacity to learn. The efforts of adult educationists like Albert Mansbridge (1876-1952) to educate the working class in Britain for democracy and citizenship is a good example of what can be done among ordinary men and women. Mansbridge's philosophy was that adults needed to be trained for citizenship, an idea that forms an integral part of continuing education. This was impossible without the proper facilities, books, lectures, tutorials, adult educational settlements, art galleries and museums. These were his words:

> Tired men and women are made better citizens, if they are taken, as they often are, to picture galleries and museums, to places of historic interest and of scenic beauty, and are helped to understand them by the power of a sympathetic guide. It is by the extension of work of this sort, which can be carried out almost to a limitless extent, that the true purpose of social reform will be best served. It is by such means that the Press may be elevated, the level of the Cinema raised, the efforts of the demagogue neutralized. (Mansbridge, 1944, p.61)

Mansbridge had an idealistic picture of the working class, and though he criticised the Co-operative Movement for being taken over by men of the "educated class who had become co-operators", it is also true to say that he himself was influenced in his idealistic description of the working class by extraordinary men of talent, like Robert Tressall, the 'house-painter who suffered', and author of the classic, *The Ragged-trousered Philanthropist;* and Alfred Williams (1877-1930), a Swindon hammerman, and author of *Life in a Railway Factory.* Tressall and Williams were a minority among the mass of workers in the twentieth century but this did not hinder Mansbridge from his vision of educating the ordinary worker. His philosophy can be discerned in his eulogy of praise of the workers in a sermon preached during the First World War in Salisbury Cathedral:

> Their welfare of body, mind and spirit must be sought by church people in yearning love. If, with our imperfect knowledge, we hate them and their doings, as some at least seem to do at this time when the actions of working-men and women, as heralded in newspapers, seem to militate against the true welfare of the nation, it is well for us to remember that there is a long history if the unwise treatment of labour by the community as a whole, and the false strike, the revolutionary action, may have had its beginnings in the disloyalty of church people to their own professed beliefs. (Mansbridge, 1944, p.69)

Mansbridge stood unflinching in that standpoint and with lieutenants of the calibre of R.H. Tawney and G.D.H. Cole the education of the working class became an important part of the provision of adult education. The situation was recognized in the famous 1919 Report of the Adult Education Committee established during the first world war by the Ministry of Reconstruction. This committee was dominated by the Mansbridge viewpoint and by the traditional University Extension Movement, formally launched by the University of Cambridge in 1837, geared to the working class but in the hands of middle-class do-gooders. The 1919 Report which was a landmark in the history of adult education saw the future as a collaboration of the WEA and the University Extension. But the movement brought into being by Mansbridge tended to become the dominion of the middle class. S.G. Raybould, a WEA tutor, and from 1936 a full-time staff tutor for the Leeds Joint Committee, released his "tract for the times" in 1949, in a book entitled *The WEA: the Next Phase*. Raybould argued like Mansbridge before him that the WEA was turning its back on its historic mission to aid the "educationally underprivileged", which was defined as those whose schooling finished at the minimum school-leaving age. Mission of the WEA to the worker existed still and indeed the emphasis on 'education for democracy' was given another boost in the writings of Ernest Green, the general secretary of the WEA, and in books by Harold C. Shearman, *Adult Education for Democracy* (Workers' Educational Association, London, 1944). R.H. Tawney in *Education: The Task before us* (Workers' Educational Association, London, 1943) argued that the task of adult education was to reform all education, so that the mass of people would know what democracy is all about. All this was in line with the philosophy of continuing education propounded by Dr. J.R. Kidd in the late sixties:

> Continuing education is no mirage in the desert, it is no dream of a religious prophet. Hard-headed, unsentimental engineers, doctors, lawyers, manufacturers, now understand that they must continue to study and learn, just to keep with the demands of their calling as well as accept the obligations of public responsibility. (Kidd, 1969, p.114)

The term 'lifelong education" is then intended to embrace a broad concept, the continuation of the educational process without interruption, to fulfil the hopes and desires, the potentialities of each individual being, and to meet the pressing demands for a world in transformation. Society is changing and therefore it is an impossible task to gear any individual, or a group, to a specific, standardised formula of educating adults.

The first meaning of lifelong education is, however, a rather narrow, limited concept, and research on new orientations is at present being carried out by bodies, like UNESCO and the Council of Europe. Dr. J.R. Kidd even goes as far as to say that a new educational system has been created in Canada as a result of education permanente, that is, the Community Colleges. It has also proved that adults have the capacity to learn and it has meant the introduction of improved educational methods of counselling, correspondence courses, television study circles as in Sweden, and group methods. The goal of education permanente, as one of its most successful proponents, J.R. Kidd maintains, is to "produce people who care and are sensitive and who are at the same time hard-headed and tough-minded" (Kidd, 1969, p.16). It is an intellectual calling.

'Lifelong Education' is concerned as we have seen with the kind of education that is provided for children and adolescents. Like John Dewey they call for an overhauling of the early stages of education, both in its content and in its methods. They claimed in a Conference at Paris in 1968 that the "traditional distinction between primary and secondary levels of education" has become "increasingly obsolete", and that "vertical structures" should be replaced by "horizontal ones". The basic aim of education in the past was dictated by the idea that once a man completed his education - primary, secondary and university - then he was equipped to face life with confidence.

In primitive societies the young were always prepared for manhood by a complicated process of initiation, ritual, ceremonies, after which the young man was ready to play his part in the life of the tribe or clan. In our societies similar rites for this transition have been developed, in the religious world through confirmation and in the secular world through examinations and diplomas. The whole ethos of education was to give the pupil facts and figures, knowledge in all fields, and then to specialise for 'O' or 'A' level examinations, before entering a further institution of learning or to start on a different training, as an apprentice, in his new sphere. The concept of 'lifelong education' changes all this pattern. The role of the primary and secondary school changes, and becomes a prelude to the real learning which starts after the person leaves formal schooling. Rather than offer courses in different subjects, it should provide the future adult with the means of expressing himself and communicating with others. There is no need to overburden the child's brain if education is a 'lifelong process'. The impact of all this thinking is on all the stages of education and practice, firstly in institutes of higher learning, then in secondary and primary schools, and beyond that in the family and the community in which it is applied.

This brings us to the second interpretation of lifelong education which is closer to the true nature of this concept, that is, all educators and in particular those who are involved in the education of adults must look again at their methods, processes, techniques, training of man in the different stages of his existence. Each period of our lives represents at once a unique and valuable experience and a preparation for future stages. This is true not only of childhood and adolescence but also of an adult in all his periods of existence. A young married couple has different aspirations and hopes from a middle-aged couple whose children have left home, and their experiences are entirely different from people who are in their late fifties looking ahead to retirement, and again their satisfactions are somewhat different from those people who have lived a few years of retirement.

Therefore, there can be no question of an age limit for education; education is a way of being aware of what is happening in the local community as well as in the world-wide family of nations. There are individuals who are very much aware of what is happening around them and write on these issues to the columns of *The Times, The Guardian,* the *New Statesman,* and other 'intellectual' newspapers or magazines, while others are entirely oblivious, uncommitted, apathetic. The task of lifelong education is to enliven interest in individuals in what is happening in society, and to make an effort to understand the complexities of a modern age.

It also means that in this process of education permanente there is no such thing as a failure or a hopeless case. Society is geared at present to the viewpoint of success and failure academically. But this needs not to happen. Failure is relative and confined to a particular subject. A man can be a first-class mechanic but a hopeless gardener or vice versa, and a woman can be an entertaining speaker on foreign travel but an atrocious mathematician. The same is true of success; it is relative and applies to one or at the most two undertakings. It is hard to visualise a man securing first-class honours in English, Spanish, Sociology, Physics, though not of a man gaining two first-class honours degrees. Indeed the combination referred to is a near impossibility in our specialised secondary school curriculum. Children are streamed into the arts or science and 'never the two shall meet'. The whole structure of society needs to be geared to this approach, but it is going to be a long process. Institutes and all kinds of employment need skilled training, diplomas, degrees and the formal adult education pattern has been slow to realise this and to respond constructively. But the tendency is for important posts to be hogged for a lifetime. An executive is appointed at 37, or a Professor of a Department, and he is there till retirement. Paul Lengrand, of the Department for the Advancement of Education, UNESCO, points to the different set up in many of the Socialist States of Europe and the world - where no one can occupy a post of high political or social responsibility for more than a limited number of years (Lengrand, 1971, p.11).

No single person has contributed more to the discussion and development of the concept of lifelong education than Paul Lengrand. It is imperative then for us to look at the theories put forward by Paul Lengrand who has contributed as a member of the UNESCO secretariat since 1948 to the formulation of the thesis of lifelong education. Paul Lengrand sees lifelong education as "Learning to Learn", that is equipping the human being with a method which will be at his disposal throughout the length of his intellectual and cultural journeys. Like many others he is very annoyed with the training and selection that is so central to the European scene, with examinations and diplomas, and people being rejected as part of the educational system. For this reason Lengrand desires a new approach with education being drawn out of the school framework so that it occupies the totality of human activities relating to leisure as well as work (Lengrand, 1975, p.61).

He is concerned with the life span of every individual. One should not allow time to acquire a minus value but to regard it as a factor of enrichment. Lengrand also is conscious that a partnership between a man and woman is part of lifelong education. This is what he calls a "sentimental education" - with the husband and wife performing a positive role of educator at every level of personality. Lifelong education comes into the understanding of parents and children for Lengrand feels that in actual fact that there is very little communication between young people and adults. He maintains that the "duologue between father and son or professor and pupil is virtually non-existent" (Lengrand, 1975, p.54). There are other areas, and in particular the professions and leisure, where a great deal has been written, but which needs to be thought out very carefully. Lengrand would like to see the day when education would prepare men to exercise their profession and when the coexistence of leisure and work had been thought out.

Lengrand admits that sport has acquired the dimensions of universal culture, and that it should take its due place in lifelong education. He rejects the view that sport is only undertaken during a brief period of life and condemns the episodic and secondary treatment of sport in the educational field. There is need for better integration of sport and lifelong education, and also centres of popular culture in which, within the same precinct, will be found both the library and the sporting facilities.

Apart from technical education and some sectors of higher education the future adult is not prepared by education to cope with his real situation, which is essentially that he is desinted to become a worker. He adds "Culture and work are considered separately as if they belonged to different worlds" (Lengrand, 1975, p.125). To the extent that education does aim to provide a vocational training, Lengrand feels that it operates very largely in a vacuum.

The same is true of education for leisure which is largely ignored in the educational system. The only way to train people to enjoy the mass media (television, radio and newspapers) is to develop their taste when young. Schools should set out to give every child a taste for and also a habit of reading. Politics is another subject which has not been given its proper place in the educational world. Most pupils reach adulthood without ever having been instructed or encouraged to think about the most important things in their public or private lives. He is of course absolutely right, if we only thought of politics in terms of peace, war, justice, social classes and the relationship between them, the nature, role, functions and structure of the state.

Lengrand stipulates that the schools find it most difficult to change for they and indeed the universities still behave "as if we were still living in the age of stagecoach and the salon, of indisputed paternal authority and of women confined to their home" (Lengrand, 1975, p.133). To Lengrand traditional education is a powerful instrument in the hands of the authorities - authorities of every kind.

> What the authorities want are docile, obedient people, people who accept meekly and without question the places and roles allotted to them, whether as producers, citizens or elements of the various structures of society; yes - men, prepared to let others think and decide for them, to fall in with the instructions of leaders, guides or heaven-sent men to tell them what to do or not to do, to tell or keep secret, to love or hate, to accept or refuse. In a sense, they live by proxy . . . In so far as education is the heritage of periods prior to the democratic conception of man and existence, its aims and activities are designed to continue to keep man in a state of protracted infancy and prevent him from becoming adult in the full sense of the word. (Lengrand, 1975, p.134)

A whole new civilisation lies between the cradle and the grave and every individual in the post-war years in the western world were obliged to choose. Man was forced by social change to be free of tradition which had outgrown its value. For knowledge and know-how accumulated in any one period of life quickly becomes out of date and loses its value. There is pressure in every profession to engage in refresher training. To Lengrand this is a clear indication of the importance of the part played by adult education. The time for education in the full sense of the word will be in adult life but the responsibility will rest on school to develop the person as a whole, instead of concentrating as they have done on the transmission of knowledge. The accent in life-long education is on the human being as Lengrand puts it in a forceful passage:

> The real education process concentrates not on a body of knowledge designated arbitrarily as the content of education, but on the needs of the human being, his aspirations and the living relations he maintains with the world of objects and persons. Education covers everything that can provide intellectual, aesthetic or spiritual sustenance for the individual and becomes an integral part of his being. To put it the other way round, the content of any teaching, whatever its importance or value, is educationally worthless if it remains external, if it is not adapted to the recipient's abilities and reactions. Life, with its needs, conditions, rhythms and expressions, is therefore to be regarded as our supreme guide in all our educational ventures. (Lengrand, 1975, p.139)

The rule of Lengrand's methodology is simply an emphasis on the pupil, rather than the curriculum, that education is to be a process and not as the transmission of knowledge; to substitute qualitative appreciation of the child as an individual for quantitative assessment which establishes artificial scales between individuals; to reduce competition to a minimum and replace it by a system of team-work; to treat children as children and not as miniature adults; and to link education to life as far as it can be done effectively for their

35

working and leisure lives (Lengrand, 1975, pp.142-143). He sees adult education as a decisive factor for the maturation of the whole process. Lifelong education is also to Lengrand the "instrument of equality", and a means of fostering fellowship. In lifelong education every man will find his own road to development since it will offer him a series of different kinds of education and training which caters for each one's individuality, originality and calling. Lengrand adds this caveat:

> Lifelong education is an encouragement to everyone to fight a never-ending battle against prejudice, ready-made ideas, dead coventions, stereotypes and the successive crystallisations of existence. In this, such education comes uncommonly close to life, following its rhythms, heeding its lessons and blazing its trails.   (Lengrand, 1975, p.155)

Lifelong education means an attempt at coherence and mobilisation of available resources and manpower as well as new lines of thought in education.

Lengrand's ideas have been accepted by a number of adult educationists and in England and Wales the idea of lifelong education has been propounded by a few adult educationists and practitioners of adult education. In 1969 a valuable symposium on continuing education was published by the Pergamon Press under the editorship of F.W. Jessup, Secretary to the Delegates for Extra-Mural Studies at the Oxford University and called *Lifelong Education*. F.W. Jessup also introduces the idea of lifelong education and in the United Kingdom context it was a refreshing reminder of the work done by pioneers such as Sir Richard Livingstone. Jessup saw lifelong education in 1969 as very desirable, for it answered in the first place the vocational need. In a technological changing society there is a continual need to train people for new jobs as automation becomes more universal. The Industrial Training Act of 1964 was a recognition of that truth. This is true also for the profesional managerial administrator and expert as Jessup rightly pointed out:

> In the professions, most conspicuously perhaps in medicine and engineering, the man who does not keep himself up to date is at the best inefficient, and at the worst dangerous.
> *(Jessup, 1969, p.19)*

But lifelong education is relevant also to those men and women who are not faced with sudden innovations due to technological development, and also relevant to those who are faced with a life of leisure in retirement after a lifetime of solid hard work. Lifelong education is also essential in the thinking of F.W. Jessup to cope with the shrinking world which has become real to all people through the introduction of transport networks (air, road, rail and naval links) as well as radio and television. Communication has made the world a global village and this means working out new human relationships which cannot be effectively done without the process of socialization. Leisure has also far reaching implications with greater access available to people to culture, and Jessup felt in 1969 that the French "socio-cultural" approach to adult education was much more relevant and rewarding than the British didactic approach (Jessup, 1969, p.24).

Jessup spelt out what lifelong learning meant. It means that every adult must take responsibility for his own education, but the opportunity to fulfil this obligation rests on the kind of society we live in. The responsibility for adult education is therefore a three-fold prong - the individual, the society to which he belongs, and the Government which accepts the public responsibility for education of its citizens. But Jessup like all adult educationists, was disappointed at the end of the sixties at the fact that the Department of Education and Science was overwhelmingly child-centred. This was the case also at the end of the seventies as well. To most local authorities in England and Wales even after the reorganization of local government, adult education remained of peripheral interest, or to borrow Jessup's colourful phrase, adult education is "regarded almost as a work of supererogation".

Jessup like Lengrand and the philosophers of lifelong education emphasises the fact that for most adults their attitude towards adult education is to a large extent coloured by their own experience of schooling. "For most people school creates an appetite for or an aversion from, education which persists throughout life" (Jessup, 1969, p.29). But lifelong learning involves a deliberate attempt by each educational institution to see how its work relates to that of the rest of the educational system, and that education does not end with their provision, whether it is a secondary school or a further education college or even a university. Jessup points out that the "open academics", that is institutions such as museums, libraries should be used to the full, that voluntary associations such as the Churches and Trade Unions have to prepare and help their members to relate their experiences to life, and the media of mass communication need to be used for education. F.W. Jessup sums up his idea of lifelong learning in one concluding sentence:

> It is a temper, a quality of society, that evinces itself in attitudes, in relationships, and in social organization. (Jessup, 1969, p.31).

Lengrand, Jessup, Houle and many other adult educationists argue that lifelong or continuing education is not as restrictive as the traditional system of adult education. Indeed to them adult education takes on a new dimension as it encompasses all aspects of life. Television, cinema, newspapers, magazines, theatre, museum all have their role to play and in some countries this has been fully realised. Romania is a good example and two andrologists could state quite categorically:

> The moulding of a new human individual with a high socialist consciousness, with a broad cultural outlook, represents a principal element in the whole activity of the revolutionary transformation of society and of the construction of socialism and communism. To this end, mass ideological and cultural activity forms an inseparable part of the process of construction of the new social system and of emancipation of human personality. (Neamtu and To pa, 1973, p.87)

To sum up the idea of lifelong education, it means:

a   Education for Tolerance

Continuing education will enable all citizens to make really free choices in their style of life, and not choices limited by the inheritance of prejudice or by ignorance of know-how or timidity. It will mean the acceptance that different life goals and life styles are to be expected in different individuals and different groups. The adult education staff of the Anne Frank House in the Netherlands, which is dedicated to the reduction of prejudice and intolerance, can testify that it calls for the utmost patience and tact, and a capacity to "tolerate intolerance" (Simpson, 1972, p.200).

b   A Comprehensive Culture

Stresses the training of man as a whole, not only its intellectual and aesthetic aspects, but also his economic and social development, his psychological and sociological culture which makes possible better relationships with those around him.

c   A Continued Development

Because an adult is in a perpetual and unfinished battle, there is no end to learning. Even in his old age man is beset by new problems. To face up to them he must learn, he must adjust and develop. He cannot stand still.

d   Collective advancement

This education has its origin in a desire to transform the world and society so as to embody in them the best chances of human progress by means of collective advancement. That is why this continuing lifelong education is seen as an involvement in social realities.

e   An Education for everyone

'Lifelong education' brings into association all of the members of the educational family. It will share in the power of education, and, as Dr. J. Robbins Kidd said of this new concept of adult education:

> It could no longer be treated as one of the less dangerous pastimes for adult leisure hours.
> (Kidd, 1966, p.12)

It had become a necessity as the learning of the rudiments of reading and writing were to Griffith Jones of Llanddowror in the Wales of the eighteenth century and as the training for skill and to participate in democracy was to Albert Mansbridge in the Britain of the twentieth century. Continuing education however is not accepted by a large number of adult educationists and certainly not by the local or national government as a necessity. For thirty years the ideas of Sir R.W. Livingstone and others were accepted in some circles but not among adult educationists, local and national governments.

38

This is why adult education was still treated throughout the thirty-five years as a Cinderella. J.R. Kidd could say in the sixties in the context of the North American continent:

> Most people in education have failed, as we sometimes have failed, to understand the full meaning of continuing education. (Kidd, 1969, p.115)

They still perceive education as they always did as a preparation for life and in preparation of young people but continuing education is exactly the opposite, and in that respect as we shall understand this philosophy acted as a rebuke as well as a challenge. J.R. Kidd and Cyril O. Houle, R.W. Livingstone and F.W. Jessup wrote with evangelistic zeal, idealism and optimism, 'equanimity and beauty' being often used as titles to describe their exciting vision. The theory was not translated with great zeal into practice more than most adult education theories, but what did take place, needs to be narrated as the ideas were propounded not only in England and Wales but throughout the western world. Indeed a point was made in one publication in 1968 to show that this emphasis has been in the education of adults since the twenties by reprinting a paper delivered in 1929 by Albert Mansbridge *(Convergence, December 1968* was the special issue).

The thirst for learning throughout life has always been present among many of the students who attend WEA classes and extra-mural tutorials. An interesting example of this was published by Basil Blackwell in a book form at the end of the second world war, namely the *Life Work of Alfred Williams*. Born in South Marston of a Welsh family, Alfred Williams started work at eleven on the farm, and at fifteen in the Swindon Railway Works. His thirst for learning was unquenchable, and in his adult life he devoured scholarship of all kind. Alfred Williams learned one of the most difficult languages of all, the Sanskrit. But as F.H. Spencer points out, he was a scholar wasted:

> This tragedy was the tragedy of being born in 1877 and born at South Marston and born poor. (Spencer, 1945, p.37)

The Open University could have rectified this tragedy and the modern ethos of continuing education would have been understood by Alfred Williams but it is doubtful whether it would have helped him to be accepted among his own people who were unable to appreciate or understand his 'desire to learn as to live'.

2   The Auxiliaries in the Education of Adults

I have already stated the importance of what can be called education of adults and this section will look at the auxiliaries that assist individuals to learn more about life and to solve the problems. The end of the second world war was the starting point for a revolution in attitudes and in the work of the auxiliaries of mass communication.

Men and women who had fought in foreign lands as well as those who had experienced intolerable war-time conditions at home were determined to build a better world for their future and their families. The General Election in July 1945 was the first opportunity of putting into practice what was felt by a whole generation. Lavish promises of David Lloyd George as Prime Minister at the end of the First World War of a 'Britain fit for heroes' were not to be repeated in its failure of fulfilment. The Election of 1945 gave a massive victory not to the Party of Winston Churchill who had led Britain to a victory in the war, but to the Party of his deputy, Clement Attlee, a dour but determined administrator. Altogether 393 Labour MPs were returned, giving them a clear majority of 146 over all other parties. The Labour Party manifesto, *Let us face the future,* had caught the imagination of a whole nation. The Conservatives were blamed for the past, for the Munich agreement, for the failure to re-arm as well as for pre-war unemployment.

The end of the second world war signalled a new awareness also among the adult educators, and in particular as Section A has indicated among philosophers of adult education in the western world. Education in general was to be given priority in the post-war period, and the Education Act of 1944, which raised the school-leaving age to 15 and established the principle of free secondary education for all, opened up tremendous new opportunities. More money was to be spent on every stage of education. The Education Act was only one aspect of a whole series of measures that in two years transformed Britain into the welfare state. Between 1944-46 the Education Act, the Family Allowances Act, the National Health Act, the National Insurance Act, the National Assistance Act, the Children's Act, were all passed through parliament. Full employment and better wages were also important manifestations of the 'new age' that had been ushered in on July 1945.

To adult education there was a new direction and a new goal to be achieved. The Education Act of 1944 placed on the shoulders of the local education authorities for the first time the responsibility of securing adequate provision for further education, and this in itself proved a blessing, but for a number of years it disturbed some adult educators. A split appeared among the adult educators. What was the purpose of adult education? The age-old argument that had cropped up in the nineteenth century once more re-appeared, and the argument has still not finally been settled. Indeed, this book evaluates and discusses the whole basis of adult education as we have experienced and visualised it over the years. Adult education is still regarded by many as the perogative of the institutions and movements. To many in Britain, adult education is synonymous with the university extra-mural departments or university extension movements, with the WEA and other voluntary movements who conduct lectures, tutorials, meetings. We are using in this section the term suggested to me by Professor E.G. Weddell, the 'education of adults' which is not so confined as the term, adult education, and which brings in all kinds of influences, approaches, methods and organisations. The most significant development in the welfare state has been the increase in the amount of leisure time. The increase in leisure time happened at the same period in time as the growth of two important developments in British society: the number of private cars and the coming of television into the homes of ordinary people. It will be argued in this book that a great deal of 'adult education' is done through the vehicles of the mass media, namely the radio, film industry, newspapers, books, and television, as well as a host of informal and formal voluntary movements, as well as the political parties, the trade unions, residential colleges, and the working class movements. This is what we mean by education of adults, and it is convenient to look at each of these vheicels for the educating of the masses.

i   Radio

The radio was a great innovation, and one which contributed immensely to the education of adults. It all began in 1922 with the establishment of the British Broadcasting Company under the leadership of a devout scottish puritan, John Reith. He turned broadcasting into his mission, and intended to use the best brains - as well as to stamp the christian morality on the masses. In no time it became an essential element to the British way of life and it soon became an essential commodity in every home. The process of educating began, in talks, music programmes, serials, and in the news bulletins. The BBC had direct political impact: speeches could be delivered direct over the air. Politics began to be assimilated at home rather than being propagated in large halls in the oratory of David Lloyd George and Ramsay MacDonald.

But the most significant and interesting experiment in the education of adults through radio began modestly in January 1941. It was the brains trust programme, and a breakthrough in adult education. Six programmes were originally planned but by popular demand they were extended for eighteen months. It was listened to in twelve million homes and for the first time an educational radio programme achieved universal popularity and the status of a national pastime (Fisher, 1944, p.46). Everyone came to imitate the method and in villages, schools, provincial towns, colleges, hostels and camps they produced their own brains trusts. Questions were asked in parliament, and many poured scorn on its educational value. N.G. Fisher in an interesting account refers to the fact that it started out as an entertainment but succeeded in being educational:

> In fact the Brains Trust succeeded not as entertainment nor as education, but as both.
> (Fisher, 1944, p.47)

The brains trust experiment had its lessons for the education of adults. It gave the public what it wanted, and what it wanted was diagnosed as education in that "entertainment is not necessarily incompatible with education" (Fisher, 1944, p.48). But this popular and far-reaching experiment however was not used as it could have been to make adult education a necessity for adults in England and Wales.

Adult education as envisaged by Albert Mansbridge, the founder of the WEA and R.H. Tawney, the socialist thinker, was for the masses. But many felt at the end of the war that adult education as a movement was out of touch with the mass of people (Bartlett, 1945, p.134). Howard Thomas, the inventor of the brains trust, had developed the habit of enquiring what his public wanted and the technique of providing it. Also he anticipated what the public wanted next and discovered what they wanted when they did not know themselves. The listener assimilated knowledge as well as finding out what he himself knew in comparison with the answer supplied by the expert. A tremendous interest was aroused, and libraries in the provinces reported a demand for books on philosophy (Fisher, 1944, p.54). The brains trust method reminded one that to be attractive to the student is a virtue, another insight which was largely lost in the adult education field.

The experience of many an adult educator at that time and since then is that radio does help. It presents the material in an interesting manner, it enlivens interest, it focuses on a topic or a subject, and is always able to stimulate discussion and thought. Though its influence declined in the fifties and sixties with the coming of television, yet one has to seriously consider its impact and influence on the education of adults at the end of thirty-five years that we are looking at. It ensures that the mass of people are given an opportunity of exploring a largely uncharted world. There is no doubt that the BBC and the new experiments in local radio stations in the sixties are doing educational work of great value, and possibly all the more valuable because it is not under guise of education.

ii   Cinema

At the end of the war the cinema was an influential factor on the education of adults. Nineteen forty six was cinema's peak year and there were in Britain some five thousand cinemas, catering for an average weekly audience of twenty millions or more (The Arts Enquiry, 1947, p.198). The cinema to a certain extent had displaced the theatre and the music hall as well as building up a clientele of its own. The cinema-goers saw often films based on literature, on the Bible; they saw films on other countries, of natural life; they became familiar with people who were famous in other parts of the world; their horizons were enlarged. It was educational.

The cinema's years of glory were few in the post-war period and the attendances began to fall critically. This decline can be stated in a statistical form: from 1,365 million in 1956 to 1,151 in 1957 *(The British Film Industry,* 1958, p.133). Between 1952 and 1958 650 cinemas were closed. The main reason for the decline of the cinema was the coming of television as a popular means of entertainment. Television had grown in six years from less than a million licence-holders in 1951 to nearly eight million at the end of 1957. According to a PEP report (1958), it was the opening of ITV stations which had the most devastating effect rather than the opening of BBC stations. This may well be because people held back from buying television sets until there was a choice of programmes available to them.

The film industry were disturbed at the trend of falling attendance at British cinemas. Pressure was upon Government and public to assist. The Government pressure was with regard to the entertainment tax and the setting up of the National Film Finance Corporation. This corporation helped with money, but the public were becoming more addicted to television. Panoramic films and three dimensional films were innovations in the industry, and the panoramic films of the two were more acceptable to the cinemagoers. First film made by this system was *The Robe,* and it had its European première at the Odeon, Leicester Square on the 19th November 1953.

But the film itself was accepted in this period as an aid in teaching children as well as adults. It was shown that adults at higher educational level learn and remember at least as much from a good film as from a traditional lecture on the same subject, and that the more intelligent students learn more from films than do poorer students. Motion pictures also could significantly affect behaviour, attitudes, emotions, although the degree and direction of the change was not always predictable.

The educational film has its own history and has taken a variety of forms. We have the *single-concept film,* often silent, which dealt with a single phase of a process in a minute or two of film time; *the open-ended film,* which posed a problem but left the solution to the audience; and *the iconographic film* in which still pictures or photographs were converted to motion-picture form by camera movement, cutting other cinematic effects.

It seems that the film technique has become an essential part of the educational system, at university level as well as in extra-mural activities. Research is still needed to bring out the full implications as well as a detailed research on the content and presentation of material in movies on television and in cinemas. It can be said that an era of new and exciting possibilities have been opened up in the field of communications in the education of adults, and it seems that the cinema has still a significant role in the process of entertaining and educating the audiences, children as well as adults.

iii   The Newspaper Press

The Press has for a century been a powerful influence on the education of adults, and all the indication points to the fact that the people of England and Wales have taken their papers seriously. Though a decline has set in, it is a startling fact in itself that in the mid 1960s Britain had the highest per capita sale of newspapers in the world - 50.6 copies for every 100 people (Hohenberg, 1973, p.423). Radio had helped as it whetted people's appetite for more news information. But the sixties saw also a more sinister development in the newspaper industry; the disappearance of some outstanding daily papers, the concentration of more than one national newspaper in the hands of a syndicate or one owner, and the growth of competing media. The loss of the *News Chronicle* with a readership in excess of one million was a severe loss.

We do not intend to study the personalities, editors and the content of the newspaper industry, except to state that editorials are used to persuade people to vote for one party more than another. The serious daily papers are important in informing adults, and in particular the *Daily Telegraph,* the *Guardian,* and the *Times.* The *Daily Telegraph,* with nearly 1.5 million circulation, has exerted tremendous influence among the middle class careerist and technocrat while the *Times* have always appealed to the intellectually-minded in all professions, and the *Guardian* appeals to the radically orientated from all sections of the community. It is believed that the *Times* is the leader of the British Press and the most important independent influence on the governmental process outside the major political parties themselves. The views and opinions of Lord Thomson of Fleet had to be considered for a long time, and in particular, his philosophy on the role of the *Times* in educating its readers. Lord Thomson has lavished a fortune on its limp pages to keep it alive. Why the *Times?* Lord Thomson's answer was simply: "It is a symbol of Britain, and more characteristic of Britain than any paper in the country" (Hohenberg, 1975, p.423). Thomson's rescue of the *Times* was a remarkable operation, and the intellect and skill of editors, such as Sir William Haley, has to be mentioned when discussing the Press. At the end of the seventies it seemed that the moulders in the task of educating the adults in Britain were the *Times* and *Sunday Times,* the *Financial Times,* the *Observer,* the *Guardian* and the *Daily Telegraph.*

But another important part of the newspaper industry is the weekly magazines and journals, and in particular the serious weekly reviews such as the *New Statesman,* the *Spectator* and the *Economist.* Each of these three magazines have exerted an influence comparable to the work of an adult education organisation and Kingsley Martin, editor of the *New Statesman* for over thirty years, was himself conscious of this role.

iv   Books

The role of books in educating adults in England and Wales has to be evaluated in the following aspects:·

(I)   The influence of best-sellers. What are these books? Who are their authors? A notable example that can be looked at is the life and work of H.G. Wells (1866-1946) who died at the beginning of our period. Wells influence was at its height as G. Bernard Shaw in an earlier period, but they were both dedicated to furthering education of adults, and cannot, therefore, be ignored. H.G. Wells had been a tutor with the University Correspondence College, and his life was a mission. He believed that the hope of mankind was in scientific education, and his monumental work, *The Outline of History,* is regarded by some adult educators as the most important book which educated adults in Britain in the twentieth century.(Cole, June 10, 1974).

The Outline of History, though hastily written, took the reading public by storm and over two million of them bought the book. Ronald Seth sums the contribution of Wells to the education of adults in the following manner:

> His writings made him, with Shaw, one of the most powerful influences of his time.
> (Seth, 1972, p.316)

The printed word is powerful and television has not diminished its influence on adults. John Lewis is very much near the mark:

> Whatever modern technology may have to offer by way of aids to learning, the role of the printed word in educational development will continue to be of paramount importance.
> (Lewis, 1970, p.36)

(II) The role played by publishers and book clubs and other organisations in using the book as an organ of education. Undoubtedly the most well-planned and successful venture in this way was the Penguin Books, which came into being on 30th July 1935. The policy of Allen Lane and his brothers from the very beginning was to maintain a high standard of scholarship, production and presentation. Allen Lane was fortunate in the advice he received from visionaries in the world of adult education, such as W.E. Williams, then secretary of the British Institute of Adult Education, H.L. Beales of the London School of Economics, and V.K. Krishna Menon, the Indian politician. Series of books were produced, such as the *Pelican Edition,* with a definite educational impulse behind them. Big sales came with *Penguin Specials,* which were a series of books that went a long way to satisfy the craving for political enlightenment. *Penguin Books* changed everything in publishing to adults, and showed also that mass-produced books can be planned with care *(Penguin's a Retrospect 1935-51,* 1951, p.1).

The *Penguin Books* made their greatest impact after the war, and their aim of supplying "something good for all needs and moods" were implemented. Penguin's millions was launched, a simultaneous issue on one day, of a million books by a single author. This was particularly big when applied to books, and the first of the Penguin millions was a set of Bernard Shaw's plays, produced in honour of his ninetieth birthday in 1946 *(Penguin's a Retrospect 1935-51,* 1951, p.12). There was another million of Wells' novels which was intended for his eightieth birthday (which he did not live to see) which served as a memorial at his death. Other authors whose works were produced (a million at a time) were Agatha Christie and Evelyn Waugh. *Penguin Classics* were started in the New Year 1946, and consisted of original translation written in good modern english. The first volume in the series was *The Odyssey* newly translated by E.V. Rieu, the general editor of the series *(Penguin's a Retrospect 1935-51,* 1951, p.14). One can understand the impact of this book by stating that by 1950 over half a million copies had been sold.

Allen Lane was full of ideas for the education of adults. As one sympathetic observer wrote:

> He is its principal source of inspiration and invention as well as its presiding genius.
> *(Penguin's a Retrospect 1935-51,* 1951, p.18)

The inspiration of Allen Lane was in the personnel that was taken on by Penguin and by the series of books on educational subjects that were published. R.B. Fishenden, an authority on colour printing, was appointed technical editor of the King Penguin Special and in 1947 Jan Tschichold, an outstanding typographer, joined Penguin. Sir Kenneth Clark was invited as the editor of the *Penguin Modern Painters Series* which became an outstanding piece of book production and a considerable contribution to the popular education of adults. The *Penguin Modern Painters Series* was just one of many series, which included *Penguin Scores* started in 1949, *Penguin Guides, Penguin Shakespeare* and *Penguin The Buildings of England,* whose first volume appeared in 1951 *(Penguin's a Retrospect 1935-51,* p.15).

The Penguin were not the only company which specialised in paperback editions. It became the most profitable means of publishing, and by the early 1960's the annual sales of 30 paper-back book publishers in the English language exceeded 250,000 copies through more than 100,000 retail outlets *(Encyclopaedia Britannica,* 1971, p.944).

Book clubs were the major innovation in the inter-war years, and the remarkable success story of *The Left Book Club* has been narrated by one of its convenors, John Lewis. It was the vision of one of the most extraordinary publishers of our time, Victor Gollancz, socialist propagator par excellence. An Oxford graduate who spent his early career as a successful teacher of classics at Repton School, but entered the firm of Ernest Benn Ltd. in 1921. He even preceded Allen Lane, Penguins and Pelicans, by issuing a series of paper-covered books on a wide range of topics in 1927 (Lewis, 1970, p.19).

Victor Gollancz had a burning passion for political education: "not merely desirable but a matter of life or death". He believed that, "as an instrument for education the disciple of politics is a disciple like no other". Victor Gollancz has given us his own thinking in two books published in the fifties, *My Dear Timothy* and *More for Timothy.* He sums up his philosophy for the education of adults in this manner:

> And this can be done in one way only - on the basis of knowledge: knowledge of facts; knowledge of ideas; knowledge of the motives that have moved human beings and still continue to move them, often so obscurely. Without it a man is at the mercy of any unscrupulous demagogue or shrieking newspaper, and we plunge on with increasing precipitancy from one disaster to another.   (Gollancz, 1953, p.156)

To Gollancz national salvation depended on the political education of the masses. He saw the urgent need of clear reasoning, of political thinking. It was political education that was needed and in the course of our study we will see that even the political parties neglected this task. As a publisher Gollancz was very successful and was enthusiastically welcomed by a large band of progressives as a visionary in propagating the gospel of socialistic education to the general public.

The Left Book Club exerted tremendous influence and undoubtedly played a significant part in creating the landslide victory for the Labour Party in 1945, and, indeed, in moulding the thinking of a generation. But Victor Gollancz felt in the late 40s that the purpose of the Left Club had come to an end; and the Club was disbanded in 1948. The work of educating adults was to continue as Gollancz spelt out in the last issue of the *Left News:*

> Political education and, in particular, the education of the electorate in the principles of socialism are more vitally important than ever but we feel that this work can now best be carried on not on a membership basis but by providing, at the cheapest possible price, suitable books for mass circulation to the general public.　　　*(Lewis, 1970, p.132)*

Victor Gollancz pursued this objective through his publishing house and through his vision succeeded to some extent in the task of "educating the electorate". A few other publishers, such as Lawrence and Wishart, MacGibbon and Kee, Sedwick and Jackson, have been willing to pursue the same task.

One cannot forget the important work carried out by the university publishing houses in the education of adults, and in particular the work of the Oxford University Press and the Cambridge University Press. In 1941 the Oxford University Press took over the publication of *The Home University Library* which had at least opened the way for the popularity of the book as a means of educating adults. One of the most important single works completed in the fifties and published by the Oxford University Press was Arnold Toynbee's, *A Study of History,* which exerted a tremendous influence on the teaching of adult classes, and in discussion groups. Another notable publication has been the *Oxford Dictionary of Quotations* described in a history of the Press as the "world's best bedside book". The Cambridge University Press have also published in the same literary tradition as the Oxford University Press, George Allen and Unwin, Dent, Collins, MacMillan and the smaller publishing houses, many of which appeared in the fifties and sixties.

v　　**The role of the Public Libraries**

A provision of books, in hard cover or in paper-back, sold by booksellers can never be as effective as the provision of books on loan through public libraries. The public libraries have taken an important part in the work of educating adults, and as Frank Gardner rightly said in 1970:

> The last 25 years have probably been the most productive in the history of British librarianship.　　　(Gardner, 1970, p.37)

Libraries can carry out their task in a number of ways. The work of giving out books to the public is carried out at all public libraries. In 1950 the expenditure on the public library system was £8,600,000, of which £2,000,000 was on books (Gardner, 1970, p.40). Staff numbered 11,000 and book circulation was 300,000,000. In 1969-70 total expenditure reached £54,000,000 of which £12,000,000 was on books, total staff 25,110, and loan of books was over 600,000,000 (Gardener, 1970, p.40). In less than twenty years the service had doubled.

The Public Libraries Act of 1964 heralded a new era. It was the first piece of public library legislation for 45 years. A new impetus was given to the public libraries, and many of them responded by providing leisure-time activities in the form of lectures, lunch-time recitals, a meeting place for adult education classes. One can discern today a well-organized institution giving an informal educational and information service. As Frank Gardner, who as Borough Librarian of Luton has been in the middle of the movement, sums up the role of the public library:

> as an integral part of the cultural and educational structure of the modern democratic
> state. (Gardner, 1970, p.40)

vi   Television

Much of television is educative, as for instance news programmes, documentaries, political broadcasts, outside programmes. All adds to the viewers' awareness of the world and society in which they live, and people learn in this way. Adult educationalists have realised the potentialities, and useful co-operation has taken place within the scope of the television cameras. The opening of a second BBC television channel in 1964 was a major breakthrough, for programmes of educational nature were shown every evening on BBC2.

The sixties saw in Britain three important experiments. The first experiment took place under the auspices of the Nottingham Extra-Mural Department under the leadership of Professor Harold Wiltshire. It took place in the autumn term of 1964, and it was a small-scale local experiment in the use of television for adult education (Kelly, 1970, p.348). The experiment was a success and reached a good percentage. 1,347 people enrolled as students and 549 of these did all the exercises for the thirteen programmes, entitled *The Standard of Living.* Professor Harold Wiltshire and his colleagues felt that television teaching can reach students who otherwise would not be reached, that television teaching can be of a high standard as well as effective if it is part of a system that involves students in active learning and in contact with tutors, and that the cost (which was a fee of fifty pence for enrolment) need not exceed that asked by any organization catering for the education of adults.

The need for a further experiment was widely recognized; and this led to the most spectacular experiment of all, the Open University. The idea originated in a speech delivered in Glasgow in 1963 by Harold Wilson, and when he became Prime Minister in 1964 he entrusted the task of carrying out the proposal to Jennie Lee, (widow of Aneurin Bevan); Parliamentary Under-Secretary of State in the Department of Education and Science. Miss Lee invited an Advisory Committee drawn from the world of education to consider the possibilities in more detail. An official statement embodying the advice of this committee was issued by the Government in February 1966. The Government accepted the findings and went ahead with the scheme, and a Planning Committee under the chairmanship of Sir Peter Venables did the essential groundwork.

The University of the Air, as it was first referred to, appointed its own Vice-Chancellor and started its teaching in 1971, being called now, The Open University. The principal end in view from the beginning was to help mature men and women, who in the past had to leave school at an early age, to be given an opportunity to develop their powers of concentration and intelligence. A new university was created, with power to grant its own degrees, and using televison, correspondent unit courses, text books, radio, seminar, tutorials, counselling. The students would be doing the assignments at home, and pursuing in the day-time their own vocation.

The only other major innovation of this kind which had been established successfully was the Schools for Adult Education by correspondence and by the oral methods in Leiderdorp, Holland. This has become a major part of adult education in other countries, such as Hungary and in Russia.

The methods, approach and success of the two important ventures needs to be evaluated in a piece of research that is, the Leidse Onderwijsinstellingen (LOI) as it is called in the Netherlands and the Open University in the United Kingdom.

The initial arguments of using television as a means of educating adults were not accepted without a debate. One of the most bitter oponents to the scheme as proposed in the White Paper (CMND 2922) was Stuart Hood, an expert in the world of television as communicator and administrator. Hood went so far as to dismiss the whole idea:

> The University of the Air is a historical fossil from the days of the Workers' Educational Association and the National Council of Labour Colleges.   (Hood, 1967, p.127)

There is an element of truth in his unfair attack for after all the education of adults should be essential in a democracy. The WEA and the NCLC had been involved in the task of spreading education, and indeed some educationalists would accept the role of adult education in exactly the way that Stuart Hood dismissed it. Twenty years before a German educationalist on a visit to Britain felt that there was a need for adult education as part of a political, public duty - a process of education for democracy.

49

Heiner Lotze maintained:

> The right to vote entails a corresponding obligation to co-operate actively in public life, and it is our task to educate adults up to this active co-operation, to an understanding based on knowledge of facts, and to a sense of responsibility.   (Lotze, 1947, p.12)

The Open University is undoubtedly an institution that comes near to implementing the essentials in the view of Heiner Lotze, namely:

I   objectivity in presentation
II striving for truth
III tolerance for the opinion of others
IV scientifically unbiased approach.   (Lotze, 1947, p.12)

Unfortunately these auxiliaries have not been regarded as essential in planning for adult education, but our survey has underlined the role which it could pay in a national strategy for the education of adults.

3   The Historical Trends (1945-1980)

1945 was a year of great excitement in Britain. The long and distressing war was over and it seemed that the United Kingdom would enter upon a new phase in the history of education, and in particular adult education. During the war a demand had arisen for educational reform, and this became a reality in the Education Act of 1944. A new classification was introduced (primary, secondary and further education). Further education was to embrace not only the vast range of technical, commercial, and art education, and the wide field of adult education of a tutorial kind but also facilities for leisure-time occupation, in organised cultural and training facilities. The 1944 Act, which came into force on the 1st April, 1945, was an imposing landmark in the history of education. For further education it promised a comprehensive provision:

i   County Colleges;

ii   Technical Schools and Colleges;

iii   Community Centre and all other post-school establishments.

It was to be administered by a single section of the newly created Ministry of Education (Lowe, 1970, p.33). The Ministry had limitless power and there was nothing to stop the expansion of adult education in any way that the Minister saw fit.

During the war adults had been introduced to education, especially in the army. This important contribution has been ably recorded by N. Scarlyn Wilson, *Education in the Forces, 1939-46: the Civilian Contribution,* and there is no need in this survey to go after the details. But it was the first time many adults had experienced education, and they were enthralled. Edmund Harvey, who represented the Combined English Universities in Parliament argued at the end of the war in favour of adult education on the basis of the war-time experiences of a great number of people. Harvey wanted to see two things happening. Firstly, the universities to throw open their doors so that the "disinherited" could study in evening adult education classes *(Hansard, Volume 411, 1355)*. He praised the great work done by the WEA, and Harvey asked the questoin, "Why can't the Government take over country houses and afford facilities to them?" Secondly, Edmund Harvey wanted to see much more done for the training of adult educators. During the war years one came across, in the Forces, gifted men and women who could contribute so much to the work of adult education. These were his words in the House of Commons debate:

> In the Army discussion groups and classes they meet together and discuss economic and political problems and other questions and they have awakened to a keen interest in education. *(Hansard, Volume 411, 1356)*

He felt also disappointed at the local authorities' response to the opportunities. They could do much more in co-operation with the WEA and a movement like the Education Settlement Association.

> We are dealing with people who want to learn, who are not compelled to go to school. They are coming at sacrifice to themselves in their spare time after a day's hard work because they are keen. Surely they deserve to be helped, and we ought to be willing to spend the money of the nation generously to help those who are willing to make sacrifices in order that they should learn. *(Hansard, Volume 411, 1356-1357)*

His plea fell on deaf ears as did his argument for the priority of adult education:

> There is no branch of the great work of education which deserves more support than this neglected branch of adult education. *(Hansard, Volume 411, 1357)*

Mrs. Thelma Cazalet Keir (a great friend of the family of Lloyd George) agreed with Lindsay and Harvey as Parliamentary Secretary to the Ministry of Education. She also said that the Minister himself - Richard Kidston Law - felt attached to adult education "and that we are both alive to adult education" *(Hansard, Volume 411, 1374)*.

The same noble and pious sentences were expressed in a debate in the House of Commons in the following year. R.A. Butler spoke from his experience on the 8th February 1946, and noted again the great interest in adult education *(Hansard, Volume 418, 2054)*. However he did not believe that proper adult education provision can be made by each authority. Essex and Yorkshire had the resources but for the rest it was doubtful. Ellen Wilkinson, a Minister, in her reply emphasised how anxious they were to encourage the local education authorites *(Hansard, Volume 418, 2065)*. Her statement and the statements of all her successors at the odd moment when adult education was discussed in the House of Commons bear out the point that there is a wide gap between official statements and official practice.

The Labour Government in 1945 had a tremendous opportunity with regard to the demand for adult education. Parliament had such an attraction. "Everyday since the new parliament met there have been crowds of people anxious to see it at work" (Johnson, 1945, p.176). It did work, and brought into being the welfare state and national health service. But adult education was never given the high priority demanded by some of the alert back-benchers, like Kenneth Lindsay and Edmund Harvey.

Another classic example is Winston Churchill's famous statement on the place of liberal adult education in a technological society. Churchill's first Minister of Education, Miss Florence Horsburgh, announced in January 1953 that there might have to be a ten per cent cut in the estimates for adult education. Sir Vincent Tewson, on behalf of the Trade Union Congress, sent a strongly worded protest against the reduction in the Ministry's grants for adult education. The Prime Minister answered in a letter dated 11th March which was later reproduced in full in the Ashby Report (1954):

> There is, perhaps, no branch of our vast educational system which should more attract within its particular sphere the aid and encouragement of the State than adult education. How many must there be in Britain, after the disturbance of two destructive wars, who thirst in later life to learn about the humanities, the history of their country, the philosophies of the human race, and the arts and letters which sustain and are borne forward by the ever-conquering English language. *(Ashby Report,* 1954, p.66)

Churchill went on to say:

> The appetite of adults to be shown the foundations and processes of thought will never be denied by a British administration cherishing the continuity of our Island life. *(Ashby Report,* 1954, p.67)

Yet after all this rhetoric the grant in 1953 was £330,000 and £33,000 was originally to have been cut. The main work of the Government is to give grants as well as ensuring that the local authorities carry out provision for adult education. It supervises standards through a constituted branch of Her Majesty's Inspectors. Government helps to finance the teaching costs of certain adult education agencies designated responsible bodies. It makes grants to long-term residential colleges and triennial grants towards admin-istrative costs incurred by certain national voluntary associations who promote liberal education among adults. It also awards ad hoc grants for special research projects and a number of mature scholarships to adult students over 25.

The bulk of the adult education in the period 1945-1980 fell on the shoulders of the local education authorities, the responsible bodies, and other voluntary organisations. All these will be dealt with in some length in the following chapters but a few generalisations will be offered on each one in this chapter.

i   The work of the Local Education Authorities

It seems that the provision of the local education authorities differ in three respects from those of the responsible bodies. Firstly, in the content of their programme. The local education authorities classes held in the evening institutes and adult centres are largely or sometimes exclusively in vocational classes. These centres sometimes offer non-vocational courses, and at other times a mixture of vocational and non-vocational classes, but the emphasis generally is on vocational classes which offer information that can be applied to the contemporary world. That is why psychology, cookery, handicraft, car maintenance, are always offered at the evening institutes. There is usually no expectation that the students will do any private work, whereas the responsible bodies lay stress upon study by the student.

Research done in Leeds permits us also to use several generalisations for this type of education. Evening institute classes have a special appeal to females. Among the juveniles the boys attend for vocational reasons and the girls for recreational activities. The institutes have a great deal of language teaching - making little direct provision for liberal studies (Hanna, 1966, pp.14-43).

The sixties saw a great deal of improvement in the evening institute provision but still at the end of our period, in 1980, there are glaring deficiencies. Most of the deficiencies turn around the buildings and the staff. Evening institutes are held often in poor accommodation. There is a general failure to design the institutes for students. One thing was clear to all involved in adult education: whenever an evening institute is given good accommodation it will flourish. The chances otherwise are slim. Many an institute functioned with the principal having no office of his own, and the classes expected by the caretakers to vacate the premises - which are usually schools - at the moment the clock struck nine. Programmes can often be monotonous and uninspiring and the pay of the adult tutors was so poor that it could not attract the most able teachers in the area. Third-rate teachers, and in some cases, people who have never taught in their lives, are invited to take classes. In adult education so much depends on the tutor, and local authorities as well as responsible bodies have to depend mostly on part-time staff. The fees are often inadequate for them to take their work seriously and this has hindered the professionalism of adult education within the local education authorities. It is a glaring example of our argument that very little is learnt from the actual situation by those who have the responsibility of providing adult education.

ii   Responsible Bodies

The period 1945-1980 saw some very encouraging developments within the WEA and the extra-mural departments. It seemed as if the responsible bodies realised that if adult education is going to be of any value then it should include variety, purpose, as well as preparing people for their vocational tasks.

There was a concern for making education relevant to the adult learner. Sir John Maud, in *The Listener* in 1949, wrote on the need to develop all skills. He saw the future of education tied up with making people to enjoy themselves in their own way, to make them aware that they were a part of a larger world, and that they had a responsibility to be better citizens (Maud, 1949, pp.224-225). The WEA and the university extra-mural departments accepted to some extent this viewpoint, and some of their most successful ventures have been achieved in residential and tutorial classes.

There is no doubt that the short-term residential colleges have a special place in the history of adult education. By 1970 there were 50 short-term residential colleges in the United Kingdom. The inspiration for the spread of these colleges came from a small book published in 1941, *The Future in Education,* by Sir Richard Livingstone. R.D. Waller was the first to put Livingstone's ideas into practice with the establishment of the University of Manchester's short-term adult residential college called Holly Royde. This college was also fortunate in securing as its first warden, Donald Garside, who became the doyen of wardens of short-term residential colleges. He was an internationally-known figure and served as warden from 1949 to 1974 *(Roscoe Review,* 1974, p.22).

The other concern was for adult education to the workers. The WEA, TUC, NCLC, the universities, as well as other organisations, were all involved in this period with educating the workers. We will see in the next chapters how successful or how disappointing this venture proved to be, but there is no denying the stimulus behind this aspect to the education of adults. The WEA and the university extra-mural departments were reminded of this aspect to the work especially by Professor S.G. Raybould, head of the Department of Adult Education and Extra-Mural Studies at Leeds University. He was a central figure in adult education from 1946 when he was appointed first head of the new department till his retirement in 1969. He was ably assisted by the Assistant Director, Albert Johnson, who was at Leeds from the inception in 1946 till his retirement in 1970. Johnson played a leading part with Professor Raybould in the expansion of university education among the working class. It was said of him at his retirement:

> His work was based on a fierce determination that extra-mural work played a leading part in the expansion of university education among the working class.
> *(University of Leeds' Department of Adult Education and Extra-Mural Studies Twenty-fourth Annual Report 1969-70, p.9)*

But to be successful Raybould and Johnson had to tempt tutors with the same motivation to work within the Department. On this score they were successful. Two examples will suffice to prove the point. Edward P. Thompson is regarded as a fine historian of the british working class and proved during his term as staff tutor in the Adult Education Department as an "outstanding tutor of tutorial classes and at WEA Summer Schools" *(W.E.A. Yorkshire North District Annual Report* 1964-65, p.11). Dr. A.E.P. Duffy was another lecturer who did a valuable job among miners, steel workers and shop stewards before he was elected a Member of Parliament in 1970. The work at Leeds was carried on at other universities and within the WEA, the Trade Union Movement and the NCLC, and we will in another chapter see how their ideas on workers education were implemented by the responsible bodies.

Another concern of adult education (1945-1980) was in academic provision for young adults (18 to 21) as well as older adults on a full-time and part-time basis. A new demand arose within university extra-mural departments for career education as well as a greater willingness to respond to it especially within the further education sector. Since the early 1950s the United Kingdom saw the development first of ten colleges of advanced technology, and then of thirty polytechnics, together with a huge expansion of higher education. A continuous debate has existed over the years within adult education and higher education with regard to 'advanced further education'. There is no doubt that Britain stood firmly for the élite tradition, and that the whole spectrum of career education favoured the minority among young adults. The Robbins Report in 1963 called for an expansion in higher education but it never changed the élite-dominated system. The great debate of the sixties was between the view of the Robbins Report and that of Anthony Crosland (the Secretary of State for Education and Science in 1965 to 1967 during the 1964 to 1970 Labour Government). Robbins was particularly élitist for he saw the expansion in terms of the universities. The figures were as follows: from 216,000 students in 1962 to 1963 to 309,000 in 1973 to 1974 and about 560,000 in 1980 to 1981, and the universities were to offer 350,000 out of the total of 560,000 for 1980. To do this, existing universities would grow and six new universities would have to be established.

The Robbins Committee defined higher education in terms of full-time students working to a degree level, with a concession to include students in colleges of education working below this level. The committee's reference excluded more than 100,000 students on part-time courses at degree level and another 100,000 students in non-university colleges on courses below that level.

It was this stage of higher education which expanded with the result that in the middle seventies there are more full-time higher education students outside the universities as inside them. This excludes the part-timers which are an essential part of the education scene.

It was Anthony Crosland who suspected the Robbins approach. In a speech at Woolwich in 1965 and Lancaster in 1967 he spelt out the invaluable further education tradition of providing opportunities for late developers. However, Crosland himself chose to carry out his policy in a manner that was not in keeping with his stated aims in the Woolwich and Lancaster speeches. The Minister designated "thirty polytechnics" as "comprehensive academic communities of higher education", and there was a feeling by 1970 that so many of the polytechnic students came from the same social background as those of the universities.

It is important to stress that Crosland was moving towards a 'mass' system in contrast to the élite and autonomous tradition of the British universities. He sought an alternative tradition and a system that would cater for the needs of more people, but unfortunately Crosland was concerned in the main with eighteen to twenty-one year-olds, and the adults who had passed their early twenties were neglected. Crosland's philosophy towards 'mass' higher education turned out to be one still for a minority.

It seems that Crosland and subsequent Ministers had not taken seriously the idea of recurrent education or permanent education or that of continuing education. The British system is not different from most of the other systems in the western world. In the past British society offered adult education to those who were interested and fairly affluent and then the trend has been to educate the trainable. While individual adult educators have conceived of education of adults in terms of education for all, there is still reluctance to extend the debate for the élitist approach is the one most acceptable to the majority of academics. Tyrrell Burgess has argued with passion in *Education After School* (1977) that the "gradual expansion of an élite system is the enemy of post-school education for all". He argues on two points. Firstly, the present élitist system is expensive and is "inclined to swallow up all available resources". In the second place, "the expansion of higher education on demand "has meant that such education has been available to the same sorts of people who were getting it already - "that is, the relatively advantaged" (Burgess, 1977, p.87). Burgess sees the Open University in this light as an inaccessible avenue. He writes:

> Only 10 per cent of its students can be described as manual workers (we are of course not comparing the social class of their fathers). The rest have mostly had some form of post-school education. The English universities are and always have been middle-class institutions. (Burgess, 1977, p.26)

Burgess' argument has a great deal of relevance - for education after school is education of adults, all adults, but so many of the institutions of learning will not allow adults to enter without previous success in education - which is exactly what most people cannot show.

Sir Sydney Caine, who had a great deal of experience of higher education, mentioned another point that so often is forgotten. That is, the content of academic education is decided wholly by the teaching staff on the basis of what they find most interesting to teach rather than on the relevance of the course for the students. This criticism could equally be applied to all post-school education. Sir Sydney Caine regretted that the pattern of education was wholly determined by the academic profession:

> Considered as an industry, education is perhaps the only industry in which the nature of the product is decided solely by the producer. (Caine, 1964, p.10)

However, at the end of our period as we have already described a most interesting experiment in higher education was put into operation, namely the establishment of the Open University. The idea was to create an university that would be really open to all the adults in the United Kingdom. But it soon become clear, and figures from the Open University substantiated this, that the student population did not really represent a balanced intake from the community as a whole. The Open University was in principle open to everyone but in actual fact it was as impotent as the WEA and the university extra-mural departments in attracting men and women who worked in manual and semi-skilled jobs. It is possible to criticise the Open University as all other adult education agencies on their ways of communication. The usual policy of the Open University, like the WEA, is to advertise in newspapers, insert leaflets in libraries, and at the adult education centres. Leaflets in libraries are ideal for the book-loving minority of our society but for the blue-collar worker there is need for a more powerful means of communication. It can be argued that in the future all adult educatin agencies, including the Open University, will have to be more educationally-motivated and that adult educators have to discuss the merits of the education of adults in the factories and the work place among the blue-collar workers. If education of adults is important then it must be liberated from the limitations that we have seen in England and Wales in the period 1945-1980, and lessons have to be learnt from the actual situation.

The Open University also, to gain academic respectability, designed courses which would appeal to people who had already been trained in different professions. It was no wonder then that in the initial period of the Open University a large number of teachers joined as students and that the factory workers were still in the minority. It is at least possible that the blue-collar worker is not attracted to subjects like educational technology; biochemistry; curriculum design; linear mathematics, or the philosophy of Wittgenstein, and that the Open University is doing what Sir Sydney Caine referred to with regard to the conventional universities. A possible but untried solution would be for the Open University to work with the adult education agencies and the TUC Education Department at grass roots level on the curriculum for the degree courses. The Open University then would demonstrate that education is something a person gets for himself, not that which someone else gives or does for him. For this to happen the Open University would have to rearrange its admission procedure and also to consider making the foundation courses less exacting. This of course would be severely criticised by the academic establishment who are very much concerned with the élitism of the Robbins Report. But it seemed even after the establishment of the Open University that there was a need for new approaches. The Open University has shown that television is a powerful medium for educational purpose - but in 1970 the full potential of television had not been enlisted in the service of adult education. On the contrary the media were often used for anti-educational purposes. The basic problems were how to use the media (in the way of the best BBC2 and Independent Television documentaries) with a view to extending educational opportunities how to reduce costs without lowering the quality of learning and how to engage the learner in the planning and management of the educational process.

The role of the mass media is crucial in our opinion on the basis of the Open University experiment to the future of the education of adults. Concern can be expressed at the present use of the mass media, especially television, for too much television time in Britain is devoted to propaganda programmes and entertainment programmes, which often depict violence and sexual permissiveness. It is possible to argue that on some evenings, and in particular during the holiday-festival periods like Christmas and Easter, cheap entertainment is allowed to dominate the screens. On the other hand, one has to draw attention to the positive effects of television in enlarging people's horizons, and to some excellent Open University television programmes which cater for a minority but which indicates what can heppen in the education of adults. The Open University's greatest asset is that it is different in its conception from the rest of the British universities. It has been and still is to a large extent, a flexible institution, and with its use of correspondence teaching, face to face tutorials, the use of radio and television, it can be a model to adult education in the United Kingdom. But this depends on its efforts to win and keep the blue-collared workers and if it is willing to learn from the actual situation.

For in the early sixties in England and Wales most of the members of the Trades Union Congress Council had left elementary school at fourteen. Acquisition of knowledge was a driving force for these union leaders who started on the shop floor. Sidney Greene, the leader of the railwaymen, started as a railway porter at Paddington Station, while Frank Cousins, the leader of the Transport and General Workers' Union was an ex-coalminer and lorry driver. But as a perceptive journalist points out on these men:

> Whatever further education they received was self-administered and was not of the kind to encourage a speculative bent of mind. (Jenkins, 1962, p.10)

The tasks these union leaders had to perform, the responsibilities they had to face within their own union, demanded a much more systematic training and indeed called for continuing education. It was denied to them by the pressure of work and lack of provision. It is a source of amazement that these men discharge their responsibilities so well when one considers the little formal education that so many of them received.

It seems also that within informal education which makes up the adult education of most of the trade union leaders and a great number of other people in responsible position there is the same ingredient as found in the rest of the country: élitism. Take the theatre as an informal educational agency. Anthony Hilton found that only $4\frac{1}{2}$ per cent of the British playgoers who were surveyed were 'blue-collar workers' (Hilton, 1971, p.30). Over half of the theatre-going men had been educated beyond the age of twenty. This corresponded to less than 4 per cent for the United Kingdom population as a whole at the time of the survey. Also Hilton found that the proportion of young people aged 20 to 24 in the audience was three times higher than for the country in general, but this is explainable as young people go out much more than their elders.

There were other trends. It depends a great deal on the attitude of the local authorities and the patronage that they extend to the local theatre. But it seems that no local theatre would 'sell out' in England Wales without the assistance of tourists. In 1968-69 Stratford-on-Avon's production of the Royal Shakespeare Company sold out while only 36% attended the Chesterfield Civic Theatre, 38% at Canterbury, and 44% at Richmond in Surrey.

Hilton found that those who attended the theatre regularly in the sixties were better educated and more affluent. But greater wealth does not mean more visits to the local theatre, and so often the theatre-going member moves out to the suburbs. This involves an increase in travelling time and this is true also of a great number of the faithful adult education students. It seems that 1% increase in travelling time causes about a 2% drop in attendance (Hilton, 1971, p.29).

Like so many adult education agencies the theatre-owners have done very little to find out who attends their theatres. As far as the theatre company are concerned it is just the public. However, there have been studies in Sweden and in the United States of America and they have found that the playgoer is a professional, highly educated and well-off member of the community. Over 60 per cent of the men and 55 per cent of the women are members of a profession, or in the case of wives, have received professional training though they no longer practice it. In its highest, truest form the theatre appeals only to a limited number of the people (Hilton, 1971, p.26).

The major problem is the conflict between education and entertainment. It seems that drama is essentially educative and modern audiences go to the theatre not only to be entertained but also because they want to learn. That is why, as Anthony Hilton shows in his pioneering study, the theatre audience at the end of the sixties was drawn from the narrowest possible band in British society - the very highly educated and relatively well-off. The policy of many theatre managers was to lower the standard and ensure that there were no productions of Shakespeare. But this drives away the true audiences and they feel alienated (Hilton, 1971, p.27). Furthermore, the plays that are put on do not appeal to a sufficient cross section of society with the result that the educational process is not as successful as it could be.

What is true of the theatre is also true of another informal adult education agency, and that is books. Books of educational value are written in the main by members of the middle class (Brown, 1972, p.34). Two out of three authors at the end of the sixties in Britain were men, nearly half had been to universities and another quarter had been to a public or a grammar school. Over half of the professional writers were solely occupied with their work, 30 per cent were part-timers, and friends and relatives of the writers came from the same well-educated class.

59

The British nation is not bookish compared with the Russian people. Thirty per cent of the secondary authors were found to be lecturers or teachers. In their spare time they prepare books on educational subjects. For it is a fact that educational and technical books make up 60 to 70 per cent of the annual total of volumes published in Britain (Brown, 1972, p.36). It is preparation of books for educated people and very little effort has been done to reach the millions who never enter an adult education class or a public library. A great number of experiments could be done on the lines of the interesting model set up in the sixties by the Cardiganshire Library Service. The librarian, Mr. Alun R. Edwards, initiated a scheme by which groups of people under a tutor would attend at least six to ten meetings every winter to discuss books in the Welsh language. The culmination of the winter's work was to take part in a quiz programme on these books. Every village group would elect four from their group to comprise the team and the winning team would be presented with a shield. As the years went by the extra-mural department at the University College of Wales, Aberystwyth, adopted the groups as part of their adult programme. The significance of this remarkable adult education experiment was the fact that these people from the villages, towns and the countryside in Cardiganshire read and discussed recent books that had been published in the Welsh language, but that many of these small groups, especially in the outlying country areas around the towns of Aberystwyth, Tregaron, Lampeter and Aberayron, met in houses, farms, as well as in the local chapel or church vestry, the village school or hall. A similar set-up could be adopted for other parts of England and Wales with the establishment of book clubs or groups as part of adult education.

With regard to the world of films, this has already happened, and the film as well as the cinema is like the book world, a definite auxiliary of adult education. There are three definite aims to the film societies:

a   to enable members to see, at a low cost, films that are not exhibited on the commercial network;

b   to revive the classics;

c   to stimulate interest in the cinema as an art form and in film making as a skilled crafts.

In 1945 the Federation of British Film Societies was formed with the task of co-ordinating the work of the film societies. The United Kingdom is divided into nine regions, and the Federation publishes *Film News,* an annual year-book, as well as the magazine, *Film.* At the end of 1966 nearly 100,000 people in England and Wales belonged to over 450 film societies, varying in size from about 100 to 1,500 members (Lowe, 1970, p.219).

Another important trend in the period under consideration has been the special educational facilities set up by employers. This is the field of vocational training, and within industry there is a continual need for developing and updating industrial skills. Old skills become redundant and new skills are needed. But the task of retraining an adult is often difficult and complicated. One has to prepare carefully and as H.W. Quednau has stipulated, there has been a change in the concept of vocational retraining. At the end of the sixties it was part of lifelong education, and it was organised as an introduction to a constantly changing world of work rather than as a specialised training for a job (Quednau, 1970, p.5). Indeed, H.W. Quednau, who in 1970 was the Chief of the International Labour Organisation Human Resources Development Department, argued that this concept should be introduced before children leave secondary schools. But all this cannot overcome the basic problem in all adult education work, and especially with regard to vocational retraining, and that is the reluctance of adults to take advantage of the facilities offered to them. D.B. Newsham found in his research a high proportion of older workers with the will and the potential for the more skilled jobs finding their way into unskilled jobs. He cites the example of an employer in the Midlands who was offering retraining for other work within the company. A machine was introduced to develop hand operations. In the first group affected there were nine men whose ages ranged from 41 to 58 years of age. Seven left the organisation in preference to retraining. Of these seven two proposed to open a business together while the other five sought their familiar job in other firms. Each of them realised that it was just a matter of a few years before mechanisation caught up with them, and Newsham felt that the Redundancy Payments Act can be a stumbling block to retraining. The adult prefers the redundancy payment and then he tries to find a similar job elsewhere rather than to be retrained.

The Newsham Report in 1969 gives the result of a survey carried out in thirty organisations who were retraining workers over 35 years of age as well as young workers for work which required a training period of two weeks. They compared the stamina of the older men and women to the younger workers, and found:

i   that higher proportion of older men than young tend to leave during the training period or soon afterwards. After this the trend is reversed, and over a longer period it compares favourably;

ii   older men tend to succeed best in those jobs requiring training period of ten to thirteen weeks. They survive less well in those requiring longer training periods or very short training periods, and least well in those requiring six to eight weeks (Newsham, 1969, p.35);

iii   the method of training has more of an influence on the older workers than the young;

iv   among women the survival rate tended to be higher than young men during the training period, in the transition period, and in the long run. It is worthwhile to consider older applicants for training and women tend to respond better to the systematic training than do men (Newsham, 1969, p.35).

There is no doubt that vocational retraining demands attention, more research, and that the training needs to be extended. For example, a repair and maintenance specialist in modern industry needs to have some degree of skill in more than one trade. It seems also that models which can be seen in other countries could well be adapted to the United Kingdom context. Norway started in the late sixties correspondence courses for technical staff, with a Summer School at the end of the course of two weeks' duration plus an examination (Nilsen, 1970, p.69). What the Norwegian model does is to point to the need for co-operation between management, labour and adult educators. This is a model what could be adapted to the British scene, where ideas have rarely been modified by facts.

It is also a fact that the training of adults is much more organised and successful within the white-collared section of the community than the blue-collared section. A case in point is the provision for the training of the police. Great advances were made in the period 1945-1980 and according to S. Lawrence, who was one of Her Majesty's Inspectors of Constabulary, "the police training has the fairest and most advanced professional training facilities possessed by any country" (Lawrence, 1966, p.506). The young applicant is trained for thirteen weeks in one of the police training centres where he is taught by experienced police officers. On completion of his course he goes into the force where he is continually under instruction. Emphasis is placed on aptitude and the police officer is trained in detective work, traffic and road safety, forensic science, and public relations. There are professional examinations that he is expected to pass, and he must pass to qualify as a sergeant and then as an inspector. An officer destined for the middle and high ranks is very likely to be selected for training at the National Police College at Bramshill. Bramshill is the staff college, the university and the management college of the service, and glowing tributes have been given to the standard and provision of the police college (Lawrence, 1966, p.506).

The police training serves a specific purpose, and cannot be looked upon as a model for education after school. But it has one thing in common with all the education after school provision: it is selective and élitist, and very little is learnt from the actual situation. It caters for a specific group and favours minorities. The domination of post-school education by the requirements of the élite means that it is very hard to make it useful or attractive to most people. Teachers in British primary schools were amongst the first to evaluate the situation. It was realised that the reforms which have produced the 'open' primary school depended on abolishing the eleven-plus examination. Primary education for all has become a fact by minimizing the influence of the grammar schools; secondary education for all will come when Britain has minimized the influence of the university. The élitist system produces inequality, and it is a fact that very little has been done to overcome the deficiency and the natural waste of talents. Robbins Report in 1963 did not propose any relaxation of the competitiveness needed to obtain a place in the

British university. On its own estimates, the Robbins Report admitted that over a million adults in Britain had over the previous three decades qualified for university entry but had not sought it, or had not been granted it. The criteria of ability and need rather than qualification would multiply that number by a few millions. As David Page admits in a critical review of higher education:

> The provision of higher education for all who want it also applies at any point in their lives. At the moment there is a critical path to higher education, and if you don't get it by the age of twenty-three or so, you might as well give up. (Page, 1970, pp.213-4).

Some countries in the world at least try to rectify the inequality. In the United States of America half the adult population is touched by some form of continuing education. More and more of this education is conducted on campus by accredited university teachers (Driver, 1971, p.283). In Britain a quarter of the adult population is touched by further education in some form or other, but the walls of the universities are far harder to jump over. A full-time residential mature student was a scarce personage in the period 1945 to 1970 in the universities of England. Those who want an external degree register with universities on a part-time basis, and in 1970 there were 33,149 such students, a body equal in size to three Oxfords. Probably some of these students would overlap with the 40,000 or so students who applied to take a degree course with the Open University.

It seems that there are a number of assumptions made with regard to the university. Firstly, that full-time education is designed to receive the survivors of the school system. Secondly, a university degree is indelible. Thirdly, it is believed that outside the university there is no academic salvation. This view has been severely challenged by Labour politicians such as Anthony Crosland and academics such as Tyrrell Burgess and writers such as Christopher Driver. Tyrrell Burgess expresses this view:

> The question to be discussed in Britain seems to me to be — not whether 20 or 25 per cent of eighteen-year-olds embark on a three- or four- year course leading to a degree, nor indeed whether these students should be accommodated in universities or polytechnics — but whether we should offer this kind of course to eighteen-year-olds at all. Should we not start by planning an education service for everyone? It is quite clear that such a service will be different from the one we have now — because the one we have now excludes most people and will continue to do so until well into the next century. (Burgess, 1977, p.87).

Burgess and others who have written in the same way raise the question of content, purpose and provision of education for adults. Joseph Trenaman, who in the nineteen fifties established that the proportion of British adults who had ever taken further education courses of any kind was 26 per cent, went on to suggest that nearly 45 per cent of the population were resistant to new ideas and cultural values, but that the other half were potentially 'pro-educational'. They were likely to be susceptible to an educational approach though in only 10 per cent was there a sustained interest in education. Trenaman also maintained that the whole provision of education for adults (both formal and informal) was a reinforcing rather than a remedial process.

Research in the United States of America reinforces Trenaman's theory. The people who want adult education are the people in absolute terms who least need it, that is the ones who have already had seventeen years in schools and colleges. The people who most need adult education, like the black poor in the United States of America and the manual workers in Britain, have no desire to use the facilities. To complicate the situation very few are asking the question of how men and women in adult life had been helped or hindered by the education they received in childhood or adolescence, and there is always the situation (as we claim in this book) of adult educational ideas rarely being modified by facts.

During the period 1945-1980 there was an obvious neglect of those adults who were unable to fit into society, adults who often are 'unclubable' and 'drop-outs' as far as the traditional adult education classes are concerned. Peter Clyne wrote in 1970 to all the 162 local education authorities and found that the provision for the disadvantaged adult was very uneven. The Inner London Education Authority was the best authority, while the Welsh counties dragged their feet and showed great neglect. They provided very little adult education for the disadvantaged. Sixteen per cent of all local education authorities which responded to the enquiry (in fact 128 responded out of 162 local education authorities) were at that time not making any special provision. Clyne saw very little evidence of a desire to provide adult education for early leavers, and he also shows the failure of the English and the Welsh secondary school system (Clyne, 1970, p.10). Workers Educational Association were much more active than the universities' extra-mural departments in most of the areas. In particular the WEA were very active in the North West, East Midland and North Yorkshire among the immigrants, in London amongst the physically handicapped, in North Yorkshire among blind students in Leeds, and in the Western District they have been involved in preparing adults in community action.

There was a need to prepare and plan for the disadvantaged adult. Most of the residential centres and colleges had no suitable premises for people confined to wheelchairs. Best facilities were at Knuston Hall in Northamptonshire but even there they were limited.

Adult education among the disadvantaged suffers from lack of finance and need for more people to be involved. The main thrust has come from the councils of social services, and in 1970 there was nearly 200 of them in number. All these were autonomous and often there was a difference of opinion between local councils of social services and the national body. The councils of social services involved themselves in adult educational work by training voluntary workers and arranging courses in preparation for retirement at centres such as Nottingham, Southwark, Letchworth, Manchester and Coventry (Clyne, 1972, p.25). A number of councils of social services have developed extensive literary and language schemes designed to serve adult illiterates and immigrants. The councils of social services in Coventry,

Manchester and Salford were the most active councils of social services in this field of work at the end of the sixties (Clyne, 1972, p.26). Leicester and York were singled out as urban centres where a great deal of teaching among immigrants was carried out.

Radio and television could also be of more value in the educational process. No one denies the educative component in many of the programmes, such as *Cathy Come Home* and the Archers' programmes on understanding various kinds of disability and disadvantage. Local radio has its potential and Radio Leicester has pioneered in a number of experiments — a magazine programme for the elderly, *Over Sixties Club;* another for the blind, *Sound Guide;* and a third, *Getting Together,* for the Asian immigrant community (Clyne, 1972, p.39).

Films are often used for educational information, to train the voluntary worker for the task of assisting the disadvantaged. Three examples will clarify this point. The British Epilepsy Association's film, *The Silent Factor,* outlines the extent and nature of the problems faced by an epileptic and how he or she can be helped; the British Diabetic Association had the same general purpose in the film *Balance of Life;* and the Spastics Society indicated their concerns and philosophy in the film, *A Place like Home.* All this is splendid, and there is always a need to extend the education among the disadvantaged adult.

Another serious problem in adult education which was touched upon in the first chapter is that of political education. The record of adult education in this field is not satisfactory. Pious noises have been heard time and time again and the National College of Labour Colleges was always emphasising in its magazine *Plebs* the need for political education among the workers. As we will see most of the adult educational provision among trade unionists and the working class is vocational and utilitarian. The Right Honourable Arthur Woodburn's hope expressed in 1953 in the *Plebs* has never been implemented by the Labour Party:

> Much of our education inculcates the 'morality' and purposes of capitalism — not how we can serve but how much we can make. Labour hopes to educate with a new moral purpose and for serivce. (Woodburn, 1953, p.242).

It is very seldom that adult education centres provide courses that could be in any way regarded as political education. There are few staff students in subjects such as International Affairs in the extramural departments. Adult education has never been successful in persuading people to study local government and classes in economics, international affairs and current affairs have dropped over the years. Yet in the same period a number of creative contributions to political theory have been made by academics in English universities. Among these are the studies of R.T. McKenzie and David E. Butler in the field of political parties, S.E. Finer on interest groups, and Herman Finer and Denis Brogan in the field of comparative government. The political parties have never really taken political education seriously for their efforts are geared to winning support at local and national level rather than educating the electorate on the nature of government or on international affairs.

All these trends that we have sketched indicate quite conclusively that at the end of our period we had reached a stage at which lifelong education should have become a reality for a great number of people. Conceptually speaking, adult education was already in integral part of the overall educational system but in its application it remained disorganised, and in England and Wales there was no agreement as to its role in the education of adults. Britain lagged behind many of the other European countries and a great deal of valuable assistance will come by looking at the European scene with regard to the philosophy of continuing education. To establish continuing education in the United Kingdom many pre-requisites must be taken into account. These can be gathered together and stated in our study of adult education.

1.   Education must become available to adults wherever they are and whenever they are free. The first step must therefore be to expand education at all times and in all places so that every adult will have the opportunity to educate himself. To achieve this ideal all the responsible agencies for adult education must have much more government aid and also must be convinced themselves of the need to provide classes and facilities for adults in every area. It is possible to talk of the "right to adult education" following the definition of "the minimal right to education" for all individuals, as proposed by the Marly Conference, which the Council of Europe organised in May, 1967. The right should comprise the following:- a basic education, variable in length according to country; a professional training, generally apart from compulsory school-attendance; and a continual education involving both the improvement of professional training (which covers all kinds of post-school activities) and access to cultural, leisure activities.

2.   Diversify levels and fields of interest.

The teaching for adults must also correspond to their fields of interest and level of attainment. Bertrand Schwartz of France has argued under this heading that an adult can only be taught effectively within a group in a particular area (Schwartz, 1970, pp.75-76). An adult is different from an adolescent for he has over the years gathered a great deal of 'intellectual baggage' and expertise. Within every group the adults will differ and each adult will be a separate case, so the task of relating the different interests, expertise will always be a hurdle to overcome for the adult tutor. The adult educator as we will see time and time again is a very special person in the field of adult education. Bertrand Schwartz expresses this point succinctly:

> One must have educators whose first task will be to bring out requirements, to transform latent needs into conscious ones.   (Schwartz, 1970, p.76).

3.   To achieve continuing education educational technology has a specific role to play in the achievement. Educational technology has shown that it can assist adult education. The mass media to some extent is willing to co-operate and while adult educationists in Britain have been slow to respond yet it is relevant to point out that the research findings are rather muddled in their conclusions. For example, television has tremendous potentiality but the work of some researchers indicates that television is not the great harbinger of culture and enlightment (Halloran, 1964, p.34). Television does broaden the outlook of people and brings the family together. But W.A. Belson felt that the effect of television depends upon the viewer's cultural and family backgrounds and upon the area in which he lives (Belson, 1959, p.127). This supports the earlier point of the need to take the 'intellectual baggage' into consideration when educating adults.

Educational technology includes correspondence education. The period between 1945 and 1970 saw an increasing demand for this and adult educationists like Professor E.G. Weddell stressed the need for a body of teachers specially trained for this type of education. Open University has taken up this challenge and a part of its teaching is made up of the correspondence texts. Each block of correspondence material is mailed to the student at appropriate times during the year.

Closed circuit television can be a powerful reinforcement in the teaching of adults and is regarded as part of educational technology. The University of Leeds set up a short circuit television centre for the benefit of all its departments. It can retail programmes to more than a hundred units at one time. Other universities have followed suit with closed circuit television provision. But it is a provision largely preserved for students in universities rather than for the mature adult learner.

Many specialists are putting all their hopes in "educational technology" to improve the quality of adult education. G. Maddison defined educational technology as "the development, application and evaluation of systems, techniques and aids to improve the process of human learning" (Maddison, 1971, p.14). The trend in the late sixties was to move away from technology in education and towards a technology of education, and the tendency was to construct pedagogic method round the student (learning) rather than round the teacher (teaching).

The consequence of using educational technology is to step up the student's personal activity. He will be led more and more to acquire knowledge and skills for himself without direct aid from a teacher. In such a context, the teacher's role is completely changed: he has to analyse the content of programmes, translate them into concrete form so that they become self-educational aids while at the same time maintaining direct contact with the student. The tutor's task is to help the individual adult to learn to learn.

Computer based and programmed learning has its place in educational technology. Programmed teaching is often very valuable, and there will be more use made of it in the future. The application of educational technology is very much a part of the provision of continuing education to the adult population.

4.   Adult education is a prerequisite of continuing education.

The concept of adult education originated in the English-speaking and Scandinavian countries in the middle of the nineteenth century. All were concerned at the growing gap between rapid material progress on the one hand, and, on the other, the cultural standard of the mass of the people who had not been given the basic right to some elementary schooling. The development of adult education in England and Wales was influenced by the idea of a second chance and catching up, of adjusting less educated adults to the norm and ideology of English society. During this period a few dissenting voices were heard pleading for a much deeper motivation and those who saw adult education as a tool for radical social change. Adult education was to liberate people rather than a means of making the lower class toe the established conservative line on social, political and religious issues. The need for continuing education is an acknowledgement that adult education as conceived in the past is inadequate and that education is a means of enriching the individual and society. It also means that one has to learn from the situation and apply it in a constructive manner.

Continuing education as the word implies is not static or conformist, but takes account of the actual conditions in which changes take place in every society.

5   Continuing education counteracts the bureaucratic, impersonal society

Continuing education is meant to fulfil people's lives, assist them to know themselves and understand society and so it must find ways of coming closer to people's lives. It must be anchored in the home, the neighbourhood, in work and leisure groups. Education with reference to both content and methods cannot be divorced from the travails of any era. In the thirties of the century the German exiled sociologist, Karl Mannheim, observed the trend of social change towards the organised society and the mass public. The breakdown and consequent disintegration of the traditional organic social structures meant the liberation of individuals and groups from the static positions they formerly occupied, with their fixed rights and duties. However, the social changes involved have tied down the individual once more, this time to the structures of organised society. In many respects life in the technological society ignores and sometimes even annihilates the personal freedom that was promised to the individual in the welfare state. People are free in name, but wherever they go they meet with bureautcratic regulations, with rights and duties of an impersonal character. Individuals resent the organisational structure in which they find themselves. This results in what we call the mass public. Communication media such as radio and television fit in with this development and serve the system accordingly. Continuing education is a disturbing element to any satisfied bureaucratic mass society.

6   Continuing education is a useful means of planning for the education of adults for the future. This to many of the theorists entails a continuous renewal, democratisation, and a continuous effort. But the crux of it all is the continuous role of the individual in society. Objectives have to be constantly scrutinised in the light of research and new insights. The educational systems have to be comprehensive and coherent and must cover all age groups and social classes in such a way as to provide an integrated range of courses, meeting the greatest possible number of individual needs. As the system of continuing education rests on the principle of a mobile social order, it demands from each member of society constant physical, mental and emotional mobility. The goal is to educate the whole man and everyone must be, and remain, a seeker.

7   Continuing education emphasises the fundamental philosophy of voluntary education, and that is to enable the adult to become an independent learner. It is true to say that this principle is forgotten in adult education and tutors tend to become demagogues or authoriatarian teachers. Education is not an independent phenomenon which exists outside a person and which can simply be grafted on to him. It can only exist inside a person. The teacher's task is not to transfer or impose education but to awaken curiosity, offer guidance, enable the pupil to discover learning and let it grow in him. The adult has to discipline himself in the task of learning, and he has to accept a great deal of responsibility for the educative process.

8   Continuing education in England and Wales could well be identified with community development. The term 'community development' corresponds with a great deal that goes on in an educational sense in England and Wales. Community development has come to mean a particular approach to all education based on certain ethical propositions — the chief of · which is that people have not reached their best unless they are involved in and committed to the upkeep and moulding of their social environment by participant membership of groups dedicated to that end. In the course of time the national and local government has taken responsibility for a number of structures which cater for cultural tastes, such as libraries, museums, art galleries. Encouragement and financial support is often given to voluntary associations in their work, and every effort made to assist those who feel left out and neglected in an affluent age. Many of these groups are made up of disadvantaged adults and at other times consist of immigrants or those in sub-cultural communities. Self help groups come in this category and we will look at the most well-known of these groups later on in the book.

9   Continuing education is a realistic attempt to ensure that everyone should be entitled to extended schooling. Bertrand Schwartz has gone so far as to work out the cost in the French context for this elementary right of adults to education. We find in his article that the right to continuous adult education will amount to 13.2 hours per year, 6.6 of which will be paid. This right applies to adults from the time they leave school until they die. Thus in

69

an active life of 50 years (between the ages of 16 and 66) we may estimate that about 660 hours would be devoted to education, that is to say only about a hundred days (Schwartz, 1972, p.110). Already many adults do educate themselves, and a large proportion of them spend more than 660 hours of their life doing so. Most adults would be very encouraged if they realised that they had the right to 660 hours, half of which would be compensated. Instead of further education and adult education for just a small percentage of the population, consisting always of the same people, who would thus benefit from more than their quota of 660 hours, the right ought to be the same for everyone and become a de facto right.

But as Schwartz admits, such a change in France or any other country for that matter would raise a host of problems and particular attention would have to be paid to: labour legislation (length of working week, hours, continuous working day), the question of educational leave or sabbatical leave is a key issue; wages, social costs, financial, organisation and intellectual matters, the establishment and equipment of new education establishments; mass media and the local situation.

10 Continuing education implies that education is important throughout life and can be resumed at any moment of an adult's life. There is a tendency to overload children and adolescents with facts in their early years and as adolescents. Ivan Illich in *Deschooling Society* (1971) opposes the concept of childhood as the educational period and in this sense his radical protest has great relevance. Werner Rasmussen of Denmark feels that permanent education will reduce pressure on adolescent education, and maintains that:

> The lifelong "journey" should in the future be supported by supply-stations all along the route. It will thereby be possible to travel more lightly which means that it will not be necessary to try to load the memories of young people as such. (Rasmussen, 1972, p.422).

This means that adult education is very important for the government and community and that it should never be left in the hands of an élite group. Continuing education will change mankind and society, and it will therefore be number one priority in the future. But in England and Wales the theory has to be implemented and this is always the difficult task for the adult educationist.

Chapter 3
Workers' Education and Trade Union Education

Workers' education in England and Wales was bedevilled for over thirty years by a huge number of unnecessary hurdles and in particular by the inability to learn the lessons from the actual situation at local and national level. While we will look at each of these hurdles in detail in the chapter it is only right to point them out briefly in our introduction. There was the continual confrontation between the two main suppliers of workers' education, the Workers Educational Association and the National Council of Labour Colleges. Between 1920 and 1960 there was unnecessary overlapping in resources and a reluctance on the part of everyone to change the pattern. The workers themselves and their trade unions were largely apathetic, and the bigger unions claimed the right to go their own way. Trade Union Congress had the task of unifying the different organisations under the NCLC's call for rationalisation and also to strengthen their authority in workers' education. The Workers' Education Trade Union Committee, which came into existence in 1919, and the NCLC, founded in 1921, would cease to function and its activities would be carried out by the Trade Union Congress education department. As it happened they were not all carried out by TUC for many of the activities were discarded.

The historical account of the confrontation of the WEA and the NCLC on Workers' Education between 1909 and 1945

The WEA was founded by one of the great prophets of English adult education, Albert Mansbridge. He had left school at fourteen and knew the advantages of attending a university education. The WEA was to serve the working class for Mansbridge realized two things. Firstly, that the university extension movement which he was most indebted to was not reaching the workers in the urbanised, industrial connurbations, and secondly, the educational facilities it was providing were too disjointed, too scrappy, to make the educational impact that was needed. Mansbridge found like-minded idealists, and in particular R.H. Tawney, who in time epitomized what was best in the WEA.

However, the Labour Movement had earlier established a College with the Wealthy American, Walter Vrooman, as one of the founders, to train working men for service to their class. The date was February 1899, and the name of the college became well-known in the Labour Movement, as Ruskin College, Oxford. Ruskin College was in the ' middle of the road' or to some to the right in the Trade Union camp, and the Trade Unions in time demanded this allegiance. Dennis Hird, the Principal, was a socialist and many of the patrons and friends of the College were not socialists. But Hird had among his students young men who were imbued with socialist and industrial unionism such as Noah Ablett of the Rhondda Valley. They brought into being a magazine called *Plebs* and instituted a movement called the Plebs League. These young Ruskin students sounded a new note: a crusade for working-class education. A strike over the sacking of the Principal's and his executive's disagreement on the teaching of sociology in March-April 1909 brought the confrontation between two standpoints to a climax. The students and some ex-students of Ruskin who had accepted Marxism appealed for a new institution and through their efforts a Central Labour College came into being and classes were organised in all parts of the country. At Rochdale, where Tawney had taken charge of an university tutorial class, an old WEA member, Harold Kershaw, set out in September 1909 to organise, in opposition to the WEA, the Rochdale and District Labour College classes (Craik, 1964, p.92). This was the beginning of great bitterness, and an issue which bedevilled trade union education for over fifty years. It was a conflict that became absurd and meaningless as the years went by (Waller, 1956, p.29).

But for a great part of those fifty years the debate was a live one. As Waller states no one would gather this by reading the outstanding 1919 Smith Report on Adult Education. But in the WEA magazine, *The Highway,* and the NCLC (which was established in 1921) magazine, *Plebs,* one comes across continual argument as to the purpose of trade union education.

The WEA standpoint can be found in the massive study of adult education by the Reverend Basil A. Yeaxlee, a member of the 1919 Report Committee. Dr. Yeaxlee's book, *Spiritual Values in Adult Education Volume II,* published in 1924, saw the NCLC position as provocative, and he condemns their materialistic basis. On the NCLC side J.F. Horrabin, who proved a great educator, argued forcefully in the same year in his book, *Working Class Education,* for the development of specifically working class education, with working class aims and under working class control. Horrabin, who had been influenced by Shaw, Blatchford, the Clarion, Ruskin and Marxism, wrote a textbook for *Plebs* classes on economic and political geography, supplemented by atlases such as the *Plebs Atlas,* and other books, such as the *Atlas of Europe* and the *Atlas of Current Affairs.* These books helped to put the Labour College Movement on the map, and one cannot overestimate Horrabin's contribution. G.H.D. Cole, on the other hand, had a great deal to say to both movements, and felt that the emphasis of the WEA on educating the workers, and the NCLC insistence on propaganda were both legitimate. But precedence belonged to education, and Cole urged both movements in the twenties to adjust themselves and co-operate in the task of educating the working people. For Cole felt that ordinary members of the trade union movement would be so puzzled by the perpetual controversy that they would abandon the WEA and the NCLC. Cole had an important point in his article in 1923, and R.D. Waller thirty-three years later suggested that the conflict caused by the rival claims of the WEA and the NCLC led the trade unions to begin making their own educational arrangements unconnected with either of them (Waller, 1956, p.29). This is a view that merits consideration, and the conflict was still simmering in the post-war period. We intend to look at the different approaches and the different movements that catered for worker's education in the period 1945-1980.

A   National Council of Labour Colleges

The National Council of Labour Colleges made its debut in January 1921, and immediately a rift and misunderstanding grew between the permanent Central Labour College in London and the new movement. There was no denying the need for a central body to co-ordinate the individual non-resident colleges which had been set up the length and breadth of the country. The Board of Governors and the staff of the Central Labour College saw themselves in the role of preparing tutors and organisers for the Districts that were to be formed. But the Plebs League, which was instrumental in calling the conference that founded the NCLC, did so without reaching an agreement with the Central Labour College. By the end of 1923 they were both competing for trade union support, and the two unions which had given annual financial support to the Central Labour College began to have consultations with the Trade Union Congress as to the future of the institution. The Trade Union Congress at Scarborough in 1925 agreed to the transfer of the Labour College into their care and also the plans for the construction of new buildings at Kew or 'at an equally suitable centre as soon as funds are available'. After the Congress, the rich Socialist Frances, the Countess of Warwick, offered her country house, Easton Lodge in Essex, to the TUC. The NCLC and in particular the General Secretary, J.P.M. Millar, opposed the Easton Lodge scheme, and at the Bournemouth Congress in 1926 the Congress declined the scheme. William Craik, who was to be the Principal of the Labour College at London, saw this decision as also the virtual end of the Labour College (Craik, 1964, p.144). At the Swansea TUC Congress in 1928 the death sentence was announced, and the Labour College ceased to function.

The NCLC General Secretary, Jim Millar, expressed his regret, while William Craik shows how the NCLC itself had not been fully behind the scheme, and at least had allowed the TUC to close down the Labour College (Craik, 1964, p.153).

The NCLC enlarged its scope in the thirties from its London office, but during the second world war the building was bombed and the organisation's headquarters were moved to Tillicoultry in Scotland *(Plebs,* 1952, p.118). The work of administration was carried out from Tilicoultry until the movement was wound up in 1964. The main educational work of the NCLC was as follows:

i   Tutorial Classes

These were held in most of the urban areas in Great Britain and the tutors were voluntary though the full time members of NCLC were also tutors. Many an academic, and in particular professional university adult educationists, criticised the standard and the qualifications of the dedicated men and women who gave their time and talent for the cause of working class education. The NCLC tutors did the work for an out-of-pocket allowance of 2/6d. plus travelling costs, and this dedication is obvious when one realises that in 1953 the tutors taking a WEA class which met 24 times in the year were paid from £80 to £120 *(Plebs,* 1953, p.45). Who were the tutors? In the main, committed socialists who were imbued with a vision of Socialism — to build a new Jerusalem in the Satanic mills of Lancashire and the depressing mining valleys of South Wales. Many of them were committed Marxists, though in the fifties this was not highlighted as much as in the early period. The tutors were in the main politically activated, and one or two examples will surface to prove the point. Take the South Wales Miners' Leader, Dai Dan Evans (1898-1974), who was most active in spreading Marxist ideas through the NCLC classes during the inter-war period in the Dulais and Swansea Valleys and sometimes as far away as Talgarth in the Breconshire countryside. One of his successors in the South Wales Miners' Union said in a tribute to him:

> Even while he was a Miner's Agent he spent at least one night a week tutoring for the N.C.L.C. (Francis, 1974, p.3).

In Division 9 in the early fifties Sam Watson, the General Secretary of the Durham Miners, tutored in a weekly class every winter. In the fifties in the Cardiff area one of the most active tutors was George Thomason, a young lecturer in the Department of Industrial Relations who subsequently became, and holds the post at present of, Professor of the Department in the University College of South Wales and Monmouthshire, Cardiff. Dr. Thomason is an outstanding academic and it seems that he was not the only one to devote his talents to the NCLC.

The local NCLC classes were in charge of a divisional organiser, and Great Britain was divided into twelve divisions. The divisional organiser was also as a rule dedicated, committed to the education of the working people, and sometimes with an ambition to become a labour member of parliament. Many of them did. E.J. Milne, who later became an MP for Blyth, was for a time midlands divisional organiser of the NCLC. William Warbey, a former organiser, won the Broxtowe Division of Nottingham in a by-election in 1953. Raymond Fletcher, who fought a few elections while a NCLC organiser in South Wales, subsequently became the MP for Ilkeston in Derbyshire. Will Owen, who was elected MP for Morpeth in 1955, was at one time an NCLC organiser for South Wales. Sid J. Bidwell, who had become active in the early fifties as a NCLC voluntary tutor, was appointed in 1955 as the NCLC organiser for North London. Today Bidwell is the Labour MP for the nationally-known largely immigrant community of Southall.

The NCLC was served also by divisional organisers who gave their services for most of their working lives to the movement. A good example was George Phippen, a Rhondda miner who retired in 1954 after 32 years' service in the London area. At first he was the only organiser for London, and the

Division ran right down to the south coast and later as the North London organiser for the NCLC and then as the movement grew, divisional secretary. Though George Phippen had a House of Commons dinner at his retirement, J.P.M. Millar summed up the work in a nutshell:

> N.C.L.C. work is back-room work — not for the N.C.L.C. organiser the excitement of elections or industrial disputes. (Millar, 1955, p.19).

Another example would be J.T. Dorricott who served between 1929 and 1954 as the NCLC organiser for Norther Ireland before taking up the same work in the North East of England. Jack Dorricott was educated at the Central Labour College, London, on a Northumberland Miners' scholarship in 1923-25. The non-residential Labour Colleges depended for their survival on the activities and enthusiasm of local committees and officials. Bristol Labour College in the post-war period was well served by B.K. Preuss as secretary. In 1955 he spent a week's holiday touring the city's trade union offices on behalf of the Labour College. Preuss, who was a native of East Prussia, was well-known also in the South West of England as a lecturer on Foreign Affairs. There are many examples in university towns of help coming from members of the staff who were sympathetic to the cause of independent working class education. Swansea Labour College was well served for a period by the family of Professor Cass-Beggs. He acted as the secretary of the College, and the daughter, Rosemary Cass-Beggs, served as a voluntary tutor. The enthusiasm of the classes sometimes was extraordinary, and nothing would disrupt them. The preparations for the coming of the huge Royal National Eisteddfod of Wales to the small village of Ystradgynlais in the upper reaches of the Swansea Valley in the summer of 1954 did not disrupt the NCLC class, which 'met as usual'.

What was expected of the class and its tutor? At least four things:

i   Commitment to the aim of the NCLC although some adult education historians suggest that the NCLC in the post-war period played down its Marxism philosophy, one has no evidence for this in the official organ of the movement, namely the monthly magazine *Plebs*. NCLC flew the flag 'Education for Emancipation' and opposed the emphasis of the WEA of having 'Education for Education's sake'. The NCLC education was based on the recognition of the class struggle which had given birth to the trade union movement, the Co-operative movement and the Labour Party. J.P.M. Millar sums up the commitment of the NCLC classes in this way:

> It believed that those who fought the workers, politically or industrially, must think against them and could not therefore be their educational friends. *(Plebs,* 1954, p.43).

This was the main reason behind the constant sniping at the W.E.A. which was often an unfair attack.

ii   The emphasis should be in the class on discussion as a method of conveying information, knowledge and ideas to the students. NCLC entered the debate in the fifties initiated by S.G. Raybould of the University of Leeds on the value of the three year university tutorial class which had been the mainstay of the WEA from its inception in 1903 till the post-war period. Academics, adult educationists within the university extra mural movement and the WEA joined hands with J.P.M. Millar of the NCLC and W.P. Alexander of the Association of Education Committees for England, Wales and Northern Ireland in debunking the exaggerated value attached to academic courses in adult education, particularly the three year course. *Plebs* comment in its first issue in 1952 was stark-real in its questioning:

> Is it not frequently the case that many of the students who undertake such a three-year course are merely taking the course for their own interest and pleasure and make little or no contribution, through that course, to the improvement of the social system in which they are living? *(Plebs, 1952, p.5)*.

To J.P.M. Millar, the most consistent philosopher in the NCLC movement, the tutorial method had its weakness. Millar felt that a solid hour's lecture was not suitable to working class students and that the most suitable method was the discussion group. J.P.M. Millar adds:

> It is high time all of us engaged in educational work in the N.C.L.C. dealt with the tyranny of the unbroken hour's lecture. (Millar, 1954, p.47).

iii   The syllabus to be working class orientated and vocational. Essential basic knowledge was given as to the history and growth of the working class organisations and this included also social history and economics. Practical subjects were taught such as courses in the English language as well as trade union problems.

iv   The tutor should influence his students with regard to the reading and of buying books of importance. J.P.M. Millar emphasised this more than once in his articles in the *Plebs* magazine:

> It is the N.C.L.C.'s job to encourage workers to get the habit of literature buying and reading.

ii   **The One-Day School**

The One-Day School proved to be a very popular method of conveying education to the members of the NCLC Movement. There are reasons for this. One-Day Schools were held in the main on a Saturday or a Sunday so that the students were fresh and not expected to go along after a day's work. The schools were held often in pleasant settings such as Dunraven Castle in South Wales, and in places which were central to the region. But the main reason for the popularity was the availability of Labour Members of Parliament and trade union leaders to lecture at these One-Day Schools. The subjects also would be topical and of interest to trade unionists and labour party activists and an effort was made to involve labour politicians who belonged to the two main divisions in British politics — the left and the right wing. In 1953 and 1954 three One-Day Schools were held in Wales with Roy Jenkins, a right-wing Labour MP, at Bridgend, Desmond Donnelly, a right-wing MP at Port Talbot, and the left-wing MP Ian Mikardo at Neath. The

Fabian, Anthony Crosland tutored at the Southampton One-Day School on October 22nd, 1955, on the future of British Socialism and one of Southampton's MP's, Dr. Horace M. King, lectured at a One-Day School a fortnight afterwards (November 12th, 1955) at Chichester. The following day at Rotherham in Yorkshire the Bevanites, Michael Foot, MP, and J.P.W. Mallalieu, and the intellectual Richard Crossman were all at a One-Day School. Christopher Mayhew and Fred Peart, both Members of Parliament, were willing to travel to Carlisle for a One-Day School during the Parliamentary recess in the summer of 1955. Some of the One-Day Schools would have a very broad theme. Ronnie Williams, MP for Wigan, spoke at Liverpool at a One-Day School in 1954 on his visit to Kenya, while Arthur Blenkinsop, MP, took as his subject at Amble, 'the future of the Social Services'. Young and old politicians alike travelled to NCLC One-Day Schools. The veteran Labour MP Fenner Brockway was the speaker at Dawlish while a new name appeared on the posters advertising the One-Day School at Swansea, Shirley Catlin, later to become a Cabinet Minister in the Labour Government and known as Shirley Williams. Some of these politicians would attract large crowds, and among the most successful were the two old Labour Central College students, and both architects of the Welfare State, Aneurin Bevan, Member of Parliament for Ebbw Vale, and James Griffiths, Member of Parliament for Llanelli, who became in the fifties Deputy Leader of the Labour Party. James Griffiths drew one of the largest crowds of delegates ever seen at a One-Day School in East Ham in 1954.

iii   Week-end Schools

The NCLC organised also Week-end Schools on the same pattern as the One-Day Schools. The Week-end Schools were largely residential and catered in the main for trade unionists, and were held throughout the country. One of the most loyal supporters of the week-end schools were the miners, and the Derbyshire Miners Council, for example, provided regularly fifty free scholarships at the NCLC week-end schools held at Eastwood Grange. The need for a residential college to serve the NCLC for week-end schools and summer schools was raised in the post-war period and at the Annual Conference of the Movement in 1954 at Scarborough a resolution was moved by a R.W. Hatton calling for a residential college. Hatton had in mind an institution similar to the old Central Labour College which had been discarded so easily in the late twenties. He argued that it should be possible for the NCLC to use the Wortley Hall premises as a residential college. A year afterwards the shelves of the library in Wortley Hall were filled with three valuable NCLC collections, namely the Fred Shaw, the Jean Dott and the Hyndman collections. B.K. Preuss of the Bristol Labour College seconded the resolution and reminded the Conference of the provision made in Denmark for workers' residential education. The National Union of Railwaymen delegate, G.E. Walton, maintained that if a residential college was to be built, then it should be built by the TUC and run in co-operation with the NCLC.

The cost was the prohibitive factor in his opinion. Arthur Woodburn, MP, was not impressed with the idea and pointed out how the Amalgamated Engineering Union paid around £9,000 a year to the NCLC and in return had some 25,000 people taking advantage of the NCLC facilities. If the same amount of money had been spent on the provision of residential courses lasting a year the number of students would have been only nine. Woodburn, like W.H. Bradley of the AEU, was afraid that long-term scholarships at residential colleges so often resulted in students becoming personnel officers and factory inspectors, and in this way being lost to the trade union movement. The opportunity had been lost thirty years before, and Walton and Woodburn were aboslutely right in their speeches. The NCLC could not hope to set up a residential college on their own. It had to be a Trade Union Congress decision. The trade unions were not extravagant by any standards as far as adult education was concerned, and they would be interested in seeing 25,000 members having some advantage from the educational facilities rather than sponsor a few young trade unionists. It was a useful debate but there was no chance of anything being derived from it, and it was another example of how the adult education movement was slow to learn from the actual situation.

iv   Summer Schools

It was at Coberhill Guest House near Claughton that the first NCLC summer school was held in 1924. It became a regular event and more than one summer school was organised. In the post-war period six to seven summer schools were held in July/August as well as a summer school in one of the European Countries. The details of NCLC summer schools for 1954 will give an idea of the subjects discussed in the post-war period:

1954 N.C.L.C. Summer Schools

Beatrice Webb House, near Dorking, Surrey	17th-24th July, 1954	Section 1 Industrial Management
Beatrice Webb House, near Dorking, Surrey	24-31st July, 1954	Workers' Control & Joint Consultation, Nationalisation and other forms of Public Control of Industry
University Hostels, East Suffolk Rd., Edinburgh	24-31st July, 1954	Training in Public Speaking and how to state a case

Continued

University Hostels, East Suffolk Rd., Edinburgh	31st July-7th August, 1954	What Trade Unionists should know about Company Accounts and Profits
Wortley Hall, Wortley, nr. Sheffield	7th-14th August, 1954	History and Policy of the T.U. Movement
	Section I	Young Trade Unionists
	Section II	Others
Wortley Hall, Wortley, nr. Sheffield	14th-21st August, 1954	Problems facing Labour
Stockholm, Sweden (2 schools of a week each)	24th-31st July, and 31st July - 7th August, 1954	Sweden and the Swedish Labour Movement

Table 3:1

The same was the pattern, and the venue and in the main the subject matter were vocational and topical. The foreign summer school naturally changed its venue every year, as for example the 1953 summer school held in Copenhagen, Denmark, on Denmark and the Danish Labour Movement; and the 1955 summer school at Oberursel-Taunus, near Frankfurt in Germany, on Germany, including the German Trade Union and the Labour Movement; and the 1956 foreign summer school held at Vienna in Austria.

The NCLC was also asked to arrange occasionally summer schools for the trade unions. In 1950 the AEU executive decided to invite NCLC to run two residential summer schools on Industrial Managements, and in 1954 the NCLC organised a summer school for the Nottinghamshire Miners at Retford. The NCLC was invited to arrange summer schools for other coalfields besides Nottingham, as, for example, the Durham miners and the Midland miners. The full-time organisers were responsible for conducting the summer schools as directors of studies.

v   Postal Courses Department

This proved to be one of NCLC's most rewarding activities and was supervised by Christine Millar who had in 1923 married the General Secretary of the NCLC, J.P.M. Millar. This domestic partnership became a most fruitful partnership in the educational work of the NCLC, and Christine Millar became a most able postal courses supervisor and acted as the General Secretary's deputy. In time more students took advantage of the postal courses than any other activity except the branch lectures organised by the NCLC. The success of the Postal Courses depended on:

i publicity. The NCLC had to use every opportunity given to them to publicise their postal course syllabuses. In 1954 the NCLC employed an outside enrolling agent to visit factories, railway workshops, to make contact on behalf of the department of postal studies with those members who could not be contacted at their branch meetings;

ii topical and practical subjects. The whole emphasis was on vocational topics and it was in the same tradition as the usual subjects conducted in the weekly classes. In 1955 there were 56 subjects available and 16,646 students who had enrolled. The total in the post-war period usually fluctuated between 15,000 and 21,000 students who participated in the Postal Courses.

The emphasis on topicality can be illustrated by the course on automation which was one of 56 courses offered in 1955 to the 16,550 students who enrolled. Automation attracted 1,717 students. This was not surprising for automation was a very popular subject for one-day NCLC schools, and in the July 1956 issue of *Plebs* a series of articles was published on the subject. Articles were contributed by George Thomason, Cardiff; Fred Lee, MP; an American, Don Slaiman and Graham Horsman, chief editorial assistant of the NCLC postal courses department.

The practical nature of the postal courses is also evident as one looks at the courses that were provided. The NCLC had two postal courses specially adapted to the needs of beginners in public speaking. It gave guidance in preparing and delivering short speeches, serious and humerous, as well as full-length speeches. A complete lesson was devoted to debating, presentation speeches, after-dinner speeches, votes of thanks and other practical points. There were courses on secretaryship as well as on the administration of the local trade union branches; chairmanship, as well as conference and committee duties. The history of the labour movement had six aspects highlighted, namely the Co-operative Movement; Labour Party — yesterday and today; Labour's post-war achievements; pioneers of the labour movement and socialism. Trade unionism, however, dominated the postal courses with twelve relevant courses, namely history of the British working class; industrial injuries insurance; industrial law; industrial management for trade unionists — elementary, as well as an advanced course; industrial relations, shop stewards and workshop representatives and their functions; time and motion study for trade unionists — elementary and advanced; trade union branch administration; trade unionism today; workers' control and joint consultation. Councillors were also catered for with courses elementary and advanced on local government in England and Wales, and a course on local government in Scotland, and if they were interested in finding out more about economics there were two courses (elementary and advanced), a course on finance; great powers and world problems; how Britain is governed; national insurance;

standard of living; cost of living, as well as a practical course on electioneering. Current affairs were included with courses on Britain's tasks today; Europe since 1914; international developments and our wages; problems of British agriculture; and the trade unionists who had an interest in historical material could study the early history of man; European history to 1914; social history as well as other historical orientated courses already referred to. The basic skill of expression was not forgotten with courses on English — elementary (grammar); English — intermediate (composition and article writing), and advanced English (article writing and labour journalism). The influence of J.F. Horrabin can be detected in the course on political geography and the unusual was catered for by an elementary course in esperanto.

vi Publications

The NCLC provided a useful service through their attractive short-texts books with a strong marxist slant. Many of these have become very well-known indeed inside the Labour Movement. An example of this would be the text-book *A Worker Looks at History and Trade Unionism* written by Mark Starr, a Welsh miner who became a NCLC organiser and then the educational director of the International Ladies' Garment Workers' Union in the United States of America. J.F. Horrabin's books have already been referred to, and they were exceptionally good in presentation. In the post-war period the striking success of the booklet, *ABC of Chairmanship,* was commented upon by Members of Parliament as well as by ordinary members of the Trade Union Movement. Nearly 15,000 copies of *Your Trade Union and You* by Frank Allaun, MP, and Ellis Smith, MP, were sold in 1955. The General Secretary, J.P.M. Millar, was exceptionally versatile as a writer, editor and author of countless booklets describing the history, aims and activities of the NCLC, such as *Education and Power,* which had to be republished in 1953. He was responsible also in the post-war period for the lively periodical *Plebs* which was way ahead of other similar publications. In adult education and the Labour Movement in England and Wales there were few monthly magazines to compare with *Plebs* in interest and presentation. Established in 1909 it was the eldest of the Labour monthlies by the fifties and on its forty-second birthday in its new format it congratulated one of the most interesting companions, *Labour's Northern Voice,* on entering the twenty-seventh year of publication under the guidance of the same editor from the very beginning in 1925, Sam Higenbottom, an ILP pioneer. *Plebs* attracted articles from Labour politicians such as James Griffiths, Arthur Woodburn, Anthony Wedgwood Benn, young academics such as George Thomason, NCLC organisers such as Raymond Fletcher, historians of the calibre of A.J.P. Taylor whose parents had been enthusiastic supporters of the Labour College Movement in Lancashire, and the doyen of them all, J.P.M. Millar, whose flair for controversy produced an interesting magazine. Socialist principles and concern for education of the working class was continually hammered upon and the pungent cover-slogans of *Plebs* and the cartoons were effective as propaganda. The NCLC, like the Owenites in the eighteen-forties, relished public disputation with anyone as a means of inexpensive propaganda.

Difficulties of the NCLC

a   Apathy of the Workers

The NCLC was as effective and in many ways more effective in the role of educating trade unionists than the WEA or the WETUC. Through its unrelentless emphasis on its philosophical aim the NCLC was able to keep the most active trade unionists within its ranks. It had the support of the large unions such as the National Union of Railwaymen, the AEU, the National Union of Mineworkers, as well as the small localised unions such as the Hinckley Hosiery Warehousemen, and the Nelson and District Weavers' Association. Powerful trade union leaders such as Sam Watson of the Durham coalfield, Les Cannon of the Electrical Trade Union, were as active in the work of the NCLC and in the Annual Conferences as the lesser-known leaders of the smaller unions, such as A. Dunne, the General Secretary of the Plasterers, and the octogenarian General Secretary of the Iron, Steel and Metal Dressers, J.H. Wigglesworth, who, on his eightieth birthday in 1956 received an appreciative gift from the NCLC. But this did not deter the leaders of the NCLC from feeling frustrated often with their task of providing a socialist-based education in order to equip the working class for service in the labour movement. They sometimes rationalised the situation by comparing themselves with the WEA who, in the opinion of the NCLC, had lost "its manual workers." The truth was that both were not very successful as providers of adult education, as can be proved by taking the NCLC figures for 1952. In that year the NCLC catered for 15,040 class students, 12,818 day and week-end school students, 79,332 students at Union branch lectures, 656 students at residential summer schools, and 18,652 students at Postal Courses. A total of 126,498 students, which seems a very good figure. But it is not a large figure when one realises that there were eight million workers in 1952 affiliated to the Trade Union Congress.

The National College of Labour Colleges realised the situation, but often its criticisms were puritanical and old-fashioned. J.P.M. Millar's generalisation on the interest of the workers in sport lacks a sociological dimension. He summed up the situation in this way:

> Millions of workers are much more interested in races, run between horses, than the race that is being run between Socialists' ideas and chaos. So long as that is the position the prospects of achieving socialism are remote. The Socialist Movement must, therefore, strive to get people to take greater interest in social questions than they do in sporting events.   *(Plebs, 1953, p.14).*

While J.P.M. Millar thundered at the sport-loving British working class, an exiled Polish sociologist, Ferdynand Zweig, had written a sociological account of the British workers, and had included some pertinent points on the way sport had taken the place of religion in the life of the industrialised worker. Zweig adds a lyrical note which substantiates Millar's condemnation:

> It (sport) captivates his imagination, refreshes and comforts him; it gives him courage and amusement, excitement and beauty. It may sound absurd, but one could say that sport has bewtiched the British worker. (Zweig, 1952, p.124).

Sport was more relevant than socialism to many of the proletarians in England and Wales and one could add that the decline in religion had removed a motivation that had inspired a large number of the self-taught workers who had attended the WEA and the NCLC classes in the inter-war years.

The NCLC also was a class-conscious educational movement. Though Britain was, as T.H. Pear has shown, in his study, *English Social Differences* (London, 1955), one of the most class structured countries in the world, a sizeable percentage of the working class do not want to be reminded of their history or of socialism. The phrase 'working class Tory' sums up the attitude of those workers who identify themselves with the standpoint of a right wing political party. Lewis and Maude (1949) showed that 40% of the population of England felt that they belonged to the middle classes. Mark Abrams, over a decade afterwards, agreed with Lewis and Maude. Abrams showed that while a third of all working class supporters of the Labour Party consider themselves to be outside the working class, half of the working class who do not support the Labour Party consider themselves as outside the working class (Abrams, 1960, p.10). The fact that a worker belongs to a trade union does not automatically mean that he would like to participate in the educational facilities of the NCLC or the WETUC or indeed of his own union. *Plebs* made this interesting comment in 1957 on trade union education:

> For our experience shows that there is no Union with an education scheme that doesn't have large numbers of members who don't know that the education scheme exists. *(Plebs,* 1953, p.160).

The main obstacle, however, was the low priority given generally by the trade union movement to the education of its members compared with many of the European trade union movements. In many ways the British trade union movement was one of the worst organised in western Europe. In Austria, for example trade union education was planned and given top priority. The Austrian TUC had two residential colleges of its own, and made use of the two colleges owned by the chamber of labour. Denmark was also another country that regarded trade union education as an important priority. A new Labour College was opened in April, 1955, at Esbjerg, and they were also rebuilding a Labour College at Roskilde. J.P.M. Millar felt that the British trade union movement should follow the example of the Austrian and Danish trade unionists and regard adult education as a matter of first-class importance. He adds:

> In Britain many unions regard it as of third-class importance and some regard it as of no importance at all and so have no educational scheme for their members. *(Plebs,* 1956, p.178).

Millar was not the only voice that was raised to protest at the apathy of the trade union movement. An NCLC member, W. Williams, complained in 1952 at the inadequacy of the British trade union movement compared with the West German trade union movement:

> Although the German trade union movement has over 5 million members whereas our movement has over 7 million, the British trade union movement has no residential college, where the German trade union movement has eight and one or two German unions have also colleges of their own. *(Plebs, 1952, p.42).*

The Trade Union Congress did move along the European model in time but not in the way the NCLC had envisaged. Zweig's memorable comment that the unions had "grown not only big but fat" might explain a great deal of the apathy which we have been discussing (Zweig, 1952, p.180).

b   Lack of Finance

The N.C.L.C. throughout its history was hampered by inadequate financial resources. When George Hicks brought the Amalgamated Union of Building Trade Workers (AUBTW) in to the NCLC in 1922 as the first national union, the union paid ninepence but the standard fee was to be three pence per member *(Plebs,* 1954, p.197). It remained on that basis for over thirty years. At the NCLC Conferences reference to the raising of affiliation fees was always unpopular by the trade union leaders, and often the message for more money was couched in vague sentences and a general appeal for an increase in the membership of the movement. J.P.M. Millar always stressed that the main reason why the European trade union movements, like the Austrians, were better equipped than the trade union movement in the United Kingdom was that the members were willing to pay adequate dues to their unions *(Plebs, 1956, p.195).*

c   Wasteful Competition and lack of Co-operation

The rivalry and the philosophical disagreement of the NCLC and the WEA/WETUC has already been mentioned in this chapter. Till the second world war the rivalry seemed to be a permanent blemish on the education of the working class in England and Wales. While it is easy to castigate the NCLC as the villain of the peace one has to remember that the attitude of the NCLC was in fact a product of circumstances. In order to justify its existence and its financial support from the trade unions it was bound to adopt, as Pashley, rightly points out, and maintain a critical and competitive attitude towards the WEA (Pashley, 1966, p.204). During the war the NCLC was beginning to support the idea of centralisation of trade union education, as J.P.M. Millar has shown in his booklet, *Post-War Education.*

The TUC started thinking of this themselves in 1946 and a report was produced and submitted as we have already seen to the 1948 Congress (TUC Report, 1948, pp.155-162). Within it are contained the attitudes to the idea of the main bodies concerned: the WEA, the NCLC and the TUC. Both the NCLC and WEA favoured the principle of centralised control of trade union education since this would rid it of the bogey of competition. The NCLC suggested its own amalgamation with the WETUC and the new body would be controlled by the TUC and carry out the work previously carried out by the two separate agencies. The NCLC therefore made it clear that it did not wish to abolish the WEA though they did not of necessity agree with a great deal that went on in the name of the WEA. The WEA suggested co-ordination could be achieved by a tripartite arrangement between itself, the NCLC and the TUC. The WETUC would cease to exist but the WEA would retain its influence on trade union education.

The TUC rejected the possibility in 1948. It gave three reasons:

i finance. It would involve a permanent levy of threepence per member per annum; ii the failure of the WEA and the NCLC to mix, and iii the fact that "concentration would possibly give it (that is, trade union education) an authoritarian and totalitarian twist which could easily degenerate into mere propaganda instead of education" (TUC Report, 1948, p.347).

The rejection meant a stalemate but it triggered off within the NCLC a recurring debate, and some of it of a high standard. H.A. Turner, who had been an assistant education officer with the TUC, argued with precision in *Plebs* (January 1952) on the need for unity in trade union education. Turner felt that the educational split kept trade unionists in two different camps. It was a rarity to see a member of the NCLC at a WETUC course and vice-versa. There was not one activity that brought the two movements together, such as the summer schools, and the consequences of this was that the unions in the main (with a few exceptions) were divided in their loyalty to one of the rival organisations.

Turner saw the dispute as a hindrance to the expansion of trade union education. Although the majority of trade unionists were covered by some kind of scheme the majority of the unions were not. In 1949 100 trade unions were not associated nationally with either educational body for it was a matter of being afraid of upsetting the balance. J.P.M. Millar answered these two points quite fairly when he stated that the competition between the WETUC and the NCLC made it easy for the Trade Union Congress to escape their obligation. Added to this was the lack of will to pay even a modest sum for educational facilities.

Turner added three points on the educational controversy. Firstly, a large number of trade unions approved of the type of education offered by each of the educational associations. Secondly, generations of controversy had done little to convince or convert different trade unions to their particular standpoint. In twenty-five years not a single union had transferred his allegiance as a result of these controversies.

Turner argued for co-ordination and saw three possible methods of securing co-operation. Firstly, amalgamation of the educational bodies. Turner opposed this method and disagreed with the NCLC proposal for an amalgamation with the WETUC was not an independent organisation but a committee of the WEA, and the unions associating together and making use of the educational facilities provided. Secondly, the TUC to provide a comprehensive educational scheme in place of the existing separate services. He admits that this was referred back because of cost. An additional £87,750 a year would be needed merely to maintain the provision. Thirdly, the possibility of channelling through the TUC all the present separate expenditures of individual unions, thus enabling the General Council to exercise a co-ordinating influence over the Trade Union Congress as a whole *(Plebs,* 1952, p.18).

J.P.M. Millar points out in reply to H.A. Turner that the sum of £87,000 was unrealistic. It covered the whole WEA provision which covered a variety of subjects of no interest to workers' education. Trade union education could have been rationalised by putting together the joint incomes of the NCLC, WETUC and the amount of money spent on education by the individual unions. Turner felt that in 1952 there was room for a dialogue between the WEA and the NCLC, and for co-operation on two tasks i the training of tutors suitable for work with trade unionists; ii the task of conducting joint (instead of competing) propaganda to convince trade unionists of the necessity for education.

The 1952 NCLC annual conference debated the need for rationalising the educational work, and this was emphasised in most of the annual conferences. NCLC was ready for amalgamation and J.P.M. Millar complained bitterly in *Plebs* of the wasting of resources, the overlapping, and the unnecessary competition. He was right. There was the overlapping in postal courses between the Ruskin College postal courses and the NCLC. WETUC was sending organisers often not to areas where NCLC was inactive but "in nearly all cases" to areas where the NCLC had been active in the trade union movement for years. The lack of co-ordination in the Labour Movement was also responsible for a great deal of wasteful competition.

> As for the competition throughout the country, it has been known for the Labour Party, the W.E.T.U.C. and the N.C.L.C. each to have a day school in the same town on the same day. (Millar, *Plebs,* 1957, p.172).

The post-war period and in particular the fifties saw a great deal of agreement as to the practical work of trade union education. When one reads the plan for trade union education suggested in 1952 by the NCLC to the National Union of Railwaymen Executive one realises that in the practical application there was very little difference between the different organisations involved in trade union education. Voices were raised continuously as to the watering down of the marxist philosophy. George McKay of Perth thought at the annual NCLC conference in 1952 that the movement had departed "from the teachings of scientific socialism", while the elder statesman of the movement, J.H. Wigglesworth from the Iron, Steel and Metal Dressers, disagreed. He saw "no reason to object to the educational work that was being done", and conference endorsed that view in 1952 *(Plebs,* 1952, p.174). J.P.M. Millar in an answer to C. Sleight's article in *Plebs* which claimed that the NCLC was no longer the leader of the workers' movement and that there was no longer any need to quarrel with the WEA, harked back to the difference between the two movements. The NCLC was proud of its independence from the state and Millar claimed that he did not know of any NCLC writer who had given up Marxism *(Plebs,* 1952, p.207). There were many like C. Sleight who felt uncomfortable with the unnecessary confrontation between the WEA and the NCLC. Others interpreted the situation as a victory for the NCLC. Among these was the lively organiser for South Wales, Raymond Fletcher, who detected by 1956 a great change in the attitude of the WEA. Fletcher saw their pamphlet on trade union education as very much in line with NCLC thinking and it was significant that the tutor to take charge of the pilot scheme in the Port Talbot area of South Wales was to be a man trained in the NCLC *(Plebs,* 1956, p.160).

Raymond Fletcher does not admit that the pilot study in Port Talbot and another two intensive pilot schemes in Cleveland and Tyneside had a specific purpose. It was to point the way to a new system, and this was the purpose of the working party set up by the WEA. The report on the 'pilot area' schemes of trade union education was presented in February 1959 by Hugh Clegg, a fellow of Nuffield College, Oxford, assisted by Rex Adams. Clegg's report analysed not only the result of the pilot schemes but the whole range of trade union education. Clegg noted the difficulties incurred in the three areas i turnover of staff in the three areas, ii difference of policy between the extra-mural department of Leeds University and the Yorkshire North WEA district which had detrimental effect on the Cleveland scheme, iii failure to develop advanced work. Tyneside scheme was the most promising largely due to their efforts in the final session to carry out advanced tutorial work and that the area included the offices of some influential union officials. Sidney Hill of the Transport and General Workers' Union was highly successful both as a tutor and as an unofficial organiser for the scheme (Corfield, 1969, p.124).

Clegg, however, extended his term of reference and took a close look at the whole range of trade union education. He examined in turn the WEA, the NCLC, the extra-mural departments of the universities, the educational schemes of the TUC and of the six highest national trade unions. Clegg's blueprint for the future contained valuable suggestions.

The need to train tutors who would be qualified in subjects like industrial relations, collective bargaining, trade union government and work study. These tutors would have to combine two roles — the teaching aspect and the research aspect. Little material was available and this called for considerable professionalism.

Teaching trade unionists had to be recognised as a specialised branch of adult education. While the NCLC had depended to some extent on trade union officers to carry out the work, this of necessity was not always successful. Union officers were not always natural tutors and effective communicators. The pilot scheme had shown the need for suitable teaching material. Books in particular needed to be produced and readily available.

Many of Clegg's ideas were never put into operation but his call for the fusion of the WETUC and the NCLC was certain to be listened to. The pilot scheme and the Clegg and the Adam Report gave stimulus to trade union education, and it was studied by the General Council of the TUC. They then referred it to the educational committee. Two years later a final report appeared, and it was adopted by the Trade Union Congress in 1961. It foreshadowed a new scheme as from 1963, and was divided into five headings:

i   Courses arranged by the education department of the TUC in the training college at Congress House or at week-end or one-week schools elsewhere, for example, at Ruskin College.

ii   Courses directly arranged by individual unions.

iii   An infinitesimal number of courses directly arranged by the trades council.

iv   Courses serviced by the WEA.

v   Courses serviced by the universities.

The NCLC was anxious to be taken over completely. They already relied for their income mainly on contributions from the trade unions, and would be unable to function without the support of the affiliated unions. No one can deny that this was a compelling reason to wind up the NCLC. H.F. Turner at the NCLC annual conference in Blackpool (1956) had pointed out the financial wastage involved. According to Turner the National Union of Railwaymen was paying £4,000 to the NCLC in affiliation fees, but they were also spending three or four times that sum of an educational scheme intended to train its own members in relation to the union's own organisation and policy. At a time when the Labour Party, TUC and the NCLC were asking for more fees, the time had come to rationalise the educational work (*Plebs,* 1956, p.160). So by merging in the TUC, the NCLC would not sacrifice anything in financial terms. Their educational programme was quite impressive — even more than the WETUC. In their annual report for 1957 they recorded 14,704 students taking correspondence courses, 11,625 attending 782 classes, and 8,163 taking part in 219 different week-end and one-day schools. They ran twice as many classes as the specifically trade unionist classes run by the WEA and rather more than twice as many students attended. However, the WETUC ran more one-day and week-end schools. But the NCLC's record was impressive, and so was their postal courses enrolment. It was considerably larger than the Ruskin College postal courses run for the WETUC. In 1957 Ruskin College enrolled 1,541 students. The NCLC's total of 14,704 represented a bigger share though the courses were often shorter and less demanding than the Ruskin postal courses. Christine Millar had built an efficient NCLC correspondence department which provided a major service to trade union education.

The TUC after taking over the NCLC found that many of the classes disappeared, and this is what they wanted to happen. Many of the classes were not of the specifically trade union type. The NCLC organisers became, after the reorganisation, TUC regional educational officers, and their future was more secure than it had ever been. In 1952 when the NCLC was advertising divisional organisers for Cambridge and Ipswich area the salary was £450 rising to £505 (*Plebs*, 1953, p.47). They were to be part of the TUC machine in the future while in the past they had to coax, win and keep the allegiance of trade union leaders. It was a voluntary partnership and a bitter blow was struck in 1947 when the South Wales area of the National Union of Mineworkers, who had been with them from the beginning, withdrew their support from the NCLC. 1952 was a good year for the NCLC when seven extra unions affiliated, including the Rhodesia Railway Workers' Union (*Plebs*, 1952, p.172). In the spring of 1958 they suffered another serious moral and financial blow when one of the biggest of the affiliated unions, Union of Shop Distributive and Allied Workers, dropped out of the NCLC scheme. This happened in spite of a strenuous campaign on the part of the NCLC to keep them in the scheme. These were ominous signs which must have weighed the balance in favour of the TUC patronage. The annual income in 1957 for the NCLC was just over £50,000, and nearly twice the WETUC's income. In 1957 it was £26,000, and in terms of affiliated unions there was very little to choose between them. NCLC had over 90 affiliated unions, which included several small unions such as the National Union of Pearl Agents and the National Union of Press Telegraphists, and eighteen separate sections of the National Union of Mineworkers. Excluding the Transport and General Workers' Union and the National Union of General and Municipal Workers, which only affiliated on a limited basis to the NCLC, the NCLC's ninety unions about equalled in membership WETUC's thirty seven. On the figures available it looks as if the NCLC was more successful than the WEA in providing opportunities for manual workers as the following table, reproduced from *Plebs* (January, 1952, p.15), indicates:

Class Students Analysed by Occupation

	NCLC (1949)	WEA (June , 1948 - May 31, 1949)
Manual Workers	86.37	20.5
Clerks, Draughtsmen, Travellers and Foremen	4.22	16.1
Shop Assistants and Shopkeepers	5.40	3.8

Continued

Continued from previous page	NCLC (1949)	WEA (June, 1948 - May 31, 1949)
Teachers	.01	12.2
Civil Servants and Postal Workers	.01	5.3
Professional and Social Workers	.01	4.8
Home Duties and Nursing	3.95	28.8
Miscellaneous	.03	8.5
	100	100

Table 3.2

But the large trade unions wanted to provide education on their own affairs and they began establishing their own educational departments. The education officers of these unions were in favour of rationalisation, and this in 1961 ensured the support to the proposal before the annual Trade Union Congress in favour of expanding the educational role of the TUC. This was carried and between 1961 and 1964 the scheme was implemented. The final period was not without its problems. It arose over problems of staff adjustment, over the constitution of the new educational body and the old WEA/NCLC controversy. The NCLC objected to the failure of the TUC to provide an established place for their Labour Colleges in the new scheme, and the NCLC wanted a local machinery and not a bureaucratic top heavy scheme. The Labour Colleges were equivalent to the WEA's local branches. NCLC had legitimate grounds for some of their criticims. In particular in the original draft scheme of 1961 the TUC had proposed a constitution in which outside interests would have been represented. But by 1964 they had revised this proposal and decided to vest the entire control in their own education committee. The TUC argued that the original proposal was designed for a scheme in which only some of the unions were likely to take part in, but under the new arrangement the whole TUC was involved. There was no need to duplicate resources.

J.P.M. Millar and the NCLC executive who were sensitive to any WEA interference was very unhappy with the choice of Miss Ellen McCullough, a member of the TUC's General Council and a Transport and General Workers' Union officer to take charge of the scheme. Miss McCullough was also in addition to her other connections a deputy president of the WEA. It was unfortunate and a petty protest for Miss Ellen McCullough was competent and knowledgeable in the world of trade union education. But J.P.M. Millar felt that "she was a bitter opponent of the NCLC and was brought in to apply Woodcock's hatchet. No one else got the chance of the job." It would have been more practical if the NCLC had continued with their objection to the absence of any local representation in the machinery. The

WEA, WETUC, Ruskin College, were all unhappy with this arrangement, and the NCLC, instead of unifying the support, discarded it by taking an individual stance in their magazine *Plebs*. Fuel was poured out on the flames by the refusal of the TUC to take over the magazine *Plebs,* and its publishing society, and to remove from the postal courses everything that dealt specifically with the Labour Party for example or socialism. The TUC also refused to accept affiliation from these Labour Parties and co-operative societies who had joined over the years the NCLC. Millar and the NCLC charged the TUC with selling the movement and of ignoring the need for political education. The TUC argued that they could not infringe the 1913 Trade Union Act which laid it down that trade union moneys could not be used for party political purposes unless they were drawn from special political funds; and secondly, that they were not responsible for providing a scheme for the Labour Party. While the TUC had administrative reasons for tidying up the trade union education provision the TUC left themselves open to relentless criticism on account of their high-handed method of arranging the scheme. The WEA in the 1964 Annual Conference were dissatisfied but succeeded in preventing an open clash.

It had taken 18 years for the scheme to materialise and the important step was largely ignored by the press and the trade union movement itself. Even in 1964 the involvement of ordinary trade unionists in any educational scheme was small, and A.J. Corfield has estimated that no more than 100,000 members took part in all the trade union educational programmes during that year. This meant that not much more than 1% of the total TUC membership participated (Corfield, 1969, p.159). It was an effort not to be lightly dismissed, and as we shall see when looking at the official union provision in this chapter, the story has a great deal of romance to it.

d   Contribution of the National Council of Labour Colleges

i   Political Adult Education to the Labour Movement

J.P.M. Millar's resentment at the TUC's refusal to regard itself as a provider of political education to the Labour Movement at the amalgamation in 1964 is understandable for the whole history of the NCLC was an attempt to provide the working class with the tools of the trade. 1926 was a watershed in its history. In the year of the General Strike the NCLC ceased to teach militant, revolutionary syndicalism, and began to teach the Labour Movement to fight the class war according to constitutional rules (Pashley, 1966, p.198). Foremost among the NCLC educationists was J.F. Horrabin, who served as a Labour M.P. for Peterborough between 1929 and 1931. At his defeat in the 1931 General Election Horrabin went back to the NCLC as Rita Hinden rightly said of him:

> He became one of the great educators of a whole generation of socialists in the
> international facts of life.   (*Plebs,* 1955, p.8).

91

The General Secretary of the NCLC summed up Horrabin's contribution as follows:

> One of Frank's outstanding tributes to the movement was to show that Socialist theory could be expressed in simple terms. In some ways he might be called the Blatchford of the Labour College Movement. (*Plebs,* 1955, p.19).

Horrabin himself expressed his philosophy of political education in 1954 on his seventieth birthday when he said:

> It means educational work in the broadest sense — books, plays, pictures, music, comradeship — they are all part of the business of making a new world. And that people should be able to enjoy these things is what we want to make a new world for.
>
> (*Plebs,* 1955, p.8).

To Horrabin and his fellow adult educationists in the NCLC socialism was the philosophy that needed to be conveyed to the ordinary men and women on the factory floor, in the heavy traditional industries, as well as in the newer technological industries.

A concern was expressed at the fortunes of the Labour Party at by-elections and General Election George Shepherd, the Labour Party National Agent, wrote after the sweeping victory of the Labour Party in the General Election of 1945 to J.P.M. Millar expressing the appreciation of the part the NCLC had played in bringing political and economic understanding to a large number of workers, and contributing on a substantial scale to the success of the Labour Movement.

At times the NCLC castigated the Labour Party and the trade union movement for not realising the value of adult political education. After Labour's poor vote in two by-elections at Cleveland and High Wycombe in 1952, J.P.M. Millar felt that the Labour Movement received what it deserved. His words were disturbing but relevant to the Labour Movement:

> It is not possible to establish a new social order without devoting really serious attention both to the education of the public and to the education of the Labour Party's own membership. The fact that there are still a number of unions that have either no education scheme at all, or a quite inadequate scheme, tells part of the story. (*Plebs,* 1953, p.13).

J.P.M. Millar as General Secretary of the NCLC complained continually of the neglect and the attitude of the members of the Labour Movement towards education. An example from his speech to the 1954 Annual NCLC Conference at Scarborough illustrates this concern:

> The average member of the Labour Movement devotes less time to Labour education and spends much more time and money on commercial recreation. Fifty years ago it was not uncommon for members of the movement to walk ten miles to a meeting and ten miles back. Today most of them find it too much effort to take a twopenny bus ride.
>
> (*Plebs,* 1954, p.164).

But a great deal had been achieved. Every year there was someone or other who had been taught in NCLC classes finding himself as a key figure in a trade union or being welcomed to Westminster as a Labour Party member of parliament. The contribution of the NCLC to political education of the British Labour Movement was far-reaching and can be regarded as one of its main contributions.

ii   Contribution of James P.M. Millar

James P.M. Millar made a substantial contribution to working class adult education. He was involved in trade unionism as a young adolescent of seventeen and received an opportunity to study at the Central Labour College in London. In 1920 he left the College and was involved from the beginning in the establishment of the NCLC. He became the General Secretary of the NCLC in 1921, after being for a year the Edinburgh and District tutor organiser of the Scottish Labour College. Millar was, therefore, one of the first educational officers and remained at the work until the NCLC ceased to operate in 1964. His consistent marxist philosophy is evident and his knowledge of the NCLC and the Labour Movement was unsurpassed. Millar prided himself on the amount of work achieved by the NCLC for the working class and nothing upset him more than to find historians of adult education ignoring the NCLC contribution. He complained critically in *Plebs* that Ernest Green, the General Secretary of the WEA, failed to mention the NCLC in his book, *Adult Education – Why this Apathy?* (1953) (*Plebs*, 1954, pp.75-76). When two Leeds University Professors, W.R. Niblett of the education department, and S.G. Raybould of the university extra-mural department, arranged a course of twenty two lectures in the winter of 1952-53 on the history of adult education without referring to the NCLC Millar was ready to protest. Professor Raybould, a WEA controversialist, replied that the course was never intended to cover the whole field. But this was not an answer to J.P.M. Millar who went on to insist that it was pure bias on behalf of the Leeds Profesor.

> Mr. Raybould may not, in the zoology of education, like the educational giraffe, but the animal does exist and is of quite considerable size.   (*Plebs*, 1953, p.57).

The examples could be multiplied over and over again throughout the NCLC history. He was willing to cross swords with outstanding adult educationists on the meaning of adult education. Millar could see no value in what he called 'academic' education taught in the extra-mural and WEA classes for the trade unionist, and the worker. His bias and prejudice so often destroyed his initial premise as when he claims that most university teachers tend to be pro-capitalists and anti-socialists (*Plebs*, 1953, p.139). One could name a large number who were as dedicated to the cause of adult education to the working class as he was. G.D.H. Cole and R.H. Tawney are the outstanding examples of adult educationists who were not pro-capitalist or anti-socialist. But J.P.M. Millar would claim that they "were striking exceptions and both appreciated the NCLC's work" and were his friends.

J.P.M. Millar was a propagandist and a socialist through and through as his articles and writings illustrate vividly his skill as a propagandist and an educator of socialism. His contribution in the history of the NCLC can be compared with that of R.H. Tawney in the history of the WEA. Millar kept the NCLC as a great force in workers education, and James Clunie a Labour Member of Parliament summed up the contribution of the movement in these glowing terms:

> To the working class, the N.C.L.C. is one of the great inventions of the century. It has opened the history book and the economics text book to the ordinary man and it raised the social questions to new heights. (*Plebs*, 1952, p.238).

But the history of the National College of Labour Colleges (NCLC) is full of lost opportunities and an inability to adapt its philosophy to the new affluent workers that bought their own homes and enjoyed the luxuries of the fifties. They were often more concerned with keeping to the philosophy that had brought them into existence than with the new social changes that were evident in the life of ordinary trade unionists in England and Wales. However their contribution was immense and deserves an honoured place in the history of workers education.

B   The Co-operative Movement

The same spirit as moved the WEA and the NCLC pioneers was also at work in the educational work of the Co-operative Movement. In the nineteenth century the Co-operative movement had supported university extension, but in the twentieth century it gave active assistance to the WEA, Ruskin College, the London Working Men's College, and in 1951 affiliated to the NCLC, and many of its members participated in the work of these working-class organisations. It also undertook a small but significant amount of adult education which we intend in this section to examine.

i   The Co-operative College

The Co-operative College was established on a small scale at Holyoake House, Manchester, the headquarters of the Co-operative Union. Over the years in Manchester the College developed and even kept its doors opened during the second world war. In 1945 at the end of the war, Stanford Hall, near Loughborough, was bought, and in 1946 the College made the most of its new premises by expanding to 98 students. In the same year the new Principal, R.L. Marshall, joined the staff and till the middle seventies he was in charge of the adult education work. His successor was Dr. Bob Houlton, a tutor at the Department of Extension Studies of the University of Liverpool.

ii   Purpose and Tasks of the College

The purpose of the Residential Co-operative College is to serve in the first place the Co-operative Movement by educating the future managers and secretaries of the movement both in the technical aspects of their work and in the social significance of Co-operation. It prepares students to share in the democratic leadership of the movement — in service to the local Societies' Co-operative Committees, in the auxiliaries, and as teachers and youth leaders. The College has to promote research into Co-operative principles and techniques and make available data, information, expertise from the study and guidance of Co-operators in the British movement and in the world-wide fellowship. The College has a competent staff under the guidance of the Principal to fulfil the purpose and tasks of the College, and sometimes external experts are invited to deliver a lecture or a series. This was happening as frequently by the end of our period as in the earlier years.

iii   Content and Method at the College

Every student is expected to pursue a general subject which may vary but which has a general and Co-operative theme. Other subjects which cut across departmental lines are the history and organisation of the movement, or economic or social history. The five main departments are:

a   Retail Management

b   Management — General

c   Retail Secretaryship

d   Social Studies

e   Co-operation Overseas

Certificates and diplomas are awarded to the successful candidates who will have been taught by a variety of methods: by lecture, by seminar, by individual tutorial and by project work.

iv   The adult educational work of the Co-operative movement

There is no denying that the Co-operative movement's philosophy can be summed up in the assertion made by one of the pioneers, Robert Owen, that a man's character is made, not by him, but for him. If we want men to co-operate then we must teach them the principles says the movement. Men will become co-operators by co-operating, and there are in the opinion of Co-operative educators a number of approaches and a number of spheres in which adult members of the Co-operative Movement can be active.

a   Consumer Education

It is believed that a consumers' movement should address itself to the education of consumers. The purpose of consumer education is to train the consumer to exercise his or her choice wisely, and use his or her purchases effectively in the everyday activities of the home. The Co-operative Movement pioneered in this adult education activity, and other large retail organisations have followed suit. How serious and successful they have been in carrying out consumer education is difficult to evaluate. G.D.H. Cole in his booklet, *Democracy and Authority in the Co-operative Movement,* pointed out that customer education was the most effective way possible for the movement to spread the Co-operative ideals. More leisure time does not mean that people want to spend it shopping. It means that they want to do their shopping in as little time as possible but without wasting their money or buying goods which will not be of use to them as a family.

b   Social and Co-operative Studies

Under this term the Co-operative movement cover a variety of activities — short lecture courses, terminal classes up to twelve meetings and even sessional classes and tutorial classes of three years. To the Co-operative movement this is regarded as one of its special responsibilities — the education that indicates the relevance of the philosophy of the movement to the solving of problems of man and society. It is unfortunately one of the spheres in which the achievements are weak and efforts are made continually to introduce new innovations as well as techniques by arranging day-time classes and by using the walls of the Co-operative stores to put over the Co-operative philosophy.

c   Education for Leadership

This ideal is accepted, but the training is haphazard at best. Like every other voluntary movement most of this education is aimed at those who have an interest in the Co-operative cause, and inevitably the people who find themselves involved are in the end the people who serve on the management and education committees and for service in the auxiliaries.

d   Recreational Adult Education

The recreational model is usually involvement in cultural activities such as drama and choral work. Co-operative Societies have a long history of drama and choral activities, and an effort is made to deal with things which are related to Co-operative experience and principles. It is also hoped that those taking part in the cultural activities will be brought closer to the Co-operative Society and find themselves involved in other Co-operative educational work. All this is part of the effort to 'self direction' inside the Co-operative movement.

e   The Adult Auxiliaries

Importance is attached by Co-operative adult educators to the adult auxiliary organisations that fulfil so much of the educational tasks that the Co-operative movement are unable to put into operation. In England and Wales there are the following adult auxiliaries — the Women's Co-operative Guild of England and Wales, the National Guild of Co-operators, and the National Co-operative Men's Guild. These auxiliaries are autonomous, and have their own separate organisation but they subscribe to the ideals of the Co-operative movement. The Co-operative movement concentrates on planning, preparing and providing short lecture courses for auxiliaries.

v   The Organisation for Co-operative Education

a   The Local Society

The local Co-operative societies are expected to be active in adult education, and they form the National Co-operative Education Association.

Every local society is represented in the association through the committee which they nominate as responsible for education. The range of the education committees varies and societies with a membership exceeding 20,000 should appoint a full-time education committee. Societies are encouraged to co-operate with other local societies and co-operate on the appointment of an education officer.

Part-time secretaries of the education committees are key figures, and ideally they receive support from the management and the Board of Directors' District organisation.

Each of the eight sections of the Co-operative Union is divided into districts, and several of the sections have district education committees to promote educational activities.

b   Sectional Organisation

In each of the sections of the Co-operative Union in England and Wales the constitution of the NCEA establishes a sectional education council consisting of four representatives from the sectional board and six representatives elected by the education committees of societies in the NCEA. In addition, each adult auxiliary in a section with a sectional organisation and prescribed minimum number of members is entitled to one representative. The council normally meets quarterly, and its main function is to stimulate, assist, develop, implement Co-operative education as well as to arrange conferences, schools and classes.

c   National Organisation

The national committee of the NCEA is the education executive and consists of:

i   one representative from each of eight sectional boards appointed by the board from its representatives on the sectional education council;

ii   one representative from each of the eight sectional education councils appointed by and from its members other than the representatives of the sectional board. The chairman is appointed each year by the executive from among the eight sectional board members.

d   The Education Department

The work of the executive is carried forward by the education department of the union, and they co-ordinate all the activities, provide syllabuses, examinations and awards in Co-operative studies, correspondence courses, and provide long-term and short-term residential courses. The chief education officers, R.L. Marshall, and after him Dr. R. Houlton, were also the Principals of the residential college in the post-war period.

vi   Evaluation of the Co-operative Movement Education

The Co-operative movement combines the vocational and the liberal aspect of adult education and in terms of technical education and training it succeeds in helping its employees to have more skills in the management of the local Societies. It is education for responsibility with a certificate or a diploma at the successful completion of the course. The adult liberal education has not the same appeal except to those who are committed Co-operative members. Why should a person choose a Co-operative society tutorial class rather than a WEA or university extra-mural class? The publicity given to the classes is much more limited than the publicity material of the main agencies (e.g. WEA or university extra-mural). Co-operative Movement lost one of its most important propaganda outlets with the disappearance of the Sunday newspaper, *Reynolds News,* and most of its domestic news is contained in the weekly paper, *Co-operative News.* Their efforts to reach trade unionists have met with sporadic success and in certain parts of the country such as Yorkshire (*Co-operative Education,* p.66). But Co-operative educators believe that it is important to arrange classes on industrial problems, industrial democracy, management techniques in industry and Co-operative co-partnership as they are worthy of attention to trade unionists. But the response is minimal. It seems that Co-operative education societies are encouraged to co-operate with the WEA, NCLC and LEA in providing classes, groups for the workers and very successful day release courses have been arranged with university extra-mural departments. These classes were primarily, but not exclusively, for employee students already in responsible posts. Generally the method used was for the sectional education council to approach societies within the area of the university concerned to release one, two or three of their younger adult staff to attend at the university for a full day each week for a period of about twenty-four meetings. The pioneer course was with the University of Sheffield and other extra-mural departments which took up the idea have included Durham, Leeds, Birmingham, University College of South Wales and Monmouthshire, Cardiff, Leicester, Nottingham and Oxford.

It seems that the most significant aspect of the Co-operative movement's work in the field of adult education and in particular the workers' education is to stress the philosophy of Co-operation which has become an essential ingredient in the witness of the Labour Movement. Large numbers of trade unionists who would not attend a co-operative class, day-school or residential school, will use the Co-operative societies' facilities as well as defend its attitude. The Co-operative Societies in some areas of England and Wales, such as the South Wales coalfield, have great attraction for the majority of the population. Its educational work cannot be ignored when discussing workers' education, but like so many of the other movements it has not been able to modify its philosophical ideas to sociological changes.

C   W.E.A. and Workers' Education

The WEA's involvement in workers' education is a complex story which demands two sections. I intend in the first section to look at the philosophy and attitude of the WEA towards workers' education, and secondly to look at the work of the Workers' Trade Union Education Committe (WTUEC).

W.E.A. and education of the workers

The WEA had a more cumbersome title in the beginning than it has at present, namely *Association to Promote the Higher Education of Working Men,* primarily by the extension of university teaching (Stocks, 1953, p.26). Original objectives were nebulous, but it hoped to bring the trade unions and Co-operative societies into closer contact with the universities. It was not the first attempt to do this, and it encountered the same problems of apathy and lack of finance on the part of the workers as the earlier attempts in the nineteenth century. Early support came from academics like R.H. Tawney and christian leaders of the calibre of Charles Gore, the Bishop of Birmingham, and William Temple.

The initiative for a new type of course — a tutorial class for workers — came from Rochdale in Lancashire and Longton, near Stoke-on-Trent in Staffordshire, in 1907. Edwin Welch has shown that the tutorial class system was not devised by Albert Mansbridge as so many historians of adult education claim, but can be traced back to two disciples of John Ruskin who saw the need for courses of lectures suited to the wants of working men. These disciples of Ruskin were Michael Sadler, secretary of the Oxford University Extension Committee, and Canon Barnett, warden of Toynbee Hall (1883-1906) in the East End of London. Barnett experimented in 1886 with a class in political economy, and it is possible that Albert Mansbridge, a frequent visitor at Toynbee Hall, knew of this experiment and also the classes in sociology, conducted by Patrick Geddes at the beginning of the century in London. R.H. Tawney, who was sent to Rochdale and Longton knew of Geddes' work.

We have spent some time on the beginnings of the WEA and the prehistory of the university tutorial class as both were re-evaluated in the period under our consideration. The purpose of the WEA was continually debated, the university tutorial class was questioned as the most effective way of teaching trade unionists and members of the working class, and indeed of attracting them in the first place into the movement. We will discuss the arguments on the role of the WEA in workers' education at this juncture as the history of the WEA as a provider of adult education will be scrutinised throughout the book.

Albert Mansbridge thought of the education of adults as a spiritual emancipation of the individual, and an opportunity to receive tuition of university standard. His philiosopy of adult education was expressed in these terms:

So the ideal of adult education is the fulfilment of capacity, the expression of the life of every man and woman at its best. (Mansbridge, 1923, p.83).

Mansbridge appealed to trade unionists to join hands with the Co-operative movement in a full realisation of the "glory of education", and to the University Extension Movement to "settle itself deliberately upon trade unionism and co-operation, where, in spite of opposition and dead days, it will finally see the day of fruition and be satisfied" (Stocks, 1953, p.24). But in the very beginning there were others who saw adult education as more a weapon for the political advance of the workers and this attitude was refreshingly expressed by J.M. Mactavish, a shipwright from the Portsmouth dockyard, at an Oxford Conference in the summer of 1907 on the title of "What Oxford can do for working people". Mactavish spoke this memorable sentence as an active member of the Labour Party;

> I decline to sit at the rich man's gate praying for crumbs. I claim for my class all that Oxford has to give.

He went on to state that the working man does not want to escape from his class, but rather to lift his class, to return to it from Oxford inspired "not with the idea of getting on but with the idea of social service" (Stocks, 1953, pp.40-41).

It was this man, J.M. Mactavish, described by Beatrice Webb in a typical vitriolic remark as a "blunt, energetic and somewhat commonplace Scot" who was appointed in 1916 to take over from the founder, Albert Mansbridge, as General Secretary of the WEA. Mary Stocks states that Mactavish was chosen to re-dress the balance on the side of the trade unions as Mansbridge admitted having tipped the balance during his tenure on the side of the universities (Stocks, 1953, p.70). Mactavish saw adult education as a weapon for the political advance of the workers, but the differing Mansbridgian viewpoint had also its adherents in the WEA in the inter-war period. It was R.H. Tawney who, in Mary Stocks view, will "probably go down to history as the greatest adult education tutor of all time" who was the effective bridge between both camps. Yet Tawney leaned to the political rather than the cultural view of the WEA's tasks, especially when the issue came, as to whether the WEA existed for the workers or for all classes (Terrill, 1973, p.44). It was Tawney himself who wrote on September 29, 1948, to the Leeds adult educationist, and vice-President of the national WEA (1949-1957), S.G. Raybould, expressing his unhappiness that WEA classes contained fewer workers than previously, that tutorial classes, the most ambitious of WEA activities, had been down-graded; that many members had little sense of the association's purpose. R.H. Tawney, who had given so much to the WEA, did not think that the WEA's specific purpose was furthered by classes on butterfly catching and medieval monasteries. He was also remembering the demand in Rochdale and Longton in 1907 against "begging people to join" classes. Tawney wanted students challenged not catered for, and education should make socialist citizens out of them (Terrill, 1973, p.100).

S.G. Raybould took up Tawney's criticism and 'the tract of the times', *The W.E.A.: The Next Phase* in 1949 sparked off a very real debate, a debate which has never really ceased. Raybould's main contentions were those of Tawney. The WEA was to equip the students to change society and the courses offered served no purpose. Neither did the WEA courses attract the educationally underprivileged for whom it was originally intended. The educationally sophisticated were throwing out of the WEA the educationally underprivileged. Raybould saw the task of the WEA as Mactavish, and later what Tawney had come to believe, as a movement geared to educating those who had had a limited schooling, and the others who were interested in education for a social purpose. The WEA was being transformed from a 'proletarian' to a 'bourgeoise' or a 'petit bourgeoise' organisation or from an association of labouring men and women to one of black-coated workers. Raybould felt like Tawney that it should concentrate on the working class. He was supported by tutors like G. Horwell who, in *The Tutor's Bulletin* (Autumn 1950, pp.7-11), called on the WEA to concentrate on the have-nots and in an article in the WEA magazine, *Highway* (October 1952, pp.2-11) G.D.H. Cole felt that the WEA was failing to act as a point of focus for the working class movement.

Raybould's contention that the WEA was losing its manual workers from its tutorials had statistical evidence in support. A post-war study in Leeds of students who attended tutorial classes had shown that the students were mostly middle-aged people and most of them women. 49% of the women were housewives and only 32% were manual workers, while 44% were administrative and clerical workers, and 19% were professional workers (Pashley, 1966, p.133). Only 25% were members of political parties which again was not very encouraging to those who, like Tawney, felt WEA education should produce socialist citizens.

A survey in Manchester added further information, and supported the main contention that the WEA classes depended to a great extent upon clerical and professional workers (Styler, 1950, p.134). To W.E. Styler, who became the Professor of Adult Education in the University of Hull, this was an inevitable process, and a process which the Raybould controversy did nothing to stop. In the decade of the controversy there was a steady decline in the percentage of manual workers attending WEA classes from 24% in 1945-46 to 16% in 1956-57 (Harrison, 1959, p.4).

Raybould's orthodoxy was attacked. The working class did not want adult education. So many of them had become middle class. It must universalise its appeal and leave the workers to come along as they so desired. A. Bullock thought, in the Summer 1952 issue of *Highway,* that it was inevitable that the WEA should assume a national instead of a sectional responsibility in order to survive (Bullock, 1952, p.6). Richard Hoggart approached the problem in a different way and to him adult education spoke to all classes of society, and this is what the WEA was doing. The WEA was in the middle because of the changes happening around them in society. Only a small minority of the workers, according to Hoggart, were interested in education for a social purpose (Hoggart, 1952, pp.46-53).

It was a difficult position for the WEA to be in as the Ashby Report, which appeared in 1953, admitted. The WEA, the Ashby Report said, regarded itself as still predominantly working class in its membership, and this might be so among the active members of the WEA branches, but among the students of its classes there was certainly not a predominance of manual workers (Ashby Report, 1953, p.14). This seems to have been the situation throughout our period, and became much more obvious as the affluent fifties and sixties brought into being fundamental social changes and the disappearance of old loyalties as well as values. It is a matter of preaching the old philosophy of education for the workers by the WEA Annual Conferences, and providing courses on all kinds of topics for the interested, largely educated, middle classes who support the WEA activities in the districts of England and Wales. It supports our central thesis that adult education movements are slow to learn from the actual situation.

J.F.C. Harrison saw the problems of the WEA in the fifties as part of the wider dilemma of the left. The appeal of the idea of social emancipation for the working class was the factor that made the WEA tick. Harrison adds:

> Not that all who came to the W.E.A. were workers, however curiously defined, or even enthusiasts for this ideal. But it was the dominant ideology of the movement, that is of the all-important minority of activists who ran it. A voluntary movement depends ultimately upon the strength of its ideals. And the undermining of the ideal of social emancipation by welfare economics slowed down the main dynamic of the W.E.A. (Harrison, 1961, p.350).

The Labour Party felt the same difficulty in the fifties, and Anthony Crosland wrote extensively re-defining the socialists' goals in terms of the affluent welfare state. His first book on Socialism in 1956 was an important landmark for the Labour Party — it was a watershed which had to be passed. The annual WEA Conference in 1958 was also a watershed. Motions calling for a 'large dose of WEA to combat the systematic triviality of mass media' was passed, and the delegates heard a Londoner, Miss E. Monkhouse, eloquently emphasising the original philosophy of getting "at the people who are on what one might call a protein-short diet" (*TES,* April 4, 1958, p.543). It was an important conference, for the leadership was changed. Dr. Harold Clay, a trade unionist, gave way to the new incumbent, Professor Asa Briggs, Professor of Modern History at the University of Leeds. As Tawney, in the interwar period, had kept the different strands together, Asa Briggs did the same in the late fifties. The view that the WEA was to offer education for people in the middle of the twentieth century voiced by adult educationists like Roy Shaw, A. Bullock, F. Pickstock, on the pages of *Highway,* was accepted as well as the original aim of the WEA to offer people who had left school early another chance through the WEA classes. Asa Briggs reflected these strands in his book published in 1960, *Education for a Changing Society,* and the same emphasis was found in the WEA Working Party Report, *Aspect of Adult Education,* which came out in the same year. The major differences between the Edwardian period, which saw the growth of the WEA, and the post-war Welfare State period had been to some extent reconciled as well as the higher standard of living which meant new tastes and interests even among the manual workers who were still attending the WEA classes every winter. But the main conclusion must still be that the WEA itself had great difficulty in adapting its educational philosophy to the sociological changes witnessed in England and Wales in the post-war period. It was still a difficult task for adult educationists to learn from the situation around them, and their inability to do this, meant that adult education itself was not as effective as it could have been in the period between nineteen forty five and nineteen eighty.

The WEA did, however, contribute to trade union education, but only as one aspect among many other aspects of adult education. It was not even a top priority, but some WEA Districts were already more successful than others and a few of them in co-operation with other agencies extended their provision. The East Midland WEA District was successful in the post-war period with the miners' day-release courses. At the beginning it was a three years' course, and afterwards two one year courses and concurrently a three year course in each stage of the development, a total of five courses. From 1962 to 1970 there were held every year two basic courses of two years' duration and one advanced course in its first year and another in its second — a total of six courses. Their combined membership has averaged 95 mineworkers per annum, and in the opinion of the WEA these day-release courses are an "outstanding piece of work". Efforts were made also to promote classes at factories and for a time they were popular. In the East Midland attempts were made to experiment in the field of co-operative employment. The first year was disappointing, and it was not tried afterwards (Allaway, 1969, p.70). But the East Midland District could claim by 1968 that it had become the foremost provider of all WEA districts of education for workers. One must state also that the co-operation of the extra-mural departments of the Universities of Nottingham and Leicester with the East Midland WEA District was an important factor in its success.

Another WEA District which co-operated and provided substantial provision for mineworkers was the Yorkshire North WEA District. in the North Yorkshire area a Yorkshire Miners Lectures Committee acted as an agency and provided facilities for mineworkers and their wives by payment of class fees and assistance in buying books and the provision of courses of lectures. In 1945 class fees for 107 students were returned, and two courses of lectures were provided. The WEA was always willing to experiment with regard to workers' education, and a case in point was the trade union weeks arranged in co-operation with the University College of Hull at Scarborough, Selby and Goole in 1949. Lectures were held every night of the week on aspects of the trade union movement but the response was disappointing.

Average attendances were 20 at Scarborough, 15 at Selby, and 10 at Goole (WEA Yorkshire North District 36th Annual Report 1949-50, p.13).

The WEA's standpoint had changed dramatically. It contented itself with being a provider of adult education for the whole community. Its working class image had altered, but the word 'Workers' had not been deleted though voices were heard in Annual Conferences demanding the removal of the word. The workers themselves were only a small portion of the WEA's clientele, and evidence was received every year of an increase in the number of housewives who were attending the classes, and a decrease in the manual workers. The increase in housewives was symptomatic of another change: an increase in the number of women who attended the tutorials and a decrease in the number of men who attended. A respected WEA District Secretary, F. Gallimore, felt that the decline in the proportion of men in classes was due to the claims of the men's occupations, in particular overtime, shift work, and travelling long distance to work. Such factors were also true of other WEA districts besides F. Gallimore's district of West Lancashire and Cheshire, which included the vast Merseyside conurbation (Annual Report 1958-59, p.2).

Like many other voluntary organisations, the WEA were faced in the fifties with chronic shortage of money in exploiting new ideas. This was particularly true with regard to trade union education, and this meant an inability to act upon the two important reports: the working party on trade union education, which reported in 1953, and the Clegg and Adams' enquiry into the trade union pilot schemes which was published in 1959. Both these reports recommended the formation of a research and education centre for the preparation of material and the co-ordination of teaching experience in trade union education. But it was found impossible to raise the money, though at the same time Oxford University Extra-Mural Delegacy managed to find enough financial resources to build up its staff for a trade union centre, and also to equip itself with a residential college designed primarily for trade union work. Like the NCLC, the WEA found it frustrating in their task of persuading the trade unions to increase their grants above the ½d. per member they agreed to pay to the WETUC scheme in 1949.

The WEA, and in particular its specialised trade union work under the umbrella of the WETUC, welcomed the TUC's initiative in bringing together all trade union education. A co-ordination policy in the eyes of the WETUC should eliminate overlapping, remove competition for the financial support of the unions, and bring together all the educational services that were available.

The WEA — WETUC statement in 1957-58 also reminded the trade union movement of the services that they had provided in all parts of the country. All the classes were open to trade unionists but the WEA reminded the TUC that they always conceived of education for the whole citizen rather than just for the trade unionist. But this had never altered the WEA — WETUC determination to give priority and importance to its work for trade unionists. The policy statement *Education for a Changing Society – the Role of the W.E.A.* issued in March 1958 reaffirmed this concern and emphasised the importance of trade union education. In 1957, for example, of the 5,351 classes held under the auspices of the WEA, 382 involving 5,900 meetings and 5,300 students were recruited specially for trade unionists and dealt with a syllabus closely relevant to their interests. Added to this were the WETUC schemes of 250 one-day and 276 week-end schools catering for 6,297 and 8,943 trade unionists respectively.

The purpose of the WEA — WETUC statement to the TUC was to demonstrate the advantages for the trade union movement of retaining its close links with the WEA which should therefore remain independent. While the WETUC would be taken over, the WEA was adamant that it should have the opportunities of conducting day-release courses, classes in factories, residential week or week-end schools. This has never ceased, and by the end of our period some WEA districts, and in particular the East Midland District, in conjunction with the Universities of Nottingham and Leicester were providing a great deal of useful training for trade unionists. New types of provision were also introduced, such as the study tours to Stockholm in Sweden, to examine industrial relations, and a course of ten meetings on the shop steward and industrial relations broadcast by Radio Nottingham (Allaway, 1969, p.87). The WEA was willing to develop its provision independently as well as through other bodies.

D   Trade Unions Educational Provision

Trade Unions are a British invention, one of the most important of the Industrial Revolution, and one that is still growing in its influence as more workers belong to the trade union movement. In the late Victorian era (1870-1901) there were some 1,300 unions in Britain, but by 1970 nearly 1,000 of these had died out or merged into strong trade unions. The large unions in particular had the resources to conduct their own education provision, and many felt dissatisfied with the WETUC as well as the NCLC provision. Trade union leaders felt the need for specialised narrow vocational kind of education which dealt on mundane union affairs of how to conduct branch meetings as well as more skilled expertise. The post-war period saw the larger unions going their own way and establishing education departments. Ernest Bevin's Transport and General Workers' Union took the lead in 1938 and other unions followed suit. The National Union of General and Municipal Workers (NUGMW) began their own educational programme in 1949. In 1954 the NUGMW appointed a full-time education officer, and in the same year the National Union of Railwaymen began to experiment with the educational courses. USDAW started out on its own in 1949, and in 1958 appointed a full-time officer. The South Wales area of the NUM established an education officer to develop their own scheme which became fully

105

operative in 1958. These individual unions and others will be mentioned in more detail in the course of this chapter, and we will look first at the educational provision of the Transport and General Workers' Union.

i   The Transport and General Workers' Union

The TGWU's education provision came into its own after the second world war. In 1942 the sum of £10 was distributed as an educational grant; it was increased to £7,544 for the year ending 31st December 1947, and to £34,764 for the year ending 31st December 1954 (Allen, 1957, p.244). The pioneering work was due to the support given by the General Secretary, Arthur Deakin. Deakin's main reason for his support was the need to improve the quality of union officials. He expressed this strongly in 1948 at Manchester, and by 1955 there were already signs that this desire was being fulfilled in quantity and quality. In 1950 only 51 students attended Summer Schools, whereas over the two year period 1954-55 there were 1,036 students. By 1955 many former union students were figuring among the successful applicants for full-time union jobs.

Separate training provision was made also for shop stewards, branch secretaries, branch chairmen and branch committeemen. Deakin and other Transport and General Workers' Union General Secretaries after him realised the value and importance of classes in letter-writing, preparing minutes, agendas as well as in the handling of accounts.

The shop steward is the key figure in any trade union. He is the one who carries out at local level the union's policy for an effective organisation. There is no doubt that every union realises the need to train shop stewards who will speak effectively for their fellow workers on matters that affect their well-being, and efforts are continually made to train these key people.

The Transport and General Workers' Union home study course called *The Union, Its Work and Problems,* enrolled forty thousand students during its thirty years of existence (1940-1970) and was replaced in 1970 by a new course, *The Union in Action.* Courses of one or two days are held on week-ends or on day-release, on special aspects of the work of workplace representatives and other branch officers. One-year full-time bursaries at Ruskin College, Oxford; Fircroft College, Birmingham; Coleg Harlech, North Wales; Hillcroft College, Surrey, and the London School of Economics for the study of industrial relations and other subjects of interest to trade unionists. The union provide one-week residential training courses at Cirencester dealing with union organisation, workplace representation, and payment systems. Intensive five-day courses at the place of work, or occasionally at the union's own training centre for shop stewards are held. There is also ample opportunity for home study on a variety of industrial and trade union matters, including joint consultation, productivity bargaining, and courses in English, Economics, Arithmetic and Statistics, History, Industry and Industrial Relations, Social Services, Government, as well as practical subjects on organisation and public speaking. TGWU works with the WEA and the TUC as well as providing its own facilities, and statistics for an average year at the end of our period would be as follows:

Union's Home Study Course Enrolments	2,239
TUC Home Study Courses Enrolments	1,407
Union Day and Week-end Schools (Attendance)	3,124
Union 1-week Courses (Attendance)	910
TUC 1 and 2 week Courses	195
TUC Week-end, Day, Day-Release and Evening Classes	3,976

The criticism voiced by Ray Fletcher in *Plebs* in 1952 seems most relevant even in 1980:

> The Transport Workers, for instance, spend thousands of pounds each year on education. Only a small percentage take advantage of it. (Fletcher, 1952, p.244).

In 1972 the sum spent by the TGWU on educational work was nearly £250,000 but it still seemed that the concept of continuing education had not been accepted by the majority of the members who belong to the largest union in Britain.

ii General and Municipal Workers' Union

Educational facilities for members of the General and Municipal Workers' Union were started in 1926 but like the Transport and General Workers' Union the expansion took place after the second world war. The annual allocation of £400 for educational work started in 1932 was increased to £1,000 in 1947. In 1948 it was raised to £2,000 and in 1950 a further increase to £5,000. Most of the educational facilities between 1926 and 1950 were limited to the day, week-end and summer schools, and the correspondence courses offered by the WETUC and the NCLC.

Leaders of the union realised two things. Firstly that the growth in membership of the union meant a particular responsibility on their part. By 1947 the total membership of the Union was 824,000, which was a big rise from the membership figure of 439,000 in 1937. Larger membership meant money to spend on educating the members.

Secondly, the need for functional and vocational training was most evident. This began in 1951 after experiments in 1949 and 1950. the early fifties saw an expansion in the range of training and educational facilities. It was decided in 1951 to award annually two scholarships to Ruskin College, Oxford, and in 1954 to organise day and week-end schools, and in co-operation with the Board of Extra-Mural Studies of the University, a summer school (for a fortnight) was held at Madingley Hall, Cambridge (Cooper, 1966, p.5).

107

General and Municipal Workers' Union appointed an education officer as Head Officer in 1954 which was an important step. Prior to that three officers had been partly responsible for the activities, one for liaison with the WEA and WETUC, another for liaison with the NCLC, and a third for the rest of the educational programme. The pattern was fixed with the following provision:

i   correspondence courses

ii   day and week-end schools

iii   summer schools

iv   training courses (technical colleges, the TUC courses and industrial consultants)

v   scholarships, and in particular to Ruskin College.

These range of facilities were increased in 1958 with training courses for branch officers and stewards being organised at the Union's headquarters. This provision was transferred in the autumn of 1964 to the Union Residential College, Woodstock, which was officially opened on 25th May 1964, by one of the remarkable leaders of the Union, Lord Williamson. The new residential college at Woodstock was situated near the Union's headquarters, and it originally catered for twenty students. By the end of our period it had doubled the number it could accommodate, and a three-stage programme was introduced in 1967.

Stage one was a one-week course designed to be taken by shop stewards and branch secretaries who had previously received preliminary training at District level. There were three educational stages in the provision mentioned, namely:

i   A general shop stewards course;

ii   A special shop stewards course;

iii   A. course which gave particular attention to the role of the branch sectretary.

Stage two was a two-week course designed to extend the training of shop stewards and branch secretaries who had attained a satisfactory level of performance on stage one. A particular emphasis was placed in stage two on explaining the procedure of collective bargaining. Stage two was a practical course, and role-playing was used to convey the Union's case, the employer's reply, and a critical assessment of the negotiations. Assessment of performance on stage two would play an important part in the selection of students to attend stage three. Stage three had an utilitarian and limited purpose of training the selected students for full-time posts in the Union. It was a four-week course, and the last week was devoted to the study of work measurement into the field of other management techniques.

It seems that the GMWU was concerned above everything else with the training of officials to serve the interests of the Union. The philosophy of continuous learning was being accepted in a limited manner, and in 1965 the National Executive Committee decided that the training of officials, which in the past had been carried out by numerous movements, should be planned and under the control of the GMWU. Before 1965 the General and Municipal Workers' Union would send along able, enthusiastic future leaders on scholarships to Ruskin College, Harvard University, Technical Colleges, Summer Schools held by the Union at Oxford, Cambridge, Cranfield, Burton Manor and Barlaston. The new course was to cover the following needs of a trade union education:

i   induction or pre-induction training covering essential skills;

ii   further training to complement experience;

iii refresher courses.

The concept of a recurrent education was being adopted in the provision made for further training. It was felt that the trade union officer needed, during the first five years of his service, an opportunity to study the economic and social factors. An annual training course was to be held at Madingley Hall, Cambridge, organised for the Union by the University of Cambridge Board of Extra-Mural Studies which would provide the social and economic background to current problems. Experienced academic, Dr. J. Ward of the University of Strathclyde, was willing to act as a Director to the Annual Training Course. Training courses for younger officials were provided by the TUC and training courses with industrial consultants were provided. Development training was also instituted, that is, training those who had shown a great deal of potential, and they are entered for courses run by the advanced management programme and the Administrative Staff College. Refresher courses of one month's duration were also implemented by the General and Municipal Workers' Union, and to be attended by each official once every five or six years. The course was designed for the Union by Professor H.A. Clegg of the University of Warwick.

The General and Municipal Workers' Union had no special relationship with the Workers' Educational Association or any other adult educational movement, but it would use their service as well as encourage all their 'students' to participate in the TUC postal courses. One important development that we find in the educational provision of the General and Municipal Workers' Union was in the training courses provided at the technical colleges. It all started and was centred for a time on Birmingham Central Technical College. Two full-time courses were organised in the autumn of 1949. It was to be a course of one month and the students were taught in the techniques of time study; motion study, and job evaluation. Ten students were enrolled in each course during the first years of its existence but then, as we will see in the table, it expanded, and by 1951 there were 13 Training Colleges involved.

1951 and 1952 were two fruitful years with 90 courses provided and 954 students attending. Demand fell in 1953 and from 1954 onwards 10 or 11 courses at three Technical Colleges attended by around 100 students every year was the pattern. Birmingham courses were discontinued in 1964, but they were carried on at Woolwich Polytechnic in London.

Training Courses supported by General and Municipal Workers' Union at the Technical Colleges (1949-1965)

Year	Colleges	Courses	Students
1949	1	2	20
1950	1	2	18
1951	13	39	424
1952	13	51	530
1953	8	22	232
1954	3	10	113
1955	3	11	116
1956	3	11	113
1957	3	11	128
1958	3	11	123
1959·	3	11	119
1960	3	9	83
1961	1	4	40
1962	2	9	105
1963	2	11	115
1964	2	7	64
1965	1	6	81

(Source: Cooper (1966) p.8)
Table 3.3

General and Municipal Workers' Union realised also in the fifties the value of organising day and weekend schools. In 1955 56 day and week-end schools were organised by the districts attended by 1,490 members. The following year — 1956 — there was a marked increase with 114 schools organised and attended by 2,608 members of the General and Municipal Workers' Union. The day and week-end schools have been organised regularly since 1955 to provide a basic appreciation of trade unionism as well as to provide a basic training for branch officers. Another innovation was the appreciation schools — usually on four week-ends — with topics being:

i   The General and Municipal Workers' Union

ii   The wider trade union movement

iii   Trade Unions and Industry

iv   Trade Unions and the State

General and Municipal Workers' Union prides itself with the training courses arranged since 1958 by the head office, and the statistics show an encouraging response at the end of the period.

General and Municipal Workers' Union Head Office
Training Courses (1958-1967)

Year	Students	Courses
1958	48	4
1959	108	9
1960	108	9
1961	120	10
1962	108	9
1963	144	12
1964	183	13
1965	396	24
1966	406	26
1967	440	28

Table 3.4

One obvious reason for the growth has been the doubling in the courses provided from 4 in 1958 to 28 in 1967. The other reason has been the support given to the courses by the Union hierarchy. This was a breakthrough which was true also in the attitude of the other major trade unions for even in the sixties most of the members of the Trades Union Congress (TUC) had left elementary school at the age of fourteen. One has to resist over-emphasising the change of the attitude for even in the sixties the trade unions were inward-looking, often inefficient, and the nature of their information and argument were often inferior to the world of management. There was a natural reluctance to change which the General and Municipal Workers' Union overcame in the middle sixties. In 1965 the National Executive Committee decided that the training of officials — which previously had been carried out quite haphazardly — should cover:

i   induction or pre-induction training covering essential skills.

111

ii   further training to complement experience.

iii   refresher courses.

The other reason for the growth was the fact that more finance was forthcoming from the Union for the training and educational programme. In 1950 the sum spent was £5,000; in the middle fifties (1955) was £15,000; in the late fifties and early sixties (1955-63) the sum was £25,000. Then there was a dramatic change as the following figures indicate. In 1964 the General and Municipal Workers' Union spent £32,992, the following year £55,480, and in 1966 the sum was £63,763. The General and Municipal Workers' Union had realised the necessity and the potentiality of educating its members. B. Willey from the General and Municipal Workers' Union sum it up:

> It has frequently been said by Union spokesmen that expenditure on training and education is one of the Union's best investments. This is axiomatic, for it is undeniable that trained leadership at all levels is the key to the efficiency which the organisation must have to give proper service to its members.   (Cooper, 1966, p.20).

iii   National Union of Agricultural and Allied Workers (NUAAW)

The National Union of Agricultural and Allied Workers is one of the smaller unions and the amount of time and money spent on educating its members is limited by its resources. Its aim is to instruct the members with regard to the history and the work of the Union, the witness of the wider trade union movement, as well as to inform the farmworkers of the broader social as well as political questions. It seems that the educational work is done on a small scale and mostly through the winter school which takes place in January of each year when some thirty students attend a one-week's course. This educational venture opened as an experiment at Folkestone in 1948 and continues because, to quote the Union's General Secretary, Reginald N. Bottini, "we feel that an informed membership will be an active membership and a membership that is both informed and active is the greatest asset a Union can have".

The school is arranged for selected members of the Union in order to instruct them in the problems confronting the trade union movement, and to give them a more intimate understanding of how the National Union of Agricultural and Allied Workers is tackling its responsibilities to the membership. At the beginning there were three sessions with around 90 attending, but due to rising costs there were only two sessions at the end of the sixties. The students are given a thorough outline of the manner in which the Union functions, with detailed accounts of the work undertaken by the various Head Office Departments. In addition lectures given by Members of Parliament in particular on the position of Agriculture, and sometimes on the history of the farmworkers' struggle. Reg Groves, author of *Sharpen the Sickle* (a history of the Union to 1947), is frequently invited to lecture on such historical topics as 'The Growth of Rural Trade Unionism'. Most of these winter schools (1949-1970) were organised by one of the most forceful personalities of the Union, Edgar Pill, who had been appointed Organiser for Lancashire in 1947. Hundreds of young and not-so-young Union members had their interest in the National Union of Agricultural and Allied Workers and the wider labour movement strengthened and activated in new directions as a result of their attendance at the winter school. Added to that was the forthright, enthusiastic manner of the school's organiser, Edgar Pill, who was also the Union Education Officer until his retirement in 1974.

The Union organisers a few week-end schools in different parts of the country every year, but these are not organised from the Head office — Headland House in Gray's Inn Road, London — but depend on the initiative of the districts. The districts corresponded in the main to the county system except for Wales, where the six counties were grouped together into a District. All this represents an attempt at adult education, and one has to realise that the National Union of Agricultural and Allied Workers is faced with a great number of difficulties. The obvious difficulty is to keep its membership, for the farm labour force declined in the sixties. In September 1959 there were around 350,000 regular whole-time male workers in agriculture. During the next eight years this number dropped by over one third. The National Union of Agricultural and Allied Workers has to try and win unorganised country roadmen to join the union. Leaflets and publicity material is continually being prepared to convince roadmen and other allied workers (such as the forestry workers) in the countryside to join. But to do this effectively demands education. The other problem is to organise a group of workers who are not in continual contact with one another. A great number of rural workers are not organised in any trade union and this is very true in areas like North Wales. On the positive side the National Union of Agricultural and Allied Workers publish a very useful monthly magazine called *Land Worker,* which incorporated another magazine, *The Labourer.* The *Land Worker* serves an educational function though most of the magazine is devoted to news of the movement. However, every issue has at least one or even more articles of an educational nature, and the annual Tolpuddle Martyrs Rally, organised by the Dorset National Union of Agricultural and Allied Workers Committee, always has articles which deal with the men who in 1834 suffered transportation in the cause of liberty, justice and righteousness. The National Union of Agricultural and Allied Workers also co-operate with the Agricultural, Horticultural and Forestry Industry Training Board by informing members of schools as well as courses sponsored by the education service of the Trade Union Congress.

iv   **The Civil and Public Services Association (formerly the Civil Service Clerical Association**

The Civil and Public Services Association, which was formed in 1922 and known then until 1969 as the Civil Service Clerical Association, is the recognised trade union for clerical, typing and machine grades in the civil service and in some public corporations. It had 16,500 members in 1922, but by 1974 it had 215,000 members in 900 branches, varying in size from less than a dozen to over 7,000 members.

The Association believes in providing educational and social activities for its members and for many years it has adopted a policy of organising week-end schools for members. No cost falls on the students. The schools are intended to give students a brief history of the Civil and Public Services Association, its scope and organisation, how it fits into the civil service trade union movement and into the wider trade union field. The syllabus covers instruction in negotiation, and the conduct of branch meetings, and the forming and carrying out of national policy through Conference, the National Executive Committee and the Headquarters of the Association. All schools are organised by area committees, while the education committee provides the lecturers.

The association also organises a yearly summer school of one week's duration. Between 40 and 50 students are selected by the education committee from amongst applications made through branches. The syllabus of the school varies from year to year, but basically it is designed as an advanced course for branch or potential branch officers. The lecturers include senior headquarters officers as well as lecturers from outside the Civil and Public Services Association, and National Executive Committee members also act as additional lecturers and discussion group leaders.

The Civil and Public Services Association work closely with other educational agencies, and in particular the Workers' Educational Association. Local Civil and Public Services Association branches are strongly recommended to affiliate individually to their local district organisation of the WEA. The Civil and Public Services Association members have opportunities of securing scholarships to WEA summer schools as well as applying for scholarships for long-term residential study at the two residential colleges for adults, Ruskin College, Oxford, and Hillcroft College, Surbiton. In the case of Ruskin College, the Civil and Public Services Association has its own 'L.C. White Memorial Scholarship' and is a participant in the college's scholarship pool for trade unionists.

The Civil and Public Services Association work hand in hand with the Trade Union Congress Regional Educational Advisory Committees. In addition, the Trade Union Congress educational trust offers a quota of scholarships to the Civil and Public Services Association each year, for training courses run at Congress House in London, for the TUC summer schools, for the TUC youth school and various schools held abroad. The Civil and Public Services Association members are expected to make use of the Trade Union Congress correspondence courses in subjects basic to their educational needs. The association has, through the national staff side, a representative on the national body of the Civil Service Council for Further Education, as well as representatives on each of the regional committees.

The Civil Service Council for Further Education does not run any classes itself, but it operates the civil service day release scheme for persons up to the age of eighteen, and it will assist any interested group to form the class it desires, or give information on almost any educational question, vocational or non-vocational.

The members are informed of these facilities through the branches, and in particular on the pages of its monthly magazine, *Red Tape*, which has been published continuously since 1911. A readable magazine, *Red Tape* provides its members with knowledgeable information and comment on union and national affairs.

The Civil and Public Services Association spent in the early seventies around £60,000 per year on educating their branch officers and members with a view to making them better negotiators, and also to improving the organisation of the union. A further indication of their determination with regard to adult education was the appointment in 1974 of a full-time education officer. A great deal more can be done as the Civil and Public Services Association is the largest union affiliated to the staff side of the Civil Service National Whitley Council.

v   Association of Teachers in Technical Institutions (ATTI)

The Association of Teachers in Technical Institutions was a small union, but one which was naturally tied up with the education of adults, for its members were to be found in all kinds of educational institutions catering for the education of adults, that is, colleges of further education, polytechnics, colleges of technology, colleges of art, and it had in joint membership the Association for Adult Education which organises full-time teachers in adult education. The Association played an important role in the development of work within the sphere of adult education as a pressure for the role of permanent or recurrent education. In its statement to the Russell Committee in 1969 the ATTI argued strongly for adult education to be taken seriously. Its ideas and arguments were most important, and unique in the history of trade unionism. The reason for this uniqueness was the particular function of the Association of Teachers in Technical Institutions — as a union which catered for the interests of a great number of practising adult educators.

The Association of Teachers in Technical Institutions argued in its 1969 statement to the Russell Committee for the following:

Non-vocational Further Education. Work should be treated as a specific sector of the educational system. Powers should be given to assist 'recognised bodies' providing adult education, and it should be a duty of the Secretary of State and local authorities to ensure that their work is co-ordinated with that undertaken by the local authorities themselves. The ATTI believed that the growth and expansion in adult education had taken place without any specific provision in the 1944 Act, but rather as reflecting the continuous pressure and demand from a growing section of the population for education of the kind which the adult education services have provided. The Association of Teachers in Technical Institutions argued that the new Act should make more specific the minimum requirements and that the local authorities should be required to provide adequate adult education facilities.

The Association in its statement included other meaningful and important suggestions such as the setting up of adult education committees to co-ordinate the work of the responsible bodies as well as to improve and provide a more adequate service; appoint professional administrative staff; to establish Area Principals who would be teachers in adult education, and the building of appropriate purpose-built premises for adult education.

Most of these useful suggestions were not adopted by the Russell Committee, but the Association of Teachers in Technical Institutions issued a very useful constructive review on the Russell Report. Its greatest disappointment was with the limitation of the terms of reference to non-vocational adult education which inevitably precluded any effective discussion of recurrent or permanent education.

The Association of Teachers in Technical Institutions felt as others have done that the Russell Committee teetered on the "edge of a discussion of recurrent education, but then draws back" (ATTI *Adult Education* (1973) p.1). But the Russell Committee were unable to ignore the wider issue totally, and in paragraphs 49 and 50 they outline the concept of permanent education as adopted by UNESCO in 1964. However, they promptly dismiss the concept in the next paragraph (51):

Permanent education is a long-term concept and we have not time to wait for it.

The Association of Teachers in Technical Institutions was disappointed with such a lukewarm approach in view of the proposals for development of in-service training for teachers and the Open University. It expressed its disappointment in this statement:

The Association regrets that the Committee was not able to make recommendations on permanent education. It accepts that the implementations would have to be over a period of time, but guide-lines for its development could have been extremely valuable.

(1973, p.1).

The educational work of the Association relating to its own members was largely organised at the subnational (or divisional) level: week-end and day-schools were organised with the assistance of national and regional officials. These were generally confined to activists and office holders within branches, and were primarily concerned with developing their roles within their branches and colleges. For instance, courses were run for branch secretaries and treasurers, and for ATTI members on the academic boards and governing bodies of colleges. Use was also made of Trade Union Congress educational courses where those were appropriate. Officials in the Head Office at Hamilton House, Mabledon Place, London, and liaison officers in the regions were responsible for the development of internal education programmes.

vi   Union of Post Office Workers

The Union of Post Office Workers is a Union which has greatly increased its educational facilities in the period under consideration. Prior to 1964 the education programme was limited to week-end schools and the TUC general education programme. In 1964 a varied educational programme was adopted, and facilities were made available for the study of useful non-vocational subjects.

The Union of Post Office Workers makes a clear distinction in its literature between education and training for union work, and the greater part of the services provided for members revolves around the Union's Three Tier Training Scheme which takes students through the three phases of induction, secondary and advanced training.

The scheme operates as follows:

i   Induction and Preparatory Training. This is the first 'tier' of the new training policy and priority of attendance is given to local branch officials. The schools are held in the spring of each year, to follow the branch annual general meeting, and the application for places comes through the branches.

ii   Secondary Training. The curriculum concentrates on specific items and on the work of departments at the headquarters in Clapham, London. It is expected that students who have attended the induction meeting will come along as well as branch officers who have been in those positions for at least two years.

iii   Advanced Training. The curriculum of the advanced training is a 'follow-up' to the induction and specialised courses, and the overall aim being to give a better understanding of the problems of the union and to foster a deeper appreciation of the social and economic life of the community.

Each district council may hold one week-end school each year linked with a normal district council meeting. The school is attended by delegates to the district council and among the subjects taken are promotions procedure; revisions procedure; trade unions and politics; the TUC and Trades Council; United Nations Organisation; the International Labour Office and elementary introduction to work study.

The next educational facility available to the members of the Union of Post Office Workers is a special branch official's course arranged for the union by the TUC. A member can complete the course in twelve monthly lessons which includes procedure, finance and English, as well as other subjects. Those who complete the course and reach the required standard are awarded the Green Triangle Union Badge. Additionally there are courses for branch chairmen, treasurers, as well as a variety of other subjects.

The Union of Post Office Workers accepts other provisions prepared by the TUC such as the courses held at the TUC Training College and the summer schools held at Ruskin College. It also awards a limited number of scholarships to One-Week Residential Schools run by the Labour Party, usually at Beatrice Webb House in Dorking, Surrey, during the months of July and August.

Since 1964, apart from a retrenchment period due to the postal strike, the Union has annually dealt with approximately 800 students each year within the programme outlined. The breakdown is approximately 300 for induction, 300 for secondary and 200 for advanced. At the induction and secondary the tutors are members of the Union National Executive who have received some training in teaching methods. The advanced schools have a number of outside people who lecture from the wider movements, but again the principal is the officer responsible for education.

vii The Iron and Steel Trades Confederation

The Iron and Steel Trades Confederation deserves a very special place in the history of trade union education for the formation of the Workers' Education Trade Union Committee in 1919 was inspired by the Iron and Steel Trades Confederation and in particular through the efforts of Arthur Pugh, leader of the newly amalgamated Steel Workers' Union. The historian of trade union education has described him in these glowing terms:

> He (that is, Arthur Pugh) has a legitimate claim to being one of the handful of great trade-union administrators in Britain. (Corfield, 1969, p.5).

The Steel Smelters' Union had a tradition of support for adult education which ante-dated Pugh's tenure of office as Assistant Secretary. In 1903 two of their organisers attended Ruskin College on a one-year course, and a third organiser soon followed. Arthur Pugh's organising ability was put at the disposal of the new venture and he became the first chairman of the WETUC. But things did not work out as Arthur Pugh had envisaged, and the reason for this was the depression which hit the industry in the twenties. In the early nineteen twenties between 40% and 50% of the steel workers were unemployed (Corfield, 1969, p.181). It can be argued that trade union education would have made a much bigger impact had the Iron and Steel Trades Confederation been able to sustain their earlier strength. In 1920 the Iron and Steel Confederation represented 2.1% of the TUC's membership, and by 1930, because of the especially deep depression in the steel industry, its proportion had shrunk to 1.6% of a much reduced total (Corfield, 1969, p.183).

The Iron and Steel Trades Confederation, however, played an important role throughout the years in conjunction with the W.E.A. and afterwards with the TUC, but the changing pattern of industrial society forced the Iron and Steel Trades Confederation to review their educational service. They felt that there was a need to equip their own members better for the rapid changes which were taking place both inside and outside the industry.

In 1969 the Executive Council of the Iron and Steel Trades Confederation decided that arrangements should be made to provide residential and other courses especially for their members, with the provision that initially the main theme of such courses would be confined to extending the knowledge of their members to all areas of the union's activities and the problems facing the iron and steel industry. The subjects and speakers were chosen to provide the most comprehensive coverage with the highest degree of teaching possible in the time permitted, and also allow the students ample opportunity to participate in full discussion. In 1973 the Executive Council approved a five year programme of education and training, which included the publication of a manual, and the training of newly elected branch officials within the divisions. It was also decided to introduce an advanced national school with a reduced and more specialist curriculum. The Iron and Steel Trades Confederation had not lost the educational enthusiasm of Arthur Pugh but they had narrowed a great deal and that at a time when recurrent education was becoming an acceptable philosophy to many trade unionists, and at a time when they needed a more broadly based education for adults.

viii   The National Union of Hosiery and Knitwear Workers

This small Union, with its headquarters in Leicester, has participated in adult education since 1950 through the aegis of the T.U.C., the Workers' Educational Assoication, and a number of extra-mural organisations in various localities. The course matter of all these participants has been allied to the trade union movement in particular, covering such subjects as wage negotiations, industrial relations, work study, time and method study, health and safety at work, and the implementation of agreements which they done with various manufacturers. A large number of the National Union of Hosiery and Knitwear Workers over the years participated in the WETUC correspondence courses which after 1964 was taken over by the TUC. Like other unions, this union in the late sixties instituted its own courses of one-day and week-end schools, and the subject matter for these courses has been industrial relations, the application of work study, health and safety at work, government legislation and aspects of the industry, both national and international. H.L. Gibson, the General Secretary of the Union, sums up the educational philosophy succinctly:

> The whole aim and philosophy behind our educational pursuits is to try and encourage the memberships to participate in the work of our Union and the Trade Union Movement in general and therefore, become a more useful member of society.

ix   National and Local Government Officers Association (NALGO)

National and Local Government Officers Association is an union that takes particular pride in its educational programme and its education department caters for two separate distinct needs among the membership. Its historian has claimed that NALGO is unique among British trade unions in its zeal for education (Spoor, 1967, p.436). The department is divided into two sections, the vocational educational section, and trade union education section. Vocational education is carried out through the National and Local Government Officers Association Correspondence Institute and the NCI, as it is called, is an integral part of the Association's education service. The National and Local Government Officers Association first provided correspondence courses in 1920 to meet the needs of members preparing for its own examination in local government administration. The success of these courses led to demands for tuition for more specialised examinations, such as those for rating officers and weights and measures inspectors. After the second world war NALGO took a new look at the correspondence courses. The 1944 Education Act envisaged many new developments; and the question was simply if correspondence tuition was still needed by NALGO members? The answer was soon found. It was still difficult to find class teachers for all subjects at the required levels, and, even where they could be found, the examinations were so specialised that it was seldom possible to assemble enough students every year to sustain a satisfactory class.

The need for correspondence courses has been reviewed by NALGO periodically, but on each occasion there has been evidence of a continuing demand. By the late sixties more than two hundred examination subject courses were available and the tutorial and advisory panel comprised over one hundred and fifty university lecturers and senior officers. NALGO was also willing to accept non-members who belong to other recognised unions, and also to cater for overseas students. The Union has been co-operating with the College of Estate Management which is associated with the University of Reading and provides correspondence courses in the field of estate management as well as the Co-operative Union Education Department and the National Extension College in efforts to promote higher educational standards. NCI provide correspondence courses for the following Diplomas and Certificates: Association of Medical Records Officers; Department of Trade and Industry Certificate in Weights and Measures; Diploma in Consumer Affairs; Diploma in Government Administration; Diploma in Housing Management; Diploma in Municipal Administration; Diploma in Public Adminstration; Education Welfare Officers Examination; Institute of Ambulance Officers Examination; Institute of Baths Management Examination; Institute of Chartered Secretaries and Administrators Examination; Institute of Health Service Administrators Examination; Institute of Home Help Examination; Institute of Municipal Entertainment Examination; Institute of Municipal Treasurers and Accountants Examination; Institute of Population Registration Examination; Institute of Rent Officers Examination; Institute of Shops Acts Administration Examination; Institution of Municipal Engineers Examination; Rating and Valuation Association Examination; Royal Town Planning Institute Examination; as well as the General Certificate of Education Examinations. NALGO prepare tuition for other courses such as the Diplomas in the Royal Society of Health and the Greater London Council.

The Union arranges residential courses for students and in 1972 some 800 students attended. Fifty separate class programmes were arranged and staffed by over one hundred and twenty tutors. the NCI correspondence method claim that every student is well catered for by flexible and individual schemes of study. To cater for the individual needs of the student the NCI introduces, in addition to the basic National and Local Government Officers Association notes on subject matter, a set of tutorial notes for each subject. The student is recommended further reading and is given practice in answering examination questions and how to prepare himself for the task of becoming a competent student.

The Trade Union Education Section is the second main concern of the National and Local Government Officers Association Education Department. Like all other unions NALGO is concerned with increasing their members' knowledge of union affairs and their ability to undertake union work effectively. It was argued in the late sixties that one way of strengthening and developing NALGO's trade union education was through the establishment of a NALGO residential training college.

The National and Local Government Officers Association provide basic courses for NALGO members described in the organisation, structure and aims of the Union and courses specifically for serving branch officers. In addition to courses provided at national level, each NALGO district runs schools for the members and officers of their particular district. The third level of trade union education takes place at branch level with the branches themselves running courses for their members and branch officers. The aim is to provide members with basic knowledge about issues affecting NALGO, about the organisation generally and branch organisation in particular, making effective use of district and national provision and facilities offered by other agencies. The National and Local Government Officers Association branches sometimes make use of the WEA to run courses specifically for NALGO officers. As NALGO is an affiliated union of the TUC it has access to TUC education facilities for its members of which they make considerable use.

x   Amalgamated Union of Engineering Workers (AUEW)

The Amalgamated Union of Engineering Workers has been in the forefront of trade union education and the Assistant General Secretary is in charge of all the arrangements. The AEU, as it was then known in the early fifties, increased and developed its educational scheme through the initiative of A.J. Caddick who retired in 1953. There was a very close co-operation between the AEU and NCLC who organised summer schools and residential week-end schools for the union members. When the Trade Union Congress took over in 1964 the Amalgamated Union of Engineering Workers supported the new provisions. For example, the Executive Council of the AUEW offer fifty-eight places at the TUC General Summer School which cover such subjects as 'Industrial Relations at the Work Place', 'Trade Unions and Social and Economic Policies', 'Workers and the Law' and 'Study of Relations with Government'. The Amalgamated Union of Engineering Workers offer places also for the specialised courses involved in the TUC Training College Scheme at Congress House, London, as well as scholarship to Ruskin College.

The Amalgamated Union of Engineering Workers provide, like all the major unions, their own residential courses. There are two such courses, namely the branch secretaries' residential course held at Worthing in Sussex, and the Shop Stewards' Residential Course at Wortley in Yorkshire and Worthing. Branch secretaries' residential courses deal with the duties and problems of branch secretaries and cover a four-week period with forty members in attendance each week. Shop stewards' residential courses are open to all accredited shop stewards and run over a four-week period with forty members in attendance each week. Lectures include subjects such as 'The Structure and Function of the Unions' 'Communications and Information Services', 'Accidents at Work' and 'Aspects of Preparing and Presenting a Grievance'. This union, like many other unions, has a very narrow approach to the needs of its members, and their activities bore out the main thesis of this book that philosophical and educational ideas in workers education have rarely been modified by the changing circumstances in the life and interests of ordinary people in England and Wales in the post-war period.

xi   Union of Shop, Distributive and Allied Workers (USDAW)

The Union of Shop, Distributive and Allied Workers insist that their priority in the education of adults is to train competent full-time and voluntary officers backed by the "active and informed support of its other members". To meet this challenge the Union's six-part home study course *Introducing U.S.D.A.W.* was designed to provide members with the basic 'nuts and bolts' of trade unionism in general and USDAW in particular. The fact that three hundred to four hundred members in the seventies enrolled annually for this course shows how successful it is in introducing members to trade unionism. For many members it is also the springboard to other and more advanced studies.

The Home Study Course Units are useful guides in the educating of the Union of Shop, Distributive and Allied Workers members. One can criticise these courses in parts for being too simplistic but reading them all together, that is the six parts (*The Essence of Trade Unionism; Union's Growth and Development, Structure, Government and Administration of the Union; The Union at Work; Wages and Conditions; Service for its Members; The Union and Politics*) a member would have an excellent bird's eye view of the historical development of the trade union movement and his own union as well. Alfred

W. Allen in his foreward to the six booklets sums up the aim of the Home Study Course:

> ... the success of the Union will continue to depend (as it has done in the past), largely upon the extent to which its members are prepared to share in its work and are willing to accept not only the rights but also the responsibilities of membership. Before members can be expected to play such an active part within U.S.D.A.W., however, they must have opportunities to come to understand what the union is and what it does. Only if and when the union has succeeded in making clear to its members the value and relevance of its aims and functions, can it expect a positive response. The purpose of this postal code is to provide such elementary understanding.
>
> (A.W. Allen, *The Essence of Trade Unionism, Part 1*, p.3).

For those who complete the elementary home study course there are other opportunities for education. In 1949 an annual summer school was established intended mainly for those who have completed the home study course. It is held at the Beatrice Webb House in Surrey, and skills essential for the active trade unionist, such as note-taking, self expression and meeting procedures, are developed. Talks and discussions on policy issues also form part of the programme.

Each year also the Union's federation of branches throughout the country arrange 40 to 60 one-day and week-end conferences at which industrial, political and economic issues are considered. Usually a union official or a Member of Parliament is invited to lead the discussions. Approximately two thousand members take part each year in seminars of this kind. In addition to the week-end conferences the regional education service of the TUC offers active members free attendance at day or week-end courses, as well as day release and evening classes on subjects of concern and relevance to active trade unionists. Each year the union offers a number of comprehensive scholarships at one-week courses arranged by the TUC, the Labour party and the Co-operative Movement. This provides an opportunity for about forty experienced members who have completed some of the basic courses mentioned previously to spend a week under expert tutors at Ruskin college Oxford.

The Union of Shop, Distributive and Allied Workers, like all other unions, arrange tailor-made training courses to equip the local branch officers for their role in the organisation. Branch secretaries, chairmen, shop stewards are catered for in the course of a year. One-week residential courses are held for branch secretaries at the union's training centre in Manchester. Many courses for groups of shop stewards in a particular factory, warehouse or store are also arranged, often with the support and participation of management. Such 'in-plant' courses normally extend over four to five days and concentrate on providing such information and practical training as is appropriate to the functions and responsibilities of the union representatives concerned. The TUC also provide courses, as does the WEA, on trade union education, and USDAW education department circulate its membership with regard to the facilities provided by both these organisations. Union refunds class fees to members who have completed a series of evening studies through the WEA and annual grants are made to adult education colleges, namely Coleg Harlech, Ruskin College and Hillcroft College for Women.

xii   The Inland Revenue Staff Federation (IRSF)

The Inland Revenue Staff Federation educational activities shows the same pattern as the other unions that we have discussed. This union provides one scholarship to Ruskin College for one year study as well as eight one-year bursaries at the same college. Furthermore, they provide eight bursaries for full-time courses of one academic year at the London School of Economics; three awards at Coleg Harlech and one award at Hillcroft College, Surbiton. Two awards are given to attend full-time residential courses at Fircroft College, Birmingham. The Inland Revenue Staff Federation make provision for interested union members to attend the Trade Union Congress summer schools as well as the TUC classes, courses and week-end schools. Many IRSF members enrol with the TUC for postal tuition. All the courses are available free of charge to members. The Inland Revenue Staff Federation is also affiliated to the WEA and members are encouraged to use the facilities of that organisation.

xiii   Association of Broadcasting Staff (ABS)

The Association of Broadcasting Staff is a relatively small industrial union with some twelve thousand five hundred members. The majority of the Association of Broadcasting Staff members work for the British Broadcasting Corporation though a significant minority are employed by the Independent Broadcasting Association. The Union has no education department or a full-time educational officer. In the period between 1945 and 1970 courses were organised in rather ad hoc manner, but in 1974 they regularised the courses and held two-day industrial relations courses. Like all unions, the philosophy is to make the branch officers better equipped to deal with the employer. There was no formal political education, and the lecturers were drawn exclusively from their full-time officers of the union.

xiv   Confederation of Health Service Employees (COHSE)

The only education courses that the Confederation of Health Service Employees was involved in during the period 1945-70 were those organised by the TUC and NCLC which was advertised and promoted amongst the members. Since 1970 they have organised courses specifically for stewards. Confederation of Health Serivce Employees did not have any formal links with either the WEA or the NCLC, but their head office at Glen House, Banstead, Surrey, always passed on queries and attempted, as far as possible, to co-operate with both movements. Also they distributed National College of Labour Colleges literature.

The union never had an education officer, and the work was carried out in the early seventies by one of the national orgnaisers. Much of the reason behind this lack of activity has been the small size of the union. Until the mid nineteen sixties it was largely content to be a small union centred on psychiatric nurses. Since that time the Confederation of Health Service Employees has increased at a tremendous rate (121, 150 in 1975), and their expectation was that an education officer could be appointed before the end of the seventies.

xv   Association of Scientific, Technical and Managerial Staffs (ASTMS)

The Association of Scientific, Technical and Managerial Staffs are very concious of the role of education in the life of their members. The motivation is an awareness of the technological problems of a highly industrialised society and of people who are employed in industries such as insurance and in medicine. The Medical Practitioners' Union is a section of ASTMS. It is expected that all those who have been in the union for some time will take advantage of the educational provision at TUC level or at the union level. The divisional councils arrange week-end schools for educational and political work and tutors who are specialists are called in. Members are also encouraged to attend the college at Bishops Stortford, and scholarships are given to members for study at Ruskin College.

xvi   Prison Officers' Association

The Prison Officers' Association has no provision of its own for the sixteen or so thousand members that belong to it. As they are affiliated to the Trades Union Congress they receive the facilities offered by the TUC, but the vast majority of the courses are conducted through the Home Office Prison Department. This was an agreement reached between the Prison Department and the Prison Officers' Association and ever since the members have been involved in the further education field.

The political education of the members is never entered into by the Prison Officers' Association as they have no political affiliation towards any political party. Mr. D. Evans, Assistant Secretary, makes this point very clear in a letter addressed to the researcher:

Our work, as you are probably aware, involves discussions with all the Home Secretaries that have held office since our existence in 1939. It would, therefore, be imprudent of us to sway our members to affiliate or have any political leaning whatsoever.

(Letter dated 18 April 1975).

xvii   Other Unions

Electrical, Electronic, Telecommunication and Plumbing Union (EETPU) is among the most active in trade union education. It has its own residential college, opened in June 1953 at Esher Place, Esher, Surrey, where it trains its members in organisational work. National Union of Vehicle Builders had an excellent programme of adult education in trade union and social studies. It is one of the smaller unions but it expects its members to give generously for their education work.

125

E The contribution of the Trade Union Congress

The TUC emphasises in all its publications that the education of trade unionists is one of the major functions of adult education. It views trade union education as a distinct sector within the total provision of adult education, differing from both vocational training and liberal adult education.

Looking at the contribution of the Trade Union Congress one has to admit that its educational provision for trade unions is extensive. It has an education department which organises its summer schools and courses of training for officers and members of the affiliated unions. The training college is concerned with giving its voluntary officers skills in their day to day union work.

The Trade Union Congress in the post-war period was very dissatisfied with the trade union education that was being carried out, and in its deliberations at the Annual Congress concern was expressed at the overlapping of facilities with regard to summer schools and tutorials in evening classes. It was a wasteful use of educational funds and introduced into trade union education competition rather than co-operation. They felt also that the NCLC and WETUC restricted the development of the Trade Union Congress educational facilities. It was an excuse for a union not to do anything and there was an apparent failure to meet certain educational needs. The need in the main of educating the trade unionists for the tasks within their unions. But the number of active trade unionists undertaking studies of this kind had not expanded to match the increased responsibilities and developing functions of trade unionists. It was felt that there was a need to equip trade unionists as well as to enlarge their horizons. This was highly idealistic as it did not happen in reality, but they were determined to replace the NCLC and WETUC with a movement that was under the direct control of the Trade Union Congress. It happened in 1964 with the Trade Union Congress Committees and Regional Committees being formed, each supported by a full-time education officer of its own, supported by funds derived from an annual levy on all unions in membership with the TUC. The District's Trade Union Advisory Committees were wound-up and the WEA were afraid that its scope would be restricted. But there was no need for the WEA to worry. Funds raised by the annual levy proved insufficient to enable the TUC itself to undertake much provision directly, and the Regional Committees were, therefore, pleased to encourage the Districts to make as much provision as their own resources, human and financial, would permit. Robert Peers criticised the TUC in 1958 on the insignificant amount spent on education and this was also partly true in 1980 (Peers, 1958, p.167).

But by 1980 there was a significant difference to the situation in 1958. There are a number of reasons for this. Firstly, the impact of the Industrial Training Board. By the seventies there were twenty-eight boards set up. The Engineering Board reported that the proportion of employees undergoing training rose from 23 to 28 per cent (Lees and Chiplin, 1970, p.34). It would be difficult to assess the quality of training, but the 1964 Industrial Training Act had led to increase in the volume of training. However, there were criticisms of the monolithic coercive nature of training boards, and Professor Dennis Lees was also concerned that they had been given the wrong job to do. He called for a root-and-branch reform (Lees and Chaplin, 1970, p.41). But setting aside the criticism one had to admit that the Training Boards were at least conscious of the task they had been set — of training ordinary trade unionists in vocational skills.

Secondly, the TUC had carried out a thorough re-appraisal of the role of the shop stewards. In 1968 there were 175,000 voluntary officials trained (TUC 1968 Report, p.96). A handbook was issued, *The Training of Shop Stewards*. The scope of the training was discussed, and the TUC proposals drew a very sharp distinction between what is relevant to the education of the shop steward in the performance of his duties and what is relevant to his education in the general responsibilities as a citizen. But the distinction is much easier to make in theory than it is in fact, and this is another instance to support our argument that ideas were rarely modified by facts in the adult educational world.

The TUC feels that it has the right to select and endorse the student as well as to judge the suitability of the courses. Many dedicated educationists found this very unacceptable, and Trevor Park, MP, wrote that the control of the syllabus as well as student selection are as important to the tutors and the student as they are to the trade unions. Park argued that these tasks would be better in the hands of professional educationists than in the hands of local or national union officers. He says:

> Training shop stewards to serve the members and training them to serve an existing union hierarchy are not necessarily the same thing.   (Park, 1969, p.99).

But Park raised a very important principle: who controls the syllabus? One can continue and ask: education for what? Should the education be political, historical, economic, sociological, or should it contain all those academic approaches? But the biggest problem is how to educate ten million people organised into thousands of different branches in hundreds of different unions and to assist the adult educationists to learn how to adapt their theories to the actual situation that the trade unionists find themselves in.

The Trade Union Congress also have the task of assisting many of the small unions who are apathetic with regard to the provisions at hand. In 1958, for example, the Trade Union Congress in the report on trade union education referred to the TUC Training College Scheme. Thirty-seven courses and 680 scholarships were offered, but forty-eight were not taken up (TUC, Report 1958, p.165). If all the unions affiliated to the TUC had taken up their full quota the total number of scholarships would have been 812. But the real culprits were the small unions — those with 12,000 or under members. There are so many of them, such as the Amalgamated Association of Beamers, Twisters and Drawers (Hand and Machine) with their head office in Nelson; Cigarette Machine Operators' Society at Bristol; Cloth Pressers Society at Honley, near Huddersfield; Amalgamated Society of Journeymen, Felt Hatters and Allied Workers at Denton, near Manchester; Healders' and Twisters' Trade and Friendly Society, Huddersfield; Laminated and Coil Spring Workers' Union at Sheffield; Military and Orchestral Musical Instrument Makers' Trade Society at Edgeware, Middlesex; Pattern Weavers' Society at Huddersfield; Scottish Union of Power Loom Overlookers at Forfar, Angus; British Roll Turners' Trade Society at Corby; Society of Shuttlemakers at Bradford; Spring Trapmakers' Society at Willenhall; Wool Shear-Workers' Trade Union of Sheffield, and National Wool Sorters' Society at Bradford — all with less than one thousand members, some with as little as 100, and the Sheffield Wool Shear Workers' Trade Union has only nineteen members. None of those named were approached for details of their educational workers, and even among the larger unions there were a number — 32 in fact — who could not be bothered to answer the queries asked or even to acknowledge the letter. This in itself is an excellent indicator of the health of trade union education. Trevor Park, who was in the 1966-1970 Parliament the Labour MP for South-East Derbyshire, as well as being sponsored by the Transport and General Workers' Union, emphasises another weakness — the need for the ordinary trade unionists to have a say in the education provided for them. Park says:

> If the fate of industry is too important to be left to the managers, can we afford to leave the fate of trade union education exclusively in the hands of trade union officials? Like the managers they are one party in the process, but they are not the only one. The others too should have their voice. (Park, 1969, p.100).

The courses are often narrow in scope and do not enlarge the horizons of the trade unionists. It has only an utilitarian basis. The educator aims at developing people's all-round potential, including their skills, but also their critical faculties, their ability to make judgments and their capacity to think independently for themselves.

Education is an open-ended process, aiming to examine roles and functions and so appraise ways in which these have been developed and how they may change in the future. In the light of such a definition trade union education in England and Wales had many deficiencies, but while there are trade union leaders like W.B. Beard, who at the 1955 Trade Union Congress said that "the most important requirement of our national life, our adult life and our trade union life, is education" there is hope (TUC, Report 1955, p.334). But one of the most urgent tasks is to learn from the actual situation and in trade union education concepts were rarely modified by facts.

Other experiments in Working Class Education.

F   The London Working Men's College

Founded in 1854, the Working Men's College is an independent institution that was inspired in its origins by Christian Socialists like F.D.

Maurice, Charles Kingsley and Thomas Hughes. The College has a remarkable record of service, and runs an average of one hundred courses a year. It provides recreational and social facilities, and as far as numbers are concerned it has kept its original appeal. In 1961/62 there were 787 students; 1962/63 918 students; 1967/68 1,677 students, and ten years later 1,906 with a slight drop in 1978/79 to 1,856 students. 1967/68 was an important year for the College admitted women for the first time.

Ian Rodger Haldane conducted a useful piece of research in the early sixties on this College, and he came up with some significant information. For the education of adults Haldane found that a "friendly atmosphere' is most conducive for study, and more than half of the sample interviewed emphasised that they chose a place to study because of that very reason. Two further factors mentioned by over forty per cent of the students to Haldane and which should be borne in mind when planning adult education provision, were the small classes, which are restricted to around twenty, and the ease of getting to the centre after work (Haldane, 1962, p.181). Six other factors were mentioned by over a third of the students, namely:

a   good library and reading room in Crowndale Road, near Mornington Crescent Tube station;

b   pleasant buildings and classrooms;

c   individual tuition if necessary;

d   opportunities to meet interesting people;

e   food canteen facilities;

f   high standard of tuition. (Haldane, 1962, p.182).

Haldane found also that the College was established to provide Working Class Education, yet the majority of students in the fifties and sixties of the twentieth century came from the lower middle classes. This was not a new discovery. Sociologists have been saying that since the second world war. T. Bottomore (1954) in an analysis of social stratification in 133 different voluntary organisations in a small country town found that cultural and educational organisation was noteworthy for having the smallest proporiton of members drawn from manual and routine non-manual occupations. Furthermore, the definition of working class is so often a subjective classification. Haldane found that between one third and one half of the students belonging to the usual criteria of the working classes used in censuses felt that they were middle class (Haldane, 1962, p.126). The research suggested that to identify an adult education movement or institution closely with one class or society — the working class — may be not merely irrelevant but may be positively detrimental to its best interests (Haldane, 1962, p.206). It may discourage any interest in it by a substantial proportion of the very members of society for whom it seeks to cater; whether or not it provides the facilities and opportunities they seek, they may be deterred from joining it because of feelings of social distance from the student body which it is assumed will be studying there. Haldane argues also that the traditional sense of social purpose has withered away due to the growth in power of the Labour Party and the Trade Union Movement. It has deprived, he argues, the adult education movement of much of its potentiality, as the activists in the Labour Party if they had time would also come along to the WEA classes.

The motives for studying are mixed. Haldane found that the middle-class students in general were motivated to study by the prospect of a better job due to an additional qualification. But he also found a continual struggle between the selfish/materialistic attitude on the one hand, and the the social/non-materialistic attitude and motivation on the other hand. Students received a general all-round liberal non-vocational education at the College. A student who came to the Working Men's College with the primary aim of studying to get on in his job and who places little value on student corporate life will inevitably remain, to a greater or lesser degree, dissatisfied (Haldane, 1962, p.171).

Haldane found a lack of awareness among adults outside the Working Men's College with regard to its aims and facilities. Only about one student in four at other institutions had any real appreciation of the true aims and educational facilities of the Working Men's College (Haldane, 1962, p.187). Educationally, the Working Men's College was conceived to be a trade-training institution of some kind, and a place which specialised in elementary education for poorly-educated men.

Haldane regarded the friendly atmosphere at the College as its greatest merit. Men were sharing experiences at the club and in the common room. Such opportunities are infrequent in society (Haldane, 1962, p.217). He cites the fragmentation of the urban areas, and the disappearance of the closely-knit communities as well as a lack of tolerance as the inner city ghettoes and the suburban communities drift further afield. Haldane sees adult education as contributing to this loss and adding a new dimension.

The work at the Working Men's Colleges was appreciated by the students who attended. Past students mentioned that their sojourn at the Working Men's Colleges had made them readers of books and magazines (Haldane, 1962, p.176). Also other leisure-time activities, radio, television, hobbies, watching sport, had enriched the lives of the students. They felt that they had benefited in their social/cultural leisure time activities from their attendance at the Working Men's College classes (Haldane, 1962, p.179). It is an interesting reaction for over a decade before Haldane another University of London post-graduate student had underlined one of the baffling things about adult education. T.H. Coates goes on to suggest that so much of adult education can be "taken" by people without very much widening of interests or rounding out of experience (Coates, 1950, p.180). Haldane found a different situation among people who had attended the Working Men's College.

G   There are other movements with the same philosophy as the Working Men's College, namely:

i   **The Working Men's Clubs**

The man who gave up the ministry with the Unitarian Church, Henry Solly, to devote his whole time to the work of the Club and Institute Union in 1863 was a disciple of F.D. Maurice and one of the original band that was inspired by the Working Men's College. Solly started the movement as a temperance answer to the cry, 'What are we to do with the reformed drunkard?'. However, the movement never gained the educational momentum expected by Solly, and its temperance origins were soon swamped by the demand for beer and entertainment.

However, the educational emphasis of Solly has not been completely forgotten even in the twentieth century. There is a national education committee and a full-time secretary. Two national one-week schools are held annually at Vaughan College, Leicester, and Ruskin College, Oxford.

The movement has great potentiality for there were in the late sixties approximately two million members with 3,900 Clubs affiliated to the Club and Institute Union (Lowe, 1970, p.171). Within the movement there are individuals who are struggling for more educating influences within the individual clubs but the concept of education for all the members has not been implemented.

ii   **·Adult Schools**

The adult school movement has been concerned from its very beginning with working people, and is the oldest of the voluntary bodies in the field of adult education. The first school was opened in Nottingham in 1798 and a century later a national council was formed. This happened in 1899 and in 1914 it became the national school union. The schools were created to meet a very elementary need — the need to read and write, and they usually met on Sundays as it was the only available free day for working people, and at times which would not clash with religious services.

The early adult schools owed much to nonconformist zeal — Methodist at first, and Quaker at a slightly later stage. It has never lost its religious attitude and the improvement of people's minds was believed to be an essential Christian duty. This led in 1911 to the publication of the first of the series of annual study handbooks which are excellent in content and approach. A wide range of human interests (scientific, literary, artistic, political, social, religious) are dealt with in the annual handbooks.

But the National Adult School Union has been unable to sustain its zeal in the post-war period. The movement has suffered a decline in membership from 14,000 in 1945 to 3,260 in 1970. One of the main reasons is the 'nonconformist spirit' of the leaders of the movement. As they have no fixed syllabus or a paid teaching staff, their applications for financial assistance to the local education authorities and the Department of Education and Science have always been refused.

The movement had around two hundred adult schools in 1970 — situated in Bristol; London; Midlands; Leicestershire; Yorkshire; in the North East, and in smaller numbers in other parts of England and Wales. The word schools is being replaced in many areas by the name group, and they meet once a week, or in some cases once a fortnight. Some of the schools still have their own premises, some meet in hired rooms, and some in the homes of the members. The pattern and format of the group is flexible, and democratic. It is the local group which decides to invite a guest speaker to open the discussion or to ask one of their own members to do this.

The movement is very flexible and within it there are wide ranges of activities. Some groups based their programme and discussion on the study handbook; others prefer to discuss topical problems not based on the handbook. In the late sixties there was a new demand for informal education either weekly or fortnightly, and this demand is met within the local or national provision. Another change which has happened is that the prayers, hymn singing and Bible reading are not carried out as in the meetings of the groups in the past.

The philosophy behind the adult schools is that people matter, and that informal methods of educational fellowship can be particularly helpful in preserving quality and essential values in the changing patterns of modern life. To extend the work, the National Council of the Union has been appointing field organisers to extend the existing schools, and to promote the formation of home and neighbourhood groups.

In addition to the weekly (or fortnightly) meetings of the groups, there are arrangements for special lecture schools, both regionally and nationally. These may be one-day events or residential occasions of several days' duration or even a full week's summer school. Professional lecturers are engaged for all such events, whereas in the regular meetings of the groups the amateur principle is preserved as much as possible, except where subjects of a specialist nature are under consideration. Occasionally, overseas visits are arranged, especially those of an educative nature.

The Adult School Movement has a special place in the history of adult education with its ideal of corporative study in which all were considered teachers and scholars, each contributing what he had to give. The *Handbook of 1911* set out deliberately to foster this "true adult school ideal of mutual co-operative study" and reminded the schools that "to evoke an effort is as great a necessity as to satisfy a need".

The movement has been criticised in our period for its abandonment of the original idealism and the temptation to depend on visiting speakers rather than learning themselves through discussion. The main task of educating adults has been described as that of "making experience articulate". The

Adult Schools have often achieved this when they were pioneers of the discussion group and of informal education.

Adult schools have a great deal to offer, and it seems that the movement has to organise itself professionally so that it can expand its valuable provision and halt its decline in membership, and it has to learn also from the actual situation — a weakness which belongs to all the educational agencies in adult education.

H   Universities and Trade Union Education

The university extra-mural departments have taken trade union education seriously in the post-war period and the result has been a new flowering of the universities' relationship with workers' education in England and Wales. It is known that the Universities of Bristol, Durham, Hull, Keele, Leicester, Liverpool, Manchester, Nottingham, Oxford, London, Sheffield, Southampton and the University Colleges of Bangor, Cardiff and Swansea within the University of Wales, have all arranged courses for trade unionists.

Hughes and Thornton suggest that the main reason why the universities were failing to attract workers in the fifties was that they had nothing to say to the employees in the work situation. The answer was simply:

> If universities are failing to recruit workers to courses established on a neighbourhood basis then why not try recruiting them directly from their industrial community.
>
> (Hughes and Thornton, 1974, p.157).

University departments of extra-mural studies such as Nottingham, Leicester, Sheffield, took the challenge seriously in the fifties. But one must mention that the University College Nottingham, as it was known then, had from 1922 made special provision for adult students to attend two days a week at the college during term time for intensive study. This provision was carried on into the fifties and mostly supported by the miners due to the support of Nottinghamshire and Derbyshire Miners' Welfare Adult Education Committee. It was an important experiment, but as A. John Allaway says, it only touched a tiny fraction of the workers in the Nottinghamshire and Derbyshire coalfield (Allaway, 1969, p.68).

A need was felt for day-release provision on a far wider scale. It was to be for three terms (each of about ten weeks duration) and release sought for its members on the basis of one day every week. The idea of the day-release course for mine-workers was born at the same time in Sheffield, and its paternity is thus in dispute between Sheffield and Nottingham. At Nottingham there was overwhelming response for the 20/25 available places. There were 168 applicants and two parallel courses were established on different days of the week with a total of 65 students. Allaway has provided us with the breakdown of the students who attended. Thirty three were coal-face workers, a 50.7%; sixteen auxiliary underground workers, a 24.6%; seven surface workers, a 10.7%; two office workers, a 3.07%; and six deputies and shotfirers, a 9.2%.

133

To get successful university courses for trade unionists everything depends on the power of persuasion. Management and unions have to be converted to the active support that liberal education is a good thing — good enough, in fact, to warrant release from work and the payment of loss of wages, subsistence and travelling expenses. It was easier to persuade nationalised industries than private industry of the merits of trade union education organised by universities. A.H. Thornton has written on the Nottingham Experiment. The extra-mural department approached seven firms, all within fifteen miles of Nottingham, and the WEA approached the unions. All the academic planning was done inside the department without any reference either to the unions or to management. It was well publicised and produced 120 applicants for twenty places. This meant selection, and it was decided that each applicant had to be interviewed and efforts made to be far in selection. The verdict of the tutors with regard to the group was that it was first-rate and capable of producing excellent work. (Thornton, 1960, p.30).

These experiments spread as the need arose for the training of shop stewards. In the London University extra-mural department day or half-day release courses were arranged for workplace representatives from the Associated Society of Locomotive Engineers and Firemen, the National Union of Railwaymen, from London Transport, local government, print, furniture, Fords, engineering and the docks. Some of these have been in co-operation with the TUC, rather more with individual unions and shop stewards' committees. In all cases unions or union representatives have negotiated day-release for education as an additional trade union right. The syllabuses are worked out by discussion between students and tutors so that the criticism voiced earlier by Trevor Park is overcome in this instance, and classes are conducted with intense participation of the students themselves, and with their trade union officers.

A syllabus from the London University extra-mural department class for ASLEF members shows the detailed, specific subjects dealt with — study of railway negotiating machinery, machinery for dealing with disciplinary cases and accident claims, basic skills of note-taking, report-making, moving resolutions, meeting procedure, preparing and presenting a case, using figures, and where to look for information. But it deals also with the aims and organisation of British trade unions, trades councils, the TUC, the Labour Party, trade union history, trade unions and the law, the law of picketing, unfair dismissal, industrial democracy, government pay policy, socialism, unemployment and inflation, the multinationals, reading company accounts, international finance and the City (Fyrth, 1976, p.83).

University academics on the whole are dissatisfied with the efforts being made for they believe that a ten-day course is not enough (Fyrth, 1976, p.83). Trade union education requires continuous study, and the clientele are there for the asking.

There are some 350,000 shop stewards in the unions amalgamated to the TUC, and they all need a short training course. However, at the present rate it would take years for this to happen. This is the immensity of the task facing the TUC, the WEA, voluntary working class organisations and the extramural departments with regard to trade union education. The other task is to understand that adult education concepts with regard to trade union education have to be modified by facts and this is a lesson that has not been learnt.

Chapter 4
The Role of Local and National Government in Adult Education

It is generally agreed that the second world war provided an impetus to adult education and the 1944 Education Act was an inevitable consequence of the new spirit abroad. This concern for extending adult education facilities, and in particular involving local education authorities, was in the forefront of the few parliamentary debates that took place between 1945 and 1947. Kenneth Lindsay spoke of the millions of people who had been brought into contact with adult education in the Debate on 11th June 1945.

> Are these men coming back to find just a few W.E.A. classes or is there to be a new set-up which brings large numbers of other people into the field of adult education? I should like to see the Ministry taking an active part. What I want to see in the central administration is not just an advisory committee but a department which will help to supply all the things that are required by a strong adult education movement.
>
> (*Hansard*, Volume 411, column 1350).

Edmund Harvey, who represented the Combined English Universities, argued in favour of an idea which has not been adopted in any significant way and that is to encourage the universities to throw open their doors for the disinherited. Small sums were spent for further education in 1945 and the total sum was only £174,320 (*Hansard*, vol. 411, column 1355). Edmund Harvey was disappointed at the local authorities response, and in particular their lack of co-operation with the WEA as well as with the Education Settlement Association. This was in 1945. In the following two decades local education authorities increased their provision for those young men and women who had left school, or who wished to continue full education to qualify themselves for their chosen trade or profession.

Our task is to look at the provision made by some of the local education authorities and we have succeeded in receiving information to a personal letter asking for information that was sent to all the education authorities in England and Wales.

A   The role of thirteen local education authorities in adult education

1   Nottinghamshire

Adult education in Nottinghamshire after the war was organised on the standard pattern of evening institutes in the main centres of population throughout the county. These institutes had a part-time principal and a management committee. In 1968, evening institutes were discarded, and replaced by an area organisation system whereby Nottinghamshire was divided into twelve areas, each controlled by a full-time area organiser, helped by full-time assistants assisted by a number of part-time centre heads, each responsible for a main centre and a number of satellite centres. This arrangement did not include the City of Nottingham which was a separate authority. The City was administered as a single unit with one organiser responsible for the provision of adult education.

The courses carried out were on the usual liberal and vocational subjects. In the late sixties and early seventies a number of innovations were introduced. These included courses for mothers of socially deprived children, aimed primarily at improving the educational prospects of the children, but nevertheless making a significant contribution to the personal education of the mothers, whose school education had been entirely unsatisfactory. There were other innovations — adult illiteracy campaign; the increasing adult education commitment to the five penal establishments, and a number of hospitals, including the hospital for the criminally insane at Rampton, the psychiatric hospital at Balderton, near Newark, the adult education involvement in joint-use community centres, which combine a secondary school, adult education facilities and high grade sports facilities, partly provided by the LEA and partly by local district councils, and the participation in the East Midlands regional scheme of training for part-time teachers in adult education. Nottinghamshire did not possess a residential college, but a residential centre, a rather small one with forty beds, was added to one of the large secondary schools with youth service money as a result of the Albermarle Report in the mid sixties. Since 1960 there has been a steady improvement in the response to adult education, so that in 1975, of a total population of 970,000 for the whole county, of which some 650,000 could be assumed to be of adult age, there were some 40,000 enrolments in adult education classes.

During the period 1945 to 1970 8 colleges of further education were established. They were set up as follows:

i   Arnold and Carlton College of Further Education located in the north-east suburbs of Nottingham was opened in 1960.

ii   Basford Hall College of Further Education, located in the north-west suburbs of Nottingham, was opened in 1969.

iii   Beeston College of Further Education, located in south-western suburbs of Nottingham, was opened in 1953.

iv   Clarendon College of Further Education, located just north of the city centre in Nottingham, originally a social club founded in 1919, moved to its present site and was designated a college of further education in 1960.

v   West Nottinghamshire Technical College, located on the southern edge of Mansfield, formerly known as the County Technical College, Mansfield, was established in 1928 and moved to its new site in 1955.

vi   Mansfield College of Arts.

When the Mansfield County Technical College moved into new buildings in 1955 and became the West Nottinghamshire Technical College, the old building became known as the Mansfield Folk College, which was largely responsible for the provision of non-vocational adult education. Immediately behind it was located the Mansfield School of Art. In 1964 the two were amalgamated under one Principal as Mansfield College of Arts.

vii   Waverley College of Further Education. This was established as Nottingham Nursery Nurses' College in 1947, and remained a very small college dealing only with nursery nursing and social work training.

viii   West Bridgford College of Further Education, opened in 1970, in the southernmost suburb of the city.

There were three other further education institutions, two dating from the nineteenth century, namely:

i   Newark Technical College. This originated as the Newark Mechanics' Institute in 1836, and moved into its present building as Newark Technical College in 1970.

ii   People's College of Further Education. This was founded in 1846, and moved to its present site in new buildings located at the foot of Nottingham Castle Rock in 1959.

iii   North Nottinghamshire College of Further Education, Worksop, opened in 1931.

Nottingham County Council was also responsible for the Nottinghamshire College of Further Education, Brackenhurst. This college, located on the edge of the small country town of Southwell, originated as the Midland Agricultural College, established in 1895. It was taken over first by Nottingham University, then by the local education authority, and was renamed the Nottinghamshire College of Agriculture in 1949. Trent Polytechnic is an amalgamation of the old Regional School of Art founded in 1843, and the Regional College of Technology founded in 1945. The Polytechnic as a separate institution was founded in 1970.

2   Northamptonshire.

Adult education activities are provided throughout the county in adult education centres and in the upper schools in Northampton as well as in all the technical colleges. Northamptonshire local education authority is responsible for the following institutions which cater for further education:

i   Corby Technical College.

ii   Kettering Technical College which was opened after the war.

iii   Wellingborough Technical College.

iv   Northamptonshire College of Agriculture.

v   Northampton College of Art.

vi   Northampton College of Technology.

vii   Northampton College of Education.

The first phase of the Northampton College of Further Education was completed in March 1972. Northamptonshire County Council is also responsible for a residential adult education centre at Knuston Hall, a pleasant country house situated between Irchester and Rushden. The Centre caters in the main for week-end courses in subjects such as spoken Italian, painting in autumn, twentieth century literature, making pillow lace, heraldry, village history, calligraphy, field archaeology and historical topics. This centre is very well supported and is a model to all local education authorities who have not provided a similar centre for the education of adults.

3   County of Avon, and in particular in the Bristol County Borough

With local education reorganisation in 1974, Bristol LEA and parts of the former Gloucestershire and Somerset local education authorities were brought together in the new County of Avon. For our purpose we will confine our study to adult education in Bristol from 1945-1974 as the material has been preserved in the prospectuses. In this period adult education in the Bristol County Borough followed the role of its title, the interesting thing being how it adapted its work to suit the changing needs of society. Looking back to the prospectuses of the years just after the war, one is conscious that the subjects offered to the general public, while reflecting a wide variety of interests, lack the sophistication of the range found in the late sixties and early seventies. For example, one can see this by studying the subjects advertised by East Bristol Institute of Adult Education for 1949-1950 and for 1971-1972.

1949-1950	**1971-1972** (additional subjects to column 1)
Art	Art (oil painting)
Athletics	(Figure Drawing and Painting)
Bee Keeping	(Creative Art)
Book-keeping and Accounts	Cake Decoration
Car maintenance	Crochet
Choir (mixed)	Domestic Electronics
Cookery	Elderly People's Courses
Dancing (Ballroom)	Flower Arrangement
Dancing (Tap)	Good Grooming
Dramatics	Home Decorating and General Repairs
Dressmaking	Home Movie Making
Embroidery	Hostess
Engineering and Workshop Drawing	Italian

Continued

140

1949-1950	1971-1972 (additional subjects to column 1)
English Literature	Judo
First Aid	Keep Fit (Women)
French	Motor Car Driving
Gardening	Pattern Cutting and Design
Geometry	Photography
German	Physics
Healthcraft in the Kitchen	Rugby Coaching
Leathercraft	Scottish Dancing
Mathematics	Shorthand (Speedwriting)
Millinery	Spanish
Music Appreciation	Travel Talks
Orchestra	Wine Making and Serving
Pottery	Yoga
Public Speaking	GCE Courses (English, Mathematics, History, Physics)

Table 4.1

One can discern in the second list the effect of affluence, new interests and foreign travel. Although the provision of education classes occupied the major role of the institutes, they engaged in many other roles. They linked up with many other official or voluntary education or semi-educational bodies - schools, community associations, youth organisations, both in educational terms and other matters. Adult Education Centres' Principals, for example, serve on the management committees of youth clubs as well as on the area and central youth committees. In their own institutes, the principals organised visits abroad conected with classroom studies, local visits, concerts (including choir concerts in hospitals), demonstrations, socials and dances. In this period, 1945-1974, at Bristol there was continuous progress with regard to enrolment. In some institutes enrolment figures doubled, but the raising of students' fees had always detrimental effects.

4   Salop County Council

The diversity of further education in the County of Salop has been well documented in a booklet published in 1966. We will follow the story in rather more detail than it is possible with most of the local authorities who responded to my inquiring letter.

i   Technical Education

In 1945 at all levels trained personnel were essential and the wastage of the haphazard organisation of pre-war technical education had to be stopped and training had to be taken seriously by all. There was indeed a new attitude which permeated Shropshire industrialists who recognised that industry needed well-trained people. To do this staff had to be released for courses. It also became clear that to achieve worthwhile technical training the students have to receive beforehand an adequate period of general education. Furthermore, the requirements of industry were more clearly defined, so that the different forms of training that the authorities had to develop could be more productively related. Two White Papers (1956 and 1961) have been landmarks on the way to the expansion and re-shaping of the system. Categories of jobs and training had been re-defined and clarified, generally in terms of four main groups: operatives, craftsmen, technicians and technologists.

The technical colleges had a much more complex job to do at a great variety of levels and in new specialisms. But in one sense the re-shaping of the system had simplified their role. For they had to confine themselves to further education beyond school age and had shed the boys and girls who had previously come to them from school for junior technical and junior commercial courses. During this period the junior technical schools at Oakengates, Shrewsbury and Oswestry closed for that very reason.

With the transfer of technical studies into the daytime, the scope of the colleges had been enlarged and the milieu liberalised. The physical shape and lay-out of the new colleges were an indication that the technical colleges were no longer concerned only with young people as potential workers, but with their development as human beings as well. Technical education is more than just vocational education; and a technical college has a social function and corporate existence symbolised in the study rooms, common rooms, libraries, assembly halls, gymnasium and playing fields.

This meant in Shropshire a rise in the number of further education technical students. Full-time students totalled 1,043 in 1965 compared with 202 after the second world war; day and block release, 3,623 in 1965 as against 1,128. It represents a huge increase in the number of students as well as in the number of trained staff.

The surge of demand presents every local authority with a number of problems. The main problem is the flux of change. Nothing is static. A plan is made on a careful forward estimate but before it is brought to completion it is inadequate. This happened in Shropshire in respect of the three original colleges as well as a demand for a county wide coverage. New colleges were planned and the first one set up was at Bridgnorth.

Despite the impressive increase in student numbers the demand was growing. This was encouraged by the publication of the Crowther, Newsom and Robbins reports of the existence of a great pool of "untapped ability". The Crowther Report recommended not only the raising of the leaving age to sixteen but the gradual introduction of compulsory day-release for all 16-18 year olds. The 1964 Industrial Training Act meant an increased demand for technical courses.

In 1966 in the county of Shropshire 1 in 6 young people aged 16-18 remained in full-time education while only 28% of those in employment received day release of any kind. Moreover, within these figures there was a very small proportion of girls (under 10%) compared with boys and the numbers released by different industries ranged from 80% and over in engineering to almost none in retail trades. It is also fair to say that versatility and adaptability are characteristics of all technical colleges and this has been true since their first beginnings in the Mechanics' Institutes of the nineteenth century. Their infinite variety, for no two colleges are the same even within the same local education authority, results from their sensitiveness and response to special local needs within the national pattern.

The County of Salop, or the old county of Shropshire, had three major colleges, namely:

Shrewsbury Technical College;

Walker Technical College;

Oswestry College of Further Education.

a   Shrewsbury Technical College

The Technical College was opened in 1938 but in the post-war period the authority bought thirty acres at a more strategic point to build a new institution. The college's new premises were planned from 1954 onwards, and were opened in May 1961 at the cost of £548,000.

Shrewsbury Technical College offers a range of courses in engineering, commerce, art and building at an advanced level. The first advanced sandwich course in the county of Shropshire was started in 1964 which led to the Higher National Diploma in mechanical engineering. Students spend six months in college followed by six months in industry, but still in touch with college tutors. Part-time day courses include Higher National Certificate work in mechanical production and electrical engineering, and in building; the college offers advanced professional courses in commerce. It is also a key centre for day-release work in agriculture and agricultural engineering.

The School of Art is a department of the college and the county centre for art education; its advanced course leading to the National Diploma in Design pioneered the way to successful careers in industry, commerce and teaching and the pre-diploma course attracts a number of school leavers wishing to specialise in art and design.

The college works in close liaison with local industry and particularly with such firms as Rolls-Royce, Hall Engineering, Norton Asquith, the Midland Electricity Board, the Post Office and the Rubber and Plastic

Research Association, all of whom co-operate with regard to the day-release provision.

b   Walker Technical College

Until 1962 the college's main work was centred on the buildings opened in 1927 at Hartshill, Oakengates. Due to wartime expansion and the need for a more strategic centre for the whole Wrekin area a new site was bought at Bennett's Bank, Wellington. The new college was opened in September 1962 at a cost of £254,000 plus £78,000 for furniture and equipment.

The college developed advanced work in mechanical and structural engineering and is the main county centre for courses in mining. In the sixties the college became, as so many other technical colleges, the base for the organisation of liberal and leisure-time classes throughout the Wrekin area.

c   Oswestry College of Further Education

Due to its crowded, cramped situation the college moved to new buildings on a spacious site with good playing fields and opened in 1957 at the cost of £173,000. Day release work in the next decade included the Ordinary National Certificate in mechanical engineering and the usual basic range of craft and technician courses in which work in welding became a particular specialism. Full-time courses for girls in secretarial work and nursing and a variety of similar opportunities for school leavers were arranged.

d   Bridgnorth College of Further Education

Bridgnorth's College was opened in September 1964 in a small workshop instalment of new buildings at a cost of £35,000 together with the hutted accommodation previously used for mining classes. The college welded together into one organisation the work formerly done by the agricultural day courses, the Highley Mining School, and the very large evening institute which itself had centres stretching out over the rural area of south-east Shropshire.

Mining education based on the collieries at Highley, Granville and Madeley has for many years been a feature of technical education in east Shropshire, and this tradition was extended at the Birdgnorth College.

Looking at the four technical colleges one can discern the same development as found in other areas throughout England and Wales — a rapid growth in the number of full and part-time students. Taking the period 1947-1965 in Shropshire we find the following figures:

Year	Full Time	Part Time	Total
1947-48	336	1,148	1,484
1949-50	321	1,384	1,705
1951-52	334	1,708	2,042

Continued

Continued from previous page

Year	Full Time	Part Time	Total
1953-54	406	2,188	2,594
1955-56	492	2,401	2,893
1957-58	695	2,611	3,306
1959-60	1,042	2,982	4,024
1961-62	1,266	3,159	4,425
1963-64	1,431	3,311	4,742
1964-65	1,116	3,657	4,773

Table 4.2

ii   **Agricultural Education**

Like most counties, agricultural education in Shropshire was largely a post-war development. Responsibility for agricultural education was transferred to the education committee and a completely fresh start was made. It was decided to co-operate with the farming community and fifty farmers volunteered as lecturers, conducting courses of highly practical significance on carefully defined subjects all over the county.

The education committee appointed a senior adviser to expand the initial evening courses; and day classes gradually expanded in length and number, for day release was a new concept in agriculture, and expansion was slow at first. By 1959-60 day release classes had been firmly established in thirteen centres in the county and attended by 293 students — all released voluntarily by their employers. The Farm Institute was developed at Walford which in time took the majority of the one-week block release course students. In 1964-65 there were 460 students attending thirty-two courses.

A comprehensive development plan for agricultural education was prepared in 1962; the long term objective was to recruit to day and block release classes an increasing proportion of new entrants to the industry and to make proper teaching facilities available in the main teaching centres. New further education centres were developed in the market towns of Ludlow and Market Drayton.

The Loveday Committee of 1947 recommended as part of its immediate programme the establishment of two new Farm Institutes in the West Midlands — one for Shropshire and Herefordshire and one for Warwickshire and Worcestershire. After discussion with Herefordshire, the Walford estate, seven miles north of Shrewsbury, was bought for £108,000 in 1948 and the Shropshire Farm Institute was opened in 1949.

The Institute has been successful in its recruitment, and in the content of its programmes, which lead to the examination for the National Certificate in Agriculture.

Shropshire also has provided part-time agricultural education for women which has come to be known collectively as rural domestic economy. This range includes rural housecraft, gardening, poultry keeping, clean milk production, calf rearing, and farm secretarial work and accounts. A varied system of day, evening and short residential courses were provided in both Shrewsbury and other market towns, and the Radbrook College provided short and longer courses in the rural domestic economy subjects.

Radbrook College opened in 1901 to give training in domestic science and dairywork. In 1947 a new stage of development was introduced with specialisation in large-scale catering and allied subjects. Another major development was the establishment in 1951 of a teacher training department to work alongisde the original technical department.

Shropshire has also introduced horticultural day release classes as well as employing a full-time adviser in bee-keeping whose work includes advice and instruction to schools as well as to private bee-keepers.

The local authority in Shropshire has encouraged voluntary agencies and its most important development was the setting up in 1948 of the Shropshire Adult College, Attingham Park, to provide a home for short residential courses open to all interests and sections of the community. The college was administered jointly by the University of Birmingham, the Walker Trust and the local education authority and Attingham became well-known throughout England and Wales, largely due to the enthusiasm of its first and only warden, Sir George Trevelyan, who retired in 1971 after twenty-four years of extraordinary service.

In the immediate post-war years the education committee appointed three full-time tutors responsible for adult classes in the county as well as working as a team with Attingham. Evening Institute Centres with vocational classes were organised throughout the county and the manifold youth activities were also catered for by the local authority as part of the further education programme. The adult education provision at Shropshire is a varied one and shows also how one local authority was able to adapt itself to the social changes that happened in the post-war period.

5   Northumberland

In 1950 an important decision was taken in Northumberland with the amalgamation of the Youth and Adult organisations into the Northumberland Standing Conference on Voluntary Organisations. The partnership has been a valuable one, for after successful experiments among young people it was decided that this had to be extended to the young adults. Education was recognised and declared to be one continuous process, schools became centres of education — housing formal day school, Newsom extended day experiments, youth and adult activities.

The head teacher had two deputies, one for day school and one for further education and youth services, responsible for a. the preparation of young people for the many aspects of adult life, and b. the organisation of further education outside the technical colleges and within the catchment area of the school. The deputy heads (further education and youth) realised a number of important points:

i   The disadvantage of the evening class system. For decades each summer long lists of evening classes were advertised to take place between September and Easter for sessions of twenty-four weeks. The range of activities varied but little from year to year. Students scurried into schools at 7.0 p.m. and scurried out at 9.0 p.m. Indeed the late visitor would more often than not find the building empty and in darkness if he were delayed and arrived at 9.02 p.m. There was no social life associated with these adult evening classes.

ii   The adult educationists realised the need for activity groups and experiments in evening class student committees, and it was agreed in 1966 to permit six experiments in adult education. These were known as adult associations.

The centres chosen differed in character, but they all shared the desire to take part in the experiment of delegating to the people concerned the administration of their educational activities. Amble is a combination of a rural and fishing town with a great deal of unemployment, while Bedlington is an urban area made up of nine mining areas where seven collieries closed in a short space of time. Morpeth is a market town and a dormitory town for many Tyneside workers, while Prudhoe is an urban area to the west of Newcastle. Walbottle is a large urban area bordering on Newcastle and again composed of several smaller communities. Whitley Bay is a seaside holiday resort and dormitory town for Tyneside. Of the six centres chosen, five succeeded immediately. Prudhoe had teething problems. In 1967, Seaton Delaval and Wallsend joined the scheme, and in 1968 came five more, including Longbenton, an overspill area of Newcastle-upon-Tyne; Glendale, the first really rural area, and the new township of Killingworth. In 1969 the number of areas involved in the experiment was sixteen. Longbenton differed from Glendale and all the other areas in that it had no stable community nor an evening class tradition. The adult association grew spontaneously from the older members of the youth association. A sudden increase in the enrolment of young adults in non-vocational evening classes and self-programming groups ensured the future of the adult associations. The other centres joined the experiment for three main reasons:

a. they were convinced that it was good educationally, b. it ensured more flexibility, and c. it gave the clients a voice in how the centre should be run.

The individual joines the association which determines the programme, and the self-determination brings vitality as well as new ideas. All the centres have benefited from the freedom afforded them in handling of finance for publicity, for purchase of equipment which the county administration might have been forced to regard as luxury provision, and for engagement of speakers and experts of national and even international repute. One centre alone paid out £512 in the year 1967-68 in fees for extra staff and visiting speakers, and the same centre sponsored the first residential conference for association committee members and staff.

The Centres have the right to close or maintain a minority interest class. Previously, when attendance at classes dropped below a certain figure for three consecutive weeks, the class closed more or less automatically. Occasionally some exceptional circumstance could allow the class to continue, but more often than not the circumstances were not even reported and permission not sought. The number of minority groups which association committees have allowed to continue has ranged from 1 to 23, the average each year has remained at 6, the total for 1967-68 being 66. Interests include subjects such as art, pottery, languages, radio, astronomy, folk crafts, such as the making of northumbrian pipes, and in the only rural association, commercial subjects. The rural association sponsored a course of ten lectures on local history, three sponsored series of talks on education today, thus going some way to meet the parents' need to understand the teaching methods and new ideas concerning their children's education, one sponsored a teach-in on prospects for the north, two sponsored training for advanced motorists, several sponsored concerts, and one had a visit from the world chess champion.

All centres have shown imagination in providing a social area where light refreshments and opportunities for a chat are available. Certain events are now annual, some terminal, and since Bedlington's success with its residential conference, most associations have now a residential conference at which they plan their year's programme. Other events have been theatre visits, old-time dances, family socials, children's parties and film shows. Sensible use has been made of commercial concerns such as ice-rinks and ten-pin bowling alleys.

The most significant change has been in the curriculum of the adult associations. Dressmaking, crafts and physical education still play a considerable part but have no longer a monopoly in the list of subjects. Crafts may involve anything from boat-building to geology, and the polishing of local stones to making jewellery, and dressmaking is no longer regarded as merely a means of saving money. Physical education may involve use of the trampoline, sailing or skiing. Art in numerous forms, music, interest in the theatre, foreign languages, astronomy, geology, archaeology, local history, psychology, trends in education, discussion circles, and interest in folk crafts, have an important part in the year's syllabuses.

The experiments in Northumberland demonstrate the need for the concept of continuing education to be taken seriously, and the success story shows that it is possible through adult education to recapture the security of the small community in the urban area. The success of the only rural experiment at Glendale indicates that the scheme has been tailor-made for certain rural communities. Rural areas such as Haydon Bridge, Bellingham and Allendale find it impossible to establish adult associations because of the low density of the population which makes it difficult to attract sufficient students to run viable courses at any particular centres and the difficulties of travel which make it impossible to centralise classes, and deter many members from joining more than one activity.

Another difficulty was the lack of programme planning (so as to avoid overlapping) with the Northumberland County Technical College, Ashington, and Northumberland Agricultural College at Kirkley Hall who ran full-time vocational courses, and in addition a number of courses which can be described as 'rural crafts'. There were two other major further education establishments in South-East Northumberland, namely Whitley Bay Further Education College established in 1949, and South-East Northumberland County Technical College opened in 1963. Both became the responsibility of the North Tyneside Metropolitan Borough Council in the local authority reorganisation in 1974.

The experiments and the programmes in Northumberland indicate that local education authorities can achieve a great deal if it so desires. But everything depends upon the vision of those who are leaders in the education sphere and upon their willingness to adapt their concepts to the changing social scene.

6   Suffolk County Council. East Suffolk Local Education Authority

In East Suffolk we can trace the development of further education in the number of centres provided as well as in the number of classes and students. The statistics are as follows:

Year	No. of Centres	No. of Classes	No. of Students
1944/45	41	237	3,316
1945/46	52	281	4,501
1946/47	66	325	5,152
1947/48	88	408	5,793
1948/49	102	442	8,019
1949/50	119	448	6,822
1950/51	120	501	6,541
1951/52	110	480	6,157
1952/53	90	426	5,396

Continued

Continued from previous page

Year	No. of Centres	No. of Classes	No. of Students
1953/54	89	434	4,937
1954/55	92	481	5,370
1955/56	96	499	5,827
1956/57	74	353	4,218
1957/58	71	356	4,257
1958/59	72	378	4,657
1959/60	70	393	4,636
1960/61	75	431	4,688
1961/62	76	472	5,732
1962/63	76	523	6,670
1963/64	87	578	7,154
1964/65	100	688	8,527
1965/66	96	827	9,221
1966/67	68	910	11,591
1967/68	-	-	-
1968/69	46	914	11,195
1969/70	43	923	12,338

Table 4.3

The number of centres have remained somewhat static over the period except for 1950/51 with 120 centres. But there has been a dramatic increase in the number of classes as well as in the number of students. From 237 classes at the end of the war to 923 in 1969/70, and from 3,316 students to 12,338 students in 1969/70, with a corps of six professional full-time heads with responsibility for very large centres of 1,000 to 2,000 enrolments, each offering 80 or more classes, and functioning during morning, afternoon and evening, with canteens as well as crèches provided. The change of name from Evening Instututes to Adult Centres was commented upon as a significant step in the East Suffolk Centenary Circular published in 1970.

But in 1970 there were still more than twice as many women compared to men enrolled in these centres, which could be regarded as a reflection on society with women having fewer opportunities to continue their education than men.

In penal establishments, classes for adult prisoners at Blundeston, and for the young men in Hollesley Bay Borstal, have been built up over the years. There were full-time tutor/organisers in both establishments and full-time teachers of remedial subjects were also appointed. Adult education is regarded as an important part in the team work required for rehabilitation.

The Adult Centres in the late sixties were beginning to look outwards beyond the classroom to the local community.

The East Suffolk Education Committee bought Belstead House from Mr. Roger Quilter on January 1st, 1948, and this was done under the provisions of the 1944 Education Act where local authorities were asked to provide residential centres for further education if there was a need for such provision. Mr. Leslie R. Missen, Chief Education Officer, thought that in a rural county such as East Suffolk, with the greater part of its people scattered in hundreds of villages, there was such a need. A warden, G.E.Curtis, was appointed, and arrived at Belstead House on the 14th September 1948 to furnish, re-wire, clean and prepare the residential centre for its first students. It was officially opened on the 26th April 1949 by Sir Will Spens, Master of Corpus Christi College, Cambridge, who declared the house "open for the enrichment of educational life".

The first courses were planned for teachers newly qualified under the emergency training of teachers scheme. Most of these teachers had served in the armed forces and had been rather rigorously selected by panels of Her Majesty's Inspectors who visited various theatres of war, including Germany, North Africa and India and recommended those who passed the tests and interviews for an intensive course of thirteen months with a minimum of holidays at a number of teacher training colleges set up especially for this purpose. They were expected to continue part-time training for two years after beginning teaching. Those in East Suffolk attended Belstead House for six terms and were visited in their schools by Frank Glover of Beccles, an experienced schoolmaster who supervised the studies as well as assisting with courses at Belstead House, which is situated three miles from the centre of Ipswich. These special courses for emergency trained teachers continued for the next five years and were staffed almost entirely by experienced teachers.

Belstead House, according to Sir Will Spens, was to "provide a forum where major problems" could be discussed, and this was arranged throughout the years. The initial course, open to the public, was held in July 1949 to consider the political history of Western Europe, and it could provide residential accommodation for forty adults.

Another important development was initiated in 1954 with the establishment of the Annual Constance Maynard Lectures to commemorate the link between Belstead House and the lady who became the Principal of Westfield College, London. Famous names like Baroness Stocks, who was herself a Principal of Westfield College, Dame Kathleen Lonsdale, Dame Kitty Anderson, Professor Stanley Alstead, have delivered the Constance Maynard Lectures.

East Suffolk Education Committee was also responsible for the Lowestoft College of Further Education, Ipswich. The first Technical Institute, built in 1898 at Lowestoft, was completely demolished in an air attack in 1941. It was not until October 1965 that the new building to house the College of Further Education was completed. Courses at the college in this period (1945-1970) reflected the needs of local industry and the community, and some courses, such as those for sea-going personnel in the fishing fleet and Merchant Navy, attract students from a wide area beyond the county. Full-time preliminary or pre-apprenticeship courses are offered in art, building, commerce and engineering. At a higher level there are Ordinary National Diploma Courses in business studies, engineering and pre-diploma course in art, as well as a marine radio officers' course. The department of English and Liberal Studies offered a full-time course for the preliminary certificate in child care, and for professional social workers there were interesting casework seminars.

The greatest volume of work lies in the provision of day-release courses for craftsmen and technicians with the large food processing firms at Lowestoft being catered for by a three-year food science course. Yacht, boat and shipbuilding, marine and diesel engine, electronic engineering and vehicle body building courses all reflect the needs of local industries.

East Suffolk Local Education Authority ensured that horticultural education for adults and rural domestic economy were given prominence. The horticultural education centre was established at Witnesham, and horticulture was provided with a large greenhouse for the industrial training of young adults taking city and guilds courses.

Hollesley Bay Borstal Centre has an interesting history, from the original Colonial College of 1888 "for the training of young gentlemen intended to be colonists" to the teaching of agriculture to the unemployed in the twenties and its transfer in 1938 to the Prison Commissioners as a Borstal. In housed in the period 1945-70 young offenders for whom East Suffolk Education Committee provided classes.

This county also shows a great deal of initiative and imagination in its provision and an awareness of the needs of people for a variety of courses in adult education.

7   Surrey County Council

Under the Surrey county development plan for adult education in 1945 two additional technical colleges were planned at Weybridge and Ewell. The county's policy for adult education was to provide part-time institutes, each under separate principals. During the 1950s the policy was established that a small number of adult centres should be set up on an experimental basis, the first of these being at Richmond. A further college was planned for Sutton. Following on the success of the Richmond experiment, and as a result of the then Ministry of Education's circular, it was decided to appoint full-time

Principals and to create adult education centres where possible. By 1965 eleven Principals, excluding the area covered by the London Boroughs, had been appointed, and two years later their number was raised to thirteen. These centres had modern facilities and were able to offer a variety of courses.

The County of Surrey had four divisions and three expected districts. Each of the three excepted districts and the northern division has a single institute. Each of the other three divisions has three institutes. The population of the institute area was not uniform but varied from about 60,000 to 120,000. Area Principals were appointed over a period of time as well as full-time organisers to deal with administration and adult teaching. By the end of the sixties Surrey had 68 full-time adult educationists.

The County's policy was that each institute should have a building of its own to house its administrative centre and also to contain a varying number of teaching spaces. These buildings had all been used for different purposes. Because of the haphazard way in which redundant schools became available, it had not been possible to distribute day centres evenly, and some institutes had a much better provision than others.

This policy had several results, and gave adult education in Surrey a distinctive character. The first result was that a varied programme of day classes had been offered throughout the county and at the end of the sixties day enrolments amounted to one quarter of the total enrolments during the year. One obvious effect was the classes differed from the evening classes in that both staff and students came fresh to the subject. Tutors and students commented, according to the Report of the Inspector for Adult Education in Surrey, A.D.N. Forgan, on the quality of the work done in day classes. Surrey is a county with a larger than average proportion of residents in the Registrar General's categories 1 and 2. Many of these people have evening social commitments and are, therefore, free only during the day.

The kind of day students (retired teachers, doctors, graduate wives) affected the methods and quality of teaching. It was felt that the students in the day classes welcomed experimental methods of teaching and that they were critical and discriminating about course content. Many of these classes were taken by full-time staff who were very conscious of the expertise of their students.

Student participation and involvement arose from the day centres. Each centre had an area for refreshments and the coffee break helps class members to get to know each other. The most active members of each Institute's Association were drawn from the students attending these centres. A number of institutes also provided light meals which enabled students to have a full day following a particular craft or one subject in the morning followed by another in the afternoon.

The duties of the Students' Association varied as did its name. Students were able to collect money to purchase additional classrooms which they

153

handed over to the authority. Institutes have also organised crèches which allows mothers with young children to attend classes at a time when they are liable to suffer from a feeling of isolation.

The Surrey Evening Institutes are open for a twelve-hour period, from 9.30 a.m. to 9.30 p.m. In the evenings there are no other competitors and the centres are the sole property of the Institute. Where a centre is based in an old house or other building which is clearly not a school, those students who are unlikely to return to school may be brought in more easily. A further development was the use of Institute premises as a meeting place for voluntary organisations. Some organisations have become adult classes.

The enrolments over the years showed a rise although one Institute had reached its peak and began to show a certain falling off. It was a special case caused by the proximity of a purpose-built Centre in a London Borough which continued to offer courses at lower fees when Surrey was forced to increase the basic fee.

Surrey County Council had a residential centre in Moor Park College, Farnham, Surrey. This is a voluntary organisation subsidised by the county and the Inner London Educational Authority. It offers a programme of week-end courses which is used by Surrey Technical and Arts Colleges for courses during the week of three days' duration.

The county was also served with technical colleges. Guildford and Reigate Technical College was already in existence in 1945. Brooklands Technical College was established in 1949 and Ewell Technical College in 1953. In one college, Redhill, there has been over the years a large programme of non-vocational courses. An agreement was made that by and large vocational courses should be offered in technical colleges and only non-vocational courses in Institutes. Since then the line has been blurred as many colleges offer courses at 'O' level and where access to a technical college is difficult, 'A' level courses are also offered in Institutes.

All four of the county's Art Schools were set up before the war, and, during the period concerned, Farnham and Guildford Colleges were combined to form the West Surrey College of Art and Design. Each Art College offered a range of non-vocational courses and their aim was to provide advanced courses to students who had achieved a high standard in Institute classes. Surrey is another local education authority which adopted a progressive attitude towards adult education, and with more financial resources it could have achieved a much more comprehensive provision for adults.

8   County of Cleveland

The present County of Cleveland, which came into existence in 1974, includes the former Middlesbrough and Teeside Education Authority, and is mainly concerned with the provision of evening classes in Further Education

Centres. No residential colleges were established, and there is a very close collaboration with the extra-mural departments of the University of Leeds, University of Durham and also with the WEA. The seven technical colleges in Cleveland County date from the post-war period, and Teeside Polytechnic had its origins in the Constantine College of Technology founded in 1929. This authority has not the same awareness as other counties we have studied of the need for a comprehensive adult education scheme and this is a good example of what one found in the urban areas of England and Wales.

9 Isle of Wight County Council

Adult education classes have been held on the Isle of Wight since 1925. The island was divided in the period under review into two Evening Institutes (East and West Wight), and a range of vocational courses was also provided at the Isle of Wight Technical College, which was renamed in the seventies the Isle of Wight Colleges of Art and Technology. In the immediate post-war years a part-time warden of further education (with his district committee) was established in each of the six principal areas of population in the island, and classes to do with languages, handwork, art, and so on, were provided at these principal centres. In the early sixties financial considerations prompted the education committee to review the arrangements for adult education and it was then decided to have two part-time wardens for the whole island. During this period under review the number of individual students in each session was approximately 1,100.

The Isle of Wight Technical College, as it was then named, was opened in 1951, but only with engineering and building departments. Subsequently, departments of commerce and women's subjects were provided, and in the seventies there was further growth in the facilities of the college to young adults. The provision in the Isle of Wight is quite limited and it seems that little has been learnt from the actual situation by those who prepare and plan adult education.

10 Royal County of Berkshire

A large number of innovations were introduced and a considerable amount of growth took place in adult education in Berkshire in the period 1945-1970. New colleges of further education were built which, except for the old County Borough of Reading, took on responsibility for adult education. But in the main Berkshire suffered from the lack of financial resources and the old story of adult education — of concepts being rarely introduced for the situation at the right moment in time.

11 Bedfordshire

Bedfordshire introduced its scheme for further education in 1948, and its work was developed in the following ways:

Further Education Centres:

These centres have developed from the evening institutes which in the past gave the educationally deprived an opportunity of elementary education. In our period they provided young people with a means of continuing their general education, and of acquiring basic qualifications to help them with skill and advancement at work. But in the middle sixties this role gradually declined as the period of full-time schooling was extended and vocational education was concentrated in technical colleges on a full-time or part-time basis. Vocational and general educational classes diminished but non-vocational classes for leisure-time education grew rapidly in both volume and variety. In rural areas where a technical college was not easily available the evening institute continued to cater as in the past, but in urban areas where technical colleges are near at hand centres became almost exclusively focal points of non-vocational classes for adults.

In Bedfordshire evening institutes became known as further education centres, and by 1969 there were forty of them comprising 480 classes with around 7,500 students. The centres ranged in size from a single class centre based on a village primary school to the very large centres based on secondary schools in urban areas, such as the Further Education Centre at Newnham School, Bedford. A wide range of subjects were available, and full-sessional classes were of twenty-two weeks' duration. These classes are offered mostly during the autumn and spring terms with some classes being arranged in the summer term. Some classes continued in the late sixties to offer vocational subjects largely as a means of preparing students in suitably equipped rural centres for the examinations of the Royal Society of Arts in typewriting, shorthand and General Certificate of Education 'O' level in a limited range of subjects. In reviewing the regulations governing the operation of further education centres in May 1968, the Bedfordshire Authority adopted a recommendation that only overflow classes in vocational subjects, which the colleges of further education were unable to accommodate, should be offered at further education centres in the Boroughs of Bedford and Dunstable.

Students attending classes at further education centres in Bedfordshire are drawn from all sections of the community. Most students attend only one class each week, and women students outnumber men by three to one. Although the term adult education is generally used to describe the provision made in further education centres, about twelve per cent of the number of students attending classes at the centres in Bedfordshire by the end of our period were young people under twenty-one years of age.

Instruction at the centres was carried out by part-time teachers of whom a large number also held full-time posts in schools, often in the school on which the centre is based. Many others were former teachers, that is, married women whose family commitments do not allow them to hold teaching posts during the day, while a third group may or may not possess formal qualifications in their subjects, and have not received a formal teacher's training qualification. Part-time teachers were paid in 1968/69 21s 6d. per hour for non-vocational and preliminary vocational classes. Higher rates were paid for more advanced vocational classes having regard to the level of work, and these rates were adopted by the authority on the recommendation of the East Anglican Regional Advisory Council for Further Education.

The administrative work of the centres was carried out by organising secretaries. At 33 of the 40 centres the organising secretaries were full-time teachers who undertook this work as a third session of their working day. All these teachers held posts of responsibility in schools, eleven of them as head teachers, and a further three as deputy heads. Organising secretaries received payment for their work at the rate of 7s. 9d. per class meeting in 1970.

The accommodation varies a great deal with over half of the centres in secondary schools, and all of these, with one exception, were modern buildings offering specialist facilities for a wide range of classes. A further fourteen centres met in primary schools in which specialist accommodation was limited. These buildings varied in age considerably, and a number of centres supplement the available accommodation by the use of local halls for certain classes. Of the remaining centres, two consisted of only one class and met in church halls, one centre was organised in HM Prison, Bedford, and one in Fairfield Hospital, Arlesey. In all schools built in the sixties some small provision was made for adult education in accordance with the Department of Education: in the case of primary schools this consisted of an adult chair store, and in secondary schools of an office for the organising secretary, a further education kitchen where light refreshments could be prepared, and storage for equipment and materials.

Each adult education centre has a local advisory committee, and the classes were conducted in accordance with regulations laid down by the authority. The authority's scheme for further education stated that the local advisory committee should be representative of all sections of the community and the committees were vested with the responsibility of stimulating demand for classes locally and of organising and supervising a programme of classes approved by the authority. Although local advisory committees did not have a uniform constitution prescribed by the authority it became the established practice for the governors and managers of schools on which further education centres are based to be invited to serve on advisory committees. Links between the schools and centres were further fostered when the head teachers of schools concerned were co-opted on to the local advisory committees.

Bedfordshire authority also required that in order to ensure a good standard of instruction each class must be conducted in accordance with an approved syllabus and by an approved teacher. Classes are open to inspection by HM Inspectors and by officers of the authority. An adult class has to have a minimum number of students, fifteen in urban and ten in rural areas, and may not continue when the attendance falls below a stipulated number at three consecutive class meetings, ten in urban and six in rural areas. In the autumn term of 1968 out of 517 classes which were offered by County Centres 130 failed to materialise and 27 classes were subsequently closed because they did not meet the attendance regulations.

Bedfordshire education authority also have adult education classes at the two Colleges of Further Education in Bedford and Dunstable where, as part of their programmes, non-vocational classes are offered in the day as well as in the evening. The classes tend to be those in type which are able to make use of the specialist accommodation and facilities available in the colleges and include classes in languages, woodwork, physical recreation and domestic subjects. Classes are staffed by either full-time or part-time teachers. At Mander College there is a department of adult education with a Grade 1 head of department and other full-time staff. The department assisted with the provision of the authority's programme of in-service for full-time and part-time teachers, and provided a one-year full-time preparatory course for mature students wishing to gain entry to colleges of education. The department was also established to plan specialist courses and conferences as required by industry and commerce and in association with professional and cultural organisations in the area. In the late sixties, classes in a wide range of physical recreation subjects were offered as part of the programme of the department, although the heads of other departments in the college were also responsible to the Principal for the provision of other non-vocational classes in subjects appropriate to their departments.

Adult education facilities were also found at the Craft Centre, Elstow, which was opened in 1967. The centre was situated at the rear of Elstow Primary School and the accommodation consisted of three well-equipped practical rooms. A full programme of classes and demonstrations in a wide variety of homecraft subjects was offered during the day and evening throughout the year. The arrangement of the programme of classes and demonstrations was the immediate responsibility of the County Organiser for Home Economics and the centre was staffed by three full-time teacher/ demonstrators and part-time teachers. In addition to the programme of work at the centre the teacher/demonstrators were involved in the staffing of classes and demonstrations for women's organisations throughout the county.

The authority had also adult education facilities at Maryland Residential Centre. Maryland Centre was opened in 1967 and short residential and day courses were provided. It has been adapted to provide accommodation for up to sixty people of whom twenty-five can be resident. On the professional side the establishment provided a warden who was responsible under the general direction of the Chief Education Officer for the organisation of educational activities at the centre.

The programme of courses and conferences offered at the centre included in-service courses for teachers, training courses for youth leaders and senior members, courses for senior pupils in secondary schools as well as courses for the general public as a means of promoting adult education in the county generally. The centre was also available to industry and commerce and voluntary and professional organisations for courses, conferences and meetings of an educational character.

The authority was very conscious at the end of the sixties that adult education was "a continuing process which begins at birth and continues throughout the whole life of the individual" (*A Report on Further Education Centres and their Future Role in the Development of Facilities for Adult Education in the County* (1969) p.8). It added the following important point:

> It follows, therefore, that there is no age at which education can be said to be complete, and accordingly any system of education must be incomplete without adequate provision for continuative adult education. (pp.8-9).

The authority agreed in their report that the needs of individuals in the continuing educational process varies greatly. Whilst many require opportunities for initial vocational training and re-training which are met by the facilities to be found in the colleges of further education, many others require facilities of a non-vocational character. The report does not belittle the provision of educational courses which satisfy the individual. It says:

> It is important to emphasise that these non-vocational courses are bona fide educational activities. They are in harmony with approved educational practice in other spheres, envisaging in their aims the promotion of the maximum personal development of the individual and supporting the belief that the betterment of the individual must inevitably benefit the whole community. (p.9).

The report realised that the demand for adult education would increase, and that it would become increasingly difficult to satisfy unless resources in terms of manpower, buildings and equipment are used to the best advantage. It saw the adult education centre as a community centre planned and equipped to meet the requirements of the following kinds of activities:

i a wide range of further education classes either provided by the local authority or in conjunction with the WEA and the extra-mural board;

ii meetings of affiliated clubs and groups which may have developed in a variety of ways;

iii meetings of local voluntary organisations and societies which become affiliated to the centre, make use of the facilities and thereby strengthen and supplement their work;

iv a range of extra-curricula activities for the school population;

v opportunities for meeting and for purposeful group activities on the part of young people through the Youth Service;

vi social and recreational activities sponsored by the centre itself, for example, dances, concerts, plays, excursions, and so on;

vii   activities arranged in conjunction with such bodies as the Central Council for Physical Recreation;

viii   the provision of a base for other community services such as the County Library and Welfare Clinics.

What the Report advocated was the conception of the Community College. This was not a new idea and was successfully applied by a number of local education authorities in the post-war period, but this concept was not implemented by the local education authority in Bedfordshire.

12   The County of Somerset

The structure of adult education in Somerset was based on six further education centres for the rural areas under the control of area principals and in the urban areas on the further education colleges. In the case of further education colleges a tutor organiser was responsible for all non-vocational education.

There were three tertiary colleges, that is, colleges in which all education for young adults between the ages of 16 and 19 would be concentrated. These were located at Stroud, Yeovil and Bridgewater. In addition a College of Arts and Technology was situated at Taunton and a further education college combined with a comprehensive school at Frome. All non-vocational education in the immediate vicinity of these colleges was looked after by a tutor-organiser who was based on the establishment of these colleges.

All these colleges dated originally before the Second World War and all have been expanded and enlarged. In an agricultural county such as Somerset one finds vocational and non-vocational agricultural education. This is based on the Agricultural College at Cannington, and some of the staff operate on an extra-mural basis in conjunction with the further education colleges and centres.

The County of Somerset has one residential adult education college, that is Dillington House which was established in May 1951, and which has provided a great deal of adult education courses for adults in Somerset and the west country. But in this instance again very little was learnt from the sociological changes that society experienced in England and Wales in the post-war period.

13   Merseyside County Council

The post-war period saw a tremendous increase in the provision of further education on Merseyside, and in particular in the decade 1947 to 1957. Most provision was for young men and women who had left school, and those who wanted to continue full-time education so as to qualify themselves for their chosen trade or profession (Magnay, 1957, p.93).

A large number of students undertook lengthy and arduous courses. In Liverpool alone in 1955/56 over 40,000 students enrolled for courses arranged by the authority. The other factor that needs emphasising was the great variety of courses offered from the most elementary preliminary work to the post-graduate classes. But on Merseyside adult education suffered from the same defects as we have noted in the other local education authorities — lack of vision, and lack of resources, and an inability to learn from the actual situation that confronted adult education in England and Wales between 1945 and 1970.

B   The Role of the National Government through the Department of Education and Science

The role of national Government through the Department of Education and Science in adult education is difficult to untangle. It has an advisory role - as well as a rule of financial support to the different agencies involved in adult education. But it seems that the department cannot compel an authority to implement its policy on adult education. In 1978 the County of Cheshire decided to do away with further education due to rising costs, and the department had to accept it. The department has to execute national policy in the following way: Firstly, through the issuing of circulars and administrative memoranda. Secondly, by advice in pamphlets and reports published for the department. Thirdly, by financial controls, direct or indirect, and by the normal processes of administration, for example, the examination and approval of annual further education building programmes submitted by local education authorities, and the annual assessment of grants to responsible bodies, and fourthly, by consultation between local education authorities or responsible bodies, and the department's officers and HM Inspectors.

It seems that adult education has been neglected a great deal and that throughout the period under consideration it was still a Cinderella. One can say that adult education lacks glamour, and the official publications as well as the debates in Parliament on adult education suggest a declining concern with adult education. It seems that the first pamphlet published by the Ministry after the Education Act 1944 was the *Red Book* on community centres, and mention of educational provision for adults was made in two other pamphlets (No. 2, *A Guide to the Educational System of England and Wales* and No.8, *Further Education*) in the first few years after the Act. In 1954 the Ashby Committee published their Report on the responsible bodies under the title, *The Organisation and Finance of Adult Education*. A number of the Ashby Report recommendations were accepted by the Minister in Administrative memorandum No. 256 of 1956, and were incorporated in subsequent grant regulations. In 1956 the Ministry issued Pamphlet No. 28, *Evening Institutes*. Though it was referred to in the context of provision for the arts in Administrative Memorandum No.9 of 1969, the last major positive statement about adult education was made in 1963 in Administrative Memorandum No.6, *Adult Education (Accommodation and Staffing)*. Subsequent statements affecting though not specifying adult education have been Administrative

Memorandum No. 15 of 1967 on Further Education, *Fees for Classes in Leisure Time Activities.*

The department has also Her Majesty's Inspectors in different parts of the country whose task is to act as liaison officers between the department and local education authorities and other bodies concerned in educational matters. About forty such inspectors operate in the name of the department and again their role is purely advisory. Most of these Inspectors are unknown even to the active adult educators in the regions.

The department is involved more than anything else in the financial provision it makes to the local education authorities, the responsible bodies and different projects that appear from time to time. But the department spokesman in Parliament and in the country is the Secretary of State. Adult education came into the higher and further education section in the sixties and was delegated to a Minister of State.

It seems that adult education has never caught the imagination of any of the Secretaries of State. For a Secretary of State has to be effective in Cabinet and to carry his colleagues along with him (Boyle, 1971, p.120). He needs to possess also a creative imagination and a concern for his department. It is generally reckoned that it was during David Eccles' first tenure as Minister of Education in 1954-7 that the status of the department was raised. But one must not blame the Minister or the Secretary altogether for the lack of status and the money spent on adult education in the post-war period. Lord Boyle of Handsworth, who between 1962 and 1964 was the Minister for Education, spoke in this way leaving Parliament:

> It cannot be too often emphasised that nearly all important decisions of Government policy are collective decisions, involving more than one minister; in particular, any decision that involved spending money — and this applies to the great majority of things most ministers want to do — requires the acquiescence, willing or (more often) reluctance of the Treasury. (Boyle, 1971, p.120).

It depended a great deal on the Minister knowing his own mind and also if he had the support of the Prime Minister. Lord Boyle mentions that political pressure could affect the outcome which suggests that adult education never figured as urgent on the agenda or manifestoes of the Conservative or the Labour Parties.

The Department of Education and Science has at Elizabeth House in London a small team of civil servants to look after the interests of adult education. The team is a mixed group of civil servants rather than a team of highly qualified adult educators. It seems that experience as adult educators and research experience in the theories of adult education are not taken into consideration when appointing a member to the team. These men will learn about adult education as time goes on and they naturally will feel frustrated by the cinderella status and the lack of an organisational structure. For if adult education was properly implemented there would be a Department of

Adult Education rather than a small team operating as an unit within a large department.

It seems on the evidence available that national governments, through their Department of Education and Science have never given adult education any priority. It is a luxury that can be discarded in difficult economic times and other times it can ignore its needs. Adult education has not helped itself by its inability to change or adapt its concept in the face of technological and social changes and in its sheer 'conservatism'. In other words, adult education within the local authorities and national government have learned little in the post-war period in England and Wales from the actual sociological changes that adults experienced in those thirty five years.

Chapter 5
Universities and Adult Education

The universities were severely criticised during the second world war for not providing the general kind of education needed by society. Adolph Lowe, in his book *The Universities in Transformation* published in 1940, summed up the criticism;

> The modern universities have never made any attempt at a comprehensive cultural education.
> (Lowe, 1940, p.15).

Sir Richard Livingstone pointed out the danger of overspecialisation in *Some Thoughts on University Education* (1948). But not everyone agreed. F.R. Leavis, in *Education and the University* (1948), argued that specialisation was inevitable. But more significant still was the argument in favour of the universities involving themselves in the life of the region.

In this chapter we will look at three developments. Firstly, the role of the new residential universities. Bruce Truscot (alias Professor Alison Peers) coined the new term Redbrick Universities and his two books, *Redbrick University* (1943) and *Redbrick and These Vital Days* (1945), urged the setting up of eleven new universities. Truscot's plea was listened to, and new universities were established which drew students in particular from their own localities. These new universities (Nottingham (1948), Southampton (1952), Hull (1954), Exeter (1955), and Leicester (1957)), received their charters, and in the sixties the Universities of Sussex (1961), York (1963), East Anglia (1963), Essex (1964), Kent (1964) and Warwick (1965). The North Staffordshire University College (1949) became the University of Keele in 1962. All these universities received support from local government, and they offered some courses to meet the needs of local industry.

The most obvious example of the role of the local community in the development of a Redbrick University took place in the University of Keele. The University Grants Committee had grave doubt as to the sanctioning of university status for Keele and might well have withheld its support had not Sir Walter Moberley and R.H. Tawney shared the enthusiasm of Lord Lindsay for a new experiment in university education. A.D. Lindsay had planned the Keele experiment as far back as 1942 and he was supported all the way by a number of dedicated local authority leaders and officials in the North Staffordshire area. There was the Reverend Alderman Horwood, vicar of Etruria and leader of the Labour group in the Stoke City Council; J.F. Carr, the Director of Education; A.P. Walker, the City Treasurer, and Harry Taylor, town clerk of Stoke. All these men were concerned with what has become known as continuing education. They felt that local industry needed the expertise that an university education could provide, and that adult education would be strengthened in a new partnership between the university and the local community. It was ironical, as Frank Jessup maintains, that by "the time the final scheme emerged all reference to the two original salient factors, namely the needs of local industry and adult education, had entirely diappeared" (Jessup, 1973, pp.170-171).

Technology was also encouraged within the universities and the emphasis on technology was very evident in the universities by the end of the sixties. Anthony Crosland, during his period as Minister of Education, encouraged what one might call the 'technical college education'. He delivered two major speeches — one at Woolwich in 1965 and the other at Lancaster in July 1967 — which brought into being a rival to the universities in the establishment of the polytechnics. The polytechnics were in line with the new universities in one way: the pressure at the grass roots for more open university education. Universities tend to be slow to change and to be socially exclusive. Even in 1970 only a minority of an age group (8%) was in the universities, and most of these students were from middle class homes (Pratt and Burgess, 1974, p.10). Loughborough College is an excellent example of the initiative of the local authorities. It was started originally with no grant at all, and afterwards became the first College of Advanced Technology (CAT) and then the first technological university. This change in status from the College of Advanced Technology to a new university happened also in eight other centres besides Loughborough. These were Aston in Birmingham, Bath in the South-West, Bradford in Yorkshire, Salford in the North-West, Brunel, Chelsea and City University in London, and the new University of Surrey in Guildford. The Guildford experiment was unique in the sense that a city centre campus was provided. It was a great advantage for both the university and the town, and it was to the credit of Richard Crossman that he gave the planning permission (*New Society,* 6 January 1966, p.4). In its former guise as Battersea College of Advanced Technology it was on a very cramped site with no means of expanding. But at Guildford all this was changed to the advantage of the new university and economically to the town of Guildford.

The lack of planning and preparation which was obvious with regard to the universities was also true of the polytechnics as Anthony Crosland so honestly admitted in 1971 in a conversation with Maurice Kogan. Crosland was advised by his civil servants to make a major speech at Woolwich on the polytechnics, and the binary policy of higher education, when he had only a 'superficial knowledge of the subject' (*The Politics of Education,* 1971, p.193). The Minister of Education admitted this:

> It's not a mistake I shall make again, to make a major speech on a subject which I don't fully understand. But, as I've said, when I finally mastered the subject I became a passionate believer in binary and polytechnics and I suppose did as much as anyone else to push the policy through. *(The Politics of Education,* 1971, p.194).

This was the case, for the decision to create thirty polytechnics was not at all in line with the Labour Party's Taylor Committee recommendation in the report, *The Years of Crisis,* published in 1963, to create a large and undifferentiated system of higher education. The plan was created by the

Department responding to the wishes of the local authorities and the 'unusual conversion' of Crosland to the idea. For Crosland was after all a member of the Taylor's Committee. Though it be wrong to maintain that the concept of continuing education inspired the Department and the Minister of Education, yet it can be suggested that some ideas in the polytechnic plan would be in line with that philosophy. The need in the middle sixties for institutions which could cater not only for the traditional full-time degree courses but for the part-time student, the sub-degree course, and the kind of education which has its roots in the technical college tradition. Crosland felt that the universities were not in a position to give the nation what was needed — that was the "expansion of polytechnic-style rather than university-style higher education" (*The Politics of Education,* 1971, p.195). The Minister had been convinced with the case for the polytechnics which had been masterfully presented by Tyrrell Burgess. Burgess had strong views on the universities which he saw as the "preservation, extension and dissemination of knowledge 'for its own sake'" (Pratt and Burgess, 1974, p.8). He felt that the university teachers were more interested in their own development than that of their students. What was needed was a teaching institution, and Burgess felt that few university teachers were even taught to teach. He and Pratt agreed with a comment made at the beginning of the century:

> A lecturer is a sound scholar, who is chosen to teach on the grounds that he was once able to learn. (Cornford, 1908, p.11).

The polytechnics were to be institutions which could cope with social changes from the technological innovations. M.V.C. Jeffreys had argued during the war that universities should strive to be "active instruments of cultural formation rather than passive reflections of social change" (Jeffreys, 1944, p.2). It was the work of the polytechnics to implement Jeffrey's vision. To what extent they have succeeded is a debatable point, and to a large extent the impetus and their role as institutions of open learning has been largely taken over by the Open University.

The universities have two channels of communication with the community in England and Wales. In the first place, there is the provision of educational opportunities for the general public on special occasions. Little work has been done on this aspect but it is an important part of the role of the universities in educating adults. It also acknowledges the place of continuing education. Public lectures are a traditional feature of university life and all universities go through this formality except Reading and Durham (Long, 1968, p.45). Lectures are one of the most important mediums for educating adults in the adult education movement and public lectures at the universities are usually very popular. A lecture in 'the flesh' lives in the memory more clearly than an article in a journal or a radio talk. What are the standard of these university public lectures? They vary in style, content and standard, though many of them, especially in the University of London and the University of Wales, are published. In some exceptional instances these lectures are published as books, as for example the Josiah Mason Lectures at Birmingham University given by Joan Robinson on Economic Philosophy (Long, 1968, p.46). There have been examples when these lectures have stirred up public controversy, and there are two obvious examples, namely Lord Annan's Romanes Lecture in 1965 on the Disintegration of the Old Culture, and Lord Snow's Rede Lecture on The Two Cultures.

The size of the audiences vary, and it is common to have 200 to 300 at the lectures. According to the research of Long sometimes as many as 400. This can be borne out in a few of the lectures that I attended at the University of Liverpool in the period 1968-1979. To be a successful lecturer on public occasions one has to be well-known because of the position one holds or because of one's personality. Lecturers who are not well-known can attract large audiences through the title of the lecture which might be very topical or controversial. The other avenue is to have the lecture as part of a regular programme for which there is wide and effective publicity.

There are some universities where public lectures are frequent. One public lecture per week during autumn and spring terms is held at Cambridge, Leeds, London, Manchester, Newcastle and Nottingham. Keele (since the college was established in 1948) has concentrated on a few lectures by people whose personality and lecturing ability have a strong appeal. London and Cambridge are in a category of their own, for the total number of public lectures each year runs into hundreds (Long, 1968, p.48). At least 150 special university lectures are given every year in the University of London by speakers not associated with the various colleges. The majority of these lectures are from abroad, and in particular from the United States of America.

The number of public lectures within the University of London varies from about five each year at Westfield College to about thirty eight at Imperial College. The subjects vary but law, medicine, theology, social sciences make up the bulk of the lectures at London. It is impossible to state how many members from outside the university staff attend the lectures, and often so much depends on the location of the colleges. King's College, near the Strand, is one of the best located of the colleges in the University of London as far as the response from the public at large is concerned. In the University of Cambridge the 130 or so public lectures are largely on highly specialised topics — such as Binocular Interaction in the Visual Area of the Cat. It means that the University of Cambridge is not interested in attracting the public at large to the lectures for the publicity is confined to the Cambridge University *Reporter*.

This again is different in the Universities of Newcastle and Nottingham where topics of general interest are well publicised. Lectures are held on the same day and at the same time. Indeed, the University of Nottingham is unique in that it arranges a lecture programme especially for members of the public as well as lectures intended primarily for university people, but open to the public. The same situation prevails in the University of Leeds and there, like Newcastle and Nottingham, extensive use is made of publicity (Long, 1968, p.50). Audiences at Nottingham varied between 40 and 300, and in Newcastle in 1964/5 the audience varied between 80 and 600. At the University of Manchester a series of public lectures are held on Saturday afternoons during autumn and spring terms on biology, geology, anthropology and architecture. Memorial lectures are also held each year. The University of Bristol has a great deal of provision, in particular Memorial Lectures. At Liverpool the university authorities lean towards the special occasions, and some of those lectures are very well supported by students, lecturers and the public. In the University of Wales there are a number of Memorial Lectures and every public lecture is very well advertised. It is felt that the public at large should attend these lectures and advertisements appear in the Press and posters are prepared as well as leaflets. At Swansea bills advertising the university lectures appear in the local buses. The benefits to students, staff and public are immense though there is great room for improvement.

Most of the universities do not make a determined effort on the scale of the University of Wales to publicise the lectures, and many of the lectures are held at inconvenient times for people at work. Manchester has the right idea of holding their lectures on Saturday afternoons. Though Saturday after-noons do not suit everybody yet the popularity of the WEA one-day school in some urban areas prove that there is a nucleus of people who appreciate an occasional educational feast at the week-end. Residential colleges also have experienced the same trend.

Universities also encourage the public to visit permanent art collections which they have at their disposal. This happens at the Universities of Birmingham, Cambridge, Durham, Glasgow, London, Manchester, Newcastle and Oxford. Regular loan exhibitions are arranged by Manchester and Newcastle to support their permanent collections and also by ten other academic seats of learning, namely the Universities of Exeter, Keele, Leeds, Nottingham, Southampton and Sussex, and the four constituent colleges of the University of Wales. Oxford possesses the Ashmolean Museum of Art and Archaeology built in 1845, and Cambridge has the Fitzwilliam Museum. Birmingham has the Barber Institute opened in 1939, and Manchester took over the privately owned Whitworth Art Gallery in 1958. The University College of North Wales, Bangor, has a permanent art gallery. All these Museums and Art Galleries serve a valuable educational purpose, but they are only a few, and a number of universities in large urban areas are devoid of them.

All this points to the need for a much more permanent and realistic relationship between higher educational institutions and local communities. One difficulty this raises is that although the concept of 'community' is much used and indeed fashionable in educational circles, all to often it is used loosely and not defined with any degree of rigour. Stronger links between schools and communities have been seen as a panacea for educational problems ranging from reading failure to delinquency. Very little has been written on the permanent need for colleges of higher education to involve themselves and their students in innovations and educational work among the adult community.

The universities have been concerned primarily with theoretical knowledge as a source of insight and understanding, and this has had a number of important consequences for the organisation of teaching and learning. By and large, legitimacy has not been given to alternative sources of knowledge. Berger and Luckmann have argued in *The Social Construction of Reality* (1966) that there are a number of competing definitions of "what counts as knowledge", and they maintain that "theoretical knowledge is only a small part and by no means the most important part of what passes for knowledge. Theoretically sophisticated legitimations appear at particular moments of an institutional history. The primary knowledge about the institutional order is knowledge on the pre-theoretical level. It is the sum total of 'what everybody knows' about the social world, an assemblage of maxims, morals, values and beliefs, myths and so forth". Berger and Luckmann's critique is placed within the context of "the sociology of knowledge" but it has wider implications and applications. For there are subjects which lend themselves to community involvement, as for example, sociology, law, education, psychology, social administration, industrial relations and politics — and those "pure" and "applied" sciences which have a direct concern with community issues such as pollution, re-cycling of waste matter and agricultural development.

All departments are very reluctant to be involved in the education process of the local community and most university departments feel that the responsibility rests on the extra-mural departments or the departments of adult education in the different universities. The Robbins' Report insisted that universities have an important role to play in the general cultural life of the communities. Most of the educating role is carried out by the university extra-mural departments, but not all the universities in England and Wales possessed such departments. There was a reluctance among the new universities to set up extra-mural departments. The Universities of Sussex (1961), East Anglia and York (1963), Essex and Lancaster (1964), Canterbury and Warwick (1965) had not by 1966 set up any extra-mural departments. There were reasons for this. In East Anglia the area was already covered by the University of Cambridge extra-mural department, and Warwick had opened negotiations with the University of Birmingham, while the University of Sussex was considering it. Lancaster and Kent had no intention of having extra-mural departments of the conventional kind, although they recognised the importance of adult education. Dr. G. Templeman, Vice-Chancellor of the University of Kent, had pointed out in a magazine article *(Nature,* 1964, p.636) that the periodic retraining of graduates was a real necessity in science subjects. This was where the real future of extra-mural studies lay, and many universities have implemented his suggestion. Templeman stated that Kent would not set up an extra-mural department. The local community was served by Oxford University, and Dr. G. Templeman also felt that extra-mural departments of the conventional sort have in 'large measure ceased to serve a useful purpose'.

The end of the second world war prompted the universities to review their role in adult education, and the Vice-Chancellors of Oxford, Cambridge and London called a conference to discuss the future relationships of universities to adult education. A statement was issued entitled *The Universities and Adult Education,* dated December 1945. It emphasised i. the need for quality in the education of adults; ii. for less formal methods of teaching adults; and iii. to cater for those in the professions, industry and the cultural needs of the community. The university extra-mural departments were to offer a comprehensive service and to serve the wider community through their educated or intellectual élite.

University extension work between 1945 and 1951 expanded at a greater rate than that of adult education generally, and certainly faster than WEA work (Pashley, 1966, p.96). There were a number of reasons for this. One reason was the energy and enterprise of a number of outstanding directors of university extra-mural departments. Sir Ifan ab Owen Edwards, the creator of the Welsh League of Youth, was singled out for praise in the 1950 Survey of the Work of the department of extra-mural studies in the University College of Wales, Aberystwyth. R. Peers at Nottingham and S.G. Rayboult at Leeds, A.J. Allaway at Leicester, Thomas Kelly at Liverpool, D.R. Dudley at Birmingham are easily added to the list of outstanding extra-mural directors.

The second reason was that a new section in society decided to devote a part of its leisure time to systematic self-education. It appears that by 1951 about 100,000 more students were each session taking advantage of responsible body provision than at any time before the war. The public that came to the university extra-mural classes were neither educationally underprivileged nor working class, and was therefore of a different character from the stereotype of the WEA clientele. In 1911 57% of the people in tutorial classes were manual workers, and 83.5% were male. By 1954/5, when the Ashby Committee reported, only 14% were manual workers and females slightly outnumbered the males. But this soon changed, and since the fifties the women nearly always outnumber the men. Wales was an exception in some years, as for example in 1960/1 when 4,064 men enrolled in courses compared with 3,873 women. One can find historical reasons for the predominance of men in university adult classes in Wales. There has been a long tradition of adult Sunday School classes, and the hope of Principal Ifor L. Evans and Sir Ifan ab Owen Edwards in a report published in 1944 that the Young Farmers' Club and Welsh League of Youth would provide a "potential reservoir of young men and women" as clientele of adult education, must have borne fruit. In London the female adult student was

171

always in the majority, as for example in 1960/1, with 4,002 men and 5,592 women. Durham area (which included Newcastle) had 1,980 men compared with 2,499 women (Long, 1968, p.24). In the period (1945-1980) the 21 to 35 age group was well represented, and in the sample at Newcastle ex-grammar school pupils formed the largest group.

It was obvious in view of all this that the extra-mural department would in time concentrate on the educated minority and this is the trend that we can discern in the post-war period. Courses for university graduates were prepared. There were the specialised refresher courses in the graduate's own, or cognate, subjects; or more general courses designed to widen the cultural background of narrow specialists. The university extra-mural department at Leeds decided in the early sixties to organise extra-mural courses in association with the internal departments of the university. This proved a high success. Adult Education Centres were set up in Bradford, Middlesbrough and Leeds, and analysis of the four hundred students who enrolled in long courses in 1963/64 at the Bradford Adult Education Centre reflected a generally high level of previous education. Almost forty per cent had attended university or college. The University of Keele department of extension studies arranged refresher courses of married women wishing to return to their professions after bringing up families. Leicester University extra-mural department, under A.J. Allaway, believed in concerning themselves with the needs of people who had already enjoyed a full-time higher education. A.J. Allaway believed that the department in Leicester, like the one in Leeds, had to re-educate their colleagues in other departments. He is quoted as saying:

> They had had to acquire a new image of our work and of their task in extension courses. The latter has to be perceived, not as a kind of intellectual slumming or a rescue of the perishing, but as analogous to what is being done inside.   (Long, 1968, p.39).

The University of Manchester extra-mural department arranged courses for which membership was explicitly limited to university graduates.

Another trend was to arrange for courses for special vocational groups. The department of extra-mural studies in the University of Leeds established an adult college in 1964 called after the founder of the WEA — the Albert Mansbridge College — and during its first academic year sixty residential courses were arranged. The truth of the matter was that Albert Mansbridge College would have been little used without the courses run for the Nuffield Centre for Hospital and Health Service studies and the probation service. It seemed that the Albert Mansbridge College had confined itself to a narrow segment of the population in comparison with the success of the Adult Education Centre at Middlesbrough which was opened in 1958. It was the special evening — 'Friday Night at the Centre' — which really attracted the adults. Every Friday there was an average attendance of ninety-four.

University extra-mural departments in the post-war period arranged courses leading to certificates as well as diplomas. This took place on an extensive scale at the University extra-mural departments of Leeds, Liverpool,

London, Leicester and Manchester. At Leeds a Prison Service Staff Course was arranged and so thereby assisted the Prison Service Staff College at Wakefield. Bristol extra-mural department, however, was the first department to provide full-time courses for probation officers.

A detailed look at the scene in the University of Leeds department of extra-mural studies will show that this trend of 'educating the educated' is only concerned with a very small minority. Extension Certificate was instituted in 1947 but in the fifties the progress was slow. Between 1961 and 1971 the enrolment figures changed from 179 to 470 students but the increase was largely due to the increase in the certificate and diploma courses. By 1971 there were 47 certificates or diplomas available in the department. Some of the courses had longer teething problems than others. The Industrial Relations and Economics Certificate course was first established in 1963 and centred mostly on the Middlesbrough area. But by 1970 it had grown and was as secure as the certificate courses in the Russian Language and Social Organisation.

The University of London extra-mural department has been involved with diplomas and certificates and offers a wide variety. A number of the subjects are to do with the mass media. By 1970 there were thirteen diplomas offered, namely, History, Economics, English Literature, History of Art, Biblical Studies, Sociology, International Affairs, Visual Arts, Archaeology, History of Music, Transport Studies, Film Study and Science. These certificates are awarded on the basis of an examination and after four years part-time study. A Certificate in Transport Studies was introduced in 1959-60, in 1963-64 a Certificate in Criminology, and a Certificate and Diploma in Film Study and a Diploma in Science introduced in 1965-66. These certificates are awarded after three years attendance at part-time courses.

In the post-war period a number of these certificate and diploma courses disappeared. At the University of London the postgraduate diploma in Psychological Medicine ceased in 1952 after being in existence for 31 years; the diploma in Theory and Practice of Physical Education ceased in 1953 after 23 years; a Diploma in Public Administration came to an end in 1961 after 23 years, and a Certificate of Proficiency in Diction and Drama ceased in 1968 after a period of 39 years. At the Vaughan College, in Leicester (run by the Department of Adult Education) the three year certificate course in Religious Knowledge ended in 1957 but two new certificate courses were introduced, namely, Criminology and Trade Union Studies.

The bulk of the university extra-mural department's work is not with the courses for the college and university trained people but for adults who are interested in being taught at university level. The title of these departments — extra-mural studies — takes its name not from the subject it teaches but from the student it teaches. It is the department which is concerned with the provision of courses for the general public.

Courses are designed to offer an opportunity for the prolonged and serious study of a subject under university guidance, as for example the Sessional and the Three Year Tutorial Classes. These classes are open to everyone. However, the tutorials had suffered a great deal during the war, and also adult educationists as a whole tended to favour the sessional and extension courses which grew in the post-war period. The tradition of shorter courses was established. Leicester introduced their own speciality — a three term thirty meeting class.

The methods of teaching used in the tutorial and sessional was very much the same that is, a combination of a lecture and a discussion. A number of points needs to be stressed with regard to the provision and the tutors who were involved.

i   It seems that a subject has a better chance of being given a fair deal if that subject has a full-time organiser responsible for it within the department. One could select examples of this from every one of the university departments. At the University College of Swansea, during the session 1963-64 reference was made in the Annual Report of the department of extra-mural studies to the increase often in the number of classes studying Welsh Literature, which was the result of an appointment of a full-time member of the staff. It was the same in Liverpool in 1962 after the appointment of Dr. G.W. Roderick as the department's first tutor/organiser in Science, and in the same decade at Leeds with the appointment of a specialist in Archaeology. Every department of extra-mural studies could add to the evidence.

In many ways this point underlines the weakness of the university's attempt at providing adequate educational facilities for the general public. On inspecting the Annual Reports of the extra-mural departments one can see that there was no lack of response if the subject was adequately looked after by a full-time tutor/organiser. But the total number of full-time teaching staff employed in extra-mural departments in 1966/67 was 304 including eighteen specifically employed to work with H.M. Forces. Leeds had 33 while Leicester had only six (Lowe, 1970, p.100). The rest of the tutors were made up of 2,313 university staff employed as part-time tutors and 2,731 outsiders employed as part-time tutors (Long, 1968, p.38).

Many of the departments of extra-mural studies in the urban areas concentrated on a policy of selecting the part-time tutors from university departments. This, however, takes time and in some areas like Aberystwyth could not be implemented. Indeed in parts of Wales many of the Ministers of Religion who were employed as part-time tutors were excellent communicators, a statement that could not be made for every university lecturer who was in charge of an extra-mural class. Adult educationists like John Lowe felt strongly on the subject; and this is a typical comment from his writings:

> Departments should try to ensure, therefore, that a large proportion of their part-time staff are drawn from internal departments.   (Lowe, 1973, p.103).

But this did not happen in the period (1945-80) as Lowe himself has to admit:

Of the part-time tutors substantially more than half are not members of a university
department. (Lowe, 1970, p.103).

One can see what Lowe had in mind that such a situation would increase the standing of the department of extra-mural studies in the life of the universities. This is a real problem. Though the universities have a duty to the adult population with regard to education, their own departments of Adult Education are often at a disadvantage within the structure of the universities. Most of the departments of extra-mural studies in the post-war period were short of senior administrative staff as well as of tutors. Of the full-time tutors (304 of them in 1966) there were fewer opportunities for them to become senior lecturers and readers than for internal staff. Many of the staff of extra-mural departments find themeslves confined to the periphery of university life with the result that they move to the security of an internal department when the opportunity arises.

ii   It seems also that in England and Wales the urban areas are catered for more thoroughly than the rural areas. A man or woman who lives in rural Yorkshire or Mid-Wales has less opportunity than the town or city dweller. This is expected. But the haphazard method of supplying opportunities is a more serious fault. Small market towns in Yorkshire, like Easingwold, Helmsley and Kirby Moorside were ignored for twenty years (from 1951 to 1971), while towns of similar size like Tadcaster or Wetherby were better provided. The south-eastern area of Yorkshire was not very well provided, and Pontefract and Castleford had only one course each in 1971. Seventy six per cent of the University of Leeds department of extra-mural courses in 1971 were concentrated in three centres, Leeds, Bradford or Middlesbrough. Nottingham extra-mural department held 50% of its classes at six centres in 1965-66, and half of the Hull extra-mural department's programmes were held in Hull, York or Grimsby (Averg, 1975, p.14). The explanation for this is that most of these cities had an Adult Education Centre and one finds that there is a better response in an area if a centre is situated there. Adults can identify themselves with a centre.

iii   Vacation courses, such as residential summer schools at home, and study courses/tours abroad have become an integral part of the department of extra-mural studies programme for each year. Even an extra-mural department like Aberystwyth, which caters for a predominantly rural area, has arranged study tours in Germany, Austria and Italy. (A tremendous breakthrough was achieved in the International Summer School held by the extra-mural department of the University of London at the Isle of Thorias in 1966). London had held summer schools of English for overseas students since 1904 (Knowles, 1964, pp.3-18).

All this indicates that the departments of extra-mural studies and adult education in England and Wales do provide a wide range of options for the educated adults. They provide in particular for two groups in need of continuing education. The first group is those who seek professional recognition or vocational training, and who can make use of the provision offered at so many of the departments of extra-mural studies. The second group desires continuing education because it will give them an opportunity to continue their formal education beyond the undergraduate or graduate level, or in fields different from their earlier studies. To apply the term 'disadvantaged' to such a group would be inappropriate, but personal development, interest and satisfaction, with no immediate vocational outcome, have always been important objectives in the history of adult education and one would argue that the universities serve the aims of continuing education when they cater for this élitist group. David Thomson saw the task of the universities in the post-war period in terms of equipping the élite as ambassadors of continuing education. Thomson states the task of university education in terms of sending out "into the professions and into the world of business and industry, a steady stream of men and women who have savoured enough of the academic life and outlook to leaven the community with its intellectual integrity and its disinterested passion for truth, its critical spirit and its ability to examine evidence objectively, its love of culture and beauty for their own sake" (Thomson, *Listener,* 13 January 1949, p.46).

The best example of an university or a department as an institution of continuing education is the Open University. The objects of the Open University, stated in the Charter, clearly required it to provide continuing education:

> The objects of the university shall be the advancement and dissemination of learning and knowledge by teaching and research, by a diversity of means such as broadcasting and technological devices appropriate to higher education, by correspondence tuition, residential courses and seminars and in other relevant ways and shall be to provide education of university and professional standards for its students, and to promote the educational well-being of the community generally.

The Open University was a great innovation for it brought university education within the grasp of people who would never be able to attend an university. It made use of television as a medium of learning, though it is debatable if they have succeeded on this score, and it must also be pointed out that it was the universities who prepared the way for this. One can mention Ulster television's successful Midnight Oil series in 1964, and others followed in East Anglia and the East Midlands. Reginald Freeson argued in 1965 in terms of setting up television 'annexe' courses run by extra-mural departments of universities. He envisaged the local centres staffed in polytechnics or secondary schools and linked to the local universities (Freeson, 1965, p.20). but the 'annexe' idea was taken over by the Open University in their local centres housed in colleges and polytechnics.

The introduction of the Open University undergraduate programme represented a broadening of access, as regards age, place and entry requirements, which made a university level of qualification and its attendant status available for the first time through an open system. When one considers the unwillingness of many a department of extra-mural studies to experiment from the traditional tutorial/session set-up the undergraduate teaching at the Open University was an unbelievable step forward. The university offered printed materials prepared for adults by course teams brought together for that particular purpose, often of an interdisciplinary nature of great relevance to adults in modern society. In many courses the printed materials are supplemented by home experiment kits and the use of a wide network of computer terminals. The television and radio programmes produced and transmitted by the BBC penetrate to very nearly all parts of the United Kingdom and provide a support for, and a commentary of, the printed materials. In every region there are local centres where the student can attend for 20 weeks of the year and meet his tutor/counsellor who marks his essays and guides the student in the course. During the first four years of its existence the Open University operated a somewhat different pattern for the student had a tutor in his course and another person to look after his counselling problems. In 1976 the tutorial and counselling roles were amalgamated. At the centre the student meets his fellow students and they are able usually in an informal learning atmosphere — usually through discussion rather than the formal lecture-type atmosphere of a WEA or university extension class — to discuss their problems as well as the correspondence they have received from the headquarters of the Open University in Walton Hall, Milton Keynes. The distance learner who does not wish, or who cannot attend the study centre, is usually contacted through telephone, tape or extra correspondence. He or she will (again some are excused on health or domestic grounds) attend a summer school of a week's duration, held at one of the redbrick universities like Keele, York, Warwick, Nottingham and Sussex. These summer schools gave added opportunity for the adult to receive more of the traditional tuition through formal lecturing as well as a chance of conducting projects, laboratory, experimental and field work. Progress is assessed by the continuous assessment of students' assignments, and by an examination for each year's course for a full or half credit. The student has a great deal of freedom with regard to the subjects he chooses as well as the number of years he takes to complete his bachelor's degree. He has to gain a number of credits and if he wants to pursue an honours course he has to gain more credits at appropriate levels. The standard of the courses is high, much higher than anything done in any other institution of adult education, and this has ensured a wide acceptance of the Open University's role in the continuing education of adults.

The Open University has also short courses on the model of the diploma and certificate courses of the extra-mural departments. These courses are called the post-experience courses, and they include a. in-service training for teachers; b. a course of courses in the 'caring-services' sector; and c. experimental short courses, some new, others drawn from existing course

177

material. At the same time the post-experience course unit has included in its post-experience programme a number of undergraduate courses which is felt are appropriate to offer to students outside the undergraduate degree programme. As well as its undergraduate and post-experience programmes, the Open University continues to make a modest but growing contribution towards continuing education at the post-graduate level through its higher degree programme.

The role of the universities within continuing education is at present haphazard and unplanned. Adult education within the university is not given priority and continuing education is hardly mentioned. In the middle fifties the figure for public expenditure on extra-mural work (1956-7) was £630,700 (*Outlook,* Winter, 1961, p.1). The concern for finance is mentioned in every department of extra-mural studies report. There is no doubt that the setting up of the Open University has given adult education and continuing education a booster, and in particular through the harnessing of technology (for example, television, radio, telephone, video and audio cassettes) to achieve fruitful and successful individual study which allows variety and flexibility. But again this does not go far enough and the Open University needs additional resources to improve and extend learning opportunities generally to adults. The universities including their extra-mural departments as well as the Open University are still only scratching the surface of the need for continuing education, and the ideal expressed in paragraph 3 of the Russell Report which has still not been implemented:

> Our vision is of a comprehensive and flexible service of adult education, broad enough to meet the whole range of educational needs of the adult in our society. It must therefore be integrated with all the other sectors of the educational system but at the same time firmly rooted in the active life of local communities; and it must be readily accessible to all who need it, whatever their means or circumstances. Only in such terms can we conceive of education "as a process continuing throughout life".

The ideal remains valid but the implementation of the philosophy has been postponed, as we have seen in this chapter. Very little was learnt from the actual situation in the post-war period but what was learnt (in the context of the Open University) was new and exciting.

Chapter 6
The Contribution of Broadcasting to Adult Education

Broadcasting has opened up the process of education to the majority of adults. It brings education into every workplace, institution or home, and there is no limit to its potential. Adult education has accepted the challenge of television and the Universities Council for Adult Education set up a broadcasting sub-committee in 1960. Why should adult education take note of broadcasting? There are a number of reasons.

The first obvious reason is that the educative influence of broadcasting is enormous. At one time or another in the late sixties during each day at least thirty million people watched television, and over eighteen million people listened to the radio (Lowe, 1970, p.204). Sir Robert Fraser, Director-General of the Independent Television Authority went further in 1966 when he stated: "There are rather more than 50 million people in the United Kingdom, and rather more than 45 million of them have television in their homes" (Fraser, 1966, p.2). Even in the evenings there is still an average radio audience of one and a half million people. One can grasp the significance of this as far as education is concerned by putting it in another way. The number of viewers for a single programme televised on one occasion is as great as the total number visiting the most popular art exhibition in London over a period of several weeks. It was estimated that nine millions viewed the documentary in 1967, on Robots, while only 460,000 over a ten week period visited the Tate Galleries to look at the paintings of Picasso in 1960 (Long, 1968, pp.76-77).

The audience for television programmes are more respresentative of the population as a whole. Fifty per cent of the audience for BBC science series were working class viewers compared with seventy per cent of the whole population.

Television and radio reaches the working class adult in a way that no other medium is able to achieve. For the impact of the mass media on what has been called the 'after-work man' is obvious. The important thing is to know what the 'after-work man' is like — yet very little study has been done on this as Brech points out:

> It is known that most people after a day's work are in such a psycho-physiological condition that they need leisure (in its true sense) to recuperate — as a compensation — yet their condition is such they are unable to participate actively in leisure activities.
> (Brech, 1963, p.83).

One reason for the acceptance of television then is the psycho-physiological after-work condition. Television has also brought to the manual worker the same kind of programme as the middle class and the upper class can view. It contacts all people, irrespective of class, income and to some extent nationality.

People of different social and cultural backgrounds see the same films, the same T.V. shows, hear the same radio programmes, the same gramophone records, etc., and in this way class barriers are broken down. All people become the same consumers, so that mass media helps in the creation of a one-class society. (Brech, 1963, p.183).

While there are sociologists who would dispute that mass media has created a 'one class society' there is no denying that broadcasting has opened the horizons for a large number of people.

The second reason why broadcasting is of value in the education of adults is that the national television and radio networks have unique possibilities for transmitting educational material. Both the BBC and the Independent Television companies contribute to the education of adults, and the Pilkington Committee in their valuable report on broadcasting distinguished between particular programmes which were unquestionably educative on the one hand and on the other programmes which are directly educational. Sir George R. Barnes (1904-1960) in October 1950 was appointed to the newly created post of Director of Television, and he immediately set to work in introducing programmes which were unquestionably educative as well as programmes which conveyed specific information. The daily news and newsreel programme was inaugurated in July 1954. Barnes in that year stressed the need for a second channel for the BBC in order to cater for the varying tastes of the public. He emphasised the need to keep standards. "To seek success in popularity alone is a trivial use of a great invention. Mass without mind always comes a cropper . . ." (Gilliam, 1971, p.68).

Ten years later, in April 1964, the BBC launched a second television channel (BBC 2) which had spread to most of England and Wales by 1966. This channel, like the Third Programme, has been very conscious of the educative role. It is interesting that the man who was put in charge of the Third Programme when it was established in 1946 was George Reginald Barnes. He aimed at the highest standards in both programme and performance, and an example of this in the early beginning was the series of programmes broadcast in 1948 on the 'Ideas and Beliefs of the Victorians'. George R. Barnes believed that public taste needs guiding, that it should be led, not followed. Coupled with this belief was his sense of responsibility towards listener minorities and the complex needs of each individual listener (Gilliam, 1971, p.67).

For broadcasting to be effective as an educative process it depends a great deal on outstanding communicators. Broadcasting has been aided by some very effective communicators. A few examples can be mentioned. The name of Gilbert Charles Harding (1907-1960) must appear when referring to communicators. He became the best-known performer in the United Kingdom after the second world war. Harding was a flamboyant person who could not suffer fools gladly, but who was able to communicate effectively as a broadcaster in an educational sense. As quiz master in 'Round Britain Quiz', 'Brains Trust', 'Twenty Questions' and the television programme

'What's My Line?' Harding concealed the fact that every successful educator has to give of his erudition and knowledge. Sir Henry Maxmillian (Max) Beerbohm (1872-1956) was another communicator who applied himself diligently to the task of a broadcaster. In this wholly modern medium Sir Henry Maximillian Beerbohm as poet and cartoonist made an extraordinary success. Some of his broadcasts were published in *Mainly on the Air* in 1946, and in an enlarged edition in 1957. He was undoubtedly the best essayist, parodist and cartoonist of his age, and his extraordinary talents were often used in the service of broadcasting (Cecil, 1971, p.78). During the last decade of his life William John Brown (1894-1960), who was returned as an Independent Member of Parliament for Rugby in 1945, became known as a broadcaster and television performer, appearing often on the programme 'Free Speech' (Hollis, 1971, p.152). These are only a few examples from a number of communicators who have been successful as broadcasters in programmes of an educational nature.

It was a Director General of the BBC, Sir William Haley, who said that the highest duty was the 'search for truth'. The British Broadcasting Corporation and an Independent Television networks have been able to fulfil this ideal in a great number of their educative programmes. A few examples of such programmes can be mentioned, such as *Panorama,* which in the late sixties had a weekly audience of six million; and then *This Week* on ITV reinforced by special documentary programmes and *News at Ten; Nine o'clock News* and discussions on BBC 2 are other examples. The Independent Television networks have improved their educative programmes and many of their documentaries are of an exceptionally high standard. In the early sixties it was believed that the more education a person received the more likely was he to view British Broadcasting Corporation programmes and the less likely to view Independent Television, but since then the Independent Television has improved a great deal with its general programmes. In 1969 over 200 hours of transmission time on Independent Television were devoted to programmes which are classified as adult education. The range of topics covered was wide, including subjects in fields as diverse as cookery, sociology and language classes, keep-fit, geography and post-graduate medicine. This wide diversity of subject matter arose, according to the ITV, as a consequence of three main factors. Firstly, the known or assumed interests in different educational topics of the potential audience; secondly, an appraisal by the Independent Television Authority and its educational advisers of the role of television in national educational policy; and thirdly, the varied regional structure of Independent Television which gives programme companies an opportunity to serve local interests and needs and to co-operate with the universities and other educational institutions within their regions.

To formulate an effective policy, Independent Television Authorities decided to undertake extensive research into the educational interests and preferences of the viewing public. The result of this research has far reaching implications for adult education. It was found that most of the sample (82%) of 1,850 adults were interested in subject areas which dealt with the home and the family, but there were other subjects of high interests, such as the sciences, history and geography, travel, religion, philosophy and human sciences stand with literature and language, as we can see in the following table.

Net Interest Levels

(The percentage of all respondents who "would definitely watch" at least one of the topics in a group)

Group		"Would definitely watch"	No. of topics in groups
1	Home and family	82%	26
	Safety in the Home*	44%	1
2	The Sciences	64%	16
3	History and Geography	59%	10
	Travel*	42%	1
4	Home Maintenance	56%	3
5	The Arts	48%	8
6	Law and Government	47%	12
7	Hobbies	47%	8
8	Theatre	45%	4
9	Careers	44%	13
	Education*	29%	1
10	Current and World Affairs	29%	1
11	Local Affairs	39%	3
12	The Car	39%	2
13	Religion, Philosophy and Human Sciences	35%	6
14	Literature	27%	5
15	Languages	13%	6
			126

Note 1* *Safety in the Home, Travel* and *Education* are extracted from the total groups because of their all-embracing nature.

Continued

Continued from previous page

2 For purpose of analysis, the 126 topics were places in fifteen groups comprising general areas of interest.

Table 6.1

The respondents also preferred to treat each topic at an elementary level rather than at a more advanced level. Over the whole range of groups of topics 65% of the public wanted the topics treated at a 'fairly elementary level' and 35% at a more 'advanced level'. Those who were interested in 'The Car' and 'Literature' tended to wish for a more advanced level of treatment than average — although even in these cases more than one respondent in two wished for an elementary treatment.

The survey also shows that the working class is more interested in the home and family than any other social group, and that languages is the only subject matter that has very little appeal.

Social Grade
"Would definitely watch" (one or more topics in group)

		ABC1	C2	DE
		%	%	%
1	Home and Family	81	83	84
2	The Sciences	65	65	62
3	History and Geography	63	59	53
4	Home Maintenance	47	60	61
5	The Arts	55	47	41
6	Law and Government	48	50	43
7	Hobbies	48	48	43
8	Theatre	51	42	40
9	Careers	48	47	35
10	Current and World Affairs	50	40	36
11	Local Affairs	41	38	37
12	The Car	39	43	33
13	Religion, Philosophy, and Human Sciences	37	34	33
14	Literature	34	25	22
15	Languages	18	11	9

The social groupings were divided as follows:

Continued

Continued from previous page

ABC1: Upper middle, middle, and lower middle class (32% of population)

(Occupations ranging from higher managerial to clerical and junior managerial).

C2: Skilled working class (41% of population) (Skilled manual workers).

DE: Working class, and those at the lowest subsistence levels (27% of population) (Semi and unskilled manual workers, state pensioners and casual workers).

Table 6.2

The British Market Research Bureau also looked in detail at the constitution of each of the topic groups with the rank order of interest level for all respondents on each individual topic, and the audience to whom the group is of greatest appeal.

Group 1:

Safety in the Home	44%	Physical Fitness	19%
Health	35%	Dressmaking	18%
First Aid	34%	Consumer Advice	17%
Cookery	32%	Flower Arrangement	16%
Care of Old People	32%	Motherhood	16%
Dancing	31%	Needlework	15%
Budgeting in the Home	27%	Domestic Science	15%
Fashion	27%	Hairdressing	15%
Sensible Shopping	27%	Knitting	15%
Child Development	27%	Beauty Culture	12%
Child Psychology	25%	Nutrition	12%
Handicrafts	20%	Embroidery	9%
Nursing	19%	Etiquette	8%
		Tailoring	7%

Table 6.3

This table indicates that safety in the home is a subject which is of great importance and most of the subjects are of primary interest to women and to heavy viewers of television.

Group 2: 'The Sciences'

Nature	27%	Biology	10%
Medicine	22%	Astronomy	9%
Progress in Space	20%	Electronics	9%
Scientific Developments	19%	Mathematics	8%
Zoology	18%	Botany	7%
Engineering	13%	Physics	6%
Farming	12%	Chemistry	5%
Atomic Power	12%	Statistics	5%

Table 6.4

This second group of topics was of greater interest to men than to women. It is probably true that the high interest level of the first five items stems from a wish for programmes which are descriptive of the topics in question, rather than any systematic study of their content from an educational viewpoint. Medicine clearly cannot be *studied* through television (except by those already qualified), although it is high in interest for viewers; and Zoology almost certainly connotes 'animal programmes'.

Group 3: 'History and Geography'

Travel	42%	History	18%
Foreign Ways of Life	22%	British History	17%
Stately Homes	22%	Famous Buildings	16%
British Achievements	19%	Geography	14%
Famous People	19%	Great English Men	13%
		Archaeology	11%

Table 6.5

Travel is a subject of wide general interest and in a somewhat different category from the remainder of the topic group. As an area of topics 'History and Geography' is of greatest interest to those whose full-time education ended at the age of 16 or over — the most educated sector of the public.

Group 4: 'Home Maintenance'

Do it Yourself	39%	Electricity in the Home	24%
Home Decoration	36%		

Table 6.6

The average interest level for the topics within this group is highest of all among the groups, standing at 33%: all topics are significantly about the general level of interest (15%). The group is of highest interest to those who have left school at fifteen or younger, but have subsequently undertaken further study, to men, and to heavy television viewers.

Group 5: 'The Arts'

Antiques	21%	Design	10%
Classical Music	15%	Painting	10%
Jazz	12%	Architecture	7%
Art	11%	Sculpture	4%

Table 6.7

Antiques in the sixties was very popular in the W.E.A. syllabus, and this is another indicator of its appeal. The Arts are of greater interest to middle and upper-middle class viewers, with the greatest amount of full-time education.

Group 6: 'Law and Government'

Taxation	20%	Civil Defence	8%
Law and the Citizen	18%	Economics	8%
Government	14%	British Constitution	7%
Politics	14%	Foreign Trade	7%
Town Planning	11%	Public Finance	7%
Law	10%	Public Administration	5%

Table 6.8

This group demonstrates that taxation and the law are problems affecting every citizen and that 'the vocational aspect' has always a high appeal to an adult. The topic group is of greatest interest to men and to those who have left school by the age of fifteen but have studied later.

Group 7: 'Hobbies'

Gardening	26%	Ornithology	7%
Bird Watching	15%	Pottery	7%
Photography	12%	Stamp Collecting	5%
Angling	10%	Philately	3%

Table 6.9

The high interest in Gardening is borne out by other studies, such as the *Reader's Digest European Surveys 1963*, which showed that 45% of the population in Great Britain attended to the garden at least once a week, and that 73% had a private garden. Hobbies also have a definite appeal, and television viewing can lead to other interests. It is by no means the passive activity that it is so often assumed to be. Another point worth mentioning is that an appeal of subject depends to some extent on the title. The higher interest in *Bird Watching* than in *Ornithology* and in *Stamp Collecting* than in *Philately* suggests the importance of simple descriptions in naming of topics when communicating with a cross section of the general public.

Group 8: 'Theatre'

Theatre	26%	Ballet	15%
Drama	25%	Opera	11%

Table 6.10

This group was of greatest interest to older people and women.

Group 9: 'Careers'

Education	29%	Marketing	8%
Careers	15%	Business Administration	7%
Industrial Developments	12%	Technical Drawing	6%
Computers	11%	Business Law	6%
Industrial Relations	9%	Industrial Law	6%
Business Management	8%	Office Methods	5%
Finance	8%	Draughtsmanship	4%

Table 6.11

This topic group dealing with business and professional skills has a markedly higher interest for men than for women. It is of greatest interest to the 25-44 year olds, and to those whose full-time education has extended longest. Also one has the attraction of using television to acquire new knowledge of vocational application — and in particular to those who have been more accustomed to systematic study.

Groups 10 and 11: 'Current and World Affairs'

Current Affairs	31%	International Politics	9%
World Affairs	27%		

Table 6.12

The interest profile of group 11 is similar to that for the previous Group 10, although there is not quite such an increase in interest as one goes up the social grade scale.

Group 12: 'The Car'

Safe Driving	33%	Car Maintenance	23%

Table 6.13

This area of interest was almost exclusively male, and also associated with a relatively high demand for treatment at a fairly advanced level (47%).

Group 13: 'Religion, Philosophy and Human Sciences'

Race Relations	184	Comparitive Religion	7%
Religion	14%	Sociology	6%
Psychology	9%	Philosophy	4%

Table 6.14

As confirmed in other studies (for example, Michael Argyle, *Religious Behaviour* (1958); *Television and Religion* (1964) religion, philosophy and the human sciences are of greater interest to women than to men and to those whose television viewing is above average in amount. It also has a definite appeal to the younger adult viewer.

Group 14: 'Literature'

Good English	16%	World Literature	8%
English Language	11%	Poetry	4%
English Literature	10%		

Table 6.15

Interest in this topic area is very highly correlated with the present standard of education of the respondent: it is markedly higher at the upper social levels and among those whose education extended to the age of 16 or over. Women are more interested in literature than men (except in certain areas like the Welsh countryside where you find a group of poets in small hamlets, such as Ffair-Rhos in the heartland of Cardiganshire in the new county of Dyfed). Those who view less television are more interested in literature than the average, or above average, viewer.

Group 15: 'Languages'

Languages	6%	Spanish	3%
French	5%	Italian	2%
German	4%	Russian	2%

Table 6.16

The final group is also as it happens the lowest in net interest level. It comes as a surprise that foreign languages, an area of wide popularity in institutional adult education, stand so low in interest among the public as a whole. There was wide divergences between sections of the population in the degree of interest expressed: relatively much higher among the younger and inter-mediate age groups, among the upper-middle and middle social classes, and among those whose full-time education lasted longest. Lighter viewers of television are higher in interest than others, and women marginally more than men: but languages remain a minority interest.

These research findings are most important as they a. ratify or correct expert opinion about the interests of the adult audience, b. they demonstrate respects in which these interests coincide with and diverge from the known interests of students, c. they reveal what people consciously identify as their main interests, so that they may be approached in terms of these, and d. they could be relevant to a purposive strategy of programming, in that they demonstrate not only the relative popularity of major topic groups, but also the likely composition of the audience for different subjects within those groups.

This survey indicates that educational programmes can be popular if they have the necessary ingredients, that is, simple and clear presentation, a catching title and relevance to the audience. In any continuing education system the results of this research have to be taken into consideration, and it does show also that a great deal of progress has been achieved. This survey also upholds the idea that television could be used for educational purposes in two ways. It may be employed to make good basic deficiencies in the educational system. Or it may be used to improve the efficiency of that system. Italy is the only advanced European country which has used television extensively to make up for the absence of educational provision. The Italian Telescuola has provided adult viewers in the impoverished south since 1958 with basic literacy courses (Fraser, 1966, p.9). Apart from such striking exceptions most educational television has been for improved efficiency rather than for remedying deficiency.

Broadcasting is immensely important in the education of adults and in particular in continuing education. It is a medium that is at work all the time, every day of the week and every day of the year. It is accessible to everyone and everybody, and for the first time in history our technical means of communication has caught up with the scale of modern industrial mass

189

society. This is an event of significance to adult education, and we know that more and more adults in Britain are daily educated through the news bulletin and other broad current affair programmes, such as *Nationwide, Tonight,* and in the Welsh language news programmes, the BBC *Heddiw* and the Harlech television *Y Dydd.*

The survey that we have looked at also suggests that those people who make most use of television are the people who make least use of other means of information and entertainment like books, theatres, concerts. The French speak of mass communication as the parallel school, and they suggest that there are now for the student outside and alongside the school, sources of knowledge and educational influence every bit as rich, as varied, and very often much more attractive than anything the tutor can offer. We have seen throughout this book that the adult education movement has always been motivated by a concern for the disadvantaged or the underpivileged. But it has been obvious that the WEA and other voluntary movements have not been able to tackle this need as they would have wished, or indeed, to have enrolled these people in any great number. Television, however, does reach them, even the mobile gypsies. Stewart E. Males, who has been in charge of the Hertfordshire Travelling School, writes in 1977 that most of the gypsy children are on the brink of literacy through exposure to television (Males, 1977, p.20). Lord Hill of Luton argued that television reaches the disadvantaged, the underprivileged, because it does not just offer a 'second chance' to enter the academic system. It offers them, he said, entry to an alternative system (Hill, 1966, p.3). They willingly attend the parallel school. How are we to evaluate television in the concept of adult education and continuing education?

The evaluation is most difficult as Jack C. Everly has indicated in a thought-provoking article on *The Evaluation of Continuing Education via T.V.* Everly maintains that television is not a continuing education system but rather an act of communication (Everly, 1971, p.84). While this is true on the evaluation side, it is not true on the other side of the coin, that is, the impact of television programmes on the general public.

There are two other strands in broadcasting which have to be mentioned. Firstly, the possibilities of education through local radio, or as Rachel Powell puts it, "education and the community". Local radio stations opened in 1967 and though Frank Gillard's vision of a "radio station in every city" has not materialised, local radio offers itself for educational purposes. While some local radio stations have experimented a great deal many of the suggestions put forward in the middle sixties have never been tried. Rachel Powell wrote a pamphlet, *Possibilities for Local Radio* (1966), and her ideas have not been implemented. Rachel Powell wrote of such an original, novel initiative as "radio" homework, aligned to correspondence or evening courses at the centre. She continues:

This could be angled not only at the registered students, but also at their wives, mothers and friends, with the idea that the best means of learning is to have to explain one's study to others. Also, of course, many of the wives and mothers will find it difficult to learn, unless teaching is brought informally into the home. (Powell, 1965, p.14).

Rachel Powell's idea has been largely taken up by the Open University. But that does not excuse the local radio stations from making much more use of the continuing education philosophy. It has an unique possibility for transmitting educational material, and it seems that, given the right economic climate, new local radio stations as well as the proposed fourth channel might be used to increase the provision of broadcasting for continuing education. It will be necessary to do everything possible to improve communications between different providers of adult education, and between adult educators and other parts of the educational system.

The second strand is the Open University. It is a system that deserves a place in our study as we did in the last chapter as it is so unbritish. The Open University has been described quite appropriately as the "most important innovation in British Education in the last half century". (Groombridge, 1976, p.42). The Open University devised, in partnership with the BBC, patterns of working relationships among academics and educational broadcasters that were new to the United Kingdom. But the relationship drew upon other experiments in the past. A number of these experiments were significant precursors of the Open University. Professor Harold Wiltshire, Head of the Department of Adult Education at Nottingham University from 1946 to 1974, was responsible for one of the most important experiments, namely a collaboration between the university and Associated Television. In 1962 Ulster Television had co-operated with Queen's University, Belfast, in an ambitious project to give viewers an impression of a range of university disciplines — forty-two half-hour programmes on medicine, law, literature, music, physics, history and economics. In 1962 Michael Young, who had already mooted the idea of an Open University in an article in *Where* (No. 10, Autumn 1962) under the title, *Is your Child in the Unlucky Generation.*, and was about to launch the National Extension College, inspired a project called Dawn University, described as "a week of 45-minute lectures at undergraduate level produced by Anglia Television in collaboration with the Cambridge Television Committee as an experiment in extending the lecture room to a wider audience". It showed what could be done, and this was followed by what is now called the Nottingham Experiment, when the Leverhulme Trust gave a grant to ATV in co-operation with the University of Nottingham Adult Education Department, to produce thirteen twenty-minute programmes on economics. These were transmitted between 27th September and 21st December 1964. Those who enrolled paid a fee, in return for which they were given a handbook and assigned a tutor. The conclusions of the research were published jointly by the National Institute of Adult Education and the University of Nottingham. A great number of things were

191

noted which are relevant to adult education but from which the adult education movement learnt very little. There were four points:

1   a television course has its charisma. It can recruit and also keep people interested for the whole course. A difficult proposition for any adult education course.

2   it was obvious that television attracted adults who would not be interested in the traditional adult education classes.

3   it was found possible to teach effectively through television provided it was coupled with active learning and brought students into contact with tutors.

4   the argument about peak times on television was also demolished. It was not necessary to televise at peak times to get good results. Wiltshire and Baylish, who wrote the report, *Teaching through Television,* argued that "tele-teaching should be recognized as a normal method of adult and further education and that a regular service of 'tele-courses' should be established under the control of a body of education: for instance, a National Centre for Broadcasting Education could be formed".

A great deal of this has not been implemented even by the Open University, and substantiates our thesis that adult education is very slow to learn and implement the results of research, and concepts have rarely been modified by facts. The Nottingham experiment, as Brian Groombridge points out, was concerned with quality teaching in one or two subjects rather than a whole degree course (Groombridge, 1976, p.45). This idea is more in line with the Open School which has been partially put into operation in Belgium, or the Open College idea which has been debated for a few years in the Netherlands and Britain.

Television has a great deal to offer adult education. Its accessibility has been noted and its universality is also an important factor for as the Nottingham experiment demonstrated in 1964, it enables adult educators to speak to people who would never be reached by the normal methods of recruitment. The success of the Open University indicates what can be done when there is a will and a determination on the part of a national government for the plan to be fulfilled. But the Open University experiment has shown also how much needs to be done. There is need to evaluate in depth a large number of important points:

i   To explore the possibilities of learner-based provision;

ii   to look at the educational possibilities of new developments in technology;

iii   to maintain the principle of interdependence between autonomous agencies and interests. Interdependence always proves to be a promoter of change both in provision and attitude;

iv   to co-ordinate the present diversity of provision;

v   to look at the decisions which are at present carried out in the name of educational broadcasting;

vi   to study the structures outlined by the Russell Committee in 1973, and in particular the following argument:

> We are arguing not only for an increase in broadcast time for adult education but for an increase sufficient to make it possible to create what we have called analogies to the Open University at a lower academic level. By this term we mean multi-media systems combining teaching at a distance with face-to-face tuition, some relatively permanent, others transitory or perhaps ephemeral. It is not likely and not necessarily desirable that a permanent institution or a range of institutions like the Open University should be created for adult education below degree level. What is desirable is not a super-organization but an organizational framework. Within such a framework learning systems could be established involving different media and agencies, despite the logistical and organizational problems known to be associated with this kind of enterprise . . .

There is already a good basis for this framework, both in the Open University experience, the Nottingham experience, and other similar projects, and the projects which have been implemented over the years by the British Broadcasting Corporation in television, radio and local radio as well as in the television networks of the Independent Broadcasting Association companies. But adult education has to learn from the research and the experiments and implement the findings for the good of all adults.

Chapter 7
The Needs of Particular Groups for Adult Education

Group or Community Needs

During the fifties and sixties adult education organisations began to concentrate upon the collective needs of more or less homogeneous groups, or at least of groups which share communities. This is a delicate subject for the educational provision is geared to minorities rather than to the majority of the population. We will look at a number of minorities, some racial and some not, but all of them in need of adult education. They have special needs which often can be overlooked, and one of the best examples of a minority which was ignored in our period was the Gypsy population.

i   Gypsy Education

The Gypsy population poses a number of problems for adult educationists. In the first place it is virtually impossible to know the number of gypsies that are travelling in England and Wales. The 1965 Census identified 3,400 gypsy families in England and Wales but new counts, notably in the West Midlands, provided evidence that by 1976 the number could be 7,000 families or some say 35,000 people. These figures refer to the number of travellers who are still nomadic as opposed to those who have settled in houses over the years.

Estimated proportions receiving education nationally in the middle seventies was as follows:

Pre-School   5 - 7 per cent

Primary   40 per cent

Secondary   10 - 12 per cent

Adult   1 - 2 per cent

(Source: Buckland, *Trends in Education,* 1977, (1) p.4).

The reasons for this lack of concern are obvious. Gypsies do not fit into the neat categories of our settled society. They are not householders and so do not pay rates. Because they are nomadic it is difficult to collect income tax or national insurance contributions from them — a difficulty which is intensified by their social isolation. Most make a living by collecting what others throw away, these characteristics of the traveller way of life — the common non-payment of taxes and the trading in waste materials are sometimes labelled as 'parasitic'. This label suggests that gypsies choose to 'live off the backs' of others, whereas, on the contrary, they strongly desire to be independent and self-employed. The second reason is more relevant for adult educationists and that is the illiteracy of the gypsies. Illiteracy is a tremendous handicap. A gypsy has no idea of what is provided for him and very little effort is made to educate him. It has been estimated that over 90% of the gypsy population are illiterate (Buckland, 1977, p.4). Language is another difficulty. Travellers tend to run words together, mispronounce some, use their own words interspersed with English. It seems that in the main they have welcomed the provision made by the local education authorities since the passing of the Caravan Sites Act in 1968 to provide education for the gypsy children. But the provision is not widespread and continuing education philosophy has taught us that for the scheme to be successful an effort has to be made also to educate the parents. There have been examples of enlightened policies by the local education authorities. Somerset, for example, in the seventies had two mobile classrooms which allowed four teachers to visit gypsy camps with books, toys, playgroup equipment and literacy material. The aim was to provide family education so that adults and children could receive educational assistance. Both need education.

Worthwhile educational projects have sprung also from voluntary initiatives. The West Midland Travellers' School has been able to involve gypsy mothers to attend a playgroup leaders' course, and to set up their own playgroups. It has also undertaken adult literacy work supported by a grant from the Adult Literacy Resource Agency. Literacy work has many problems to cope with and the main is the resentment of the gypsies to officials and bureaucracy. Many of the rights exercised by local authorities, such as the power to close his traditional stopping places, he sees as an attack on his way of life, and as an attempt to prevent him making a living. Gypsies also resent the attempt to prevent them from collecting together quantities of scrap in unauthorised places, the requirement that as scrap dealers (metal) they must be licensed, and the serving on them of nuisance abatement notices under the Public Health Act. The result, over the years, of the continual brushes with authority is that the traveller has developed a deep distrust of other people which is a difficult hurdle for adult education. It seems from the experience of teaching gypsy children that a mobile adult education unit is essential to reach a group which is continually moving or being forced to move.

The other hurdle is the attitude of the gypsies to education, and in particular to adult education and even to the basic skill of all education, the ability to read and write. It can be said that the majority of gypsy adults actually survive extremely well without it, and are not particularly concerned that their children should acquire such skills. To some gypsies the ability to read and write comes low on their list of priorities, while others genuinely wish to see their children as well as themselves literate. But the attitude of the gypsies like the attitude of many other similar minorities can be summed up in one word: apathy or indifference.

A gypsy caravan in the main has very little of the tools of knowledge around such as books and magazines. There is no perseverance among them to master literacy. Adult gypsies expect instant results, and their plea to Stewart E. Males, the teacher in charge of the Hertfordshire Travelling School after the mobile unit was set up in 1975, was simply, "When you've got a spare ten minutes teach us to read" (Males, 1977, p.19). Males felt, however, that the contact with the parents was getting more and more important as time went on in the educational process of their children for the whole concept of education can be unacceptable to the children through the misconceived prejudice of the parents.

It seems also that the voluntary movements which are interested in the gypsy people and in gypsy education, namely the National Gypsy Education council (NGEC) and the Advisory Committee for the Education of the Romany and Other Travellers (ACERT), the National Gypsy Council and the Romany Guild, have to work together to persuade national and local authorities of the need for continuing education to this minority group in British society. It is also known that the Showmen's Guild is very interested in providing education for Fairground people and also circus people. Both ACERT and NGEC have been given grants by the Adult Literacy Resource Agency and in the seventies working parties were established and programmes prepared, aimed at bringing as much practical help as possible to adult gypsies. The Romany Guild purchased a double decker bus and equipped it as a mobile classroom so that teams could visit gypsy sites and start literacy schemes. Travellers were beginning slowly to respond and a genuine demand for literacy was evident to D.C. Buckland, HM Inspector with special responsibility for the education of travelling children. Buckland, however, is conscious that the provision amongst gypsies and their families is patchy, lacking co-ordination, and hardly touching on the predicament of the majority of travellers. He also explained and emphasises two points which are in line with the aim of continuing education, namely that in all projects educationists must work closely with the travellers themselves so as to involve them in "decision making" about "the trend of provision necessary", and "that a great deal needs to be done before the situation of travellers and their children can be regarded as at all satisfactory" (Buckland, 1977, p.8).

A great deal needs to be done in educating gypsies and it seems that very little has been learnt by adult educationists from the actual situation of these travelling people. It reinforces our central argument of how adult education concepts are rarely modified by facts, but if adult education is to have an impact on the gypsies, this has to happen.

ii Immigrants and Minorities

Many countries in Western Europe in the period after the second world war were faced with the task of absorbing immigrants and this was very true in Britain. Like the gypsies, there are no comprehensive official statistics about minorities but despite this, we have a great number of studies which enable us to present estimates of the larger minority groups.

The largest single minority group is the Irish. Looking at the 1966 Census we find that there are 698,000 Irish immigrants in England and Wales, though J.A. Jackson, in his book on *The Irish in Britain* (1963), estimates the Irish-born at over one million. The Jews follow next with a total of 410,000 estimated for 1965. The largest coloured minority is the Jamaican, numbering 273,800 in 1966 (E.J.B. Rose et al, 1969, p.99). If we put together all the coloured minorities the estimate for these given for 1968 is 1,113,000 (E.J.B. Rose et al, 1969, p.1). But this includes diverse groups which must be regarded as distinct minorities, such as 223,000 Indians, the 119,000 Pakistanis, and the 50,000 from West Africa, and 60,000 from the Far East. Other sizeable minority groups are the Poles who number about 130,000 (Zubrzycki, 1956, p.63), and the Cypriots about 100,000 (Oakley et al, 1968, p.23) .

Then come the smaller groups where we have no reliable estimates. Francesca Wilson has described many of these immigrants in her book, *They came as strangers* (1959). There were over 90,000 of these 'strangers' who settled in Britain after the second world war, and they included Ukrainians, Latvians, Lithunanians, Estonians, Czechs and other nationalities. Between 1956 and 1957 early 15,000 Hungarians settled, and in 1968 numbers of Czechs came as a result of excessive Soviet-inspired totalitarianism. At the same time there are other European nationalities such as Italians (96,000) living in Britain (Krauz, 1972, p.39). Ernest Krauz has summed up the numbers of the larger minority groups based on the 1966 Census for England and Wales in the following tables:

Size and Percentage of the Larger Minority Groups

Minority Group	Size	Per cent of population (in 1966 the total population of the ethnic and immigrant communities was 4 million)
Irish	2,000,000	4.2%
	(a very general estimate)	
West Indian	454,000	1.0%
Jewish	410,000	0.9%
Indian & Pakistani	359,000	0.8%
Polish	130,000	0.3%
Cypriot	100,000	0.2%

Table 7.1

These figures are important for they do indicate that all these groupings are very much in the minority. All the colour groups only represent 2.4% of the entire population. Adding together all the minority and immigrant groups (apart from the Ulstermen, Welsh and Scots) in 1966 in England and Wales we find the figure was somewhere around four and a quarter million, or 9% of the total population. But the other point is that so many of these immigrants have come since the second world war, the Irish and the Jews came in large numbers in the nineteenth and the first two decades of the twentieth century, while the European and the Commonwealth immigrants flocked in after 1945. In 1947 114,000 formed the Polish Resettlement Corps, thus opting to stay permanently in Britain, and this group had another 33,000 dependents brought over (Krauz, 1972, p.37). The period 1951-1961 saw a large influx of immigrants from the Commonwealth, mainly from the West Indies, India and Pakistan and Cyprus.

As we look at these differing and numerous minorities we find all the ingredients of the adult education scene: sketchy provision, apathy, voluntary efforts, experiments by the WEA and local education authorities, hostility and encouragement, and an inability to modify adult education concepts by the facts. The ethnic and coloured minorities do not pose a problem to most local authorities for the minorities congregate in large numbers in certain towns and cities. Of all the Irish in Britain one third live in London, over 10% in South East Lancashire and Merseyside, and over 8% in the West Midlands (Jackson, 1963, p.301). The story for Poles, Jews, Cypriots and other minorities is similar. The largest Polish community (of nearly 40,000 Poles) is to be found in London, and then comes Manchester, Bradford, Birmingham and Bristol (Zubrzycki, 1956, p.68f). The Italians, the Cypriots, the Chinese and the West Africans are mainly concentrated in London, besides the Soho and Clerkenwell districts. Bedford has a large Italian community numbering six or seven thousand (Huxley, 1964, p.69). The Cypriots are mostly concentrated in London and the Home Counties, but there is a large community in Liverpool. The West Africans are mainly in London and especially in Wandsworth, Kensington, and various parts of North-West London. As for the Jews, 68% live in the metropolis and 88% are concentrated in the six largest cities: London (280,000), Manchester (35,000), Leeds (20,000), Glasgow (13,000), Liverpool (7,000), and Birmingham (7,000). The Commonwealth immigrants are also attracted to London and cities lik Birmingham, Leicester, Nottingham, Preston, Blackburn, Bradford. These immigrants are found in large numbers in some areas, as, for example, 56% of the total Jamaican population in England and Wales is concentrated in 13 of the London boroughs (E.J.B. Rose et al, 1969, p.102).

A number of generalisations can be offered with regard to adult education and the ethnic and coloured minorities. Adult education agencies have not ignored the communities altogether but there is a certain reluctance on the part of both the 'host' community and the minority communities to see the need for continuing education directed at a specific group. The host community's attitude is often summed up in saying, 'These people should learn our ways when they come here', and the minority community's attitude can be summed up in their desire to preserve their own language, culture and customs. Both emphases need to be encouraged. Adult education should have courses to cater for the immigrants with regard to basic linguistic skills as well as on the immigrants' culture, language and traditions. Very little of both was attempted in 1945-1980 period. But there have been attempts as in Nottingham. In 1958 after racial tensions the local authorities in Nottingham appointed a West Indian, Mr. Eric Irons, as the organiser for educational work amongst the coloured immigrants. This was a good move for the majority of the coloured immigrants in Nottingham were West Indians. In 1954 it was as little as just over 1,000; by the end of the decade it was at least 6,000 and may have been as many as 10,000 (Noburn, 1972, p.298). Irons worked with the WEA East Midlands District and the Adult Education Department of Nottingham University in arranging educational activities for the coloured immigrants. A very successful partnership took place between the WEA and local education authority in provision for coloured immigrants throughout the sixties. But the experiment as good as it was suffered from the usual limitation associated with formal education of adults. It only attracted a small number of immigrants. By 1972 the immigrant population of Nottingham was estimated at 18,000 (5.9% of the whole population) and the local education authority and WEA were only catering for a tiny fraction (Norburn, 1972, p.302). The immigrant himself was not fired by the need for education, and the reason for this is very much tied up with immigration itself. Immigration is usually the result of economics, and the first concern of an immigrant in a new and sometimes hostile environment is to have a job and a home for his family. Many of those who showed interest were on shift work, and this accounted for the poor attendances at some of the classes. However, the tutors who were involved laid some emphasis on the informal aspect to the education scheme as a means of promoting racial harmony. This is stressed also in the findings of other similar experiments such as the work done in Oldham in Lancashire. Though very little was done by the authority in Oldham compared with Nottingham, it did organise an Urdu Class which attracted a number of social workers, teachers and police. The same thing happened in Nottingham when two Pakistanis were invited to conduct two courses in Urdu, and the courses were attended by English civil servants, local government officials and teachers. All of them felt the need to know something of the mother tongue of 3,000 of Nottingham's population.

Much more of this is needed, and such education should try to express the essential nature of pluralism.

It seems that the most ambitious attempt at educating an Immigrant community took place among the Polish community. The Polish Re-settlement Act of 1947 appointed a committee under the chairmanship of Sir George Gater to administer Polish education in Great Britain. For seven years (from April 1st, 1947 until September 30th, 1954) it co-ordinated the educational activities.

The Polish community in Britain had been well served during the war and this activity culminated in the autumn of 1946 in the Polish University College. The first Principal of the Polish University was Professor E.C. McAlpine who held office from 1947 until his death in 1950, and was

200

succeeded by Sir Harold Claughton, who held office for the rest of the life of the college. The college was served by a brilliant team of exiled Polish academics. Admission was by competitive examinations and all the students were adults. Each one of the men and women was an ex-service Polish veteran of the second world war. The student population was as follows:

1947-48	1,100 students
1948-49	981 students
1949-50	859 students
1950-51	719 students
1951-52	349 students
1952-53	183 students

The Polish University College had scattered premises, but the administrative offices of the college were centred at 5 Princes Gardens, London, SW7. It was an unique experience in adult education among an ethnic community and besides the lecturing, a great deal of informal education took place at the Students' Union and the Library of the Polish University College which was housed in Buckingham Palace Road. The student could choose any of the 65,000 volumes from the Library.

But this was not the only educational agency working among the Polish community. Grants were provided for vocational training at the School of Foreign Trade and Port Administration at London. Polish adults received in intensive training in commerce. Adult education took place also in Polish hostels and on the housing estates. The hostels which were National Assistance Board Hostels had an educational organiser whose task it was to organise English classes and promote other educational activities supplied by the WEA.

The achievements of the Committee in those seven years (1947-1954) was immense as one can see when reading the Report by the Ministry of Education, *Education in Exile* (1956). The work among adults could still be regarded as a blueprint for all immigrant and ethnic communities, and the achievement was summed up in this way:

> . . . they tackled the urgent problem of equipping humbler workers with a sufficient knowledge of English and with some understanding of the British way of life so that they might settle as fellow citizens in a new community. (*Education in Exile,* 1956, p.48).

Adult education provision is also being pursued by the immigrant and ethnic minorities themselves. A great deal of this informal educating process takes place around their place of worship. To the Jew the synagogue is a central point, to the Pakistani a mosque is important, to the Irish a Roman Catholic Church has its appeal, to the West Indian a Gospel Church, and to the Indian a Temple. Community councils and clubs of all kinds have been set up and all these assist the immigrant or the ethnic person to retain his separateness as well as assisting him to be assimilated to the most community. Sometimes there is more tension between the ethnic minorities than between them and the local community. Alan Barr suggested that for Oldham there was a greater tension existing between the "Poles and Ukrainians than between either of them or the host community" (Bruen, 1976, p.21). This was the situation also among the Asian immigrants as they are not homogeneous. Some of the immigrants came from Pakistan, Kashmir and Bangladesh, while most of the Pakistanis came from Azad. Kashmir belongs to the Wahabee sect while the West Pakistanis are Sunnis. The leaders at the two mosques organise their own school for two hours every evening to teach the Koran to the children. The Bangladeshi community is limited to the old area of Glodwick in Oldham and to a little more than 30 households in three small streets. They have their own language and travel outside Glodwick to their own place of worship. To complicate the scene further there is a Pakistan Society of Oldham and a breakaway group called The Pakistan Welfare Association (Bruen, 1976, p.23).

That situation is found in all the ethnic and immigrant communities, and so the host community has to be very sensitive in its approach and to have much more consultation with the immigrant groups with regard to the education required. Arthur Stock, Director of the National Institute of Adult Education in England and Wales, has expressed this plea for relevance and functionally in educational programmes in a sentence:

> Coping skills related to real life situations as *perceived by immigrants* should include oracy, literacy, numeracy and social skills, but with the consciousness of whole-person development and full participation in mind.
>
> (*Education for Adult Immigrants*, 1976, p.137).

Stock also saw that the media have a particular role to play in educating immigrants and ethnic minorities. The BBC in 1965 held meetings with immigrant communities to find out what the needs were, and the Asian communities were the only ones to ask for a special programme. As a result both sound and television programmes were broadcast twice weekly for the Asian community. These programmes have been concerned with giving advice to immigrants on how to settle in Britain, and giving views of the communities in different parts of Britain. In the seventies the BBC offered TV programmes for Asian women in their homes and it was estimated that there were around 250,000 of them (Matthews and Cooke, 1976, p.36). Many of these women — it has been estimated as about 70% — are even illiterate in their own language. The programmes devised by the BBC dealt with the interests of these women and at the same time encouraged them to start learning English.

Looking at the overall picture of the immigrants and the ethnic minorities in England and Wales it is true to say that the provision is very inadequate. There is no adequate provision for any of the groupings and there is need for educational television programmes for all immigrant groups. The Italian immigrants have similar problems to the Asians in that their women have few contacts outside their homes. In responding only to articulated requests as the BBC admitted in the case of the Asian immigrants, there was a danger of overlooking those who for a variety of sociological reasons might not be willing to ask for help. The difficulties of devising programmes which applied to all groups are many but not insurmountable to a nation which gave priority to adult education. Because that permanent education, continuing education, and recurrent education are concepts which have not been taken seriously in adult education, the immigrant and ethnic minorities are to a large extent ignored. This is also a reason for neglecting the education of the host community with regard to the ethnic minorities. Adult educational concepts have not been implemented among the immigrant and ethnic minorities and little has been learnt by the adult education agencies like the WEA and the local education authorities from the actual situation that the immigrants find themselves in in England and Wales. The situation demands flexibility on the part of adult educationists as well as a burning passion to adapt their philosophy to the elementary needs of the immigrants.

iii Adult Education in Rural Areas

In developing countries rural development is widely recognised as a top priority. But in the more developed countries rural areas are often victims of neglect. In England and Wales the need was recognised as far back as 1919 in the Ministry of Reconstruction Final Report on Adult Education. The report recognised the need to give special consideration to adult education in rural areas and emphasised the role of the village institute, the extension of libraries and museums and the development of adult classes, as well as the need for summer schools. The *Russell Report* 1973 had only paragraph on adult education in rural areas, and this in itself is an indication of the serious neglect of adult education in the countryside.

The Russell Report (1973) does not however go into detail as to the provision of adult education in the countryside and this aspect of education has not been written on at any great length. It seems that adult education is conducted in the following way:

a Agricultural and Horticultural Education

Before the second world war agricultural and horicultural education was provided by a few colleges and extra-murally by staff of the Ministry of Agriculture, universities and some county councils. The Luxmoore Report, published in 1943, suggested that local authorities in England and Wales should consider the establishment of centres for agricultural instruction. However, it was the De La Warr Report in 1958 which persuaded the government and the local authorities in co-operation with industry to cater for young adults and to expand the number of agricultural and horticultural centres. In the early seventies there were forty-eight centres in England and Wales.

Agricultural education classes are mostly carried out through the county colleges, and the county college has five main objectives, which are:

1   To provide a systematic educational provision which is progressive in nature and allows students to develop towards a sound career.

2   To be aware of the needs of the industry in an area by ensuring that the courses provided are compatible with the jobs available.

3   To ensure that the rural community is serviced with educational and training provision to meet the demands of the country woman, the established worker, and the farmer.

4   To develop the College Farm, horticultural and other units in such a way that techniques of commercial production can be demonstrated and the results readily available for discussion with farmers and growers.

5   To increase the awareness of conservation among adults living in the countryside.

The provision is many sided and it includes preparation for full-time further education as well as residential full-time agricultural education. Education provision has to be matched to the job opportunities available, and as the degree of specialisation in farming increases, educationists must be certain that courses are meeting the needs not only of the student but of the industry which employs him. Farmers and growers play a valuable role in helping the county college meet its objectives. In some cases they examine students on full and part-time courses but their guidance and advice in sought in a number of ways. Ad hoc committees, whose members are chosen from the agricultural industry, advise on these courses, and farm unit projects. Farmers participate fully as both speakers and chairmen at the many conferences, courses, seminars and discussion groups arranged by the college. Educational provision is regarded as a team effort and it also recognised the countrywoman's own educational needs in both a vocational and non-vocational way. Many counties in England and Wales are served by a rural Home Economics Department often based at the County Agricultural College. Women attend day, evening and week-end courses, and a close liaison exists with Evening Institutes.

Retraining is as essential in agriculture as in any other industry. Evening Institutes, County Agricultural Colleges provide throughout the winter, practical evening classes in welding, metalwork, tractor, and machinery maintenance, farm carpentry as well as building repair. The importance of these type of classes can be illustrated in the increase in the numbers of tractors in England and Wales from 78,000 in 1946 to 420,000 in 1970. The farmer also is catered for and many colleges organise management discussion groups. In these classes farmers have an opportunity to discuss with agricultural and horticultural experts problems that are special to their environment. Residential week-end seminars, teach-ins and conferences play an additional role in keeping the farmer and manager in touch with new developments that have arisen. The College Farm is an integral part of the agricultural education establishment. It is the working laboratory for the teaching of science and practice of farming. Staff are encouraged to be managers of the College Farm which allows a close liaison between the classroom and the farm.

b   The Village College

The Village College was established for a specific purpose and by a man of vision. The problem was a common one to all rural areas in the twentieth century and that is, the drift from the land to the town, and the genius behind it all was Henry Morris, Director of Education for the County of Cambridge from 1922 to 1956. Morris drew up an impressive memorandum, called *The Village College,* published in 1924. In the opinion of Henry Morris education was a continual and continuous process and he argued that the concept of lifelong education should be accepted in the rural areas of England and Wales. All this Morris outlined in his memorandum and part of paragraph xvi deserves to be quoted in full as an important statement of the need for continuing education in rural areas.

> The village college would change the whole face of the problem of rural education. The isolated and insulated school, which has now no organic connection with higher education, would form part of an institution in which the ultimate goal of education would be realised. As the community centre of the neighbourhood the village college would provide for the whole man, and abolish the duality of education and ordinary life. It would not only be the training ground for the art of living, but the place in which life is lived, the environment of a genuine corporate life. The dismal dispute about vocational and non-vocational education would not arise in it because education and living would be equated. It would be a visible demonstration in stone of the continuity and never ceasingness of education. There would be no "leaving school"! — the child would enter at three and leave the college only in extreme old age. (Morris adds a footnote, "In all seriousness it might be said that "school leaving age" would be lifted to 90"). It would have the great virtue of being local so that it would enhance the quality of actual life as it is lived from day to day. Unlike non-local residential institutions (such as the public schools, the universities, the few residential working men's colleges, and, to take a continental example, the Danish High Schools) it would not be divorced from the normal environment of those who would frequent it from day to day, or from that greater educational institution, the Family. There has never been an educational institution that at one and the same time provided for the needs of the whole family and consolidated its life — its social, physical, intellectual and economic life. Our modern educational institutions provide only for units of the family by time and space so that they may educate it apart and under less natural conditions. The village college would lie athwart the daily lives of the community it served; and in it the conditions would be realised under which education would be not an escape from reality, but an enrichment and transformation of it. For education is committed to the view that the ideal order and the actual order can ultimately be made one.   (Morris, 1925, pp.22-23).

Morris's plan was accepted and the first college was founded in Cambridgeshire at Sawston in 1930 and forty years later there were ten village colleges. They represent one of the most successful experiments in the history of rural adult education. Morris chose the sites of his village colleges with care, and saw to it that they were surrounded by natural beauty and enriched with art.

The Village College is the cultural centre of the region, and closely involved in the affairs of the community. Morris believed that the community must be involved in the affairs of the college and this involvement is obvious when one considers the number of organisations which use the colleges regularly, (from the Parish Council to the Bridge Club) and that the Governing Body contains representatives from the parishes which make up the Rural Region as well as the adults who attend classes. F.W. Bowen, warden of the Village College, Linton, Cambridge, gives an idea of the involvement and the pattern of a Village College when he stated in 1973:

> The Horticultural Society, the Music Society, the Folk Song Club, the Bridge Club, the Amenity Society, the Pig Breeders' Study Group, the local section of the Royal Observer Corps — all meet at the college. At week-ends the Assembly Hall is used for dances, dinners, wedding-receptions, concerts, sales of work, plays. At week-ends, and when school is over for the day, on to the playing fields come the golfers, the archers, the cricketers, the footballers, the netball and tennis players in their seasons. This kind of involvement, embracing a wide range of interests, is found in all the village colleges. The details differ, the emphasis varies from one college to another but the pattern is the same.
>   (Bowen, 1973, pp.102-103).

In this way the ideal of Henry Morris expressed so clearly in 1924 has been fulfilled. Morris saw the village college as providing "a theatre for the free and unfettered activities of the Voluntary Associations of the countryside" (Morris, 1925, p.19).

But the memorandum puts the onus for the implementation of the policies on the head of the village college. It is his responsibility to maintain the continuity of education which is at the heart of the village college concept. F. Watson Bowen, after complaining that Morris was looking for the impossible, gives an indication of the importance of the warden in these sentences:

> He must see that the life of the community is enriched by lectures, recitals, demonstrations of skill, dramatic presentations, concerts, displays, discussions, of all kinds and at all levels by people from within and without the region. He must, by providing facilities and showing a sympathetic and informed interest, stimulate and encourage the formation of group activities of all kinds — from a study of mediaeval architecture to Scottish Country Dancing.   (Bowen, 1973, p.103).

The specific work of adult further education is administered by an adult tutor who has to develop satisfactory personal relationship with his part-time staff, students as well as other adult organisations.

The Village Colleges possess two remarkable virtues. They practise the ingredients of continuing education. A conscious effort is made to bridge the gap between leaving school and adult education. Children are taught to regard adult activities as an important as well as an integral element in the life of the college and in their final year at school they are encouraged to attend adult classes. The second virtue is that the Village Colleges transcend the artificial barrier that often exists between vocational and non-vocational adult education. This happens due to the involvement of the community in the work and life of the Village Colleges. Vocational and non-vocational students mix together so that there is no conflict of interest present among the students.

It is easy to exaggerate the importance of the Village Colleges but the ideal itself has not been taken up enthusiastically throughout England and Wales. The misfortune of Henry Morris was that his ideas did not gain acceptance outside Cambridgeshire for a long time, and then only in the counties of Oxford, Cumberland, Monmouth, and from 1967 the county of Devon. In view of the remarkable success of Cambridgeshire in implementing a policy of education for adults in a rural environment it is most disappointing that the majority of the other rural authorities have not been inspired to adopt the same pattern to their own areas.

iv   Women and Adult Education

Women as a group appear to appreciate adult education in England and Wales. In the Open University housewives as one of the fourteen categories form 10.8% of the total intake (Wilson, 1977, p.21). This was evident before the establishment of the Open University. Women were the first 'automated' group in society to confront the new freedom of leisure. Economic work has been largely removed for the home so that the housewife must look for a role. Myrdal and Klein see a three phase scheduling in operation (work, home, work) where the women see home and children as a break between periods of paid employment. Enid Hutchinson, an adult educationist with a varied experience, wondered whether this picture is out of date, having been superseded by the desire for a continuous career.

The personal experience of the researcher in the sixties and seventies bears out the contention of Margaret Hughes and Valerie Wilson that women join adult education classes as much as for the incentive to improve one's capabilities as the social incentive. It seems that the friendly atmosphere of a WEA class is as attractive to a housewife as the urge to know and learn more of the subject. Females exceed males in most areas of adult education — around 60% of the total. Among the 60% there are more married people than single and the more education a person receives the more favourably disposed he seems to be towards adult education (Wilson, 1977, p.24). Margaret Hughes discovered also when interviewing applicants for the part-time craft teachers' certificate at Liverpool, that most of the applicants had sufficient 'O' and 'A' levels to enter college or university but preferred to train part-time six hours per week, with no guarantee of employment at the end of the course because of the unpredictable market for evening work. The drive to train was not economic but social.

But the most significant aspect of adult education are the women's organisations, and in particular, the Women's Institute, the Towns-women's Guilds and the National Association of Women's Clubs. These organisations try to achieve three very different objectives within the same organisation: to

207

provide social and recreational activities, educational facilities and to act as a pressure for women's views. The three functions are not really compatible but there is no doubt that women can take advantage of adult education as a lifelong process. Enid Hutchinson would like to see adult education play a significant role in maintaining contact and providing a special function for women by creating a continuous education process. She saw adult education as a way of helping to form opinions, a move towards the continuous education of women and a way back to study (Hutchinson, 1971, pp.241-4).

It seems also that adult education offers women a great deal of scope as senior citizens. As a tutor of a WEA Current Affairs class at the Royal Institution, Liverpool, every Monday morning (for thirty weeks of the year) I am very conscious of the ability, enthusiasm of a large number of women who though in age are senior citizens yet are very articulated in their arguments. In this class I have at least three women who are in their early eighties and I am always reminded that some of the world's leading scientists and philosophers did their greatest work after seventy years of age. Research proves that if the mind has been kept active, it is never too late to learn (Axford, 1969, p.13). As Roby Kidd has pointed out in a number of his writings, the factor of experience in the life of the adult learner is of immense value. To understand the adult learner — man or woman — we must continually be aware of three related points:

i   adults have more experiences;

ii   adults have different kinds of experiences;

iii adult experiences are organized differently. (Kidd, 1959, p.45).

But the most encouraging aspect of women's adult education is conducted by the informal adult education women's organisations.

a   **Women's Institutes**

Though Women's Institutes are not confined to the villages of England and Wales yet they have exerted a tremendous influence on the life of villages. They began modestly with fifteen Institutes established on a Canadian model in 1915, and though they declined during the second world war, they increased remarkably after 1945. In 1931 there were in England (including Jersey, Guernsey and the Isle of Man) and Wales 7,606 Institutes and 446,529 members (Baker, 1953, p.67). By August 1968 there were 9,006 Institutes and a total membership of 461,153 (Lowe, 1973, p.139).

The Women's Institutes recognise that there are four ways of fulfilling their function of social and educational agents. Firstly by allowing their members the opportunities of acquiring knowledge and expressing themselves in creative work. Secondly, by regarding the whole structure and organisation as a means of training women in the modes of citizenship. Thirdly, by involving the members in contemporary problems and issues. At national level the Women's Institute movement has provided admirable reports on the design of rural dwellings, on education, and on water and sewerage. At the 1950 Annual General Meeting of the National Federation a report was presented and based upon the replies of Women's Institutes to a questionnaire designed to find out what the villages of England and Wales needed as communities. Fourthly, the Women's Institute insist that their members should engage in educational activities. It is possible to criticise the educational provision for a number of reasons. The time given to discuss an educational matter is often extremely short and the subjects have very often to be of a 'popular' nature such as flower arrangement, cookery, and soft furnishing. On the positive side the Women's Institutes have given women in villages training in citizenship, confidence as speakers, and opportunities to become leaders. Very often the President of a local Institute has social pre-eminence, and a great number of Institutes choose as their President a woman who is able to combine the skills of leadership.

The Women's Institutes could enlarge their educational activities a great deal on the lines suggested by John Lowe, of extending the monthly education period, the value of continuity in planning a programme, working more closely with the Responsible Bodies on their programmes, introduce more liberal studies courses, and finally appointing full-time education officers within the movement (Lowe, 1973, p.142). To do this the movement will need more financial assistance and a more clear commitment to the need for education among women in the countryside and elsewhere. There was no sign in the early seventies that this was happening, though women have involved themselves more in adult education since the second world war than in any other period. This trend has been a world wide phenomenon and programmes have been arranged on every level for the education of women. In the United Kingdom besides the Women's Institute there are another two organisations which need to be mentioned, namely the Townswomen's Guild and the National Association of Women's Clubs.

b   The Townswomen's Guilds

The object of the Guilds is educational and since their establishment in 1929 they have encouraged women in the towns and cities of England and Wales to become responsible and well-informed citizens and activate latent intellectual interests. The Guilds co-operate with the WEA and the university extra-mural departments (apart from Aberystwyth and Bangor) in providing one day conferences and extension courses for the Guilds. Also the Guilds make heavy demands upon the residential colleges and the movement had its own educational office by the end of the sixties.

Every Guild has some kind of educational programme. The standards fluctuate. Some Guilds invite a few speakers during the year to come and address the members on topics of a popular nature. While this cannot be ignored yet one feels that much more could be achieved among the Townswomen's Guilds' members. Considering that in 1968 there were 216,000 in the Guilds one feels that the original object of encouraging 'the

209

education of women' has not been fully reflected in the work of the whole movement. However, it can claim that it has done a great deal to meet the intellectual needs of women of all ages and all classes.

c   The National Association of Women's Clubs

The National Association of Women's Clubs came into being during the period of great unrest and unemployment in 1926 and since then it has grown. It caters for women of all classes though the majority of its members come from the working class. Like the Townswomen's Guilds the National Association gives education a high priority and it receives an annual government grant (1966-67, £4,800) in recognition of its educational work. Schools, training courses, lectures are arranged for the members.

The movement is much smaller than the Townswomen's Guild or the Women's Institute. In 1968 there was an approximate membership of 35,000 found in 870 affiliated clubs (Lowe, 1973, p.147). Meetings are arranged in the afternoon and the evening and an educational programme is planned for these meetings. It has a wide range of subjects, from home crafts to music. They pay great attention to consumer education, and there is no doubt they contribute a great deal to the educational needs of women who often live in new impersonal communities or in inner city areas.

This chapter has drawn attention to the needs of groups and minorities which have been largely neglected and to certain dimensions in adult education such as the County College experiments in Cambridgeshire which has not been universally accepted by other local authorities. The work in adult literacy among immigrants and gypsies has shown that many adults in the community have need for programmes to improve literacy, numeracy and basic education, and the informal adult education work carried out by the voluntary women's organisations indicate what could be done if there were fiancial resources available. This chapter indicates once more our basic argument that in adult education in England and Wales very little has been learnt from the actual situation by adult education organisations and they are unable to adapt their concepts to the need for the continuing education of adults to enable them to respond to technical, economic and social changes. The implications of changing patterns of employment, of social and family relationships, the needs of special groups all need to be better assessed and better understood by the adult education movement in England and Wales.

Chapter 8
Self Help and Pressure Groups and Adult Education (1945-1980)

The period 1945 to 1980 saw the rise of a great number of pressure groups and self-help organisations. Many of them arose from bureaucratic frustration, others from a desire to do something for other people. An extraordinary number of organisations were started by individuals (often women) who wrote a letter to *The Guardian, The Observer* or *The Times,* and the newspapers and television have helped these new organisations by giving them publicity. It is education through responsibility, and all these organisations have at least understood some of the basic concepts of adult education, that is, involvement and interest in other people, and that the task of adult educating never ceases from the adolescent stage to the grave. We will evaluate a number of campaigns and organisations as well as analyse their involvement as well as their educational activity.

A   Campaigners
The Campaign for Nuclear Disarmament (CND)

The real catalyst for setting up a campaign against nuclear arms came in the fifties from an article in the *New Statesman* by the novelist J.B. Priestley entitled "Britain and the Nuclear Bombs". Priestley argued that Britain should give a moral lead to the world and contract out of the nuclear arms race. In early January 1958, at a meeting held in 2 Amen Court in the City of London, CND (as it became known) was born. The chairman was to be Canon John Collins of St. Paul's Cathedral, and five thousand people attended the first public meeting at the Central Hall, Westminster, in February 1958. At the beginning the movement tended to concentrate its energies on converting public opinion, and it was very successful in persuading Christians of all denominations to become involved in the work of the movement.

By March 1959 over two hundred and seventy local groups and twelve regional committees had been formed in all parts of Britain, but they were particularly strong in the London area and the North West of England. A distinctive badge was designed and the members were allowed ample opportunity to conduct educational meetings. Lectures, discussion groups, campaigning were all part of the educational programmes of local regional as well as the national Campaign for Nuclear Disarmament. However, unlike nineteenth century moral crusades it lacked a vociferous working-class following. Like adult education as a whole, the Campaign for Nuclear Disarmament was essentially middle-class. The members were mostly people who felt passionately on international affairs. Indeed, many of them from one's own experience were much more knowledgeable in international affairs than in local or British affairs.

211

The movement was also forced to make a choice on its educational approach. Was it to spend all its energies on the long-term approach of converting all men of reason to its cause or was the movement to take the short-term strategy of converting one of the political parties to accept its philosophy? Attempts to attract all-party support in 1958 was not very successful, and the Conservative Party showed no interest in the movement. As many of the CND's leaders were members of the Labour Party it was felt that the only way to success was through the Labour Movement. The Historian, A.J.P. Taylor, among many others, wrote articles on the need to "convert the Labour party" just as the Anti-Corn Law League in the nineteenth century converted Sir Robert Peel.

The Campaign for Nuclear Disarmament was assisted as a powerful educational power group dedicated to one principle by a number of factors. In the first place its moralistic and idealistic writings made a lasting impression on a number of traditional middle-class Labour Party activists. Many of these people were the sons and daughters of the Independent Labour Party pioneers at the beginning of the century, and they were ready for the educational propaganda of the CND. In 1956 the Soviet invasion of Hungary led to a mass exodus from the British Communist Party, and many of these Marxists moved into the Labour Party and so strengthened the left wing.

Within the Labour Party there were small but very active movements, and in particular the Keep Left Group led by Barbara Castle, Ian Mikardo and Richard Crossman who questioned Britain's subservient support for the Atlantic Alliance. The Left became intensely anti-American, a sentiment which was reinforced by the appearance of John Foster Dulles at the State Department in 1952 intent on launching a crusade against Communism, and by the McCarthy 'witch-hunts' in 1953 and 1954. The independent Left-wing weekly paper, *Tribune,* led the struggle for unilateralism, and within a short time at least sixty Labour M.P.'s had shown support for the aim of the Movement — which was to persuade the British people that Britain must reduce the nuclear peril and stop the armaments race.

The Campaigners

Frank Parkin, in his book *Middle-Class Radicalism* (1968), has given us a great deal of information on the composition of the CND. Dr. Parkin's survey was based on eight hundred activists, and he found that they were mainly from the more creative and socially orientated professions. They were people who had received secondary and higher education, and who took an interest in adult educational provision. One can find the coming together of a variety of interests in the CND campaigners.

There were the traditional pacificists, and in particular the Quakers. It was a useful partnership for the Quakers had meeting houses which could be used for committee work and gatherings. Quakers helped to set up the local and regional committees as well as the Christian Campaign for Nuclear Disarmament.

Communists joined CND, and in particular hundreds of young communists worked in the youth campaign. These dedicated marxists were well-versed in the skills of education and in particular discussions and debates.

Another important strand was the more militant pacifists who called themselves the Direct Action Group. It was they who set the tone and provided the commitment to non-violence and radicalism. The dominant leaders of this grouping were Hugh Brock, then editor of *Peace News,* April Carter, Pat Arrowsmith and Michael Randle. It was they who initiated and ran with an ad hoc committee the first 1958 march from London to Aldermaston.

Then there was the Labour Left and the New Left. Before 1958 the Labour Left had been in the Anti-H Bomb Campaign and it was this group which swung the CND behind the idea that victory would come through the Labour Party. The New Left attracted a great number of young intellectuals from the universities, and they provided a political leadership to what was basically a moral crusade.

Then there were the members who belonged to no grouping, and they have been classed as absolutists. Parking describes them as young people who were more interested in working for a more just and humane society than in finding themselves a good job. They believed that the bomb immediately threatened the future of civilization, that it had to be banned very quickly or armageddon would arrive. In sociological terms the Campaign for Nuclear Disarmament was absolutist and compulsive.

The CND achieved a great deal in a short time as far as activity was concerned. Its main educational plank was the holding of public meetings and the publication of pamphlets and leaflets. Peggy Duff,who became one of the leaders of the movement, gives us a rough idea of the actual figures involved:

> We organised hundreds — indeed, over nine years, (1958-1967) thousands — of public meetings. We distributed millions of leaflets. We sold hundreds of thousands of pamphlets. We must have sold millions of copies of our monthly newspaper, *Sanity.*
> (Duff, 1971, p.145).

From the beginning the Campaign for Nuclear Disarmament realised the importance of the educational work through the mass media. A Press and Publicity Group was established under the guidance of J.B. Priestley and Gerald Barry. To many, the major success of the group was the televising by Granada Television of Priestley's play called *Doomsday for Dyson.*

The Campaign for Nuclear Disarmament also allowed a great number of sub-groups within the movement, and each one of these groups was able to conduct its own educational work. As far as prestige and academic expertise, the Scientists' Group was in a key educational position. They produced for a time a very professional CND Scientists' Bulletin as well as a series of leaflets and pamphlets on radiation and fall-out. The Scientists' Group also gave reliable information on the effects of nuclear weapons in terms of damage, fire, loss of life, and their writings were very authoritative. It can be argued that the educational work of this group was far-reaching for gradually over the years the public came to accept the facts and in time the Test Ban Treaty was signed. Peggy Duff sums up the influence of the Scientists' Group in forming public opinion in this sentence, "They also helped us to create in Britain and throughout the world an awareness that nuclear war meant annihilation" (Duff, 1971, p.158).

The Architects' Group was somewhat different in style from the Scientists' Group. It was established very early in 1958 and a large number of its members worked for the London County Council. One of its most important contributions was the setting up of the Hampstead Exhibition *No Place to Hide*, which travelled all round Britain and to the Continent.

The Christian CND — another of the sub-groups — never became a large organisation but it produced excellent literature which was very widely used by CND groups and sympathisers within the churches. The Campaign for Nuclear Disarmament also had the colleges and universities CND and the Youth Campaign (YCND) and both were active and involved in producing literature as well as in organising educational activities. The YCND newspaper, *Youth against the Bomb,* was informative and educational.

But the CND as a campaigning movement was unable to carry on its momentum, and it seems that the main reason was that their objective of 'converting the Labour Party' to unilateralism was achieved at the 1961 Labour Party Conference. CND had lacked any educational strategy of what to do once they had gained the upper hand at the Labour Party Conference. The campaign was frustrated also by Hugh Gaitskell's determination to carry on the struggle through the winter of 1960-61. Despite continued criticism and personal abuse, he toured the country, arguing with tremendous fervour as well as carefully argued speeches, against unilateralism. Again a pro-Gaitskell body was set up to reverse the Scarborough decision and mobilise Right-wing opinion. This was the Campaign for Democratic Socialism which proved a most successful educational campaign within the Labour Party.

The campaign suffered from its own success. With the creation of a mass membership, a delegate system to Annual Conference which enabled rotten-borough branches to sprout in the country, and the growth in the number of full-time organisers, CND became ossified. The Aldermaston March began to lose the moral impact of the early years, and its carnival atmosphere deterred a great number of older people from supporting it in the early sixties. Although the national press, radio and television, tended to ignore CND at the beginning, for the period 1959 to 1961 they gave a reasonably sympathetic coverage to the activities of the movement. However, the more militant grouping, Committee of 100 unnerved the CND as did the personal wrangling between two of the leaders, Canon John Collins and the philosopher,

Bertrand Russell. As the more militant groups, such as the Committee of 100 and 'March must Decide' Committee, increased their strength within CND, the Labour Left began to leave. At a time when the economic and strategic implications of unilateral disarmament were being worked out the militants took over the CND Movement. The CND began to lose its support in the Labour Party and the accession of Harold Wilson to the leadership of the Party in February 1963 also helped to weaken CND. Support within the Labour Movement for CND began to dwindle, and as the 1964 General Election approached, leading party members like Anthony Greenwood, Judith Hart and Michael Foot, withdrew from the CND Council (Duff, 1971, pp.196-197). Unilateralist resolutions disappeared from TUC and Labour Party Conference agendas. The new Labour Prime Minister, Harold Wilson, swept the unilateralist message under the carpet. It was obvious that CND was no longer in a position to dictate its policies to the Labour Party, but it did not give up its campaign. In the sixties it produced at the Labour Party Conference and the Trade Union Congress a daily *Focus* which was a duplicated six to eight page magazine, distributed to each one of the delegates. It was the method used of putting the CND case at Conference and the *Focus* was read avidly by the delegates. But it did little to change the Labour Party's decisions after the October 1961 Conference.

There were a number of reasons why the Campaign for Nuclear Disarmament lost its impact as a mass movement in the middle sixties. The most obvious reason is this: CND never evolved from being a movement of emotional and moral protest. It was one of the last of the radical movements. The Oxford historian, A.J.P. Taylor, and one of CND's most popular speakers in the early years, delivered his Ford Lectures at his own university on such a theme in 1956. A.J.P. Taylor saw himself often as the John Bright of the movement. Just as Bright denounced the Crimean War and sought an acceptance of the principle of non-intervention by Britain in foreign wars, so A.J.P. Taylor sought to revive the moral sentiment of nineteenth century liberalism to combat the nuclear menace.

Secondly, its educational work was marred by disagreements among the leaders of the Campaign for Nuclear Disarmament. This happened more than once, and in particular within the Disarmament and Strategy Group. CND's educational campaigning was much too limited. Activists with a social conscience believed that the movement should concern itself with a broader dissenting programme, such as housing and race, but this was resented, and most of the local groups wanted to campaign on unilateralism and nothing else. It was this intransigence which drove out in the end people as different as the sociologist Professor John Rex and the veteran campaigner, Peggy Duff, from the Campaign for Nuclear Disarmament.

The CND, however, did provide its active members a means of making their presence felt in British politics. It brought warm fresh air into the stuffy atmosphere of British politics. The learning process has not been abandoned and at the end of the sixties eighty-five per cent of its work was still on nuclear weapon research. The monthly newspaper *Sanity* with a circulation of from nine to ten thousand still explains what nuclear disarmament means. It is movement of conscience and continuous education, and as such its impact has been more than many a social historian is willing to admit, and its educational activity has a great deal to offer the adult education movement.

The end of the seventies has given CND a new boost and the historian E.P. Thompson who spent a large part of his working life as an adult education tutor, has worn the mantle of A.J.P. Taylor as a rational voice to be respected and listened to.

It is surprising also that a large number of those who worked for the CND in its hey-day were still involved as CND activists in the seventies. Not all adult movements could boast of such loyalty. In a questionnaire completed by 1,403 respondents between April and June 1978 it was found that between a fifth and a quarter were still members. All the respondents, one should add, had been CND activists for at least part of the period 1958-1965 (Taylor and Pritchard, 1980, p.15). It was obvious that these activists had not got tired of pressure-group activists.

B   Other Campaigners

The sixties in particular were a decade in which persons other than professional teachers participated in broad educational activity geared to a campaign. Neighbourhood committees concerned with traffic and pollution problems, village associations, workers' and students' co-operatives give their members the possibility of a wider vision of the issues concerned, and the means of making their presence felt in community life. The learning process, as we have found within the CND Movement, is specifically geared to action and direct intervention, and for this very reason a high level of motivation is maintained. A rich and independent associated life promotes lifelong education.

There are a number of campaigning movements that come within the broad field of education. Educational institutions often adopt a didactic attitude towards parents and refuse discussion on the basic issues concerning education. Educational changes often are unable to be implemented because of a lack of commitment on the part of parents. The Comprehensive Schools Committee (CSC) founded in September 1965 by Richard and Jo Pryke had its aim to give support to an educational principle of comprehensive education. Richard and Jo Pryke felt that a government committed to comprehensive education, without legislation, was going to need a lot of support from an organised pressure group whose sole aim was to help comprehensive education to flourish. The original committee included seven who were, or had been, teachers in comprehensive' schools, four parents of children attending comprehensive schools, three who intended their children to go to comprehensive schools, and four other supporters. It is a body that brings teachers and parents together in co-operation. The committee offers advice and help to local groups who are compaigning for reorganisation and the ending of the eleven-plus system.

Comprehensive Schools Committee has an extensive system of educating its members and the public. A magazine called *Comprehensive Education* is published three times a year with supplements, and it includes articles by practising teachers, by parents and by researchers on the problems involved in comprehensive education. They have a Speakers' Service for all types of meetings from small discussion groups to mass teach-ins. In its first year of existence CSC arranged for over a hundred speakers to address meetings all over the country. It also provided speakers for radio and television programmes on the subject, manned several deputations to the Department of Education and Science, and arranged links, visits and discussions for experts in comprehensive education overseas. A National Conference has been organised each year. The first *Unstreaming in the Comprehensive* in 1966 was attended by four hundred people, the second was held the following year on *The Sixth Form and the Comprehensive School,* and in 1969 on *A New Education Act* and the 1970 Conference had as its theme, *Teacher Training.* This Association grouping teachers and parents has an important educational contribution to make, and so has every similar organisation, such as Confederation for the Advancement of State Education, The National Association for Gifted Children Limited, Pre-School Playgroups Association National Association for the Welfare of Children in Hospitals which are all worthy of a reference as well as examples of projects slanted towards lifelong education. That is the case because in themselves these groups constitute lifelong education experience for their own members and, secondly, because they can contribute to the strengthening of other components in the educational process. But educational institutions do not always appreciate the contribution of these associations, particularly if these self-help groups have loose or no formalised structural organisations. Paradoxical as it may seem, it can be said that vigorous spontaneous initiative calls forth in educational institutions a preference for strongly structured associated life. Educational institutions, for instance, are sometimes prepared to accept associations only when the initiative is slipping from their control.

The Confederation for the Advancement of State Education (CASE) sprang into being through the efforts of a group of educated parents who felt that there was room for improvement in State education. The spark occurred in Cambridge when a group of mothers complained about the poor toilet facilities and teaching space in a local primary school. A local official suggested that they should look at some other schools which were in a worse situation. Shocked to learn that theirs was an advantaged area compared with other parts of the country, these mothers formed the Cambridge Association for the Association for the Advancement of State Education in 1960. This Cambridge initiative triggered off similar groups up and down the country, and the number had grown to sixty when the first annual Conference of the Confederation for The Advancement of State Education was held in September 1963. By 1971 there were over one hundred local associations and a number of colleges and institutes of education have insititutional affiliation. The part played by parents was soon acknowledged by Sir Edward Boyle after he had, as the then Minister of Education, received a deputation from CASE Sir Edward Boyle mentioned the traditional partnership in education of teachers, local authority and government, and said:

> But we are being increasingly reminded of a fourth partner, who, if once asleep, has been roused to a new awareness; the parents of the seven million children now in the schools and of the two or more who will shortly be arriving there . . . Many parents who would previously not have felt personally concerned about state education are now, either by necessity or by deliberate choice, turning to it for their children. And they feel that their voices have a right to be heard no less than if their children were being educated at their own expense, in independent schools. (Jerman, 1971, p.8).

CASE through their autonomous local branches and the serious debate carried out at the Annual Conference have disseminated a great deal of information to parents so that they are much better equipped to understand education. They have improved communication between parents and the schools as well as the local education authorities. CASE works to make consultation with parents on educational matters as normal as consultation with trades unions or the church.

The National Association for Gifted Children Limited is an entirely different association from CASE. It also deals with parents and their children, but in this instance with parents of very intelligent and gifted children. Like CASE, the association was formed in the middle sixties as a result of a book, *Gifted Children,* written by Margaret Branch and Aubrey Cash. Margaret Branch estimated that there were about 140,000 gifted children of school age in the country. By June 1968 there were local groups in twenty-two counties. These organise meetings of parents with specialists such as eductionalists or psychologists. Groups also organise children's activities. Associations such as The National Association for Gifted Children Limited have an important part to play in enabling children to establish relations with the adult world on an independent basis. Children do not become members. It is their parents who join, but the children are able to partake in activities, such as the activity day or the Saturday morning club at some colleges of education. There students and the children would mix together in the activities.

The Pre-School Playgroups Association is another interesting self-group, for the relationship between the family and the school is only one aspect of the relationship between education and the family. Within the family itself there is a particularly significant educational life, especially in areas where the number of children not in school attendance reaches considerable proportions. It was to fulfil this need that the Pre-School Playgroups Association has done a valuable service. By the end of the sixties playgroups had become an established part of the British family life.

It started through the determination of a mother, Mrs. Belle Tutaev, who in 1961 wrote a letter to *The Guardian.* She had found the need in her own experience, and by the end of the decade over 100,000 children were attending playgroups. Since Pre-School Playgroups Association started, about a quarter of a million children have enjoyed playgroup facilities they would not otherwise have had.

The movement has taken education seriously. Helpers had to be trained and this demand for training in understanding the needs of small children is in many ways the most significant contribution of the movement. The student-mothers have initiative and they are trained in a short time to be very competent. Parents become involved, and many of them get involved in the voluntary administration of local and area groups. In 1966 a National Adviser, Brenda Crowe, was appointed and her booklet, *The Playgroup Movement,* describes the work of the movement in its early beginnings. Adults still seem to have an incredible lack of understanding of the under-fives, and Brenda Crowe's report demonstrated that mothers need the playgroups quite as much as their children. It allows the mothers to meet each other, and to be encouraged as well as assisted to cope with their children. Brenda Crowe felt that the movement should be more firmly established with full-time advisers who could organise the Pre-School Playgroups Association on a more permanent basis. It is a voluntary movement which grew out of an education demand in British society, and it is a movement, if given more financial resources, could do more valuable work than it has done in the past.

Another outstanding example of a grass-root group responding to an obvious need can be discerned in the National Association for the Welfare of Children in Hospital. It all began when a group of mothers discussed three *Observer* articles on children in hospitals. They were together in Battersea Park, and one of them, Jane Thomas, was among the eight thousand mothers who wrote to the author, James Robertson of the Tavistock Child Development Research Unit asking how mothers could be with their children as much as possible during hospital treatment. The 'Battersea Project' became Mother Care for Children in Hospital, and the name was changed at a later date to the National Association for the Welfare of Children in Hospital (NAWCH).

The National Association for the Welfare of Children in Hospital has been a movement which has influenced medical and nursing opinion to a large extent. It believed in reasoned arguments and using every channel to bring to the attention of the public the aims of the movement. Leaflets on the importance of visiting have been printed even in Urdu, Hindi, Bengali and Punjabi; playgroups are run by volunteers in hospitals, and a highly informative newsletter reports national and local activities. It is a movement which combines reason and militancy. NAWCH believes in educating parents in the importance of using good facilities to the maximum benefit of their children, and to demand these facilities when they do not exist. It is a movement that offers like most self-help groups an opportunity for participation in the welfare of the child and in the democratisation of the hospital system. All these groups and associations point to a most important factor, and that is, group structure can foster the educational relationship. This group interest has grown tremendously in the field of medicine, a sphere which was often sacrosanct and not an area for lay people. But the groups that have mushroomed in England and Wales have one thing in common, a concern for those who have been born or have suffered in their life a physical or mental disability which makes them less able to fend for themselves. These groups are in the main the initiative of individuals, and on the other hand, of ordinary men and women who are determined to help and educate each other with regard to their difficulties. An Association For All Speech Impaired Children (AFASIC) sprang up due to the initiative of a Senior Speech Therapist at St. Bartholomew's Hospital, London, Margaret Greene. AFASIC came into being in June 1968 to help parents, teachers, and all concerned with language handicapped children. Available literature includes books for teachers and parents, and the association at all times emphasises the views of these two groups.

Ignorance is often the main enemy of these specialised medical groupings and associations. The Association for the Prevention of Addiction was formed as a result of a heartbreaking article in *The Guardian* (24 February 1967) from a mother of a boy who was a registered drug addict. Six hundred letters were received and a Chelsea social worker, Mollie Craven, began to sort out the correspondence and organise the new movement. Manchester and Liverpool were the first regions to be established, and panels were formed to co-ordinate the knowledge and research available. The educational panel has a key task of informing the public through lectures, teach-ins, discussion groups, pamphlets and films.

The Disablement Income Group was formed as a result of another article in *The Guardian* in 1965, and The Leukaemia Society was formed in 1967 following a Granada Television programme *World in Action* report on the death of the daughter of the Parliamentary Correspondent of *The Times*.

All these movements and many more (such as Association for Spina Bifida and Hydrocephalus Limited; Children's Chest Circle; National Association for Deaf/Blind and Rubella Children; The National Deaf Children's Society; The National Society for Autistic Children; National Society for Mentally Handicapped Children) employ the traditional educational methods of teaching, persuasion by word and pamphlet, research, and literature to achieve their goals. They work with local and national governments and highlight the needs of their own members. Adult education in its widest sense as a lifelong concept is of interest to all self-groups. All the children who are in constant need of medical and psychological care were enjoying better facilities in 1970 than they did in 1945 or even in 1955 and 1960, and in no small measure this was due to the work of these societies and associations that we have looked at. Many of these movements have expanded tremendously. The National Society for Mentally Handicapped Children is a case in point. Judy Fryd, who had a daughter in 1938 who was classed as 'ineducable', battled for years, and in 1949 managed to form an Association. This Association grew in strength and influence. Its educational work was most successful and especially its research into the causes of mental handicap. The Society's headquarters houses the Institute for Research into Mental Retardation which was set up in 1966 to stimulate and co-ordinate research, the College of Special Education; the Federation of Gateway Clubs, the trusteeship bureau and the Society's Centre for Learning Disabilities which evaluates educational aids for the mentally handicapped.

The basic assumption underlying the concept of lifelong education is that anybody can be an educator. Self-help groups' organisations have demonstrated this. Most of the founders of the self-group organisations were not highly trained or qualified practitioners in medicine or education. They were in the main ordinary intelligent men and women (with women in the majority) who responded to their own family problems or to a situation that had gripped them. In a few instances the individuals who took the initiative had no premeditated idea of doing this. Hilda Burd had planned to go to a cinema on 18th February 1964. As the bus did not turn up on time she went to a meeting at the Woodberry Down Health Centre, North London (where she worked part-time as a physiotherapist) to a lecture on cervical cancer. The audience was apalled at the facts disclosed to them, and Hilda Burd became secretary of the Stoke Newington group which was formed that evening. Peggy Freeman was discussing at the Clinic the problem of coping with her child when the teacher remarked that it was a pity there was no organisation for the parents of deaf/blind children where they could help each other. That chance remark in 1955 triggered off the National Association for Deaf/Blind and Rubella Children. Peggy Freeman was the educator and served as the secretary of the Association until 1966. That year she was asked by the Inner London Education Authority to teach their children with this handicap, and after two and a half years she handed over to a qualified teacher who was available. But Peggy Freeman was as much an educator as the 'qualified' teacher who replaced her. The study of these initiators of self-group organisations and campaigning movements into the wide arena of the informal educational system makes it possible to understand much more clearly the assumption which underlies the concept of lifelong education. These new 'teachers' of public opinion, of the disadvantaged as well as the disabled, are able to increase the initiative of other people who are often in the same predicament as they are or have been, or in some instances they respond to a situation that they have come across in their professional work. The Reverend Mary Webster, a Congregational Church minister in South London, found through a survey that one household in ten contained an unmarried daughter caring for her relatives. She assessed the national figures as the same. From this piece of scientific research the Reverend Mary Webster published a blueprint of a National Council to illuminate the situation and to

221

help single women. From this emerged in 1965 the National council for the single Woman and Her Dependents Limited.

All these movements and associations emphasise the need for a continual appraisal of the problems. Most of the problems are recurring ones, and in particular problems that face individuals, such as alcoholism, gambling, divorce. Al-Anon Family Groups UK and Eire, which started spontaneously in Britain in 1955, is to help relatives of alcoholics, while Alcoholics Anonymous is a fellowship of those who are alcoholics. Again we find the same pattern with regard to gambling. Gam-Anon allow wives of gamblers to let off steam while Gamblers Anonymous is to help the obsessive gambler to give up gambling. The National Federation of Clubs for the Divorced and Separated was formed as a result of initiative taken by a trained social worker, Mercia Emmerson. The Clubs are to provide a 'supportive' framework for men and women who feel distressed and depressed after the breakdown of their marriages. All these movements use the traditional educational structures to achieve their aims, and the contribution of each one of these groups that we have noted in this chapter is important to adult education and in particular to the concept of lifelong education, and that individuals can be an effective adult educator once they are motivated or determined to fulfil their 'teaching task'.

The self help and pressure groups are not regarded within adult education as relevant, but as we spelt out in the Introduction and in this chapter, they have a great deal to offer to adult education. These campaigns have implemented many of the concepts that have been written about by adult educationists and they emphasise the role that individuals can play to solve their own difficulties and build a better world for their children. There is certainly a growing awareness by adult educationists of the need for the continuing education of adults to enable them to meet more fully their own personal interests, needs, and inspirations.

Chapter 9
Opinion and Participatory Study of W.E.A. Students

A   Opinion survey of adult students in one Liverpool Adult Centre
i   Introduction

The Royal Institution in Colquitt Street, Liverpool, is a Victorian building which is regarded as part of the Extension Department of the University of Liverpool. This adult centre caters also for a large number of WEA classes including One Day WEA Schools. Personally I have conducted at the Royal Institution a number of adult WEA classes and the first draft of the questionnaire was given out to my Monday morning Current Affairs Class which I describe in my participatory survey. The questionnaire before being used for the pilot scheme was sent to David Connor of the WEA office at Liverpool and to Professor Rhodes of the University Extension Department as they and their organisations are heavily committed at the Royal Institution.

The final questionnaire was sent to a sample of 52 people who had been chosen from the WEA registers of the Autumn Term 1977. In the registers (including a very popular day school) there were 520 people and one chose at random the tenth person. The questionnaire was sent out to the 52 adult students and 42 of them replied. The high percentage of returns is due to the fact that a comprehensive letter accompanied the questionnaire, that I was known to many of the WEA students at least by name, and that a stamped addressed envelope accompanied it. An opportunity was given also to the adults who answered the questionnaire to contact me personally if they wanted any assistance or explanation. At least four of the adult students did this.

One must also point out in this introduction that 37 out of 42, that is 88.1 per cent regarded themselves as belonging only to WEA while the other five adults, that is 11.9 per cent looked upon themselves as adult students who identified themselves more with other adult agencies or organisations.

I offer this as an opinion survey which brings out many aspects of adult education which have been discussed in the course of the book.

ii   The Result of the Survey

From our opinion survey it seems that an adult education student who attended the Royal Institution centre in Liverpool during the Autumn term of 1977 came from the professional class. In the first question on the occupation of students one found that the WEA class member usually comes from the teaching and clerical profession. There were seven from the teaching profession, that is 18.9 per cent, while there were eight, 21.6 per cent, who were involved in clerical work. The housewife is also attracted to the adult education facilities, in the WEA one found that 18.9 per cent were housewives while there were 40.0 per cent on a smaller response attending other adult education classes. It is of no surprise that there are only 2.7 per cent from the semi-manual occupations and 5.4 per cent from the manual occupations. This bears out what we have found in research, in observation, interviews and in adult education surveys that the typical WEA student is one that has already received a great deal of education. The more education one receives the more one values further or adult education. These students ae unrepresentative of the population as a whole and this bears out the findings of other surveys. John Lowe in 1963 carried out a survey simultaneously in a number of different places and found a high socio-economic status of adult students in all areas except Leeds. Manual workers were found in small numbers and Lowe also found out that there were a large number of married women. Teachers formed a large number as well as trained nurses. Housewives were also numerous (Lowe, 1970, pp.238-252).

This is borne out in the section on leaving school. While 24.3 per cent left school at fourteen years of age and 40.0 per cent of those attend other educational facilities (local education authorities), the biggest grouping is among those who carried on with further education. They make up 32.4 per cent from the WEA members and 20 per cent from the other adult students. When one considers the fact that on the questionnaire one had included the ages of 17 and 18 and that 8.1 per cent and 10.8 per cent of the WEA students had left school in form five or form six one is tempted to reinforce the argument that has already been put forward.

The WEA student is usually an adult learner who will take advantage of other adult educational facilities. 59.5 per cent of the adults had attended a local education authority class while only 31 per cent had attended an university extension class. Sixty nine per cent of the students had never attended an university extension class though they had come along to the Royal Institution which is part of the University Extension Department. Ten of the adult students had been through the Technical College classes and six (14.3 per cent) through the Trade Union tutorials which in the sixties became an integral part of the WEA programme on Merseyside. However there was one notable omission and that is no adult and experienced a National College of Labour Colleges (NCLC) course. It supports also the claim made by the NCLC during its turbulent history that it was catering mostly to workers who otherwise would have no provision of adult education. The NCLC devoted a great deal of its energy to attacking the education provided by the WEA and in some areas the debate was fierce. South Wales proved to be such an area with the South Wales Miners Federation and the Steelworkers Union supporting the NCLC financially. But even in South Wales WEA leaders could claim that they had more miners as members of their classes at the end of the second world war in 1945 than any other group (Evans, 1945, p.31). But in time this picture changed in South Wales as it did in the rest of the United

Kingdom. One was surprised also that only 7.1 per cent had experienced residential adult education courses, and one of these students told me that the "happiest time of my life was in Burton Manor". Burton Manor is a residential short term adult education centre run by the Univesity of Liverpool in co-operation with the Merseyside Local Authorities. He complained also that the cost for the courses had increased over the years making it impossible for "pensioners to attend the centre". This adult student was very critical of the introduction of the bar facilities to Burton Manor as he saw no need for one. The financial cost should always be an important factor in planning adult education provision.

Though the philosophy of adult education insists that no groups or individuals in society should be denied access to adult education we see from our survey that participation is not as broadly based as it should be. It is fair to note that some adults lack the time and resources to participate in education. Paid study leave, day release and security of employment during study leave would change the situation and the promotion of workers' education and trade union and co-operative education would also be helpful. It seems that the traditionally under-privileged groups as was mentioned in the Introduction is still outside the adult education provision of the WEA in one Liverpool centre and a possible reason for this is the lack of advertising on the part of adult education orgnaisations, such as the WEA. A tutor comes across students every year who have joined the class through hearing about it rather than by a newspaper advertisement. Advertising has a particular role and in 1977 the brochures of the WEA and the University of Liverpool Extension Department were very attractive and professionally produced, and yet only 11.9 per cent had information about adult education classes through the university brochure. Eighteen of the adults (42.9 per cent) came to the adult classes through the WEA brochures distributed in public libraries and six adult students (that is 14.3 per cent) because they had heard of the tutor. Eight students, that is 19.0 per cent, had heard of adult education classes through their friends and only five (11.9 per cent) through advertisements in newspapers. But the brochures are still a useful method of advetising the adult education classes, and they could be more widely scattered so as to attract the attention of more adults. But the brochures are not as effective as one's own motivation, and 33.3 per cent of the adults joined the classes through their own initiative. Local radio was another heading but the result was disappointing. Only two, that is 4.8 per cent, knew of adult education provision through local radio and there is ample room for improving the co-ordination between local radio and the adult education agencies with special information programmes designed at the beginning of each term. Local radio has tremendous potential but it is not geared to the need for continuing education. It has no specific commitment or policy through the local BBC Radio Merseyside station or the commercial radio, which is called Radio City. BBC Radio Merseyside has done a great number of local radio programmes which had an educational content and were designed to educate adults.

The motivation of adult students in adult education is crucial. Why do people attend WEA classes or for that matter any adult education class is a question that needs to be asked and the questionnaire provided an opportunity for asking the question. The researcher believed that the subject matter is important as well as the belief in continuous education. The WEA has over the years provided adults with a liberal education and the small number of people in our survey, that is 7.1 per cent, who attended for the purpose of qualifications is a reflection of the ethos of the WEA movement. If one asked the same question in a local education authority adult centre one would have had an entirely different response.

Another significant motivation is the belief in continuous education which is very encouraging with 35.7 per cent opting for this as their reason for attending adult education classes. It can be argued as the researcher does that continuing education has not been discussed among the students who attend adult education classes. The questionnaire could be criticised for taking too much for granted in stating a belief in continuous education as a reason for attending adult classes, and perhaps one should have stated in general terms what continuous education meant, or at least could have added the phrase lifelong education. The statement made by Paul Lengrand would have added to the participant's understanding of the concept: "What we mean by lifelong education is a series of very specific ideas, experiments and achievements, in other words, education in the full sense of the word, including all its aspects and dimensions, its uninterrupted development from the first moments of life to the very last, and the close, organic interrelationship between the various points and successive phases in its development". Such an illuminating definition I am sure would have gained more support from among the sample but for adult education in the future it agurs well. For the motivation to improve oneself could easily be regarded as part of the concept of continuous education, and that was the third reason with 33.3 per cent of the respondents accepting it as their own reason for attending an adult education class. The desire to improve oneself educationally has always motivated adults in their search for knowledge and continuous education has also accepted this as a fundamental part of its philosophy. A response from one of the members sums up the attitude: "I enjoy coming to the WEA class and I would not miss it for it is profitable".

Reasons given for attending Adult Education Classes

	Response		Percentages	
	Yes	No	Yes	No
Belief in continuous education	15	27	35.7	64.3
A desire to improve oneself	14	28	33.3	66.7
To pass the time	2	40	4.8	95.2

Continued

Continued from previous page

	Response		Percentages	
Companionship	6	36	14.3	85.7
To become a better equipped citizen	3	39	7.1	92.9
Earn a qualification	3	39	7.1	92.9
Fascination of the subject	33	9	78.6	21.4
Other reasons	2	40	4.8	95.2

Table 9.1

Another problem in adult education is its apparent lack of attractiveness. Table 2 of the opinion survey is concerned with a number of statements that are often made to explain the relatively low response from the general public to the adult education provision. The result of this opinion survey indicates quite clearly that the generalisations often made as to the inability of adult education to attract vast numbers are not felt by those who enjoy the benefits of adult education. When an adult is sufficiently motivated to attend an adult education centre such as the Royal Institution the meeting place is not a deterrent, neither is the enrolment form that he has to fill in for the WEA class.

The reasons as to the lack of popularity of Adult Education Classes

	Response		Percentages	
Reasons	**Yes**	**No**	**Yes**	**No**
The meeting place was more convenient	9	33	21.4	78.6
There was a better choice of subjects	13	29	31.0	69.0
The admission was simplified (e.g. no form to fill when registering)	5	37	11.9	88.1
Advertising was more extensive or attractive	20	22	47.6	52.4
The tutors were better communicators	4	38	9.5	90.5
Cost of classes were less	11	31	26.2	73.8
Subjects were more interesting	5	37	11.9	88.1
Other reasons	2	40	4.8	95.2

Table 9.2

Through our opinion survey we have details of the WEA students within this final result. The nine students who regarded the meeting place as one reason for the lack of popularity of adult education classes were all WEA students. Eleven WEA students out of the thirteen regarded the choice of Subjects as another reason for the unpopularity of adult education classes. It should be stated that the WEA in Liverpool have an excellent record for responding to popular demand. This is not true of some of the other adult education organisations which are much more rigid in their provision.

A great deal of time is often wasted at the first lecture of a WEA or an university extension class at the beginning of the session when enrolling the members. The enrolment itself demands literacy and ability to fill in an enrolment card. To the researcher this has its drawbacks and this is why in the question of popularity of classes it was included. The only students who felt the need for a simplified admission procedure were the WEA students, five of them or 11.9 per cent of the total number of 42.

It is often said that the adult educational classes should have more extensive or more attractive advertising and this was included in the questionnaire. Eighteen of the WEA students, that is 48.6 per cent from the total of 37 WEA students or 47.6 per cent from the grand total of 42 adult students compared with 2 or 40.0 per cent from the small figure of 5 other adult students felt that this was a matter that should be looked at. On the delicate issue of the tutors being better communicators it is highly significant that out of the whole sample of 42 only 4 (that is 9.5 per cent), and all belonging to the WEA section, felt the relevance of the statement. In actual fact the WEA have always been very fortunate with their full-time and part-time tutors. Every region has had its remarkable tutors. It is true that a tutor like R.H. Tawney (1892-1962) is an exception in any adult movement but the WEA have been able to find tutors of tremendous ability as communicators and educators. These men have lectured and kept classes under the most trying conditions. A good example in the North Wales District of the WEA is the Reverend Gwilym O. Roberts who gave up a lucrative lectureship in the United States of America to return to his beloved Caernarvonshire. The North Wales District Secretary, C.E. Thomas, was surprised when he called at Gwilym O. Robert's class at the village of Garn Dolbenmaen in the winter of 1953. The lecturer, Gwilym O. Roberts, was presenting his subject of psychology in a very attractive manner to over thirty members, the majority being young people. There were only a dozen chairs in the room and the rest of the adults had to sit for two hours on hard benches without any support to them (Thomas, 1954, p.38). The following year Gwilym O. Roberts attracted over 250 adults (mostly from his Lleyn peninsula WEA classes) to a one day school at Pwllheli. Every WEA district seems to have at least one or two of the Tawney's and a dozen of the Gwilym O. Robert's in every generation with the result that the WEA is used to the outstanding tutors.

The cost of the adult education classes are often mentioned as one of the main reasons for the drop in the number of adults attending adult education centres. It is of interest that this is borne out to some extent in our results. At least eleven adults (ten of them being WEA students) felt that this warranted a mention. The last statement in this section was simply to do with the subjects offered in the adult education syllabuses. Five of the adult students, that is

11.9 per cent, regarded this as a reason for the lack of appeal, and of the five, four were WEA students.

While one was unsure (as it has been admitted) if the respondents to the questionnaire had understood the meaning of continuous education there is no doubt that 57.1 per cent had realised that the only way adult education can become an integral part of modern society is by adopting the philosophy of continuous education. The respondents in the opinion survey are in tune with a great deal of the resolutions passed at the International Conferences on Adult Education held at Elsinore, Denmark, in 1949; Montreal, Canada, in 1960 and Tokyo, Japan, in 1972. Adult educators and leaders of member states of UNESCO who organised the Conferences discussed the merits of lifelong education. "Learning to be" is what a meaningful system of education should aim at as its principal goal was the verdict of these International Conferences. This was the verdict (on a less unanimous agreement) by these Liverpool Royal Institution adult education students.

The other statements were not as important as the statement on continuous education. Indeed as it turned out all the other statements were not accepted as valid by the WEA students at the Liverpool centre. 35.7 per cent felt that centres like the Royal Institution would be the way to make adult education an integral part of life while 64.3 per cent disagreed. It was the same on every one of the other statements including the controversial question of the allocation of the fourth channel. This was a surprise for television has an important role to play in the opinion of many who have looked at the mass media in the education of adults. The majority of the adult students disagreed with the argument — 76.2 per cent — that allocating the fourth television channel to adult education would make that strata of education an integral part of life-long education.

Acceptance of Adult Education as an integral part of life

Statements	Response		Percentages	
	Yes	No	Yes	No
By a more formal organisation (e.g. adults education centres)	15	27	35.7	64.3
Raising the status of adult education tutors	3	39	7.1	92.9
By giving the money to appoint full-time tutors	5	37	11.9	88.1
By increasing central government support for the W.E.A./University Extension classes	17	25	40.5	59.5

Continued

Continued from previous page

Statements	Response		Percentages	
	Yes	No	Yes	No
By appointing a Minister for Adult Education in the government	7	35	16.7	83.3
By allocating the television fourth channel to adult education	10	32	23.8	76.2
By adopting the philosophy of continuous education	24	18	57.1	42.9
Other ways of giving adult education an important place in society	2	40	4.8	95.2

Table 9.3

Table 3 in the opinion survey indicates a number of very intriguing points. It seems that the WEA student is not conscious of the need to develop adult education through the appointment of more full-time tutors. Only 7.1 per cent were in favour of raising the status of adult education tutors and 11.9 per cent who were willing to give the money to appoint full-time tutors. It seems on this result that the WEA student is ignorant of the administrative structure of the WEA. One WEA student asked me at the Royal Institution in Liverpool: "Can you tell me if the government gives the WEA any money?" At least 40.5 per cent realised the need for this, but it is worth repeating, that 59.5 per cent did not accept the statement. It seems that the point made by many of the District Secretaries in their Annual Reports is partially responible for the result. In these reports they stress the need for the adult students who attend the WEA classes to belong to the WEA branches. The adults who enrol in the WEA classes attend for personal reasons and not from any commitment to the Workers Educational Movement. A committed WEA branch secretary would accept most of the statements in the quesionnaire as central to the acceptance in society of adult education as an integral part of life. He would like to see the adult education centres (only 35.7 per cent were in favour of these), he would support the appointment of a Minister for Adult Education in the government (only 16.7 per cent were in favour of this), allocating the television fourth channel to adult education, and by increasing central government support. The most significant response is that 57.1 per cent believed that by adopting the philosophy of continuous education one would see adult education disappearing as a cinderella and being accepted as an integral part of British life.

The Workers Educational Association have always placed a great deal of emphasis on student participation and in the early period of our study the students were often encouraged to write assignments for the tutor.

230

Preparation for an Adult Education Class

Statement	Response		Percentages	
	Yes	No	Yes	No
Reading Books on the subject	26	16	61.9	38.1
Talking over the course with friends	13	29	31.0	69.0
Following the tutor's comments	18	24	42.9	57.1
Written Exercises	7	35	16.7	83.3
Collecting material on the subject from newspapers/magazines	9	33	21.4	78.6
Listening to programmes on the radio that are relevant to the subject	17	25	40.5	59.5
Listening to programmes on television that are relevant to the subject	17	25	40.5	59.5

Table 9.4 .

Table 4 of the opinion survey indicates that reading books on the subject is the most common way of preparing for an adult education class, with 61.9 per cent, and this finding is in itself important. For reading a book demands literacy as well as certain level of education, an arousal of curiosity, interest and motives for enquiry, aspirations, spare mental energy, free time, all characteristics that belong to the middle class in England and Wales. Some parts of England and Wales have always in the WEA circles laid a great deal of emphasis on reading. At the beginning of our period David E. Evans, tutor/organiser for the extra-mural department in the University college of South Wales and Monmouthshire (and a noted collector of books) pleaded for the WEA branches to organise reading circles on the model of New Zealand and Estonia (Evans, 1945, p.30). In North Wales a doyen of the Labour Movement, David Thomas, was concerned in the same period at the inadequacy of the books that were available for WEA classes. He felt the need for a central library provision for the district (Thomas, 1947, p.110). In Liverpool in the seventies there was no provision of books for the WEA classes except for the joint WEA/University extension department adult classes. These boxes of books were prepared by the librarian of the extra-mural department in Abercromby Square and by the deputy librarian of the Royal Institution.

Table 4 of the opinion survey also shows that television and radio for the WEA student has not taken the place of books in preparation for a tutorial course with 40.5 per cent listening to radio and watching television and that following the tutor's comments (42.9 per cent) is even more important than the mass media.

The practise of writing exercises has obviously been discarded by most tutors in the WEA centres (like the Royal Institution) with only 16.7 per cent having done or at present carrying out the exercises. There is no doubt that more research is needed on the relationship of the mass media to the needs of an adult student and the view propounded often in Adult Education Conferences that the mass media should educate, inform as well as entertain has to be thoroughly discussed.

It is often said by the WEA students that they would like a broader choice of subjects in the different sessions. It was natural then to ask the question: In which of the following subjects would you like to attend the class? The students were given the choice of eight subjects, Local History, History, Current Affairs, a Biblical subject, Antiques, Woodwork, Religion and a practical subject without stipulating what the subject would be. Five of the eight subjects (Local History, History, Current Affairs, a Biblical subject, Religion) are taught in WEA classes at the Royal Institution, while Antiques are taught at the University Arts Library (which is another WEA centre). Woodwork is an exception on the WEA programme. It seems that in Liverpool over half of the adults would be interested in Local History, that is 54.8 per cent. History would attract seventeen of the adults who completed the quesionnaire, a 40.5 per cent of these seventeen, fifteen were WEA students. Current Affairs which is a subject that at one time (particularly in the nineteen twenties) was very popular with the WEA was not in the sixties or seventies hardly included in the adult education brochures. There are three very popular Current Affairs classes in the Merseyside region, and one of them will be evaluated in our participatory survey. It seems from our findings that there is no desperate need for the WEA or other adult education agencies to increase their provision of Current Affairs classes. Current Affairs would have interest for only 23.8 per cent of the total, and 24.3 per cent of the WEA students. A Biblical subject would have more of an appeal with 27.0 per cent of the WEA students and 40.0 per cent of the other adult students stating their preference for such a class. Out of the total of 42 there were twelve adults interested in a biblical subject, that is a 28.6 per cent. Antiques would have a clientele of nine, that is 21.4 per cent and Woodwork has even a smaller appeal, an attraction for three (19 per cent). A practical subject would appeal to fifteen, or 34.3 per cent.

This reinforces the point that in the main the WEA student is more concerned with academic liberal subjects than with the vocational practical subjects that are offered by local education authorities in adult centres and similar institutions.

The eight subjects noted had a limited appeal and the next question followed this up by asking the question: What kind of class do you prefer? Five choices were given, namely i. a tutorial in which the tutor delivers a lecture for the duration of the tutorial, ii. a tutorial in which the tutor divides the time into two periods: first half for lecturing and the second half for comments, iii. an informal atmosphere where the tutor and the class discuss the subject as he proceeds through his notes, iv. where the tutor uses audio-visual aids (film strip or cassettes) to supplement his lecturing, v. other methods. It seems that the most popular class is the one conducted in an informal atmosphere with the tutor and the class discussing the subject as he proceeds through his notes. Twenty three of the adult education students opted for this method, a 54.8 per cent. The next most popular class is the one where the tutor uses audio-visual aids, with twenty of the adult education students opting for it, that is a 47.6 per cent. It is right to point out that 52.4 per cent on the other hand prefer an adult education class without audio-visual aids. We know also that of the twenty, eighteen were WEA students, that is 48.6 per cent from their total of 37, and two (40.0 per cent) from the rest of the group.

If this finding could be verified in similar research at other WEA centres it would be of value to adult education for it seems that the traditional lecture and the newer approach of enlisting audio-visual aids are not popular to the average WEA student. He prefers on the evidence of this opinion survey the discussion method, and educational end-in-itself and to participate in discussion is to share in one of the most difficult educational exercises. Class discussions differ very widely in quality but the effort can be very rewarding. I would on my experience as a WEA tutor add that educational discussion has to be in a completely free and open setting. In my WEA classes at the Royal Institution I see myself often as a chairman of the discussion class. At the end of the sixties 'learning through discussion' became an acceptable part of adult eduction. W.F. Hill in his book *Learning Thru' Discussion* published in 1969 sets out detailed practical guidelines for his particular method, which allows the group members to take responsibility for their own learning within a carefully defined framework which protects the group from repetition and confusion. While *Learning Thru' Discussion* is more of a handbook for the Open University than a WEA class - yet it is important for an adult tutor to give his own contribution as an individual participant and also to ensure that it remains discussion throughout the time allocated. This survey to some extent invites further research into the place of technique in adult classes.

In our effort to portray the WEA student we asked a further question: Have you ever been attracted to the course of one of the following institutions but have not applied? A list of institutions were given starting with the success story of the Open University; then Wolsey Hall, Oxford, which provides correspondence courses; the National Extension College and their correspondence courses; Coleg Harlech which in 1977 celebrated its Jubilee as an adult residential college; short term residential adult college courses; the University Extension Certificate or Diploma Courses; University of London External Degrees or Diplomas, as well as part-time courses at a polytechnic.

Only eleven students (26.2 per cent) had considered the Open University, an institution which attracted enquiries from 43,000 adults in the first year of its existence. These adults had made enquiries as Sir Walter Perry rightly said 'before they could judge the quality of its courses" (Perry, 1971, p.98). The answer according to Sir Walter Perry why so many did apply for the Open University courses can be summarised under four headings. It was associated with the use of the mass media and especially television. The Open University was a large scale experiment in the education of adults. The openness of the entry and openness of the teaching programmes were also crucial in the appeal of the Open University. It is obvious also that though a large number of WEA students regarded continuing education as extremely important very few of them saw the Open University in the same light as Sir Walter Perry, one of its leading academic administrators. He wrote in 1971 these words:

> I believe that it is in the area of post-experience courses that the fullest potential of the Open University is realisable. I believe that in the last analysis it would not matter if we never produced a graduate; what would really matter is that we helped in this process of continuing education.　　　　　　　　　　　　　　　　　　　　(Perry, 1971, p. 105)

Years afterwards adult students in Liverpool were oblivious to the role of the Open University in continuing education in the United Kingdom.

Wolsey Hall, Oxford, who advertise regularly in the educational magazines and newspapers was of no importance to the adult students in our survey, with 97.6 per cent having not thought of using their correspondence course facilities. The National Extension College at Cambridge which was the prototype for the Open University was of no importance to the adult students and the same was true of Coleg Harlech which has always been a genuine college of second chance. Nineteen per cent had been attracted to the short term residential college courses and 7.1 per cent to the long term residential adult college (other than we presume Coleg Harlech) courses. 11.9 per cent had been attracted to the University Extension Certificate or Diploma Course and 7.1 per cent to the University of London External Degrees or Diplomas. With regard to the part-time polytechnic courses 14.3 per cent had thought of applying but in the end did not apply. This indicates that the Open University followed by the polytechnic do attract a small percentage of WEA students, but it seems that the vast majority of those who do apply to the Open University come from the adult population who are outside the WEA and other traditional educational agencies.

Question 13 was included for two reasons and proved a non-starter. The question asked: Would you agree with special adult educational provision for immigrant adults and the following ethnic group minorities? The ethnic group minorities were the Cypriots, West Indians, African Negroes, Indians and Pakistanis; the Chinese; Irish; Jews; Poles and East Europeans. The first reason for the inclusion of the question was to test the liberalism of the WEA students as they are often portrayed as internationalists and members of the left-wing political parties in British politics. Secondly, it was to test the awareness of these adult students of other cultural groups which are to be found in most of the major British cities, and especially in a cosmopolitan city like Liverpool.

Special Adult Educational Provision for Immigrant Adults and Ethnic Group Minorities

	Response		Percentages	
Groups	Yes	No	Yes	No
Cypriots	12	30	28.6	71.4
West Indians	13	29	31.0	69.0
African Negroes	14	28	33.3	66.7
Indians/Pakistanis	15	27	35.7	64.3
Chinese	12	30	28.6	71.4
Irish	12	30	28.6	71.4
Jews	10	32	23.8	76.2
Poles and East Europeans	12	30	28.6	71.4

Table 9.5

Table 5 indicates that the WEA student has no strong opinion on the need for special adult educational provision for immigrant adults. Indeed it seems that he is opposed to special treatment, and in my experience in Liverpool the immigrants and the ethnic group minorities are never involved in the WEA classes. The only ethnic group which attend classes regularly are the Jews. At least three of the respondents were disturbed at the inclusion of the question in the opinion survey and one of them told me:

> We are providing enough for them at present, and if they are keen on education, why don't they come along to the WEA classes.

The lowest support was for the Jews who have their own facilities at the Childwall Synagogue in co-operation with the local adult centre, a mere 23.8 per cent in favour of special provision, and the largest support was for the Indians and Pakistanis, a 35.7 per cent support. The Indians have their own Hindu Centre in Edge Lane and the Pakistanis have a centre in Liverpool 8. It seems that the colour of the immigrants has not influenced the respondents of the questionnaire, for the group which had the smallest support were the Irish who as it turns out is the largest immigrant community in England, Wales and Scotland, and especially in Liverpool. Scotland Road in Liverpool in the nineteenth century and early part of the twentieth century became an 'Irish Town' and the Irish have played a most important part in the development of the Labour Movement on Merseyside. There are special local education authority facilities for the Irish in Liverpool but it seems that the WEA students are not in favour of such provision; 71.4 per cent are definitely opposed to special adult educational provision for the Irish. Two of the respondents told me:

> The Irish element is more responsible for the militancy of Merseyside than anyone else. They have given us a bad image;

and the other:

Let the Irish take advantage of the WEA classes as the rest of us do.

iii Public Libraries

The WEA student in our opinion survey is a person who at least enjoys books but does not attend public libraries as often as one would have expected. Only 2.7 per cent go to the public library daily while 18.9 per cent of the WEA students go along weekly and 32.4 per cent on fortnightly visits. The same number, 32.4 per cent, go along monthly and 5.4 per cent once every six months. Among the other group of adult students 20.0 per cent attend fortnightly, 40.0 per cent monthly and 20.0 per cent yearly while 20.0 per cent never attend compared with 8.1 per cent (from a larger sample) of WEA students. This indicates that to a WEA student the public library has a place in the educational process.

iv The Impact of Television and Radio

Television has a major role to play in arousing people's awareness of the problems of twentieth century Britain. One adult confessed that television had made him read less, "I don't read as much as I did before television came but my wife will buy all the books which have been serialised on the screen". Another WEA student regarded television as a fine medium of education: "There is a lot you can learn from programmes like *Panorama*". "It helps you and the whole family" was another reply made by an elderly person. It was decided in preparing the questionnaire for the opinion survey to select television programmes which had definite educational aim and content. *Panorama* is a BBC television programme which has an educational aspect to it, with an investigative role on current affairs. It is a programme watched by over half of the WEA students, 59.5 per cent compared with 40.0 per cent of the other adult students.

World in Action is an Independent Television Channel programme with a similar format to that of *Panorama*. The same number of people in our opinion survey watched the *World in Action* programmes as watched *Panorama*. *Tonight* was a late night current affairs BBC programme (usually after 10.15 p.m.) which has not the same attraction for the adult students. The number of WEA students who watched *Tonight* was fourteen, or 37.8 per cent while 40.0 per cent watched it from the rest of the adult education group. *Nationwide* which is a BBC news and current affairs programme at one of the peak viewing periods (6.00 to 7.00 p.m.) had a larger number of adult education students looking at it. At least 73.0 per cent of the WEA students watched *Nationwide* and 80.0 per cent from the rest of the adult education group. The Open University provides programmes for their own students and 24.3 per cent of the WEA students also watch these educational programmes. It is significant that no one from the other adult education group watches the Open University programmes, and this result is in line with 26.2 per cent of WEA students that had considered applying to the Open University.

236

News programmes were also included in the list of educational programmes, specifying in brackets two examples, the *Nine o'clock B.B.C. News* and the *ITV News* at Ten o'clock. Thirty three of the W.E.A. students out of 37, that is 89.2 per cent watched the news bulletins compared with 60.0 per cent from the other adult education group. It meant a massive total of 85.7 per cent.

The popular BBC *Mastermind* programme under the chairmanship of Magnus Magnusson was the next educational programme in the list. *Mastermind* proved to be a popular programme, with 73.3 per cent of the W.E.A. students watching this programme, and 80.0 per cent of the other students.

It is obvious that television has an impact on adult education students — WEA as well as those who attend regularly other adult educational centres. The WEA student enjoys factual and informative television programmes on both channels, and the only programme that proved to be unpopular was *Tonight.* The time that the programme is televised could be one reason for its unpopularity compared to earlier programmes.

Looking at the educational programmes on radio, one does not get the same interest as in the television programmes. Eight programmes were chosen. The first programme was *From Our Own Correspondents* on Radio 4 which brings together short and informative educational talks from different parts of the world, written and spoken by the BBC correspondents. From the WEA students there was a 35.1 per cent response and from the rest of the adult students it was 40.0 per cent. The *World at One* on Radio 4 was very evenly matched, with 40.5 per cent from the WEA group and 40.0 per cent from the other group. *Kaleidoscope* is a nightly arts programme which looks at literature, the theatre, poetry and any other subject or on a festival which is taking place that week. At least 27.0 per cent of the WEA students do listen to *Kaleidoscope* and 40.0 per cent from the adult education group. *Radio News* was included. It was found that 62.2 per cent of the WEA students listened to *Radio News* and 40.0 per cent from the other adult education groups. Schools Radio has invariably a large number of educational programmes but it is obvious that very few of our sample listened to these excellent programmes. The number was 24.3 per cent of the WEA students and no one from the other grouping. This in itself is highly significant for it seems that the WEA student is aware of educational programmes of the Schools Radio while the rest of the adult students are not interested in the provision. *Yesterday in Parliament* on Radio 4 was listened to by 29.7 per cent of the WEA students and by 40.0 per cent of the other adult students. This programme was first broadcast in 1947. The *World Tonight* attracted 40.5 per cent of the WEA students and 40.0 per cent from the small sample of adult students.

Another part of the mass media is the newspaper world, and it has been claimed that there was a very great increase in newspaper reading during the second world war and a list of quality and popular newspapers were included in the question: Do you read any of the following newspapers? Table 6 gives the results of the questionnaire.

Daily Newspaper	Response		Percentage	
	Yes	No	Yes	No
The Guardian	13	29	31.0	69.0
The Times	3	39	7.1	92.9
Daily Mirror	9	33	21.4	78.6
Daily Telegraph	12	30	28.6	71.4
Daily Mail	5	37	11.9	88.1
The Sun	3	39	7.1	92.9
Daily Express	11	31	26,2	73.8
Liverpool Daily Post	21	21	50.0	50.0
Other Daily Newspapers	11	31	26.2	73.8

Table 9.6

Interpreting Table 6 of the opinion survey and interviewing some of the sample one realises that the average WEA students which attended the Liverpool centre are not readers of the quality newspapers and the only newspaper which has a reasonable attraction is the local newspaper, the *Liverpool Daily Post* which is read by half of the students, that is 50 per cent (made up of 45.9 per cent of those we have classed as WEA students and 80 per cent of the other adult students). The *Guardian* has only an overall readership of thirty one per cent, twelve of the students being committed WEA students, that is 32.4 per cent. The *Times* has a very limited appeal of only 7.1 per cent, and the other popular newspapers, the *Daily Mirror, Daily Telegraph, Daily Mail, The Sun* and *Daily Express* all having a very limited readership among these adult students. they have a more limited appeal among adult students than the rest of the adult population, and it seems that the WEA students are not as dependent on the press for their information and knowledge of everyday events. Newspapers have to exist in a world in which information is a commodity dealt with by many different agencies. They are one among many agencies and this is reflected in the response to this question from a sample of adult students. One adult student told me — "There iş no need for me to read the newspapers for news. I get it on the television. I am also sufficiently interested to attend adult education classes for my general education. What newspaper will provide the same in depth education as I receive in the WEA class at the Royal Institution?"

The situation with regard to the weekly magazine was very similar as Table 7 indicates.

Magazines	Response		Percentages	
	Yes	No	Yes	No
New Statesman	7	35	16.7	83.3
Economist	3	39	7.1	92.9
New Society	5	37	11.9	88.1
The Listener	11	31	26.2	73.8
Times Educational Supplement	6	36	14.3	85.7
The Spectator	1	41	2.4	97.6
Others	12	30	28.6	71.4

Table 9.7

Interpreting Table 7 of the opinion survey one is forced to the conclusion that the average WEA students who attended one Liverpool centre are not avid magazine readers. The only magazine listed which had any sizeable readership among the WEA students was the *Listener* (the BBC weekly magazine) with a 26.2 per cent response. All the other magazines were below 16.7 per cent with the *Spectator* which has one of the lowest circulations having only one student reading it. The *Economist* had three readers, a 7.1 per cent, the *New Society* had five (three of them WEA students and the other two adult students) so that means an overall total of 11.9 and a WEA response of 8.1 per cent as against a 40.0 per cent from the rest of the adult group, and the *Times Educational Supplement* with an overall total of 14.3 per cent, which is again interesting in view of the fact that the weekly newspaper TES had a very high standard of reporting and articles. All these magazines and weekly newspapers are regarded as educational in nature and even under the wide umbrella of others there was only a response of 28.6 per cent. The vast majority of students at the Liverpool Royal Institution Centre did not feel that the highbrow weekly magazines were essential to them, and all these magazines were also to be found in the library or the lounge/cafeteria of the Royal Institution.

A question was also asked on their reading of the Sunday newspapers. Seven newspapers were listed and the response was very similar to the Daily newspapers as Table 8 indicates.

Sunday Newspaper	Response		Percentages	
	Yes	No	Yes	No
The Observer	12	30	28.6	71.4
Sunday Times	13	29	31.0	69.0
Sunday Telegraph	6	36	14.3	85.7

Continued

Continued from previous page	Response		Percentages	
	Yes	No	Yes	No
The People	5	37	11.9	88.1
Sunday Express	13	29	31.0	69.0
News of the World	0	42	-	100.0
Sunday Mirror	4	38	9.5	90.5
No Sunday Paper	8	34	19.0	81.0

Table 9.8

The most popular of the Sunday newspapers was the *Sunday Times* with 31.0 per cent regarding it and the *Sunday Express* as essential reading once a week. The *Observer* came next with 28.6 per cent and the *Sunday Telegraph, People* and the *Sunday Mirror* having a very low response of 14.3 per cent, 11.9 per cent and 9.5 per cent. It is significant that the *News of the World,* one of the Sunday newspapers with the largest circulation was not read by any of the WEA students or indeed by any of the adult students, while 81.0 per cent did not receive any Sunday newspaper. Looking at the more detailed breakdown of information we find that with two of the Sunday newspapers, the *Observer* and the *Sunday Express* (60.0 per cent) are read by the adult students, and by 24.3 per cent and 27.0 per cent of the WEA students. It seems therefore that the WEA student in Liverpool is not as interested in Sunday newspapers as the rest of the population.

The next question was devised to find out how gregarious the WEA student is and how committed to society in a political or a religious way. Table 9 gives the overall result.

	Response		Percentages	
Attending Organisations	Yes	No	Yes	No
Pensioners' Club	1	41	2.4	97.6
Church	12	30	28.6	71.4
Chapel	3	39	7.1	92.9
Townswomen's Guild	2	40	4.8	95.2
A Ward Political Meeting	1	41	2.4	97.6
Community Council	3	39	7.1	92.9
A Society (e.g. Literary Society, etc).	9	33	21.4	78.6
Others	14	28	33.3	66.7

Table 9.9

This table in the opinion survey shatters the image of the WEA as a movement which has produced left wing political activists. It seems that the typical WEA student at one centre in Liverpool is a person who does not attend any other formal organisation in large numbers. The other organisations which were not named have the largest support and of the organisations and institutions named the one with the largest support is the Church tradition with 28.6 per cent, which could mean either the Established Church of England or the Roman Catholic Church. Some of those interviewed expressed strong views on the need for religious affiliation. One was a Nonconformist who always identify themselves with the Chapel tradition. He said: "Life is empty and meaningless without faith. It sustains me and motivates in all my activities". But he was in the minority and the Chapel allegiance was only 7.1 per cent. This would be different in other areas of Britain, and in particular, in North Wales where there is a strong Nonconformist tradition. But others interviewed did not give religion any consideration, and one comment went so far as to state: "I am not interested at all in religion. I think that the WEA provides me with plenty of activities and if I got involved with religion then I would not have the opportunity of attending as I do three WEA classes a week".

Another surprise in Table 9 of the opinion survey is that only 2.4 per cent attend a ward political meeting in view of the large number of politicians who have been nurtured in WEA classes or who have passed through the WEA organisations as tutors, as for example George Wigg (later Lord Wigg), Hugh Gaitskell and in more recent times Neil Kinnock, the Labour Member of Parliament for Bedwellty. It is hardly surprising that only 7.1 per cent of the students are involved in the work of community councils when we find that only 2.4 per cent attend a ward political meeting. It must be said that this does not reflect the impact of the WEA in other areas, as for example in the South Wales coalfield. A cultured miner who was badly burnt at the coalface was David Rees Griffiths (1882-1953) who was known in the world of Welsh literature under his non-de-plume of Amanwy. A brother of the Labour politician, James Griffiths, Amanwy admitted in an article in the Welsh weekly newspaper *Y Cymro* at the end of his life that though "the W.E.A. started in England it reached its pinnacle of its glory in Wales. It shook the life of the industrial valleys of South Wales to its roots. This is seen in the number of councillors and the majority of the Members of Parliament from South Wales who have belonged to the W.E.A. at one time or another". Either the Merseyside experience has been different or the political involvement of the WEA members belonged to the earlier phases of the adult education movement and not the more affluent post-war period. Some of those interviewed were hostile to the idea of WEA members parading their political allegiance. "The W.E.A. has nothing to do with politics. I am not interested in politics but I am attracted to the W.E.A. for it offers classes on a variety of subjects, such as Antiques and Literature"; and "You surprise me that the W.E.A. has nurtured a large number of left-wing politicians. But I must admit that I am ignorant of left wing politicians and also of the history of the W.E.A."

Considering the number of pensioners or senior citizens who attend WEA classes, in particular morning or afternoon classes, it is surprising that only 2.4 per cent belong to a pensioners' club. Again it seems that the WEA student does not feel a need or motivation to belong to the organisation, and only 21.4 per cent belong to any kind of formal organisation, such as the literary societies. The largest percentage belongs to the unnamed other societies who have 33.3 per cent belonging to them. But this is again a small percentage considering in a city like Liverpool the number of societies that are active and flourishing, such as the English Speaking Union, to name just one society.

It also seems that the WEA students are not at all that interested in pressure groups as Table 10 of the opinion survey indicates.

Statement	Response		Percentages	
Belonging to Pressure Groups	Yes	No	Yes	No
Royal Society for the Prevention of Cruelty to Animals	1	41	2.4	97.6
United Nations Association	2	40	4.8	95.2
Shelter	2	40	4.8	95.2
The Howard League for Penal Reform	0	42	-	100.0
CND	1	41	2.4	97.6
"Fabian Society"	2	40	4.8	95.2
Other Pressure Groups	11	31	26.2	73.8

Table 9.10

There are two points that need stressing. Firstly, the response of the WEA student is extremely apathetic to these pressure groups. No one belongs to the Howard League for Penal Reform, and only 2.4 per cent to the Royal Society for the Prevention of Cruelty to Animals and the Campaign for Nuclear Disarmament. The United Nations Association, Shelter (a pressure group in the field of housing) and the Fabian Society with its emphasis on gradualism in British politics and an important pressure group within the Labour Party has only a 4.8 per cent response. Secondly, all the students who did belong to the pressure groups were from the WEA group with only 20.0 per cent from the other adult group belonging to some other pressure groups rather than to the seven pressure groups named.

The next question was to do with reading tastes and five well known paperback series were noted as well as two Book Club series, the Left Book Club in the thirties and forties, and the Home University Library series.

Statement	Response		Percentages	
	Yes	No	Yes	No
Have you in your home a book from any of the following Paperback Series or Book clubs?				
Corgi Paperback	24	18	57.1	42.9
Any book in the Left Book Club Series	7	35	16.7	83.3
Any book in the Home University Library Series	7	35	16.7	83.3
Paladin	10	32	23.8	76.2
Pelican/Penguin paperback	35	7	83.3	16.7
A Mayflower paperback	8	34	19.0	81.0
An Abacus paperback	8	34	19.0	81.0
Other paperbacks	24	18	57.1	42.9

Table 9.11

This table of the opinion survey indicates that the adult student and in particular the WEA student prefer the popular but scholarly books that are produced on a variety of subjects by the Pelican and Penguin series. A very high percentage — 83.3 per cent — has in their possession a Pelican or a Penguin book. Breaking the figures into two groups — 86.5 per cent from the WEA students and 60.0 per cent from the other adult education group — have in their possession books from the Pelican or Penguin series. These factual books have attraction to the WEA students and one said: "I am only interested in factual or serious books". In interviewing a number of the students one found that the factual books were books of biography, history, hobbies and that the Penguin paperbacks catered for this group. A WEA student from our opinion survey is in the main a person who loves in particular paperback books and has certain types of books in his possession. The only point that is raised by Table 11 is the fact that 16.7 per cent have in their homes a copy of the Left Book Club Series and yet only 2.4 per cent attend a ward political meeting. The zeal of the thirties for political discussion has to a large extent disappeared and it is possible also that some of these Left Book Club books could have belonged to other members of the family. Between 1936 and 1948 the Left Book Club produced 256 titles and most of them do not make interesting reading in the late sixties, though a few are regarded as classics such as Gedye's *Fallen Bastions,* Koestler's *Spanish Testament* and Orwell's, *The Road to Wigan Pier.* Again the 16.7 per cent might be explained by the simple fact that the sales of Left Book Club books were immense at the time. A choice would sell 100,000 and then there was the alternative choice and alternative alternative *(Guardian,* 8 April 1978, p.11).

The same arguments could be used for another Library Series, that is the Home University Library Series which had a response of 16.7 per cent made up of the WEA students, and from within what we have called the WEA group a 18.9 per cent response. The other adult group seems to have in its possession the more popular paperbacks, 60.0 per cent had the Corgi books, 60.0 per cent had Paladin books, and 40.0 per cent Abacus books and 80.0 per cent other paperbacks. The WEA student then had more Pelican/Penguin (86.5 per cent as against 60.0 per cent), Left Book Club and Home University Library series than the other adult students but less Corgi books (56.8 per cent as against 60.0 per cent), Paladin (18.9 per cent as against 60.0 per cent), Mayflower (18.9 per cent as against 20.0 per cent), Abacus (21.6 per cent as against 40.0 per cent) and from the other paperbacks (54.1 per cent as against 80.0 per cent) but as I have stressed all along on a much smaller sample than the WEA sample.

Looking at the interests of the WEA student it seems that books make up an important part to his life. Table 12 indicates this. At least sixteen (38.1 per cent) has book collecting as one of their

Pastimes of WEA students

	Response		Percentages	
Pastimes	**Yes**	**No**	**Yes**	**No**
Book Collecting	16	26	38.1	61.9
Stamp Collecting	1	41	2.4	97.6
Antique Collecting	10	32	23.8	76.2
Allotment Gardening	6	36	14.3	85.7
Watching Football	9	33	21.4	78.6
Watching Rugby Union or Rugby League	3	39	7.1	92.9
Watching other Sports	9	33	21.4	78.6
Other Pastimes	17	25	40.5	59.5

Table 9.12

pastimes compared with stamp collecting (2.4 per cent) and even Antique collecting which has a response of 23.8 per cent. Allotment Gardening is not popular with adult education students with 14.3 per cent opting for it as their pastime, and Sport also has not a significant part to play in the lives of these students with 21.4 per cent watching football, 7.1 per cent watching either Rugby Union or Rugby League, and 21.4 per cent watching other Sport. Even under the heading of other pastimes one has only 40.5 per cent.

Table 12 indicates that a WEA student is not a very active person physically and that his tastes and pastimes are to do with the refined world of collecting rather than the world of sport and allotment gardening.

The WEA as well as other adult education organisations after the second world war introduced study tours as part of their educational activities In all parts of England and Wales this became a regular WEA feature. As an example to prove the point from the early period, Gwyn Illtyd Lewis led 25 WEA students from the Swansea Valley and Glynneath area on a fortnight study tour in Holland in the summer of 1950 (Lewis, 1950, p.44). Because of this long-standing tradition to various parts of Europe it was felt appropriate to give the name of various countries where tours are regularly arranged by a large number of organisations to discover if travel was a characteristic of a WEA student in one Liverpool centre. Eight countries were listed as well as a general heading for others. Table 13 gives the results.

Visit to a Country on an Educational Tour

	Response		Percentages	
Countries	Yes	No	Yes	No
France	9	33	21.4	78.6
Germany	8	34	19.0	81.0
Italy	9	33	21.4	78.6
A Scandinavian Country	3	39	7.1	92.9
Russia	3	39	7.1	92.9
Greece	5	37	11.9	88.1
Israel	5	37	11.9	88.1
Yugoslavia	6	36	14.3	85.7
Others	16	26	38.1	61.9

Table 9.13

It seems that in one Liverpool centre WEA students do not regard the study and educational tours when planning their holidays and it is often a difficult task to persuade the rest of the family (that is, a husband or a wife) that they should see France on an educational tour. The schedules are restrictive to a large number of people and it is not surprising considering the number of educational tours offered that only 21.4 per cent have been to France and Italy, 19.0 per cent to Germany, 14.3 per cent to Yugoslavia, 11.9 per cent to Greece and Israel, and 7.1 per cent to a Scandinavian country or to Russia on an educational tour. Study tours had been arranged to other countries and 38.1 per cent had been on those educational visits which can take the form of a summer school. Denmark and Finland are two countries where the WEA have over the years strong contacts and we come across in the history of the WEA continual references to the summer schools held in these countries. A large Welsh delegation, for example, in 1946 attended the summer school of the International Folk College at Elsinore, Denmark. An outstanding lecture was delivered at this summer school by the Welsh adult educationist, Dr. T.

Hughes Griffiths (Lewis, 1946, p.136). But these educational tours, study-tours, summer schools are exceptions and few and far between due to the reluctance of the WEA members to participate on these educational tours.

The WEA has to exist and co-operate with other adult educational agencies, and in particular with the local educational authority. A question was asked: Do you accept the need for the local educational authorities to fulfil the following provision? Table 14 gives the results.

The Role of the Local Education Authorities	Response		Percentages	
	Yes	No	Yes	No
Encourage by special efforts those adults who never attend any kind of adult class	27	15	64.3	35.7
Give special consideration to the deprived areas of our cities to set up an adult education centre in every ward of the constituency	18	24	42.9	57.1
Appoint a full-time adult education organiser for every adult education centre	12	30	28.6	71.4
Set up community adult education newsletters to inform the people of the provisions	22	20	52.4	47.6
Hold morning and afternoon classes from Monday to Friday	19	23	45.2	54.8
Hold one-day schools on Saturdays	18	24	42.9	57.1
Do something else	3	39	7.1	92.9

Table 9.14

The WEA student is conscious of the need to reach those adults who never attend any adult education centre and over half of the respondents (that is 27 or 64.3 per cent) would like to see a situation where the LEA would be allowed to implement plans that would reach the majority of the adult population who never attend any tutorial or adult educational class. This standpoint is strengthened by the fact that 22 WEA students — 52.4 per cent — would like the LEA to establish community adult education newsletters to inform the people of the provisions available in the education of adults. This is already done in certain areas on Merseyside such as St. Helens where a newspaper is produced giving details of the provision of the LEA, University Extension and the WEA and distributed to every household in the area. However the WEA and adult students who answered our questionnaire did not realise in sufficient numbers that to introduce such a plan entails more staff, having convenient adult centres at ward level, and introducing a continuous educational programme, morning, afternoon and evenings as well as a large number of one day schools. This was not understood or accepted by the majority of the adult students though a sizeable minority realised as the statistics demonstrate. Eighteen people, that is 42.9 per cent, wanted action in the deprived areas of our cities and another nineteen, that is 45.2 per cent, were in favour of morning and afternoon classes to be organised for five days of the week. Eighteen people, that is 42.9 per cent, were also in favour of the continuation of the one day Saturday schools which the WEA occasionally organise but this time to be arranged by the LEA, while twelve (that is 28.6 per cent) would like the implementation of the appointment of a full time adult education organiser for every adult education centre. This would only come however when government, LEA, voluntary bodies and those who reap the benefits of adult education centres will be convinced that the education of adults is not a peripheral activity for the British people. Public authorities have been all too happy to leave the provision to public bodies of which it may be said that many of them have more goodwill than expertise or resources and it seems that there are still a large number of WEA students who will accept such an unsatisfactory situation.

It was natural to ask a further question: Would you like the WEA/or the University Extension to concentrate its resources? Eight options were given and Table 15 gives us the results.

Priorities of University Extension/or WEA

Statement	Response		Percentages	
	Yes	No	Yes	No
Trade Union Education	5	37	11.9	88.1
Education among Immigrants	11	31	26.2	73.8
Political Education	8	34	19.0	81.0
Adult Education for Illiterates	20	22	47.6	52.4
Education for Retirement	20	22	47.6	52.4
Education in Factories	5	37	11.9	88.1
Education in the Inner City Areas	11	31	26.2	73.8
Continuous Education	21	21	50.0	50.0

Table 9.15

There was only one priority to the WEA students who filled in the questionnaire and that was continuous education which appealed to 50.0 per cent of the respondents. This has come through in a number of instances in this quesionnaire and is a highly significant point to emphasise. It shows that adult education students are often sensitive to the need for extensive opportunities throughout the life span of every individual. But unfortunately this group stumbles with the other priorities. Adult education for illiterates and education for retirement also have priority bestowed upon them with 47.6 per cent in favour of such provision. The most surprising result is the low priority given to trade union education with only 11.9 per cent in favour of this provision. One has to remember that in the sixties the WEA has concentrated on education for trade unionists and yet the WEA students cannot agree that trade union education is a priority compared with continuous education, education for illiterates, education for retirement and indeed education for immigrants. Education in factories has a low priority (11.9 per cent) and so has political education (19.0 per cent). It can be stated without any contradiction that political education has never been seriously on the syllabus of any adult education agency though periodically an interest in it will be manifested. This happened after the second world war but by the mid fifties much of the sense of urgency for political education had diminished. The same was true in the sixties and Harold Entwistle could claim at the end of the decade that "not a single English College of Education offered a course in political studies" (Entwistle, 1971, p.3). Only eight of the adult students (19.0 per cent) would be perturbed at such a situation.

Education in the inner city area had eleven people, that is 26.2 per cent, who regarded this as a priority. But this again is disappointing when one is reminded of the pioneering work of Tom Lovett and the support of the WEA in Liverpool for the schemes in the inner city area. Eric Midwinter's *Priority Education: An Account of the Liverpool Project* published by Penguin in 1972 sums up the exciting development that took place and largely unnoticed by the students who attended WEA classes at the Royal Institution, an inner city area of Liverpool. But while Lovett and other WEA tutors met the working class in the informal groups at public houses and other centres, the WEA tutors at the Royal Institution met the middle class, the majority of whom had travelled in from the suburbs to study in the setting of a noble and well-kept building. The differences could not have been greater and summed up in a nutshell the problems faced by the WEA in Liverpool and throughout Britain.

The WEA as an adult education movement had been fortunate in the intellectual and charismatic leaders that belonged to the movement — men full of energy and enthusiasm. The most influential of these, as we have shown in this book, was R.H. Tawney (1880-1962) who soon after he left Oxford University joined the Workers' Education Association as a tutor. Here he consolidated his concern, respect and affection for the ordinary man and became an advocate for an education which would develop the full potentiality of every individual. Tawney's ideas were firmly based on his beliefs in christianity and socialism, and his influence has been significant, especially among intellectuals of left-wing inclination and the specific group of working men whom he taught in WEA classes.

Some of these intellectuals like Hugh Gaitskell and Asa Briggs became firm advocates of the WEA's concern for educating the ordinary people, and Tawney worked closely with Mrs. Mary Stocks, historian of the WEA and broadcaster, and Professor S.G. Raybould of the University of Leeds. Another outstanding social thinker of his generation was Professor G. Douglas Cole, a friend of R.H. Tawney while Lord Edward Boyle was unusual in the fact that as a Conservative Party politician he identified himself so closely with the WEA. As one comes across the names of these intellectuals and WEA figures it was appropriate to ask the question: Among the competent well known adult educators of the last 30 years in England and Wales I would name the following. Did you hear any of these lecturers at any time?

Names	Responses		Percentages	
	Yes	No	Yes	No
Professor G. Douglas Cole	3	39	7.1	92.9
Lord Edward Boyle	6	36	14.3	85.7
Professor R.H. Tawney	4	38	9.5	90.5
Professor Asa Briggs	5	37	11.9	88.1
Rt. Hon. Hugh Gaitskell	13	29	31.0	69.0
(Lady) Mary Stocks	12	30	28.6	71.4
Professor S.G. Raybould	5	37	11.9	88.1
Others	16	26	38.1	61.9

Table 9.16

Table 16 of the opinion survey can be interpreted in a number of ways. In the first place the WEA in comparison with a large number of other organisations do not personalise their academics and the opportunities for these men to speak in the different regions are very limited. Secondly four of these seven were in the forefront of the WEA's activities in the thirties and in the war years. In the post-war period their influence had declined substantially. This could explain why only 9.5 per cent had heard the greatest name in the annals of the WEA — R.H. Tawney, who was at his peak in the period 1908-1938. Hugh Gaitskell (1906-1963), leader of the Labour Party between 1955-1963 was a man of outstanding qualities, and of the seven names given he is the one whom most of the respondents had heard at some meeting or other. The historian of the WEA, Mary Stocks, comes next, and all the other academics were well behind, having been heard by less than fifteen per cent. The WEA is obviously a localised movement with the national leaders not having the same function as we find in other movements. Its impact depends not on its national leaders but on the provision provided in each locality.

The next question was to do with the qualities of these well-known WEA personalities as lecturers.

Statement	Response		Percentages	
	Yes	No	Yes	No
Academic ability	15	27	35.7	64.3
Effective presentation	16	26	38.1	61.9
Simplicity of expression	12	30	28.6	71.4
Charisma of personality	12	30	28.6	71.4
Interesting subject matter	7	35	16.7	83.3
Command of language	11	31	26.2	73.8
Interesting anecdotal material	4	38	9.5	90.5
Ample use of illustrations	3	39	7.1	92.9

Table 9.17

This table does not convey what it should as the respondents had never heard R.H. Tawney, G.D. Cole, Boyle, Briggs, Gaitskell, Stocks or Raybould lecturing in a WEA setting. But it is of interest to note that those who had heard these distinguished men and Lady Stocks were convinced that effective presentation (38.1 per cent) and academic ability (35.7 per cent) were important qualities. Simplicity of expression and charisma of personality (28.6 per cent) were also noted, with command of language (26.2 per cent), interesting subject matter (16.7 per cent) with interesting anecdotal material (9.5 per cent) and ample use of illustrations (7.1 per cent) not being of any significance.

The WEA's strength lies not in the outstanding names that have held office in the movement but in the full-time and part-time WEA tutors that have taught and lectured regularly year after year. They are able to keep the WEA classes together through effective presentation and academic ability and the questionnaire should have named seven of the West Lancashire and Cheshire WEA names of the 1940 to 1970 period rather than using the names of national W.E.A. communicators.

The WEA like all other adult education agencies constantly complain of the lack of support it gets mainly from the central government. Professor Thomas Kelly sums up the attitude of adult education organisations:

> At no time, except for a few brief years after the second world war, have the adult education agencies been provided with anything like the funds needed for the full development of this sector. (Kelly, 1969, p.9).

It was decided to find out how the students looked upon the apparent neglect of the educational system of adult education.

Statement	Response		Percentages	
	Yes	No	Yes	No
Lack of interest by central government	11	31	26.2	73.8
Apathy of the public	23	19	54.8	45.2
Poor facilities of the educational agencies	10	32	23.8	76.2
Lack of finance	16	26	38.1	61.9
Appeal of the mass media	15	27	35.7	64.3
Not enough preparation in the secondary schools for continuous education	19	23	45.2	54.8
Lack of interest by local authorities	7	35	16.7	83.3
None of the above	6	36	14.3	85.7
Others	4	38	9.5	90.5

Table 9.18

The findings in Table 18 of the opinion survey indicates that the central government is not responsible for the apparent neglect of adult education. It seems that the blame lies with the public themselves and 54.8 per cent of the respondents state that apathy on the part of the public is the chief reason. Again it is very significant that the next reason stated is that there is not enough preparation in the secondary schools for continuous education. 45.2 per cent felt that this was a reason for the neglect of adult education in the educational system of England and Wales. Lack of finance and the appeal of the mass media are noted by a large proportion though 61.9 per cent and 64.3 per cent dismiss this as being of any significance. It seems that the typical WEA student blames the ordinary public for the apparent neglect of adult education and then the schools for not preparing the young people for continuous education.

Continuing education always stresses the role of informal education in the task of educating adults, and magazines have an important role to play. Question 30 of the quesionnaire asked: Would you regard any of the following magazines (*Woman; Woman's Own; Woman's Realm; Pins and Needles; Motor Mechanic; Home Maker; Reader's Digest*- others) as educative in any way?

Magazines	Response		Percentages	
	Yes	No	Yes	No
Woman	7	35	16.7	83.3
Woman's Own	8	34	19.0	81.0

Continued

Continued from previous page	Response		Percentages	
Magazines	Yes	No	Yes	No
Woman's Realm	9	33	21.4	78.6
Pins and Needles	13	29	31.0	69.0
Motor Mechanics	17	25	40.5	59.5
Home Maker	17	25	40.5	59.5
Reader's Digest	27	15	64.3	35.7
Others	9	33	21.4	78.6

Table 9.19

The magazine *Reader's Digest* which has a large circulation is regarded by 64.3 per cent as educative while the do-it-yourself magazines, *Motor Mechanic* and *Home Maker* are regarded by 40.5 per cent as being educative. All the magazines that cater for women, *Woman, Woman's Own, Woman's Realm* and *Pins and Needles* are not looked upon as being educative by the majority of the respondents.

Two factual questions were asked with regard to television and the cinema, two more auxiliaries of informal adult education and continuing education.

The question on television viewing asked: For how long do you watch television every day? There were eight blocks — one hour to seven hours, not at all, and the results are given in Table 20.

Viewing Television	Response		Percentages	
Daily	Yes	No	Yes	No
1 hour	7	35	16.7	83.3
2 hours	15	27	35.7	64.3
3 hours	8	34	19.0	81.0
4 hours	2	40	4.8	95.2
5 hours	2	40	4.8	95.2
6 hours	2	40	4.8	95.2
7 hours	2	40	4.8	95.2
Not at all	4	38	9.5	90.5

Table 9.20

This table indicates that the WEA student is not too interested in television, but on the other hand, television has a place in their lives.

Cinema

The cinema in the sixties lost its hold — except among unmarried teenagers — and audiences dropped from 1,365 million in 1951 to 415 million in 1962, producing a fall in expenditure from £108 million to £60 million (Sampson, 1965, p.619). As the cinema has its role in continuing education it was decided to ask the question: How often do you go to the cinema? The choices were numerous: every night; weekly; twice a week; fortnightly; monthly; yearly; never, and on a special occasion when there was the exceptional film. It seems from Table 21 that the WEA student has very little time for the cinema, and that the vast majority, 64.3 per cent, attend the cinema on a special occasion where there is an exceptional film, and that 19.0 per cent never attend the cinema.

	Response	Percentages
Cinema-Going	Yes	Yes
Every night	1	2.4
Monthly	3	7.1
Yearly	3	7.1
Never	8	19.0
On a special occasion (for example exceptional film)	27	64.3

Table 9.21

Theatre-Going

Some adult educationalists, notably Harold Wiltshire at Nottingham, have been very much in favour of involving the theatre in the provision of liberal adult education. It can be claimed that some of the Nottingham University adult centres, like Pilgrim College, Boston, moved into the field of practical drama, out of which in the 1960's developed a small theatre and arts centre, Blackfriars. But in most cases the Boston experience was an exception.

The question asked for factual evidence: How often do you go to the theatre? With the students being given the choice of answering — every week; every fortnight; monthly; yearly; never; or on a special occasion. Table 22 of the opinion survey provides the answer.

	Response	Percentages
Theatre-Going	Yes	Yes
Every fortnight	1	2.4
Monthly	7	16.7
Yearly	2	4.8

Continued

Continued from previous page	Response	Percentages
Theatre going	Yes	Yes
Never	5	11.9
On a special occasion	27	64.3

Table 9.22

The same pattern is to be seen in the theatre-going as in the cinema-going, with the WEA student opting for the theatre on a special occasion though twice the number — 16.7 per cent — go monthly to the theatre than go to the cinema.

Leisure activities have changed in the post-war period and club entertainment, bingo, have come to be popular with the working class. Since the Betting Act of 1961 made them possible, bingo halls have taken over from cinema shows. Four out of five British adults gamble in some way, and bingo has provided a safe new excitement for housewives. The old and the new leisure pursuits were introduced in question 34, as Table 23 indicates.

But the findings are most revealing. They indicate that the WEA student is more likely to attend a concert than attend an amateur dramatic society's performance. At least 71.4 per cent attend concerts while only 23.8 per cent would attend the amateur dramatic

	Response		Percentages	
Entertainment	Yes	No	Yes	No
Club Entertainment	6	36	14.3	85.7
Amateur Dramatic Society	10	32	23.8	76.2
Bingo	0	42	-	100
Concerts	30	12	71.4	28.6
Others	6	36	14.3	85.7
Never	8	34	19.0	81.0

Table 9.23

society and only 14.3 per cent were used to club entertainment. The most significant point of all, however, was the fact that none of the sample attended bingo sessions and indicates that those who attend bingo sessions are not also interested in the activities of the Workers' Educational Assoication's educational programmes. And yet in the sixties bingo was the new national sport — in 1963 there were over 14 million members of bingo clubs.

What are the hobbies of the WEA student? Question 35 offers a number of options — such as Do-it-yourself; Sewing; Knitting; Yachting; Mountaineering; Skiing; Keep Fit. Table 24 gives an indication that hobbies do play some part in the life of a WEA student — that is the traditional self-help hobbies — of knitting, sewing and do-it-yourself. The more expensive hobbies such as yachting has no one of the respondents intersted while skiing fare little better with a 2.4 per cent. Mountaineering has a surprising result — of 16.7 per cent.

Hobbies	Response		Percentages	
	Yes	No	Yes	No
Do-it-Yourself	14	28	33.3	66.7
Sewing	12	30	28.6	71.4
Knitting	12	30	28.6	71.4
Yachting	0	42	-	100
Mountaineering	7	35	16.7	83.3
Skiing	1	41	2.4	97.6
Keep fit	7	35	16.7	83.3
Other hobbies	20	22	47.6	52.4

Table 9.24

The WEA student was also asked for his attitude or concern with social and environmental needs.

Social or Environmental Needs	Response		Percentages	
	Yes	No	Yes	No
Adult Education	14	28	33.3	66.7
Delinquency	19	23	45.2	54.8
Housing	10	32	23.8	76.2
Traffic	8	34	19.0	81.0
Play Areas	13	29	31.0	69.0
Primary Education	5	37	11.9	88.1
The Elderly	11	31	26.2	73.8
Planning	9	33	21.4	78.6
Smoke Control	6	36	14.3	85.7

Table 9.25

Delinquency is the main concern of the WEA sample followed by the need for more adult education. But again it is significant that the WEA student is not really worried at any of the social or environmental needs. The majority of the students are not concerned with any of the social needs apart from 45.2 per cent who opted for the problem of delinquency while 54.8 per cent of the respondents felt that even delinquency was not a major concern.

Environmental and Travel Education

The WEA have been pioneers in providing courses in pleasant surroundings or in arranging study tours. A question was asked: Would you like an adult education course provided for you in any of the following areas? Table 26 provides the results.

Adult Education Courses in following areas	Response		Percentages	
	Yes	No	Yes	No
Hereford and the Welsh Borders	9	33	21.4	78.6
The Lake District	9	33	21.4	78.6
9 day study tour of the archaeology of Wales	10	32	23.8	76.2
Georgeian Yorkshire: a study of John Carr of York (1723-1807) and his circle	4	38	9.5	90.5
Hadrian's Wall and Northumbria	12	30	28.6	71.4
Fenland Abbeys	10	32	23.8	76.2
None at all	5	37	11.9	88.1
Others	8	34	19.0	81.0

Table 9.26

The WEA students were not over-enthusiastic with the options presented and none of the study tours made a great appeal. Hadrian's Wall and Northumbria were the most popular but with only 28.6 per cent interested, and the others having much less appeal. Georgian Yorkshire providing the least attractive with a 9.5 per cent response. It seems that the WEA student is quite content with the provision offered to him at his Liverpool centre.

B   Participant observation in a W.E.A. class

i   Introduction

Though adult education has been an important aspect of the educational system in England and Wales in the twentieth century, and outstanding tutors have given their time and talents to the work it is quite surprising that there are so little participatory studies of adult classes in the literature of adult education. It is right to point out that one finds a great deal of literature on individual and group needs, methods of teaching and description of actual classes but a scarcity of case studies on actual WEA or university extra-mural classes.

I have been involved as a tutor in both types of adult classes but I intend to look at an established WEA class that I have known as a tutor in Liverpool.

I must stress that this is a participatory study of one adult education class, a class which has been in existence for a long time and I do not claim that it is representative of similar WEA classes on current affairs in the Merseyside area. But I know that it is very different to the class that was described in *Adult Education* in May 1979 by an anonymous full-time adult educationist. He visited the class on the ninth meeting out of the course of ten meetings. Nineteen students had registered for the class and thirteen were present. Notices and handout material (not relating to the course on Church history) were handed out at 7.05 p.m. The tutor then read a text from a book, five pages long and the reason for this was not given to the students. Most students had notebooks. Then at 7.20 p.m. the tutor started to deliver the new lecture, the text must have been related to the eighth lecture. At 7.25 p.m. a student comes in late but there was no change in flow from the tutor and he does not take notice of the late-comer. As the anonymous staff tutor states the tutor "never challenges them with eye and rarely with questions" (Anonymous, 1979, p.24). He does not use the blackboard and at 7.59 p.m. there is a break for coffee. When they return more notices are given out and then he proceeds with his lecture till the end of the time allocated to him at nine o'clock.

The full-time tutor has a word with him, a brief word, and the part-time tutor admits that he is conscious "that he has talked too much". But he felt that he had to get to St. Augustine before the end of the meeting. Furthermore, he has to dash off to catch his transport home (Anonymous, 1979, p.26). The full-time tutor did not open his mouth nor did more than five of the fourteen students in all.

Taking this case study as an example I would make the following observations.

i   The tutor of the class was obviously not aware of the valuable books and pamphlets that have been produced on communicating with adult students. It reinforces also the point made by adult educationists like John McLeish and C.D. Legge that we had at the end of the sixties more lectures of the uninterrupted discourse type than ever before, not only in universities but throughout the whole range of educational work with adults. C.D. Legge's questions and observation in 1969 was most valid:

> In how many technical institutions and colleges of further education, as well as in extra-mural courses and W.E.A. classes, do we still find it to be a standard method? In planning their programmes, do voluntary organisations deviate from the system which has served them for so long? In just two major women's organisations, the Townswomen's Guilds and Women's Institutes, it can be estimated that there are 20,000 lectures per month, and the mind boggles at the annual consumption of lectures by all the hundreds of organisations in this country. (Legge, 1969, p.85).

In my experience a lecture is not enough and one needs a combination of lecture and discussion to convey information and knowledge in an effective way to adult students. This I will bring out again in the course of this participatory study of a WEA adult class.

ii   The tutor's relationship with the class does not exist. It is obvious that he should have told the latecomer to the class what he was doing and he should also have involved his guest during the course of the evening. I would also claim that the tutor should never rush off without a prior warning at the end of the class and this is a frequent complaint of part-time WEA tutors in the Liverpool area.

iii   The matter of giving out notices is a difficult one and should be looked upon by all adult education classes. I feel that the registration which takes place at the beginning of the course is a time-consuming work which should have taken place outside the class time. Students should be told that they have to arrive 15 minutes earlier for registration.

iv   In my own experience and when reading the case study that has been evaluated it seems that all adult education movements should hold a one-day briefing session for all full-time and part-time tutors. This briefing session should be part of the contract and all tutors obliged to attend. Jindra Kulich in his study of the training of adult educators in East Germany (1969) makes the point that the East European states are far ahead of Western Europe in provision for training both professionals and volunteers. Be he also adds a salutary warning for adult educationists in the western world not to be overawed:

> However, it is rather illustrative of the relative fringe position of adult education in most countries that in spite of the special importance assigned in East Germany to upgrading and qualification of adults in all fields, training and qualification of adult educators is one of the last fields to be adequately developed.   (Kulich, 1969, p.17).

The situation can be improved by research and tutors in adult education should involve themselves in participatory studies and invite other researchers to study their students, syllabuses and institutions. The growing use of research findings and of opportunities for further research should spur on more research. It is this that adult education in England and Wales needs as every adult practitioner knows from experience. Books such as *Teaching Techniques in Adult Education* (1971), edited by Dr. Michael Stephens and Dr. Gordon Roderick are a valuable tool for tutors.

ii   The WEA Current Affairs Class

This class is a well-established WEA class which has been in existence since the fifties. It meets at the Royal Institution in Liverpool on a Monday morning for at least two sessions a year, with an option of a further session in the summer. The year starts at the end of September or the first week in October for a twelve week session, and then at the beginning of January for another twelve weeks. Adult students, therefore join at the end of September or the beginning of October for at least twenty four weeks. A choice is usually given for a short term class after Easter for six weeks and the most enthusiastic members of the class join for this brief term as well. Most of the adults who join the class are housewives (if they are under retirement age) or people who have retired from professional occupations (such as teaching and medicine). The high ratio of students in the 60-80 age group is due mainly to the timing of the class, that is on Monday morning. Many of the students also fall into the category of the students mentioned by B.W. Abrahart on a sample survey of students in the county of Northumberland, and that is people who have been students in adult education organisations all their lives (Abrahart, 1951, p.220). Their comments are re-echoed by Mrs. So   and Mrs. Ho   "I have attended more classes than I can count" and "I have been a student all my adult life". Abrahart found as I have done that continuity in adult education is much greater in university and workers' educational association than in those provided by local educational authorities. The WEA keep students together and provide the feeling of belonging which is a marked characteristic of the current affairs class. Effort is made to remember special occasions in the life of the older members of the class and to concern oneself if he/she or a member of his family is ill or has been in hospital. The pastoral role of the tutor is needed for the continuity of a class and explains, to some extent, the regular attendance of the adult students even when the weather is bad or the transport system is at a stop because of an industrial action. There are other reasons for the success of this class in terms of attendance and allegiance, namely:

a   The location of the study centre.

The current affairs class is held at the Royal Institution, Colquitt Street, Liverpool, which is an adult centre for the University of Liverpool Department of Extension Studies. In the opinion of many an adult educationist the Workers' Educational Association is always at a disadvantage because it has no centres of its own in the large industrial cities and conurbations in England and Wales. G. Brian Stapleton as warden of the Swarthmore Centre in Leeds has written of this serious disadvantage for the WEA and argued in favour of a grand comprehensive adult education centre (Stapleton, 1964, p.16). The Royal Institution at Liverpool could be regarded as the nearest model for a grand comprehensive adult education centre in the inner city area of Liverpool. A large number of Extension Studies Classes are held at the Royal Institution as well as WEA adult classes, and facilities are given to other educational movements if there are rooms available.

The centre then is not far from the railway stations of Lime Street and Central and is near to the main bus routes out to the suburbs of Mossley Hill, Allerton and Woolton. Around the adult centre there are parking meters and some of the adults make use of these and come to the class in their motor-cars. The class starts at eleven o'clock and goes on to twelve-thirty which is just right for a two hour parking meter. Others make a day of the occasion by ordering dinner at the cafeteria in the building, and either attend another adult class at the centre in the afternoon, or visit a friend or a relative in the neighbourhood or visit a friend or relative who is in hospital or go with another adult student around the shops before starting their way home at around four o'clock.

b   The tutors

The Monday morning WEA class in current affairs has been extremely fortunate in its tutors in the last twenty years. For half of this period the class had as its tutor a retired history master, Lloyd Morgan, who was a most articulate and accomplished lecturer. Many of the members still mention the qualities of Lloyd Morgan as a tutor and friend to the class. These are typical comments: "Lloyd Morgan took us through the whole of the Treaty of Rome and none of us were in favour of it." "He was a tremendous tutor and he really gave us so much to think about". "Lloyd Morgan had a gift of imparting knowledge and of keeping friends. He would appoint a class secretary and for nine years I was his class librarian. At the end of the spring session he would invite the class secretary and the librarian to his home for a meal". "The class really declined after the sudden death of Lloyd Morgan".

The class, however, did not disappear and for a few years it had a number of different tutors which again is a disadvantage for the continuity of a class. But then the WEA invited a young academic, R.M. O'Grady to be the tutor for the class and his personal charisma and breadth of scholarship (in particular, American affairs) endeared him to the class. He was there long enough to be able to re-build the class but not in any way comparable to the golden era of the class in the time of Lloyd Morgan. O'Grady, however, was appointed to a full-time lecturing post and in another critical phase in the history of the class I was appointed as a tutor in the class. When I took over the class there were around twelve members, all of them women except one man. It was an interesting experience for there were at least two very vociferous students, one pro Lloyd Morgan and the other pro O'Grady. But the task was to build the class and especially to attract some men to the class. One of the most glaring weaknesses was the inexact nature and amateurish way the course had been publicised in the annual handbook. This I was determined to put right the following year, and though one was expected to explain the nature of the session in fifty words, I spent some time in preparing this. It paid off with a larger class, and one felt accepted with comments like "You remind us of Lloyd Morgan" from the older members of the class. It seems also that members of the class were determined to make the class one of the most successful on Merseyside and in the whole region. It is a common occurrence to see during a term a new face who has come with one of the most regular of the members. Before the start of the class she (or he) is introduced to me as one who has come along to sample the class and as a prospective member (if he (or she) likes it) in the following session. The majority of those who come in this way to the class enjoy what they find and in time enrol as members of the class. Many of the members of the class are involved in other organisations (such as Townswomen's Guilds, Ramblers Association) and they speak to some of the more politically minded members of those organisations as to the enjoyment and enrichment they find in the class. A few have also come through my own initiative and due to my many contacts in the city. Sometimes I will mention the existence of the class if I am invited to speak on a political topic at a Townswomen's Guild, and in time this initiative will bring forth a new member.

This reinforces the point that is often made by adult educationists that so much depends on the tutor for the success of an adult education class. But it is important to underline also that a class will succeed not only because of its dedicated tutor but through the enthusiasm of its members, especially if the class is an annual and continuing effort. This has been proved from the WEA class that I have tutored in for three years on current affairs.

c   The Subject Matter

Current affairs at one time in the history of the WEA was an extremely popular subject in many parts of England and Wales. In the post-war period the popularity of current affairs classes ceased and in large cities it is an exception to find more than two or three WEA classes. In Liverpool during the sixties and into the seventies there was only one current affairs class in the day-time and an average of two classes in the evening. Professor W.E. Styler in an important review of adult education found this one of the serious problems facing the adult education movement. To Professor W.E. Styler the record of adult education in the field of what he terms 'political education' is not at all satisfactory. He mentions specifically international affairs as an adult education subject, and the fact that classes dropped with few full-time staff tutors in charge of the classes. In 1974 there were only two hundred classes in international affairs (which is another title for current affairs) out of nearly ten thousand in this field (Styler, 1975, p.12). During the agitation about the American involvement in Vietnam, Professor Styler offered a class in the city of Hull. Only five students turned up which was a big disappointment in particular to Professor W.E. Styler and the department. He makes a very forceful point when he states that a student who studies literature is "paying for pleasure" but the student who studies the Middle East, Rhodesia is "paying for pleasure and also for the privilege of being a better informed citizen". All the students who attend the current affairs class would agree with the criticism of W.E. Styler as well as his intriguing remark on paying for pleasure and for the privilege of being better informed citizens.

In my experience it is impossible to prepare a detailed syllabus for the whole 24 or 30 lectures, and not only an impossible task but also an unnecessary task. I interpret current affairs in three ways a. the important international issues that appear from time to time or the developments which have far reaching implications for the whole of mankind, b. national political debate which can include a referendum on devolution for Scotland and Wales or the issues of a General Election or a survey of what each political party stands for, c. local issues which have a specific bearing on Merseyside, the closure of factories, rising unemployment, the lack of political will to tackle

261

difficult problems by local politicians, transport, education, leisure and any other issue which the members would like to discuss and to be more informed.

During a typical twenty four sessions one remembers tackling all these issues, and one tries as a tutor to make the curriculum of interest to all the members. It is unusual to spend more than one session on a topic, but this does happen if the subject is of such a nature that one cannot do justice to it in one session. A good example of this was the topic of social changes in Liverpool which took three sessions and the European Economic Community which demanded two sessions. The Middle East issue, Northern Ireland, energy, education are topics that appear more than once and one has to prepare for the unexpected as well as to take a more detailed look at a subject which has already been discussed a few weeks or months earlier in the class. In some sessions an opportunity is taken of tackling a subject in depth, as for example, the role of continuing education, the place of assurance in the life of an individual, pressure group democracy or to borrow the phrase of S.E. Finer 'the lobby in an anonymous empire'.

d   Discussion in the weekly class

Professor James Stuart, one of the great pioneers of university extension lectures, was led in the nineteenth century to initiate a special period for discussion because of the unquenchable curiosity of the working-men who attended some lectures on astronomy which he gave for the Equitable Pioneers Co-operative Society in Rochdale. James Stuart has recorded the experience:

> One day I was in some hurry to get away as soon as the lecture was over, and I asked the hall-keeper to allow my diagrams to remain hanging till my return next week. When I came back he said to me, 'It was one of the best things you ever did, leaving up those diagrams. We had a meeting of our members last week, and a number of those who are attending your lectures, were discussing these diagrams, and they have a number of questions they want to ask you, and they are coming to-night a little before the lecture begins'. About twenty or thirty intelligent artisans met me about half-an-hour before the lecture began, and I found it so useful a half-hour that during the remainder of the course I always had such a meeting.   (Styler, 1952, p.5).

In this way the idea of holding a class for discussion in connection with the lecture was introduced as a feature of university extension work, and the idea of adult education class as distinct from a lecture course began to emerge. Discussion was discovered by experience to be the completion of instruction and the sound adult education principle of 'no instruction without discussion' is part and parcel of the WEA.

Every adult education class that I have been involved with over the years have different methods. But in this current affairs class the members have come along not only to learn from the tutor but also from their fellow students. These students in the main have a lifetime of experience and it is important that they have an opportunity to impart their knowledge (which often is of a specialised nature) to the tutor and the rest of the students. In my opinion the only method for this is the discussion method where the student is allowed an opportunity to come in at any stage of the proceedings. The tutor's role is that of an effective chairman who allows discussion throughout the hour-and-a-half allotted for him. I must agree with what W.E. Styler wrote in a WEA pamphlet:

> Adult education of the type with which the W.E.A. is associated is distinctive because discussion is so important in its classes. Discussion, it may be said, determines its character; the 'instruction' the tutor imparts fits into a setting made by the questions and discussion which are a necessary part of the proceedings. Because of this setting the tutor himself becomes, at the same time, something less and something more than an instructor. He is less because the discussion period enables students to challenge his authority: he is more because discussion makes the class situation one in which he is the leader of a group engaged in a co-operative quest for knowledge. (Styler, 1952, pp.6-7).

These words of Professor W.E. Styler have been a source of inspiration to me since I first read them in the WEA study outline as a young adult tutor. But it is only in WEA classes that I am able to practise the wise counselling of Styler. In an university extension class it is expected by many of those who attend as well as the full-time tutors that one keeps to the usual requirements of a tutor lecturing for an hour and then the class discussing the substance of his lecture for the other hour or half-an-hour. But in the Monday morning WEA class it is obvious from the regularity of attendance as well as the enthusiasm of the group that the discussion method is another reason for the popularity of the class. One of the members informed me of the pleasure that she received from the valuable social experience but also in the intellectual sphere. This class has for every weekly meeting a defined and limited purpose and the intellectual stimulation is assisted by the psychological benefits of a full and frank rapport between the tutor and his students and between the students and each other.

e   Case Studies

Looking in more detail at individual members of the class one is able to see how these adult students contribute to the WEA class. I do not intend to use their personal names and surname or to give too many personal details which are of any significance to the function and work of the group. They will be classified according to the seats in which they usually sit in the Monday morning class.

Student No. 1

Mrs. P....... is the oldest person in the class and I had the opportunity of sending during my first year as a tutor a birthday card to her on her eightieth birthday. Brought up in difficult times she never romanticises the past or indeed ignore it, but as a hard headed realist she is able to criticise the past and the present for its failures to cope with its problems. Mrs. P....... is always listened to with a great deal of admiration by her fellow students. She is one of the most regular members of the current affairs class and travels by bus from the Walton area of the city. She never gives the impression of having very strong convictions on religious or political issues but she is evidently attracted to those who are moderates in the political arena as well as in the religious sphere. It is obvious that she is not very partial to those who disrupt proceedings or who destroy property and Dr. Ian Paisley and the Welsh Language Society have both been condemned by her in discussion. But on the whole Mrs. P....... is kind in thought, generous of spirit and very impartial in judgement.

Student No. 2

Next to Mrs. P....... on the front bench sits Dr. S......., who is a Jewish doctor and a man of erudite knowledge, particularly with regard to the State of Israel and the National Health Service. Dr. S....... is not a strong person physically and he depends on a pace-maker, and due to his commitments, his occasional journeys to Jerusalem, and his health he is not one of the most regular members of the class. But everyone is excited when he is present for he will always add new insights and knowledge to the discussion and he does this in an objective manner. He has great admiration for the tutor and supplies him with material on Middle East affairs and an occasional copy of the *Jerusalem Post*. A 'born gentleman' Dr. S....... will also speak out on matters that he feels strongly about and he has strong commitment (especially in his younger days) to the Labour Party. He admires in particular Aneurin Bevan, one of the architects of the Welfare State, and the class is always an exciting experience when Dr. S....... is present.

Student No. 3

Mrs. K....... is another regular and never misses though she has to cross the River Mersey from Wallasey. It has been known for her to walk 2 miles in times of a bus strike to be present and she belonged to the O'Grady class. Mrs. K. .... does not take a very leading role in the discussions but it is obvious that she gains a great deal from the class. Like Mrs. P....... she is a moderate and has a great deal to say for politicians like Mrs. Shirley Williams who avoid dogmatism in their political beliefs. A shy person Mrs. K....... does respond and is able quite forcibly to put her thoughts into orderly form.

Student No. 4

Mrs. N....... is an exiled Scotswoman who also, like Mrs. K. ...., belonged to the current affairs class long before I took over. She travels from Crosby, north end of Liverpool and she hardly misses a meeting. Mrs. N....... is extremely gregarious and she is one of the best members in the class for asking pertinent questions that trigger off discussion. Her son is an active member of the Scottish Nationalist Party and Mrs. N....... is very knowledgeable on matters to do with Scottish affairs.

She is a committed member of the class and was largely responsible for introducing Miss H....... to the class. I had met Mrs. N.... in an university extension class at Waterloo before I took over the current affairs class, the only member that had attended any of my other adult WEA classes. Well-travelled, Mrs. N.... is extremely keen on educational tours and she in many ways would be a good representative of the W.E.A.

Student No. 5

Miss H.... is a newer member of the class and drives from the south of Liverpool to the class. She has many commitments in other movements, movements of differing philosophies and commitments. Helpful in her manner, Miss H.... will bring in literature to the tutor from her many interests. One week it could be the writings of the nineteenth century land reformer Henry George and the following week a pamphlet or a booklet from the Moral Rearmament. Miss H.... has a serious facial paralysis and it is extremely difficult to interpret what she says. But this I do for it helps the members of the class to feel that she has a great deal to add to the class and it helps them to feel also that there is no-one who is not able to join in the discussion.

Student No. 6

Mr. T. P.... is a retired banker and a man of left wing persuasion. A son of a Church of England clergyman Mr. T. P.... has his roots in Cumberland and in Wales and he has tremendous knowledge on any topic that is under discussion. A member of the Communist Party and an avid reader of left wing publications, *Morning Star, Labour Monthly, Soviet Weekly,* Mr. T. P.... is admired for his erudite knowledge but he is offputting to other members of the class for his blind allegiance to the Soviet Union. He has been to Russia twice and whenever any discussion arises he brings in Russia. This tends to aggravate the more pro-Western students and the tutor has to be very careful in his judgements. Mr. T. P...., like Miss H...., supplies the tutor with literature that he feels he should be aware of, and the Soviet Union is brought in to every class. Mr. T. P.... has his admirers in the class but Dr. S.... on Middle East affairs will not allow him to go unchallenged. The stress and challenge of debate is very evident when Mr. T. P.... and Dr. S.... cross swords in debate. Mr. T. P.... is another recruit from my period and came largely through my persuasion.

Student No. 7

Mrs. W.... is the middle aged wife of a busy general practitioner. She is a housewife and a Jewess and extremely knowledgeable on current affairs. An educated person, she possesses an university degree, and finds the class a refuge and strength for her busy life. Mrs. W...., like Mrs. N...., is always willing to ask questions but often decides that the security and cosiness of silence is better than the stress and challenge of debate. She is somewhat overpowered by the unrelenting arguments of Mr. T. P.... and especially his pronounced pro Russian views. As a member of a Jewish family who knew of persecution in Russia she is extremely wary of his strong Russian line though she is attracted to his left wing opinions. Mrs. W.... always defends the role and work of the general practitioner and will also be tempted to say something on Israel if Dr. S.... is present.

Mrs. W.... is one of the most popular members of the class and she is one of the youngest members of the Monday morning class. When she is unable to be present she is very grieved and will phone the tutor to apologise for her absence.

Students Nos. 8 and 9

Mr. and Mrs. H.... are the only married couple in the class and both are very keen walkers and outdoor people. Mr. H.... has very strong and sometimes controversial views which have been modified through discussion at the class. He has known poverty in his younger days but there is no doubt that the strong left wing views of Mr. T. P.... and the 'socialist' principles espoused by Dr. S.... have made an impact on him. Mr. H.... is an old WEA student who came into the movement through the Ramblers' Association and is also keen on organising a WEA Current Affairs Week-end School at Burton Manor. Both he and his wife enjoyed those occasions, and in his own phrase 'learnt a great deal' at these residential schools. Mrs. H.... is shy and intelligent and allows her husband to do most of the debating. He does not surrender very easily and can be tough though not pigheaded. If he feels that his point of view has not been considered thoroughly he will revert to his original point in the argument. He has not the same breadth of knowledge or intellect as Dr. S.... or Mr. T. P.... but he is a very likeable member of the class who does not lack the powers of self-expression.

Student No. 10

Miss S.... is a retired schoolmistress and a liberal in all matters to do with social, political and religious questions. A committed Unitarian in religion Miss S.... listens regularly to the radio and television and reads carefully books, magazines and newspapers. She is well travelled and has visited a large number of countries in Europe. An anti-marketeer she is able to combine her own personal observation with what she has read and combine them in her own careful exposition. Like many others in the class Miss S.... is very careful with regard to prejudice and preconception, and this is why she is always critical of the views of Dr. Ian Paisley or Enoch Powell. Miss S.... will acknowledge as she did in one discussion that the causes of prejudice and preconception are not only intellectual but also emotional. "This is why it is difficult to remove them" she stated. But it is people like her who assist the tutor in making other members of the class to be aware of these prejudices and preconceptions and to see that they can be a barrier to one's intellectual development. It is a source of self-righteousness to have strong convictions but they can also severely limit one's mental horizons, and in this Miss S.... would agree. She also has been a regular member of the class for years.

Student No. 11

Miss S.... has a friend who usually comes with her in the car from Woolton.

266

They both live in the same road and Mrs. W.... is a shy person who at the beginning of her first year in the class kept silent. Tutors should develop a practise and have the ability to put shy students at their ease and persuade them to speak up. Mrs. W.... was one of those people whom I have encouraged in different ways to speak, and it has been interesting to see the development in her power of self-expression.

Student No. 12

Mrs. So.... is one of the oldest students and she has also been a member of the class for at least 20 years. A teacher by profession of Welsh parentage, Mrs. So.... is a committed Methodist and a liberal in politics. She is a committed WEA student who has been a member of the movement for 50 years and more. Mrs. So.... is very articulate and has a very keen sense of history as well as great deal of details of historical events. Her contributions are always a delight and she gets a very good response though sometimes she allows a prejudice to determine her line of argument. She speaks a great deal of Lloyd Morgan and had great admiration for him. Mrs. So.... has been and still goes to Europe and North Africa with WEA study tours though she has passed her eightieth birthday. There is no doubt that Mrs. So.... is an asset to a current affairs class, as she has extensive powers of self-expression, determination to put her point of view over, and a very detailed and keen memory.

Student No. 13

Mrs. H.... like Mrs. So.... has been a long serving member of the class, and Mrs. H.... speaks with admiration of Mr. O'Grady's time as tutor. A widow of a railwayman and a committed member of the Labour Party Mrs. H.... lives in Bootle and is unrelentless in argument. There is no need to coax her in any way to express her own opinion and the tutor and Dr. S.... are often her targets. She has a strong voice and her powers of self-expression are excellent. Like Mrs. So.... she commands universal respect in the class for her confidence and her keen-ness as an adult student. Mrs. H.... never misses the class and she is the only member of the group who depends on radio for her information. She has no television set which can be a loss in discussion as so many excellent current affairs programmes are to be seen on television. But Mrs. H.... makes up for it by her astute observation and detailed knowledge of events and an inexhaustible appetite for knowledge.

Student No. 14

Mr. D.... is a native of Scotland and his strong Scottish accent is very evident. It seems that he has joined the class to learn more about international, national and local affairs, and he travels at least 17 miles one way every week (that is from Aughton) to the class. He feels more confident to join the discussion when the topic deals with the topography of Scotland or Scottish affairs. But he is very grateful for the information and discussion and often comes on at the end to thank the tutor for his contribution.

Student No. 15

Mrs. H.... is a Welsh speaking housewife from the anthracite coalfield of East Carmarthenshire. Married to a Liverpool Comprehensive School Headmaster Mrs. H.... is very conscious of the need for continuing education. She regards the class as an important aspect of her life and she is one of the most regular members. She is friendly with a number of the members of the class and regards the class as an educative process and a social occasion. Mrs. H.... does not speak at length but at every class she will express herself succinctly and to the point.

Student No. 16

Mrs. J.... is a retired person who has moved to live with her daughter in the Allerton area. She knows some of the members of the class through her interests in rambling and she also enjoys the class and its contributions. Mrs. J.... does not take part often in the class, she is more of a passive student. But she does think for herself and she is also prepared to receive new insights and information.

Student No. 17

Mrs. M.... lives in the Aigburth area and is again a newer member to the class. She will talk a great deal but not of the same standard as Miss S.... or Mrs. H..... It is obvious that the participation she gets in the class has given her a keener appreciation of current affairs and that she now avoids commonplace generalisations which she was very fond of in her first few contributions to the discussion.

Student No. 18

Mrs. B.... is a friend of Mrs. M.... and lives in the same area. She takes very little part in the class but it is possible to get her to respond to some topics, especially Northern Ireland.

Student No. 19

Mrs. C.... lives in Allerton and is a staunch worker for the Townwomen's Guild in Woolton. She is very knowledgeable of legal matters and will take part in the discussion without any coaxing. One of the newer members of the class.

Student No. 20

Miss H.... is a taster of adult education classes and attends at least three a week throughout the winter. A daughter of a Methodist missionary who spent his life in China, Miss H.... will speak about her own upbringing in China when asked by the tutor. The topic for that current affairs class will be China or the New China. She hardly misses a current affairs class and thoroughly enjoys the atmosphere. Her cousin who has since passed away introduced her to the class.

Student No. 21

Miss V.... like Miss H.... is also shy and listens rather than participates though she will speak occasionally. One of the newer members of the class but a most faithful and interested student.

Student No. 22

Miss .... is a retired civil servant who is very knowledgeable and will often add valuable insights into the discussion from her own extensive experience in local government and in the field of taxation. Another of the newer members of the class she has 'radical and liberal' views and often admits that bureaucracy can stifle innovation and progress.

Student No. 23

Mr. P.... has a very pronounced conservative standpoint and he and Mr. T. P.... disagree over the actions of the East or the West, and in particular the involvement of the two super powers, Russia and the United States of America in world affairs. Mr. P.... will not compromise with his views and he also knows how to conduct himself in debate with skill. He attends other similar groups and has had experience before of discussion circles. A new member of the class who, like other members of the class, are interested in outdoor pursuits.

Student No. 24

Mr. .... is a young unemployed person who is obviously overawed by the considerable skill in debate of the other men in the class. It is impossible to get him to come into the discussion and he is one of the few in the class who takes notes.

Student No. 25

Mrs. .... is another adult whom it is very difficult to get involved in the discussions of the class but she hardly misses a current affairs class. She listens attentively to the discussions that take place and will with some prompting from the tutor put over her considered viewpoint.

These then are the regular members of the current affairs class under consideration but another three members registered but due to the usual factors did not attend the class regularly. These factors have been classified by C.F. Palfrey in a survey that he carried out as Deputy Warden of Carleon Community College in Gwent. Palfrey found that adults had not returned after the Christmas holiday because of a number of reasons:

Family/business reasons	38 per cent
Moved from district	19 per cent
Illness	19 per cent
Change of shift	12 per cent

Continued

269

Lost interest	9 per cent
Other reasons	3 per cent (Palfrey, 1966, p.225)

I am unable to place these three students into any of these categories as I did not make contact with them after they ceased to attend the class. It is more than probable that if the class was smaller in number that I would have been in contact with them by letter. But in this particular case there was no real need for such a personal involvement, as there were twenty five other regular adult students.

What then have I learnt from this remarkable class of adults? I must stress three points in my conclusion of the participatory survey. Firstly, that real learning takes place in the current affairs class on the part of tutor and students. I often feel humbled by some of the details that the students are able to add to my generalisations or to a theme that I have developed. These details are often derived from a lifetime of reading or from personal experience of the adults. Real learning is often expressed through debate and discussion and this is sometimes felt in the tension between the people we are and the source of new information outside ourselves — a tension which demands potential adjustment on both sides. We are not only affected by the reality around us, whether it is economic or sociological reality, but we also as individuals and members of a society have the power to affect reality, or at least to equip oneself for participation in the wider world. The words written by C.R. Atlee in the 'golden age of the WEA' are still very relevant for members and the tutor of a WEA class in current affairs:

> For those who wish to take up public work there can be no better training than to join a W.E.A. class as tutor or member, and discuss the problems that arise with some of the best brains among the workers. (Attlee, 1920, p.285).

Secondly, that a friendly dialogue between tutor and student is an effective method of imparting knowledge. While there is need for briefing sessions for all adult tutors yet there is an obvious common-sense about the whole relationship of tutor and his students. It is obvious that the main qualities expected of an WEA tutor are the qualities expected of any one who is in contact with other adults. He should remember that a friendly dialogue must take place between all the members of the class and between the adult students and the tutor. C.R. Attlee rightly pointed out that the essence of the WEA spirit was a co-operation of tutor and students in the search for knowledge "rather than the teacher speaking *ex cathedra* to the student" (Attlee, 1920, p.284). The concept of the tutor as the 'educated man' dictating to other adults that they should be brought up to a respectable level of educational attainment is doomed to fail whether applied to the inhabitants of Acacia Avenue or Coronation Street (Rees and Edmunds, 1971, p.164).

Thirdly, the adult members who attended this current affairs class in Liverpool reinforces the élitism that is such a marked characteristic of the adult education scene in England and Wales. Out of the 28 members there was only one member one could call 'disadvantaged', namely the person who was unemployed. All the others had been in the centre of the educational system all their lives and had involved themselves in the adult education facilities. If adult education is so important to society then it seems to me that an effort must be made to seek ways and means to mobilise the least privileged into this framework, and in particular into classes on current affairs which discusses the operation of the political, economic and social systems. But the relevance of current affairs for all sections of the community is very evident to the members of this Liverpool WEA class, and many of the participants express a wish to involve more adults from every stratum of society. Though the majority of the members of the class belong to an élitism, yet they do not want to perpetuate an élitism in the education of adults.

From the standpoint of sociological analysis, this current affairs class belongs to the middle class in attitudes, ethos and life style. Of the 28 adults analysed in this participatory study 1 is a doctor, 1 a retired bank manager, 3 who were in the nursing profession, 7 who were clerks, 6 as teachers, 2 in managerial positions, 1 unemployed and 7 of the members are housewives. Though the overwhelming members of the class are middle class in orientation, housing, interests, yet at least 60 per cent of them were born into working class families, and through education and personal initiative, cultural tastes and occupations, they were initiated into the middle class. While they are middle class in values and environment, the most intellectual members of the current affairs class have kept their commitment to the working class as exemplified by Dr. S.... and Mr. T. P..... They all fit into what I call the 'Tawney image' of the WEA, a concern and respect for the working man and advocates of an education in which class distinctions do not operate. R.H. Tawney was one of the greatest of the WEA tutors and he always spoke of adult education as promoting fellowship. The individual's self-fulfilment cannot be acquired through the extreme individualism of the nineteenth century; it must be sought, according to Tawney, in social relations. At least eighty per cent of the current affairs class also, like R.H. Tawney, were not uncritical of the working class movement in England. Mr. T. P.... and Dr. S.... and Mrs. H.... and many of the others were very critical of the apathy and indifference of the British workers. Capitalism, according to Tawney and the most articulate of the WEA members in the Liverpool current affairs class, was as much maintained by the poor who admired the rich and the poor who would like to be capitalists, as by the capitalists themselves. Tawney's awareness of the working class contribution to their own oppression was a significant critique of English society. The majority of this class would agree with Tawney and continually mentioned this in our discussion on contemporary society.

One cannot but quote at the end of this participant's observation what Sir Richard Livingstone wrote at the beginning of the post-war period on the contribution of the WEA movement:

Its service to political democracy in England cannot be overestimated. Its great weakness is one for which it is in no way responsible; it only touches an intellectual élite. (Livingstone, 1946, p.65).

The WEA current affairs class in Liverpool in my opinion cannot wash its hands completely from the verdict that it still touches only an 'intellectual élite', and it has been shown also that nearly all who attend this class belong to the category mentioned by Sir Richard W. Livingstone in his evaluation of the WEA movement.

Chapter 10
Education of Adults in the Seventies

Adult education and education of adults in the seventies suffered from a lack of vision and resources to implement the growing concern of educationists. But it is true to say that in the seventies a vast amount of written material appeared in the form of books and articles in journals on adult education and the need to accept the varying concepts which had appeared at the end of the sixties.

The underlying argument of this book was still valid in this decade, that is an inability to put into action the concepts and concerns of adult educationists, and a reluctance to accept the enormous impact that societal change is having on education. One cannot deny that the knowledge explosion is a fact of life in the western world.

> Every forty minutes enough new information is generated to fill a twenty-four volume encyclopaedia.   (Cross, 1974, p.88)

Adult education has to accept this situation and indeed it has to come to terms with it for education at any stage in life is a never-ending process as K.H. Lawson ably puts it in a book published at the end of our period.

> To seek education is to ask for horizons to be extended, for new doors to be opened and for new problems to be defined. When we solve problems of which we are already aware by methods already at our disposal, we are not educating ourselves or being educated in any usual sense of the word.   (Lawson, 1979, p.88)

New horizons were extended to a great number of people and new doors were opened to adults who had not been given at home or at school the support that they needed. There were four main concerns in this period, a concern for academic adult education, a concern for basic skill adult education, a concern for education of the whole man, and lastly exciting experiments, local initiatives and the traditional activities of those movements that have been outlined already in the preceding chapters.

Academic adult education became a most important aspect of the adult education scene in the seventies. Rapid social change was an obvious reason as Sir Alec Cairncross, an university administrator, admits at the beginning of the decade.

> The more rapidly the world changes the more important education becomes, precisely because change imposes a continuing need to learn. It is no coincidence that the more rapid pace of social change has led, not to the eclipse of the universities, but to the creation of a great many more.   (Cairncross, 1972, p.7).

The sixties saw many new universities in England and Wales (Universities of Sussex (1961); Keele (1962); East Anglia at Norwich (1963); York (1963); Lancaster (1964); Essex at Colchester (1964); Warwick (1965); Loughborough (1966); Aston in Birmingham (1966); The City University and Brunel University (both in London and both starting on their work) in 1966;

Universities of Bath and Bradford in 1966; University of Surrey at Guildford in 1966, and the following year Cranfield Institute of Technology at Bedford and the University of Salford. Then at the end of the decade the Open Unviersity in 1969, and it was this university which dominated in adult education terms the following decade.

The work at Birbeck College in the University of London had shown for a very long time and especially the Birbeck College adult degree courses that there was a need to provide for mature adults on a part-time basis. The work done at Ruskin College, Fircroft, Hillcroft, Plater College, Coleg Harlech, Co-operative College and other second chance institutions indicated that there were thousands of adults who could follow an academic university education. Part-time learning suited adults and professional education as well as becoming a necessity.

The Open University can be looked at in the light of the words uttered by Lord Crowther, the first Chancellor, at the Charter Ceremony on July 23rd 1969. He spoke of four ways in which the Open Unviersity was to be open:

(i)   Open as to People.

It has managed to reach adults without entry qualifications. Any adult can apply and can be accepted without any 'O' Level or 'A' Level qualifications. But because of resources and facilities it has proved impossible for the Open University to accept every applicant. In 1970 42,000 adults applied and 24,000 were accepted. Many an educationist has been dis-illusioned with the relatively small number of working class adults who have become Open University students. Tyrrell Burgess went so far as to say:

> One would indeed predict that it will go the way of the W.E.A., providing ornamental knowledge mainly to middle class people.

But there is another side to the coin as Naomi McIntosh, Professor of Applied Social Research at the Open University, has pointed out so often in articles and interviews, and that is, the amount of social mobility among Open University students is phenomenal. She has pointed out that at the end of the seventies forty per cent of the educationally unqualified graduated which, by any standards, is a tremendous achievement. There is no doubt also that a large number of the middle class students grew up as working class and did not have enough educational opportunities than even though as adults they are now regarded and even regard themselves as middle class. The fathers of fifty-two per cent of Open University students in 1971 (both male and female) were in the "manual workers' categories, a further twenty-eight per cent were in lower grade "white collar" jobs and only twenty per cent had fathers in the middle class categories. The fathers of Open University students are much more likely to be in the working class categories than those of students at conventional universities (McIntosh and Woodley, 1974, p.89). Naomi McIntosh has pointed out that the majority of teachers who are non-

274

graduates did not get two 'A' levels, would not have been able to go to universities, were working class, and entered the working class five 'O' level route into teaching. These teachers form a sizeable group and given the career structure in comprehensive schools many of them have indicated a desire to become graduates. Another group who have become highly motivated and interested in the Open University courses are women. The application rate of women has risen from thirty per cent in 1970 to forty-four per cent in 1978. It seems therefore that in the seventies the Open University has made degree level education available for adults, not on the basis of their prior qualifications but on their innate ability. It has shown also that it is possible for adults to succeed in higher education even if they start without the entry qualifications normally demanded of school-leavers. It is possible to devise courses that are appropriate to adult learners.

ii and iii Open as to Places and as to Methods

The Open University has a very flexible system - with study centres and regional offices, a central office and summer schools. Each place has developed its own functions. The study centres have become to most foundation centres essential places, but it is still possible for a student to pass a foundation course without attending one tutorial at a study centre. The course units are sent to the student from Walton Hall by post and all the basic learning material is available to everyone. The correspondence package is the only essential, for the television and radio programmes are aids rather than essential. For the foundation courses, however, summer schools are compulsory. This was a concession that the Open University accepted largely on the advice of Howard Sheath who had a great deal of experience and expertise. Howard Sheath had been responsible for running an external degree programme in the University of New England at Armidale, New South Wales, and was convinced from experience that adults were retained to a considerable extent in the system because they were stimulated and re-motivated by attendance at compulsory summer schools. To a large extent Howard Sheath has been proved right with regard to the Open University summer schools.

The regional centres have become to a large extent a clearing house for adult education. Take as an example the Open University North Regional Office at Newcastle. Annabel Ferriman wrote on that region in 1976; a region which stretches from the river Tees to the Scottish border. The Open University office had dealt with about 150,000 inquiries in one year (that is, 1975) and many of these inquiries having nothing to do with the Open University. In effect the Open University was running through its northern office at Newcastle an adult education advisory service. This would be true of other regional offices, and in that respect serve a most important need.

Not everyone has been pleased with the openness of the Open University in its teaching role. Dave Harris and John Holmes are two who have been critical of the élitist approach of the Open University. They claimed in an article in the *Times Educational Supplement* (14 February 1975) that it was élitist because of its teaching system which to them was "designed to concentrate powers in the hands of the experts at the centre". This in my experience is largely an unproved criticism, for while it is true that the material is prepared by the Open University academics, the teaching is carried out by Open University part-time tutors at the local study centres and they are given plenty of freedom to present and discuss the material without any restrictions.

iv   Open to Ideas

The Open University has a commendable record with regard to ideas as one is conscious when reading the correspondence material. As far as adult education is concerned the Open University has blazed an important trail with regard to the need for continuing education. Walter Perry saw in continuing education the challenge required to keep the Open University open. The Open University has taken up the challenge and the first definitive result was the appearance in December 1977 of the full time appointment of a Pro Vice-Chancellor (Continuing Education). Professor Ralph Smith who was Professor of Mathematics at the university was appointed with effect from February 1978. A Conference was arranged to discuss Continuing Education with the Trade Union Congress and the Confederation of British Industry. This was in line with the thinking of the Russell Report, the discussion document *Higher Education into the 1990's* and the setting up of the Advisory Council for Adult and Continuing Education (ACACE) by the Secretary of State for Education in October 1977. It provided as Naomi McIntosh admits "the first tangible sign of a government committed to this new concept" (McIntosh, 1979, p.245). The Open University has shown in the seventies that a large number of adults will respond to educational opportunities when available. Peter Venables who did a great deal with other academics for Continuing Education within the Open University believed that the eighties would be the decade when the Open University would have to face the challenge of continuing education. These are some of the last words that Peter Venables wrote before his death in June 1979: on the challenge to the Open University of its commitment to continuing education:

> Less dramatic, less prestigious perhaps, but it will affect (that is the Open University) the lives of a far greater number of citizens in the community at large.

Peter Venables goes on to argue in his article in *The World Year-book of Education, 1979* that the Open University would have to co-operate with many other established institutions and agencies in the field of adult education to achieve its object of enhancing the lives of individuals by its provision of continuing education.

The Open University has already learnt that continuing education is a concept more readily acceptable to industry business as well as adults than other educational concepts, such as recurrent education. Recurrent education has tended to concentrate on the notion of alternating periods of work with periods of education. The Open University has shown in the seventies that many adults wanting a degree appear to prefer to study while they continue to work. This has to be taken into consideration as well as the trends within the Open University in the seventies. It seems that the adults who apply to the Open University come from the more affluent south than from the rest of the country, and that more people apply for the arts courses than for technological courses. In 1979 9.7 per cent of Open University applicants came from the south as opposed to 8.9 per cent in 1977; 10.2 per cent came from East Anglia as opposed to 9.4 per cent two years ago; and 8 per cent came from the southeast as opposed to 7.7 per cent in 1977. The percentage of applicants from the West Midlands went down over the corresponding period from 8.3 per cent to 8.1 per cent; from Yorkshire from 6.6 per cent to 6.3 per cent; the northern region from 5 per cent to 4.8 per cent; north-west region by 0.9 per cent from 11 per cent to 10.1 per cent. The low number of applicants for technological courses in 1977 was 11.6 per cent compared with 34.65 per cent of arts applicants out of the total applications to the Open University (Hempel, 1978, p.28).

The Open University has proved to be one of the most successful efforts for adult education in Britain in the twentieth century. It has triggered off other ideas. A National Open College on the model of the Open University has been suggested. This Open College, if established, would have to be different in its educational outlook and to operate with greater flexibility. It should start, as was pointed out by Gerard Macdonald, from an assumption of general adult ignorance among the mass of people and with more attention paid to course organisation (Macdonald, 1978, p.10); for to rely so much on print as the Open University does is indeed a limitation and out of place in a technological age. A National Open College could use the latest equipment, such as video-cassette recorders, video disc players, recorded and retrieval television as well as the more traditional tools.

The proof of the academic respectability of the Open University is that it managed to survive in a decade which witnessed the cutting down in public expenditure. It was not a surprise to many of us within the Open University institution to read in the *Times Educational Supplement* (16 April 1976) the comments of Mr. William van Straubenzee, Conservative MP for Wokingham in 1976 at a meeting in Bristol that the Conservative government elected in 1970 had considered shutting the university completely as part of their policy of cutting public spending.

It would have been a very great tragedy if the Open University had been closed by the Conservatives for the seventies saw a growth in higher education - it more than doubled in size between the publication of the Robbins Report in 1963 and 1977 (Williams, 1977, p.6). Added to that growth in the redbrick universities and the older universities was the impact of the Open University.

One could adapt the words uttered by R.H. Tawney to Lord Robbins for the British scene as well as the United States of America.

> You cannot exaggerate the extent to which the United States has benefitted from the fact that so many of its people have had at least a smell of a university(Williiams, 1977, p.12).

This happened to a greater extent in England and Wales in the seventies than at any other period. A case in point would be J. Elwyn Hughes, a hill farmer from Bwlchgwyn in the Denbighshire uplands. J. Elwyn Hughes had been nurtured in the WEA tradition for years like so many other people in Wales. For a number of years he attended WEA classes in Bwlchgwyn and one class was devoted for three years to the work of the Welsh poet, Dr. Bobi Jones of Aberystwyth (Hughes, 1974, p.85). Adult education had become one of the "great pleasures" in his life. It was a natural step then for J. Elwyn Hughes to take - from the WEA class to the Open University. After all the WEA have in the seventies in many areas worked closely with the Open University. At Liverpool and Newcastle and other areas the WEA have arranged preparatory courses for adults who are interested in joining the Open University. J. Elwyn Hughes converted an old granary on his farm into a study which provided him with easy access at "opportune times during the day without disturbing the rest of the household" (Hughes, 1974, p.86). His attendance at the summer school at Keele was a brand new experience - "the first holiday off the farm in twenty years". The only criticism he voices is with regard to the Welsh language:

> Welsh is my mother-tongue, and I should have liked to do the courses in Welsh. The Open University in Wales must press for this in future.   (Hughes, 1974, p.86)

It seemed that the academics in Wales were more concerned with general television programmes in Welsh than with having Open University courses translated into the Welsh language for Welsh speakers, like J. Elwyn Hughes. The idea is not as far-fetched as one would imagine. One in four courses out of the one hundred and fifteen Open University courses offered in 1979 had fewer than two hundred students and nearly half of the Open University courses had fewer than four hundred students. The concern of the Open University for disadvantaged adults and for continuing education augurs well for the future of adult education within the British Isles. At least they are open to ideas. The Open University has stimulated interest in external degrees in other parts of the world and in adult education generally. An American adult educationist, Fred Harvey Harrington, has maintained that the Open University "may prove to be the most important experiment ever undertaken in off-campus credit work for adults" (Harrington, 1977, p.59).

This has not been generally understood or indeed has the urgency of adult education been recognised. Even in the seventies the normal route for most young people was straight out of school into the working world or to experience the frustration of unemployment. Seventy per cent of children in 1973 left school at the age of sixteen or under (Hutchinson, 1978, p.167). We are still an under-educated people and the new deal mentioned by Enid and

Edward Hutchinson is very much a priority. Their call has urgency to it for it is based on a long and distinguished service to adult education in Britain.

> Nor can needs for adult education be defined only by reference to the outstandingly disadvantaged and deprived, the rejectors and the rejected, as is the current mode. Their needs are patent enough, but the response too easily smacks of the soup kitchen and the construction of an alibi for failure to face up to the true scale and character of need.
>
> (Hutchinson, 1978, p.185)

But what can someone do when there are needs which call for the 'soup kitchen' approach. This happened with the Adult Literacy Campaign in the seventies. It began in the sixties on a small scale under the umbrella of the Cambridge House Literacy Scheme. The scheme provided highly confidential tuition under the supervision of a personal volunteer tutor who gave this service in his or her spare time. Gradually other schemes of a similar character run by voluntary organisations and local authorities emerged in various centres. It proved to fulfil a desperate need even in a country which had an universal and a compulsory system of education.

The challenge was taken up by the BBC and the ITV who provided publicity and teaching material for adults who were without the basic skills needed in an industrial society. A.H. Charnley and H.A. Jones have divided the work and campaign of adult literacy into four phases:

i   Phase 1 up to mid 1974 was an activist phase. The main concern was a demand for action.

ii   Phase 2 from the autumn of 1974 to the beginning of 1976 was a period of preparatory organisation. The BBC established their adult literacy project and undertook to produce two television series *On the Move* (level I produced in 1975) and *Your Move* (level II which started in 1976). Another innovation was the introduction of the telephone referral service in London, Wales and elsewhere. At the beginning of 1975 the central government through the National Institute of Adult Education established an Adult Literacy Resource Agency (ALRA) for one year only and with the task of being the administrative unit responsible for allocating a grant of one million pounds. The local authorities were busily training volunteer tutors.

iii   Phase 3 was from early 1976 to early 1978 and it was the period of improving the quality of provision. The ALRA agency was given a reprieve until April 1978 and a further grant of two million pounds which enabled them to appoint full-time and part-time staff.

iv   Phase 4 was from early 1978 and in this period the main concern was for the quality of provision which included educational progress beyond literacy. In April 1978 ALRA was replaced by an adult literacy unit.

The Adult Literacy Campaign from the adult education perspective was important for it grew out of a demand made by a pressure group. It really emerged from a Conference held in 1973 and organised by the British Association of Settlement under the title of *A Right to Read*. Through the influence of this pressure group society was persuaded to allocate the resources (human and financial) to provide a service for a section of the population whose needs had hitherto been largely ignored. But like so many worthwhile schemes financial support is not available, for in a society which appreciates education there should always be a place for adult illiterates whatever their number. This campaign caught the mood of the times and offered an opportunity to implement at least one of the recommendations of the Russell Report. Adult education benefited in at least three ways from the Adult Literacy Campaign:

i   The use of broadcasting and its effectiveness.

Radio and television lend themselves to a campaign of this nature and many of those involved would have welcomed a permanent programme. Indeed the BBC and the ITV could prepare many more programmes which would involve minorities and groups who have special needs as well as giving acces to groups who have a viewpoint to present. If Canada can prepare and finance community television for the Eskimos it is feasible to argue that the minority groups including those who need basic skills in England and Wales could also benefit from community television (Coleman, 1975, p.6).

ii   The contribution of the volunteer tutors

Adult education depends on tutors and the ALRA has shown how it is possible to train and use adults to become effective communicators. It has also exploded the myth that adults in the post-war period were unwilling to give of their time and talents without a financial reward. If the cause is sufficiently urgent then people will respond.

iii   The effective work of the ALRA

In a short period of time the Adult Literacy Resource Agency (ALRA) was able to forge a link with the local education authorities and encourage them to examine their existing service. Local literacy committees were established which brought together people of experience and who were highly motivated. The emphases of the local committees was always on action to be taken and the urgency of the campaign. The ALRA also knew that the task was a huge one - which would entail a long campaign. Unfortunately due to the short-sightedness of central government the campaign was not given that essential support. For example in 1979 more than twenty per cent of those in penal establishments were illiterates or lacking in basic skills. The ALRA showed that basic adult education is concerned with home and family, work, stages of adult life, leisure and citizenship.

The other main strand of adult education in the seventies was the continuation of community education. As this aspect has already been written upon in the Introduction it only needs for me to enlarge a little on a few aspects to community education. The biggest problem in the community schools is that adult education is never given its rightful role. Graham Mee and Harold Wiltshire have pinpointed a number of difficulties which arise in the community school situation. Adult education is still too often the unwelcome borrower of other people's premises or alternatively the unequal partner in a sharing situation (Mee and Wiltshire, 1978, p.79). Though the concept of lifelong continuing education is built into the philosophy and structure of the community school, in actual practise it is difficult to implement the philosophy. It has been questioned whether these community schools are all that beneficial to adult. Adults are generally there on sufferance. It seems that the presence of adults in sixth form classes is of more value to the sixth formers than the adults. This whole provision was on a small scale as were other experiments to reach the working class adults.

Liverpool was among the pioneers due mainly to the initiatives by the Social Studies Division of the Institution of Extension Studies of the University of Liverpool in 1972-73. It was decided to concentrate on Scotland Road, an area which has seen poverty and deprivation since the middle of the nineteenth century. The people who live in and around Scotland Road are mainly poor, unskilled and mainly of Irish-Catholic background. A Poetry Workshop under the initiative of David Evans was set up on 24 September 1973. Nine adults turned up but in time the enthusiasm and the involvement was rewarded. Similar experiments were witnessed in other inner city areas, that is in London, Brighton, Bristol, Manchester, and Newcastle. All these workshops were concerned with working class writing in one form or another. The Scotland Road group became a model for others in Liverpool. Since the Scotland Road Writers' Workshop was established, other groups have emerged in Liverpool 8, Cantril Farm estate, Shaw Street and Skelmersdale.

The whole 'movement' has produced some quite talented writers, like Norma Igbesoko from the predominantly black Liverpool 8 Workshop and Chris Darwin and Jimmy McGovern of the Scotland Road Group. Michael Reilly perhaps was the one writer who produced the most apt and poignant description of jobless Liverpool in the seventies as "Calvary City". But like all other interesting and lively unorthodox adult education experiments the universities in England and Wales are reluctant to finance these courses and classes. David Evans at the end of the seventies felt somewhat depressed at the uncertain future of adult education in the inner city areas:

> I cannot help feeling that an opportunity to do great work is being missed through timidity and the wrong kind of analysis.   (Evans, 1979, p.53)

Adult education in the inner city areas could be enlarged and the history workshops, political workshops, writers' workshops all indicate the richness, vitality and the opportunity for expansion in the inner city areas. David Evans asks the question:

> Will they seize the chance (that is the adult education agencies) to help create a more representative culture, or will they continue with the safer - but surely increasingly sterile business of providing orthodox courses and classes for the relatively privileged?
> (Evans, 1979, p.53)

There are others of us besides David Evans who believes that adult education in the inner city should be the responsibility of the University Extension or

Departments of Adult Education as well as other adult education institutions and organisations like the WEA. But there was very little commitment and far less finance available in the seventies for such 'unorthodox' adult education.

It was part of the anxiety that adult educationists had to face. Adult education in the seventies faced cutbacks proportionately more severe than those imposed upon any other part of the education scheme. This is reflected throughout England and Wales in annual reports from all adult education agencies. The long established Cambridge House and Talbot which has been giving service to the people of Camberwell since 1879 had this to say in its annual report for 1978-79, from the pen of its head, Colin Rochester:

> It's been a good year for Cambridge House in every respect except - alas - finance. As Angus Gilroy points out in his Treasurer's report we need to raise a substantial amount of extra income. If we don't, then the only alternative is to cut expenditure and it is impossible to see how that can be done without cutting back on activities that are clearly needed.

The annual reports that I have read in the seventies, in particular from adult education centres, reflect the difficulties created by the inflation-ridden economy and from the squeeze imposed upon them by local and central government. There is no question that adult education has borne the brunt within the cultural scene. Adult educationists themselves felt the anxiety. J.W. Saunders, warden of the University of Leeds Adult Education Centre at Middlesbrough from its inception in 1958 had a complete breakdown at the age of fifty-nine shortly after those very difficult years 1977/78 and 1978/79.

Adult education even though it has not received the financial support it deserves, yet kept its morale to a large extent by stressing that people matter. Most adult education agencies had enough initiative to respond to new needs that arose in the seventies. Toynbee Hall, the Universities Settlement in East London, saw the need of the Bengali community. The two neighbourhood primary schools, Canon Barnett and Christ Church Spitalfields, consisted of children whose parents came from Bengal. It was in the spirit of Toynbee Hall to respond by establishing English as a Second Language Classes for these parents. This initiative has grown in its scope with a Bengali school and a youth club as well as a drama group for adults from Bengal. But these centres and adult institutions are often regarded as providing 'mere' recreation which does not merit public funding. The wrong concepts have been associated with adult education for too long and it has been a stumbling block to the ordinary person. Richard Hoggart has underlined this malaise:

> But in Great Britain one half of those who leave school at sixteen never set foot in an educational establishment for the rest of their lives.   (Hoggart, 1978, p.6)

It has been mentioned more than once in this book the the more education a man has the more likely he is to want more and the better able he is to get it. Adult education students tend to be middle and lower middle class rather than working class. However, there are exceptions like the University of Leeds Adult Education Centre in Middlesbrough which has an overwhelming working class clientele. J.W. Saunders in his 1979/80 Annual Report states that 99 per cent of the Middlesbrough students were either "working-class" or "first-generation middle class", that is those adults who have risen in census-status because they took advantage of opportunity not available in the years before 1939 (Saunders, 1980, p.3). But the number of adults in Middlesbrough and throughout England and Wales who are completely literate are not as numerous as one would expect in a highly industrialised country. News-papers, to use Hoggart's phrase, are in the business of "aborted literacy". He adds:

> Yet the general level of social, personal and political literacy is below that which a modern society should be content to accept.　　　　　　　　　　　　　　　　　(Hoggart, 1978, p.8)

Hoggart pleads for continuing education to be taken seriously while others plead for recurrent education. But whatever concepts one is in favour of there are measures that have to be introduced into society if it is to have a chance of succeeding. The measures would include reform of upper secondary education, extension of school leaving age to seventeen or eighteen, a more flexible post-secondary system and commitment from employers and em-ployees. New pedagogies are needed which would combine theory and practise. In other words it demands a radical change. This change is not universally accepted by either conservatives, liberals, or socialists. The Russell Report saw permanent education as a long term concept and argued that Britain had no time to wait for it. Britain has dragged its feet and in particular in the seventies. J.W. Saunders gives 1972 as the year of the decline in adult education, a decline which has been most marked since 1974 (Saunders, 1978, p.4). The decline occurred during the Heath Conservative Government but the trend was not reversed by the incoming Labour Government of 1974. They ignored their own philosophical concepts of equality and adult education became a threatened service. Mee and Wiltshire noted a decrease of about eight per cent between 1975 and 1976 in the number of students recorded by 56 authorities (Mee and Wiltshire, 1978, p.97).

Institutions which had been brought into being by the Labour Government, like the Polytechnics, were allowed to be ignored by adult education. There was almost no recognition of their potential (Ellwood, 1976, p.70). It is of no surprise for the Russell Report which was published in 1973 devotes only one paragraph and concludes that the "special contribution which the Polytechnics may make to adult education is likely to result from initiatives taken within their own institutions". In the seventies some polytechnics indicated that they were able to take such initiatives. An excellent example is the work of the Extra-Mural Centre of the Polytechnic of Central London. This centre was established in 1971 and the centre came into existence in the context of Liberal Studies Programme. Since its inception the centre has made a considerable contribution to the adult education provision of the inner London area.

One has to cite other countries as examples of what could be done and what was done in the decade that we are looking at. The most radical analysis of education and society was not the Russell Report but the Report of the Commission on Post-Secondary Education in Ontario, published in 1973, under the title *The Learning Society*. Recurrent education through the writings of J. Bengtsonn was given the support of the Swedish Government. A subsidy scheme was implemented in 1976 in which the central government makes a grant out of general tax revenues to an employer to support the release of workers to undertake education, in return for which the employer hires replacements who are twenty five years old or younger. In addition training grants are made to employers so that workers who are not needed during slack demand can receive education as well as income instead of being laid off (Nollen, 1977, p.71). To be fair to British governments one has to applaud the establishment of the Employment and Training Act in 1973, Training Opportunities Scheme (TOPS) and Industrial Training Board Schemes. An estimated two million workers out of a labour force of 24 million received training of some sort in 1971. But it is another question if one can regard all this as recurrent education. Professor Stanley Nollen from Georgetown University was not at all sure if that kind of training found in Britain in the early seventies could qualify as recurrent education (Nollen, 1977, p.72). There are others of us who share his uncertainty. The Manpowers Service commission and its training programmes was a sign of hope for it gave for the first time in the United Kingdom opportunities to people other than those already highly qualified to receive vocational education. The Advisory Council for Adult and Continuing Education is a valuable pressure group that has received government support and has produced pamphlets and organised conferences which gives a platform for adult education concepts and schemes. This is very much a necessity in view of the unemployment situation at the end of the seventies and the strategy of the Conservative Government that was elected under the leadership of Mrs. Margaret Thatcher in May 1979.

After reading this book and sharing the visions, experiments, concepts and philosophies of adult educationists and agencies since 1945 one is bound to feel bewildered, disillusioned, ashamed of the lost opportunities and angry at the lack of vision displayed by the Department of Education and Science and local authorities in England and Wales. There was no possibility at the end of the seventies for the new initiatives thought of by educational settlements, WEA, extension departments, further education colleges to be implemented. Indeed there was no promise made or acknowledgement given to the necessity for adult education as a means of cushioning the closure of factories and work-places. Local education authority adult education schemes became a national scandal. Humberside and Hampshire decided to abandon adult education for at least a year. Nottinghamshire decided to cut a substantial part of its provision indefinitely and the Inner London Education Authority was willing to consider adult education as an area where substantial savings could be made (Fullick, 1980, p.2). Adult education was again to be sacrificed, courses to be closed and part-time lecturers, in most cases, to be allocated less work. Full-time adult educationists like Leisha Fullick knew the political value of stressing the importance of adult education and in arguing a case for its survival:

> So let us please promote one urgent political message with a big P amongst colleagues, students and the neighbourhoods we serve. The good old adult education lesson about the value of group and collective action as a means of developing the individual and giving that person the confidence to take control of his or her future is never so important as now. Adult education could be a key factor in deciding the shape of our society - we must work together to keep it. (Fullick, 1980, p.2).

It is a plea that will largely go unheeded for sometime but it is a plea that has to be heeded if Britain is to utilise the abilities and the energies of its people. The eighties could witness the social revolution of the twentieth century with continuing education or life-long education and all the other concepts being utilised for the good of the individual and of society. It could turn Britain and our society on to a completely fresh track. But everything depends on learning from our failures and on realising that the 'knowledge industry' can never be dismissed or closed down. To fulfil this task, therefore, entails commitment of a kind that never gives in, for after all it is education that will be available to every adult throughout his life.

Chapter 11
Conclusions and Implications for Policy

In this book, I was concerned with aspects of adult education in England and Wales between 1950 and 1980, and a thorough evaluation has been carried out of the provision offered by the responsible bodies and in particular the work of the WEA in the education of adults. There are three distinctive strands which are interwoven into the book and which will be dealt with in this final chapter. But in this introduction to the concluding chapter, I am underlining briefly the contribution of this book to the literature of adult education.

This book indicates how adult education policies have been based on theoretical concepts and how very little has been learnt from the actual situation. Philosophers of adult education such as Sir Richard Livingstone have argued that adult education is a fundamental right of every adult person in England and Wales and that adults need education for pleasure and enjoyment, sometimes for vocational reasons and at other times for the extension of the adult's intellectual and spiritual growth. This philosophy is acceptable as we have seen to the adult education organisations but these organisations are unable to implement the philosophy as they are not given the financial resources by central government to implement the concepts and the ideas. This has been true in other spheres of adult education. Trade Unions have educational programmes for adults but they are not willing to spend the financial resources needed for its provision. Adult education philosophers argue that adult education should give the individual an opportunity of pursuing liberal education for its own enrichment and vocational training so as to meet the changing needs of an industrial society but the financial resources for the implementation of this concept are not available. We have seen how other adult educationists argue that adult education must be provided wherever there are people and whoever they are, that it must cater for the needs of special groups and minorities, for those who are disadvantaged either mentally or physically, environmentally (that is, inner city areas) or by their own deviant behaviour. But we have also seen how little financial resources local and central governments are allocating for the implementation of these concepts.

It is true that in the last two decades of our study (1960-1980) adult education has come to cover larger and larger areas. Concepts have been proclaimed in conferences and in articles in journals such as continuing education and permanent education. But very little was done to implement these philosophies on a national scale. Everything depends, as we have seen throughout this book, on the political will to accept and implement these philosophies by central and local government in a partnership with all the different parties that work in the adult education world in England and

Wales. The basic weakness is what I have argued in this book, and that is an inability to adapt philosophical ideas or concepts to the actual changing technological society in England and Wales. Every adult education organisation has its own axe to grind and due to the cinderella status of adult education it is very easy for governments to ignore and to be unimpressed by the continual debate of the adult education practitioners.

Considerable progress has to be made if the situation is to be improved and if England and Wales are to emulate some of the Nordic countries, as for example Sweden. In Sweden employers pay a special payroll contribution for adult education. This money is used to help the adult students to pursue further study, to finance study circles in high priority subjects, that is, Swedish, English, mathematics and social science as well as outreach programmes at work places and in residential areas. Outreach programmes are aimed at establishing contact with people having less than nine years of primary schooling. This provision is much more advanced than what is still being provided in England and Wales and though the Trade Union Congress, for example, have a deep seated philosophical commitment to the educational opportunities for workers they tend in reality, as we saw in the chapter on workers' education, to have a very narrow curriculum geared to the training of men and women to be efficient office holders within their own unions.

The second contribution of this book is a thorough analysis from within of the WEA movement. The WEA has been written about extensively in the post-war period in articles by WEA tutors and by other adult educationists from other movements. My position is somewhat different. I have served the WEA movement for eighteen years as a part-time tutor and as one who is totally committed to the philosophy of the WEA movement. I do not look at the WEA as so many academics have done through the windows of other movements in adult education but as an insider who realises that the movement needs to be evaluated in a critical manner. The most serious criticism of the WEA is the change in the student that has taken place over the years. At first most of the students were associated with the trade union organisation but as the curriculum became wider other people were attracted to the WEA classes. Quite a number of 'black coated' workers, professional people such as teachers and civil servants enrolled with the result that the WEA changed its character (Curtis and Boultwood, 1962, p.320). It was taken over by the middle class and our opinion and participation study of WEA students and a WEA class in Liverpool is a further evidence for this change. Albert Mansbridge would have been opposed to this change but it is worthwhile considering a number of issues which I came across in my research and in my interviews with adult students in Liverpool. The opinion study was valuable as an indicator of the trends that one has to recognise.

For it seems that the middle class are in a better position to enjoy the facilities of the WEA than the working class. We saw in our piece of research in Liverpool that the majority of adult students join the WEA classes through the influence of other adult students. This is the most successful method of selection, and because a large number of middle class men and women are members of the WEA classes they inform their middle class friends and neighbours of the provision that is available at the WEA centres. Even the WEA brochures are mostly available in public libraries which again are frequented by men and women who love books and reading, a characteristic of the middle class.

The whole pattern of work, leisure, home and personal intersts allow middle class people to take advantage of the WEA and other adult facilities. A few generalisations can be offered on the basis of the research, namely

i   The networks assist middle class people to make use of the WEA facilities.

ii   Leisure. Middle class people are more often than not in work that allows them leisure opportunities in the evenings. A teacher, for example, starts his day at nine in the morning and completes his duties at around 4 o'clock in the afternoon. This gives him time to organise himself for an evening class while a working class individual has to work on a shift basis or works in an industry where there are opportunities for overtime. If regular overtime is worked by individuals over a longer period, overtime working becomes not only a habit but what is even more important, overtime money becomes part of the regular wages, the standard of living is raised and the worker is at his place of work for a long time. Ferdynand Zweig gave examples of this in his study of the worker in the early sixties:

> A man of fifty-eight worked 66 hours; weekdays from 7.30 a.m. to 7.00 p.m., Saturdays from 8.00 a.m. to 5.00 p.m.; Sundays from 8.00 a.m. to 1.00 p.m. He owned a car and apparently these long hours were paying for the car. But actually his only free time was Sunday afternoon, and he was so tired that he had to go straight to bed on that day. Another man of thirty-nine with one boy worked 63 hours, two hours longer than the normal time, three times a week, Saturday, 8 hours and Sunday, 5 hours. A number of skilled men worked 62, 60, 58, 56½, 54 hours and so on.   (Zweig, 1961, p.75)

The leisure that is available for these workers is then to be spent within the home and within the activities of the family.

The 'cultural horizons' to borrow Zweig's phrase is also an important factor in the appeal of adult education for the middle class and the relatively small appeal it has amongst the working classes. The social investigator, Ferdynand Zweig, was dismayed at the enormous amount that needs to be done in the field of adult education after interviewing workers in different parts of England but he did not ask the question: Why is this not happening? This study has been concerned with the reasons for the apathy and the non-involvement as well as realising the difficulties encountered by working class people. We have already established that the love of reading is a basic tool for an adult student. Many working class people compared with middle class people have not the facilities to pursue their reading interests. The houses are often small. In many of the terraced houses in Liverpool and elsewhere as well as in the council estates catering for working class people there is one room where all the activities of the family are pursued. The television, record player, the conversation of the family and a number of other interests are all together in one room which makes it difficult to read or learn from factual books. This situation is not as restrictive for middle class people who often have a room which can be used for studying and where books can be kept. All this has to be realised when evaluating the task of the WEA and other adult organisations.

This study also has taken the definition of adult education in its widest context. The adult education movement is scrutinised in its various aspects but also the concept of the education of adults. It was Professor E.G. Weddell in two interviews at Manchester who indicated to me the need to regard the auxiliaries of education such as books, do-it-yourself hobbies and the various voluntary improvements, mass media, as contributing to the education of adults. This standpoint I have accepted throughout the study for those familiar with the English 'tutorial-class' tradition will recognise the tradition and value of independent study. The Russell Report recognised this tradition and even the right of a citizen to enjoy educational facilities. The words written by a Mr. Hardman in the weekly newspaper, *Times Educational Supplement* (13 April 1946) were still a vision at the beginning of the seventies:

> We needed a conception of adult education as something which touched the whole adult population and not merely a select few, and which embraced the whole range of human interests, intellectual, aesthetic, physical and practical.

This is what I have striven to emphasise in the course of this book. But it seems that there are at least eleven priorities that needed to be analysed and evaluated by all those involved in adult education in England Wales.

i   The concept of continuing education.

Continuing education is a concept according to J.R. Kidd and a great number of other adult education philosophers that politicians, policy-makers and adult educationists have to take seriously if the economic and social well-being of industrial countries are to be maintained in the modern world. As I have indicated in the book, post-school education in England and Wales in the post-war period tended to reinforce inequality by allocating the greater share of financial resources to those who had gained the highest attainment at secondary schools or in higher education and least on those individuals with the greatest educational and social needs. Even the adult education movements who were established for the specific purpose of assisting the working class and the underprivileged have been unable to reach those very people in the post-war period for whom the movement in the first place was set up for, that is the army of labour. There are reasons for this as we have already indicated in this chapter and Workers' Educational Association is the classic example. The WEA is after all a movement which has tremendous sympathy and allegiance to the education of working people but which has largely been taken over and largely serves the self improvement of the middle class.

It seems reasonable then to argue that there is need for a radical shift on the part of the central government in the allocation of financial resources for continuing education and for a massive campaign to implement the concepts of continuing education through the adult education world as well as in society at large. We have seen in this study concepts in adult education not being adapted to the existing situation and not being of any real relevance to the actual situation.

ii   Adult education for leisure.

The four main qualities of leisure according to the literature that has been published are:

a   release (release from primary obligations, i.e. occupation, family and social obligations);

b   voluntariness (not for material or social gain);

c   hedonism (the search for satisfaction);

d   individualism (reaffirmation of the individual in the face of society).

Leisure has become one of the greatest challenges to adult education, a challenge that it has largely ignored. It is the mass media (books, magazines, newspapers, television, radio, cinema) that largely cater for the leisure time activities of adults and involves them in an educational process. As John Robinson rightly points out in a survey of fifty years of broadcasting:

> Adult education as a service by enthusiasts for enthusiasts is no longer enough. We have to involve far wider sections of the community.   (Robinson, 1974, p.231)

This is true as we have pointed out when discussing adult education and broadcasting and in our survey of the auxiliaries of the education of adults.

But it seems on the evidence available that England and Wales lag behind the European countries on what can be called 'training for leisure'. Holland created a new Ministry in 1965, the Ministry of Culture, Recreation and Social Work. The sphere of this ministry includes television, radio, outdoor recreation, youth services, adult education, sports, culture (museums, arts, opera), old people's welfare and relations with various professional bodies involved (actors, musicians, youth leaders). This ministry co-ordinates a wide diversity of services and incorporates adult education with sport and the mass media, all of which are important leisure time pursuits (Green, 1971, p.68).

In the United States of America there are leisure officers and this is another inevitable development in a number of countries in the western world. Leisure books is another innovation that can be adopted by all local authorities. Wiltshire County Council produces annually a booklet entitled, *Leisure in Wiltshire,* which is a brief guide to the facilities available in the countryside for the resident. This idea is implemented by a number of authorities in England and Wales and has proved beneficial to those who are able to enjoy leisure activities. Some have argued for Leisure Shops for every large shopping centre where leisure facilities can be described, illustrated and located. All this is part of the task to prepare adults for leisure and this study provides evidence for the need.

iii Basic Education Skills

An emphasis is placed by the adult education movements on intellectual discussion and learning but for many adults in England and Wales this is too much to expect for they lack basic skills in literacy and numeracy. Whatever else is to be included as part of the adult education curriculum, there is no doubt that the basic skills of the 3 R's - reading, writing and arithmetic - must be given to those adults who for a variety of reasons have not been able to master these basic skills. We have seen how the WEA in particular has recognised that basic education has to be a part of the adult education provision throughout England and Wales.

The Adult Literacy Scheme that was implemented in the seventies underlined what we have seen all along in the post-war period, that is, the need for literacy tuition. It was estimated that only five per cent of those in need of assistance took the opportunity, and many others who could have been helped were unable to make use of the scheme. Like so many other schemes of real value the Adult Literacy Scheme was not given the financial resources it needed and this impaired its influence. It is clear to me that in the long term adults who need these basic skills which are so essential in a technological age will have to receive paid educational leave to attend such courses and this paid educational leave should be extended also to all adult students.

It seems in the light of this research that the right to paid release is crucial in any extension of educational opportunity for all adults. Trade union education became much more acceptable because unions in many industries were able to negotiate paid leave for their members.

iv State Schools for Adults

In Sweden there are two adult schools, at Norrköping and Härnösand, which are directly administered by central government. These schools are intended for students who do not have access to adult education in their home towns and people who cannot attend regular day or evening courses. The courses take place either entirely on a correspondence basis or by correspondence combined each term with relatively short and intensive in-school courses. The success of correspondence education, the National Extension College, indicates that there are thousands of people who find attendance at adult centres difficult and who are able to cope with the learning situation without having to attend adult education centres. These people enjoy self-education and education by correspondence as Professor E.G. Weddell has pointed out, and there are people living in remote rural areas of

England and Wales where an adult class is an impossibility but who would take advantage of the facilities offered by the region's adult state schools.

v   Opportunities for Women.

It has been recognised for decades that if women are to achieve social and economic equality with men, it is important that women achieve equality of educational opportunity. Women and girls were disadvantaged throughout the educational system in the post-war period, but most severely in further and higher education. Discrimination by employers against young women workers plays a major part in the patterns of disadvantage. The percentage of male workers under eighteen years of age released by their employers for part-time day courses in 1970 was a meagre 38.2 per cent, the percentage for girls was a mere 9.6 per cent. Whereas almost four out of ten males received day and block release, only one in ten females were given release. The following table indicates the lower proportion of women than men at all ages in post-school education - except, notably, the colleges of education and evening-only courses.

Per Cent of Population Receiving Education, Aged 15 and over, 1969-70

	15-17		18-20		21-24	
	Males	Females	Males	Females	Males	Females
Full-time and Sandwich						
Schools	41.9	40.5	2.6	1.7	-	-
Advanced Further Education	-	-	2.5	1.1	1.6	0.4
Non-Advanced Further Education	5.1	5.7	2.7	1.7	0.8	0.3
Universities	0.1	0.1	6.5	3.3	3.5	1.1
Colleges of Education	-	-	1.2	4.6	0.6	1.0
Part-time Students in Further Education						
PTD	20.3	6.3	21.0	2.7	-	-
Evenings only	11.5	12.9	8.3	8.9	-	-

Source: **The Future of Further and Higher Education** (Association of Teachers in Technical Institutions, 1973, p.16).

Table 11:1.

It would be revealing also if the percentages in the above table could be further analysed for it seems also that for the daughters of working class parents the educational disadvantages are added to social and economic disadvantages. Continuing education in the opinion of the TUC, for example, should concentrate on expanding opportunities for girls, particularly in the further education sector in which girls and women so rarely enrol for technical and engineering courses *(Priorities in Continuing Education* (n.d.), pp.6-7).

vi   The role of the WEA and the University Extra-Mural Departments.

It is impossible to conclude this book on aspects of adult education in England and Wales without giving a section to the two movements that have been thoroughly evaluated, namely the WEA and the University Extra-Mural Departments. Both movements have been starved of financial resources, as one can see in the table devised by John Vaizey and John Sheehan and compare it with other tables that are found in their book, *Resources for Education: an Economic Study of Education in the United Kingdom, 1920-1965,* that was published in 1968.

Adult Education, England and Wales, 1920-1965

(£'000)

Year ended March 31st	a Teaching	b Administration	c Total	d Total at 1948 prices
1920	8	4	12	36
1930	22	9	31	90
1940	64	27	91	180
1950	379	162	541	300
1955	555	245	800	420
1965	1,432	533	1,985	806

Sources: Ashby Report; Board of Education estimates; W.E.A. Reports; University accounts; Statistics of Education 1965 Part 1 (Vaizey and Sheehan, 1968, p.166).

Table 11.2

But both adult education movements have changed, as we have seen, their respective roles to a large extent with the University Extra-Mural Departments emerging from obscurity into predominance into the education of adults. There are many whose names have been noted in this book who believe that university extension has found its true role in the post-war period, that of satisfying the adult education needs of the country's educated élite. But though this is accepted by many as its role (this is the position, for example, of A. John Allaway of the University of Leicester) there are others who dispute this, as for example, Professor Maurice Bruce of the University of Sheffield who regarded the department's involvement with industrial day-release courses as the most important contribution made by his staff during his twenty-one years in the department. It seems that the university extension departments or extra-mural departments or the adult education department (all terms used in the University of Wales and the English universities) have at least given consideration to the following:

a. Continuing education or lifelong education or to borrow the phrase used by Professor H.A. Jones of the University of Leicester "education without terminus".

b. An effort has been made to bridge the false dichotomy of liberal and vocational adult education, and bridge the gap between further and adult education. Much was done in the late sixties to encourage co-operation between extra-mural departments and further education institutes, and the expansion of professional staff in local authority service has made co-operation essential. The university extra-mural departments have a splendid opportunity of providing guidance and support to further education agencies and to the efforts of the WEA.

The WEA is the last bastion of non-vocational adult education which the university extra-mural departments have largely deserted. But the WEA has, as I have documented in this book, abandoned its role as a purely workers' education. Roy Shaw has documented this in an article published in the May 1971 issue of *Adult Education* and though Michael Barratt Brown defends the WEA in the September issue, there is no doubt, in my judgement and on available documentary evidence, that the WEA has not been able to influence the working class as it would have liked. But Roy Shaw's point that the WEA achieved its highest reputation when it was an organising body concerned with building a bridge between labour and learning, that is between the working class and the university, is well worth remembering. It is worth considering his recommendation that this situation should be restored (Shaw, 1971, p.13).

But the WEA has the important task, in my judgement, of providing the initiative for a concentrated and never-ending evangelistic campaign for continuing education. It can co-ordinate the activities of universities and local authorities and its own activities, and it should not lose its pioneering and innovatory spirit. The WEA should concentrate on preparing people for the Open University as well as providing adults with what they need in their actual situation, be it information to cope with the problems of the inner city or a search for happiness.

vii   Educational opportunities for Ethnic Minorities.

In the section on ethnic minority groups and immigrants in this book, one realised that though the efforts to educate adults from a different culture does exist there is still a very urgent need for new educational opportunities to be made available to help counteract the most difficult social prejudices and economic disadvantages that ethnic minority groups have to put up with. There is always the need to provide basic courses in English language skills and television can be a powerful instrument in the hands of adult educationists for this task. Keith Travis mentions in his dissertation a Polish housewife whom he calls Helena as an example of the power of television as a means of teaching a language:

> Her spoken English was excellent both in vocabulary and in grammar, this she attributed to watching television and having bilingual children. She rarely went out except for shopping and visiting her family. (Travis, 1971, p.60)

Very little systematic information is available as to the use made of adult education by ethnic minorities but in reading the Community Relations Commission publications the following points can be made:

a   a large number of students from ethnic minorities do use the further education service;

b   the use is very patchy, that is some recruit large numbers of minority group students and more often on lower level full-time courses than on advanced ones;

c   adult immigrants prefer to be together in a learning context and also to be under the tuition of one of their own leaders or kinsfolk;

d   that so often and we know this from research done in West Yorkshire the Asian tutors are themselves middle class in values and attitudes while their task is to teach working class Asian women at home the use of the English language;

e   that there is ignorance about what further education and adult education has to offer ethnic minorities;

f   the experiences of ethnic minorities in the school system are particularly relevant in understanding their needs for further and adult education. The difficulties that children from ethnic minority communities face in the school system and even in the pre-school years are well documented. A local study carried out at the beginning of the seventies (in actual fact in 1972) by Sheila Allen and Christopher Smith in Bradford and Sheffield and published in 1975 by HMSO *Minority group experience of the transition from education to work in entering the world of work: some sociological perspectives,* shows that in a sample of 668 drawn from 14,000 school leavers not one of the Asian or West Indian leavers had reached 'A' level standard at school. Furthermore whites achieved a mean of 2.08 passes in CSE and 'O' level taken together and blacks a mean of 1.09 passes.

It seems that adult education has an opportunity to be involved on the two fronts, the further education and the adult needs of the immigrants. In the further education field the colleges can prepare themselves for the task, by appointing qualified tutors from all ethnic groups on the teaching staff and they can use every opportunity available by making contact with the minority communities including meetings, broadcasts on local radio in minority languages, working closely with the local community relations council and working with detached youth workers. The wider issue of education in a multi-cultural society - the education of the white community for multi-racialism whether they live in multi-racial areas or not - is also a priority that many of the WEA leaders are concerned with.

In the adult education field the need for English tuition amongst ethnic minority adults, especially women, will remain urgent for a long time. According to the study carried out by Political and Economic Planning (1976) on racial disadvantage, 42 per cent of the Asians interviewed who were over 15 years old, and born, or both of whose parents were born, in India, Pakistan, Bangladesh and East Africa spoke English "slightly" or "not at all". Analysed by sex, the figures are 30 per cent of all Asian men and 59 per cent of women, who spoke English slightly or not at all. Taking the 1971 Census figures for people born in India and Pakistan (East and West) only, this proportion of 42 per cent would reflect a total number of people appraoching 200,000. This is a large minority of adults who cannot cope with simple everday ordinary duties at home or in the wider society (Mobbs, 1977, p.19).

Our analysis and evaluation of adult education among minorities will need additional finance to pay for the teaching material, tutors and the mobile resource centres that will have to be created in each region where there are a large number of ethnic groups. The centres could provide a bank of materials and teaching guides, resources for all learning situations, and could be available for schemes during tutor training sessions, and at other times, so that the local organiser would have easier access to information on new developments. I would like to see these mobile resource centres being available also for other disadvantaged minority groups, and in particular the gypsies and travelling people who are connected with the entertainment world or as scrap metal dealers. A great deal more needs to be done in co-operation between adult education agencies in cities and other areas where there are sizeable ethnic communities. Local colleges of education, adult institutes, WEA and the extra-mural department and local Community Relations Council could hold one-day seminars, workshop sessions for all the schemes in a given area (Mobbs, 1977, p.52). Mobbs makes the point on the same page that "because of the nature of the settlement pattern of the ethnic minority communities, very few schemes within one area are so isolated as to be more than about fifteen miles away from the next one". Subjects for discussion as Michael C. Mobbs suggest could include: making visual aids; the language of a particular domain; difficulties currently experienced by minority communities in the locality; and further expansion of any of the topics of the tutor training courses. There is a great and urgent need for much more to be done in the post-school education sector among immigrant communities and ethnic groups.

viii   Adult education and the Welsh language.

In the post-war period (1945-80) there grew in Wales a spirit of resistance to the manner that the central and local government had ignored the place of the Welsh language. The epoch-making BBC lecture delivered by Saunders Lewis, a past president of the Welsh Nationalist Party, in 1962, brought into being the Welsh Language Society with its aim of compelling the law courts and local government to use the language in its institutions. The language was given equal validity with the law courts and while all this determined struggle was carried on, very few realised that outside the Christian Churches and Chapels of Wales, the only other institution which respected the Welsh language was the adult education agencies.

In the late fifties and early sixties, before the call of Saunders Lewis in his lecture *Tynged yr Iath* (The fate of the language) a quarter of all the extra-mural classes organised by the four colleges (Aberystwyth, Bangor, Cardiff and Swansea) of the University of Wales were conducted in the Welsh language. Within Wales the variation was astounding and reflected the strength and weakness of the language. In the two most anglicised and heavily populated counties of Wales, that is, Glamorganshire and Gwent in the South Wales coalfield, 95 per cent of the classes were in English, in West and Mid Wales the two languages were equally balanced while in North West Wales (Caernarvonshire, Anglesey and Merionethshire) the Welsh language was supreme as the language of adult education. In the county of Caernarvonshire ten out of the sixteen university tutorial classes held in 1959 were in Welsh, and of the thirty-seven WEA classes only one was in English (Llywelyn-Williams, 1960, p.287). The WEA in that session (1959-60) in the six counties of North Wales had a total number of 71 WEA classes in the English language and of these 50 were in the anglicised county of Flintshire.

The adult education movements in Wales, particularly the responsible bodies, have given as much leadership on the matter of providing classes through the medium of the Welsh language as one would expect from many of the men of literary talent who served the WEA and university extension in Wales. Alun Llywelyn-Williams, who is himself a poet of merit, maintained as the Director of the Extra-Mural Department at the University College of North Wales that an "adult education movement which provides classes in Welsh presents a positive assertion not only of the educational value of the language but also of its social significance" (Llywelyn-Williams, 1960, p.288). Dr. Cyril Parry in a pioneering study of socialism in Gwynedd has a great deal of valuable material on adult education. Working men, according to Dr. Cyril Parry, saw education as a means of improving their conditions. The growth of the adult education movement in Gwynedd in the early period is linked through men like Silyn Roberts with the development of socialism in the area. But throughout its history the WEA in North Wales has been very conscious of its role in furthering the Welsh language as a vehicle of communication.

It seems therefore that in the Welsh context adult education has always had a responsibility to the bilingual society and in a period when the Welsh language is in numerical decline that the WEA and the extra-mural departments could be asked to undertake a constructive role in the work of teaching the Welsh language to adults in Wales as well as teaching all subjects through the medium of the Welsh language. The Welsh language will survive, in my opinion, if both needs are met. More people have to be taught the Welsh language and science, technology and allied subjects as well as Welsh literature and Biblical subjects have to be taught also to Welsh-speaking adults. Alun Llywelyn-Williams in a revealing article as adult educationist puts this need in a nutshell:

> If Welsh is to be merely, or even mainly, a language in which we discuss local antiquities and the delights of *cynghanedd* but which we discard for English when we talk of other matters, then clearly it has no future and the full life in Welsh Wales are bleak.
> (Llywelyn-Williams, 1960, p.289)

We can prophesy also according to Alun Llywelyn-Williams that if the Welsh language disappeared that those "specifically Welsh characteristics" will disappear as well. He does not specify what these characteristics are but one can mention two observations that are of significance. The first comes from the lips of Alfred Zimmern who told the Welsh adult educationist, John Thomas, that Welsh adult students had some of the characteristics of the Greek students. The university tutorial class discussion amongst Welsh students in particular reminded Alfred Zimmern of the Socratic discussion in the philosophy forums of Athens which he had so brilliantly described in *The Greek Commonwealth* (Thomas, 1958, p.4). Another outsider and observer of the Welsh scene was the Polish sociologist, Ferdynand Zweig, who in his study of the British workers wrote on the Welsh workers:

> Nearly all those I met had been to Sunday School and Chapel and had an interest in religious problems, although not all of them were believers....... (Zweig, 1952, p.52)

Zweig identified one of the most important strands in the adult education scene in Wales — the place of religion and the supporting role played by the Sunday School movement in the enthusiasm discernible at times in the adult education movements in Wales.

The Sunday Schools in Wales have always had adults attending the classes and the adult classes of the WEA and the university extra-mural departments were a natural extension of an earlier and very successful institution especially among the Welsh-speaking population. Even in our period (1945-80) some of the Sunday Schools in the Welsh-speaking industrial areas were extremely well attended, and I remember attending in 1970 a Presbyterian Church of Wales Sunday School at Rhosllanerchrugog in the Wrexham area which had an attendance of 212 adults in twelve different Welsh-speaking classes each under its voluntary unpaid Sunday School teacher. It is not a surprise then to learn that in Rhosllanerchrugog the adult education classes are well supported in the winter months. For the Sunday Schools in the Rhosllanerchrugog - Ponciau - Johnstown area are natural recruiting ground for these adult education classes. The same was true in many other areas of Wales in the twentieth century and this introduced into the Welsh adult education scene a dimension that many have commented upon and that is a search for spiritual values. Adult education in Britain would be the poorer, in my opinion, if the Welsh language died and if Welsh Nonconformity declined to such an extent that its adult Sunday Schools disappeared. This is why Wales and adult education in the Principality is a priority with regard to its relationship with the language and culture of the country. Because the Welsh language and its culture is under a threat of survival, it would mean that adult education itself would be impoverished, as Alun Llywelyn-Williams maintains, within the context of Wales.

ix   Trade Union Education

The history of Trade Union education was documented in detail in Chapter 3 and it is a peculiar phase of English and Welsh adult education, and even of British education as the NCLC had its headquarters in Scotland. It is a 'peculiar phase' as it developed into a conflict between the two providers of trade union education, the WETUC and the NCLC for the soul of the Labour movement. The conflict, though it was fought in the educational arena, was part of a wider struggle between 'liberals' in the WETUC and 'Marxists' in the NCLC for the soul and mind of trade unionists and of trade union education and indeed of the soul of the Labour movement. It was the WEA through the shrewd leadership of Ernest Green, which consolidated and gained strength and deepened the association's roots in the moderate wing of the Labouar movement. But the NCLC was able to consolidate its roots in the left wing camp of the Labour movement till its work was taken over by the Trade Union Congress.

It was after the second world war that a new situation arose with individual unions devising their own schemes, which were to train union members in the organisation of those individual unions. The WEA was taken unawares by these developments (Marsh, 1958, pp.30-31). The Report of the Working Party on Trade Union Education called for by the WEA's Annual Conference in 1951 came as something of a shock to many, for it was made explicit in the report that there might be a difference between the workers and trade union education.

Adult educationists were concerned at this new development and it was at this stage that F.V. Pickstock at Oxford and Michael Barratt Brown at Sheffield took the initiative and involved extra-mural department in the field of trade union adult education for workers in industry. These courses were concerned at Sheffield and at other university centres with how to think rather than what to think and included a considerable measure of good liberal adult education. This section of liberal adult education grew in the post-war period as the need for it developed. Other bodies also got involved in the task of educating trade unionists, namely some colleges of further education and the BBC further education department.

All these two strands were present at the end of our period and one welcomes the variety of adult education that has been outlined. It seems that all two strands have to be supported, enlarged, and offered to the millions of trade unionists in England and Wales. One cannot visualise a period in the near future without the two strands being a part of trade union education. To summarise the two strands:

a.   Adult 'role' education is designed specifically to assist those engaged in voluntary union work to carry out their trade union duties more effectively. TUC and union courses are also designed to assist full time trade union officials to be more effective negotiatiors and trade union officials.

b.   The liberal adult education approach of the WEA and university extra-mural departments contribute to the all round education of trade unionists and broadens their mental outlook.

But at the end of our period the Trade Union Congress gave particular attention to continuing education and it seems possible that this will become another strand of their approach to the education of trade unionists. The two earlier strands can still be present but the Trade Union movement has to argue (as they have done) for paid educational leave and a major review of the place of student grants and assistance for more trade unionists to attend courses in adult education centres. For there are still trade unions around who have a 'narrowness of mind' with regard to the wider role the trade union movement should be concerned with in the life of the country. Unions should add to their courses some provision for an understanding of forms of industrial demo-cracy as a necessary part of the moves towards greater involvement of the workforce now taking place within industry.

x   Higher Education

It was pointed out in the course of this book that the proportion of young people from working class homes who go on to higher education is and always has been severely restricted - and there were no indications that this proportion was increasing, even after the expansion of higher education which took place in the nineteen sixties. There is need for policies that will widen the opportunities of working people to enter higher education, to advocate the opening of higher education places to more mature entrants, and to students without the traditional 'O' and 'A' level entry qualifications for universities and polytechnics. A few schemes were introduced at the end of the period and these schemes have been developed subsequently in many of the polytechnics. Universities can also examine their own entry requirements and admission policies; and the range, content and form of provision (including part-time courses) to meet the needs of adults in modern society. The universities have a golden opportunity of taking the needs of adults seriously and involving themselves in the task of educating not only the educated but the society that it belongs to. It could have a policy of the 'open door' as the newer of the universities has shown, the Open University.

To adult educationists the Open University is an exciting attempt at opening opportunities for adults in higher education, but it will demand a great deal of campaigning for the other universities to follow suit. It seems that the polytechnics in certain cases are willing to do this but the pressures of conformity and academic respectability has its restrictions in opening up higher education to unqualified adult students who have already shown a need for additional and more systematic training by their involvement in WEA or university extension classes, correspondence courses or trade union education.

xi   New target groups in adult education.

Up to the sixties adult education was mostly addressed to people who took the iniative themselves by attending the adult education courses or attending the summer schools and other educational facilities. The sxities brought major changes as we have noted, in the introduction of comprehensive secondary schools and the lengthening of compulsory schooling and in new emphasis on continuing education and education for life. As a result more active recruitment methods could be used to awaken an interest among certain categories of adults. These are to be noted in this chapter as priorities for adult education in the present and to the future.

i   Adult education for the unemployed.

Unemployment has reached in the seventies a proportion that was not tolerated in the full employment period of the post-war period. While employment is a business of central government yet there are often forces outside the control of any government to deal adequately with. But this does not mean that governments should abandon their role or introduce schemes, like the Manpower Services Commission for adult re-training. It seems to me that the unemployment situation in the seventies demands the setting up of a National Unemployment Market Board (NUMB) on the lines of the Swedish model.

The Swedish system has conditions that must be met before training allowances are given to individuals: the applicant is unemployed or runs the risk of becoming unemployed in the very near future; he is difficult to place in employment; he has reached the age of twenty; he is seeking work through the public employment service and training can be expected to result in permanent employment which would not have been possible without such training *(Fact Sheets on Sweden,* 1978, p.3). Courses used for labour market training must fulfil special requirements. As a rule, the training should lead to specific occupations rather than to occupational branches, and the importance of limiting the period of training is often greater than in other forms of training. The courses have also to be arranged to avoid unnecessary delay for the unemployed on a continuous admissions system and not to be split into terms.

This scheme is, in my opinion, a necessary one in England and Wales and the expertise of adult education institutions could be used for this important task of equipping the unemployed for a society which will demand continual re-training from its workers by hand and brain.

ii.   Adult education and the 'apathetic mass'.

The largest group of adults are those who have left school after seven or nine years full-time study and who have never enrolled for any further education. The educational needs of these people, as we have shown throughout this book, is ignored as they are apathetic and never turn up to any of the adult education centres. The telling points made by Professor E.G. Weddell deserves our attention. He states firstly that adults in the main expect adult education to be provided on an open-ended basis without an obligation to join a voluntary society or a particular worthwhile centre. In other words adult education has to be without strings (Weddell, 1965, p.122). Secondly, according to E.G. Weddell, adult education must be attractive:

> Adult educators do their cause much harm by undervaluing their work and being content with the second best.   (Weddell, 1965, p.123)

In Weddell's opinion, throughout the years from 1945 to 1965 those concerned with adult education have been content to accept a seat on the sidelines. However, at the end of our period there were signs of a change of heart and that the recognition of continuing education as a lifelong activity for all citizens was beginning to have an influence on adult educationists.

Adult educationists have to realise that adult education should be flexible and open ended. To attract those who have never been involved demands this. For example, to many an adult if he is retired morning or afternoon is a better time for classes than in the evenings, to others the summer is a better period than the winter or the spring. H.A. Jones, when he was Principal of the City Literary Institute in London, realised that there was a clear demand for classes in the summer months.

> In regularity of attendance and seriousness of mind the Midsummer students were more than a match for the rest of the year, indeed many of the tutors reported on the stimulating sense of urgency and purpose that infused their classes and were somewhat surprised to find this, especially through weeks of unbroken sunshine.   (Jones, 1965, p.245)

This also is a clear call for adult education movements to be flexible if they are to be effective and popular for adults who are outside the system.

A great deal can be learnt from the surveys that have been carried out on adult students in evening institutes. An example will suffice from a study conducted of students in ten evening institutes in the East Midlands. One institution was rural, five serving working class areas of a city, four served a scattered area of small mining towns and villages. All met in schools, and there was a total enrolment of 2,032 adult students in 114 classes. The researchers had returns from 1,171 individual students. Seventy per cent of the adult students were women and thirty per cent men. By and large women kept the institutes going, and they also had the majority of subjects as we see in the breakdown of the curriculum.

Curriculum	No. of Classes
Women's crafts (including dressmaking and cookery)	49
Men's crafts (including motor maintenance)	30
Arts (drama, music, pottery, etc.)	16
Physical recreation (including dancing)	13
Languages (mainly French)	6

Table 11:3

The difficulties facing these evening institutes are the difficulties facing all institutions of adult education, and that is publicity for the courses that are held every session. Thirty-four per cent of the adults had come along through friends, twenty-two per cent had heard of the course through a printed prospectus, twelve per cent through leaflets, ten per cent through posters, seven per cent through a school talk, three per cent by a newspaper advertisement, and eleven per cent by some other means. This survey by H.C. Wiltshire and his team is a call for more attractive leaflets and this opens up a whole area that is hardly ever dealt with in adult education literature (Wiltshire, Brookes, Dickinson, Huckle, Marsden, Moore, 1964, pp.113-116). It is the need for consistent and unceasing flow of information through the local press, radio, leaflets, of the facilities offered for all adults.

Information, however, is not enough. The nature of the courses and the subjects offered have also to be looked at and if possible suggestions from the adults themselves should be given a hearing by those planning the syllabus. J.A. Simpson who was Staff Inspector for Further Education in the Department of Education and Science wrote in 1968 on the need for adult education to cater for the whole family (Simpson, 1968, p.355). He argued for the short courses or even single lectures and demonstrations that would appeal to a family grouping. This could entail a course on cultural touring or the use of a car as a means of a family sight-seeing. Simpson felt also that very little use is made of television and television programmes for literary, dramatic criticism or ethics. Most of this type of adult education is carried out by the local education authorities rather than the responsible bodies (Simpson, 1968, p.356).

The Swedish experiment with study-circles has a great deal to offer us in England and Wales for the simple reason that the participants and their leaders plan the scope, contents and speed at which the study is undertaken as well as the individual study done between the meetings of the group *(Workers' education in Sweden,* no date, p.2).

It seems that adult education in England will have to look again at many of the experiments carried out in Sweden and also in the Netherlands for a formula to reach those men and women who are outside formal adult education. These experiments indicate that too much effort is often spent on discussing what to do and how to reach the people rather than in developing the thesis that formal and informal adult education must be accepted as intrinsic components of the educational system.

iii.   Adult education in retirement.

The adult education movement has given some thought to the task of educating the elderly and adult educationists of the calibre of Sir Ernest Barker wrote in the early twenties of the need for education as a continuous process and that people must be prepared throughout their lives to enable them to use their leisure during retirement in a wise and purposeful manner. All the evidence that we can gather leads us to believe that adults in England and Wales are totally unprepared for retirement: society does not give the manual worker paid educational leave during his working life, but rather treats adult education as an optional extra in the educational budget.

The needs and interests of the elderly are as varied as those of any other age group; the elderly are not an homogeneous group. Their interests range from those subjects that one can classify as self development - arts, music, drama, to those described as spectator sports, and to those subjects requiring study in depth. There are three principal problems according to Alan Charnley facing the adult education service, both formal and informal sections of the movement. Firstly, the type of education which should be offered to adults in retirement must be suitable for those who have had no continuous experience of education or of the problems of leisure (Charnley, 1974, p.5). Secondly, the adult education movement has to try and provide a range of learning activities and thirdly, education has to be brought into the neighbourhood (Charnley, 1974, p.6).

No adult is too old to learn, maintains Charnley, and this is the reason that the elderly have to be included in the pattern and provision of adult education. The intriguing ideas of David Selby that the adult education movement should offer retirement packages should be considered. This is what David Selby wrote.

> Retired people should be given the opportunity of passive retirement with every need catered for. There should be a Butlins near every large city especially for the retired, allowing for various shades of passivity or activity through to those retired people who want to do a full-time voluntary job, a university degree or academic research. Perhaps local authorities should take over the holiday camps during the off season for their retired citizens, in the same way that they hire steamships for educational cruising. The new recreation department, together with social services and education, could combine to provide the whole programme which might include a first class counselling, psychological and medical service as well as events and classes of various kinds. This type of approach could well get through to the retiring industrial wage earners who would not see it as the same threat of exposure that education is to them.   (Selby, 1974, p.9)

These ideas have to be taken seriously for they bring out the ingredients of a successful programme for the elderly, that is, plenty of variety, an opportunity for companionship, an opportunity for those who want to do educational work in depth, as well as those who want to be educated in a more entertaining manner. John Briggs of the Department of Adult Studies, Harrow College of Further Education, argued for flexibility of approach when discussing the elderly in education and concluded with this wise pleading:

> We argue that adult education has a role to play in the continuing education of the elderly. It may influence the other educational sectors to educate the young in such a way as to encourage helpful attitudes towards the elderly. It may also help to influence the education administrators to allocate to the elderly the national resources which they so richly deserve. (Briggs, 1974, p.14).

iv.   "Adult Concern" Courses.

In addition to the needs of the unemployed, the apathetic mass, and the retired for education, there is also as we have discussed in the book, a crucial need for the further development of courses which can be identified as "adult concern" courses. In a democracy this is an essential demand and adults must have the opportunity of understanding and being involved in the democratic institutions. A strong and flourishing and effective system of continuing education is necessary for this. Political education is part of the 'adult concern' and it is an area which is so often ignored because of the dangers involved in conducting classes on subjects which arouse people's passions. But this should not be a reason to ignore political education in the education of adults and the ignorance of the electorate on the European Economic Community is a classic case in point.

To many other people in modern society their work is often dull, monotonous and boring. Studies have been produced on the monotonous work of car assembly workers and many of these adults complain at the lack of satisfaction that they derive from their work. It is my view and the view of many of those who accept the concept of continuing education that one of the major roles for adult education is to help in remedying the damaging social consequences of this state of affairs. These adult courses could bring a new awareness into people's lives and new solutions found for new problems. It is an important aspect of education of adults to the future.

But all these activities and developments and implications for policy found in this chapter will not take place without new financial resources being committed to them. The framework has been developed with the National Advisory Committee on Adult and Continuing Education as a body which can co-ordinate experiments and activities. But this body and all the educational movements that cater for adults in England and Wales can do very little without financial support.

Financing adult education.

Adult education if it is to be effective in people's lives has to be given the same status and financial support as the rest of the educational system.

Every effort has to be made by adult education organisations to assist adults to attend summer schools, residential courses abroad and in England and Wales. These are always valuable experiences and adults could receive travelling grants so that they can make full use of the facilities. I know from conversation with people how valuable many of these summer schools are, and I can mention one of the oldest of the summer schools, namely the Glamorgan Summer School. It was first held at Barry in 1906, and apart from a break of eight years (1940 to 1947 inclusive) the school was held annually throughout the years. In 1965 the student enrolment was 743 compared with 543 in 1963 (Heycock, 1966, p.23). There are three main purposes in the Glamorgan Summer School — to provide refresher courses for full-time teachers, part-time teachers and lecturers; to train part-time teachers for the non-vocational further education in Glamorganshire; and make it possible for men and women to follow courses in chosen subjects and to pursue them for pleasure.

Another good example was the decision of Liverpool University Extra-Mural Department (as it was then called) to provide study courses in the Isle of Man. It has also arranged each year an Autumn School for visitors to the island, dealing with its history, archaeology, political institutions, natural history, folklore — and, indeed, every aspect of the island's life. Then in 1967 the University of Liverpool made arrangements with Manx Radio and the Manx Board of Education to broadcast twenty half-hour programmes dealing with a range of subjects very similar to that covered in the Autumn School (Kelly, 1967, p.116). These study courses have to be supported financially.

Adult education if it is to expand has to receive a fair share of the government budget for education. Local authority expenditure on adult education can always be increased. But to do this depends on the will of politicians and an awareness by the adult population that they need education as they need other basic commodities in their everyday living as citizens of a democracy. As we have seen in this book, the impact of adult education on the population of England and Wales was restricted in the post-war period (1945-80).

> At any time there are about $1\frac{3}{4}$ million students in adult education classes, about five-sixths of them in local education authority classes. All told they account for about one in sixteen of the adult population. (Simpson, 1970, p.366).

The task therefore facing adult education in England and Wales is a daunting one for as we have seen in this book the theoretical and philosophical ideas of the adult educators have rarely been accepted by central government or by the adult population at large. Adult education policies are based on theoretical concepts but it can be questioned as I have done in this study if a great deal has been learnt from the actual situation. This book does not claim more than any other academic evaluation of adult education that I have read to be a blueprint but it has brought together the important trends and findings of this post-war period in England and Wales and in this concluding chapter a few suggestions for policy changes in adult education.

Bibliography

A   **Primary Material**

1   Interviews in depth conducted with:

    a. Professor E.G. Weddell at the Department of Adult Education in the University of Manchester; b. Professor Thomas Kelly at the Department of Extension Studies at the University of Liverpool; c. Mr. E.R. Morgan of the Department of Education and Science, London; d. Dame Margaret Cole at her home in Ealing; e. David Connor, Secretary of the West Lancashire and Cheshire WEA District and Ernest Stebbing, Development Officer of the WEA in Liverpool; f. Mr. Arthur Stocks, National Institute of Adult Education at London.

2   Correspondence with:

    a. J.R.P. Millar of the N.C.L.C. (30/9/76) and b. Dr. Michael Young, Dartington Hall, Totnes, Devon (4/3/75).

3   Interviews and participatory observation of WEA students in Liverpool as outlined in Chapter 9.

4   A Quesionnaire which was the source for the Opinion Survey outlined in Chapter 9.

5   Letters and informative material (that is, pamphlets, articles, cycostyled material) from

a   Trade Unions

David Basnett, *General Secretary of the General and Municipal Workers' Union* (29/11/74).

Paul Bennett, Education Officer of the *Association of Teachers in Technical Institutions* (7/4/75 and 16/4/75).

Reginald N. Bottini, *General Secretary of the National Union of Agricultural and Allied Workers* (8/4/75).

Kenneth Carter, MA., LIB., DPA, Education Officer of the *National and Local Government Officers Association* (22/4/75).

D.M. Evans, Assistant Secretary of the *Prison Officers' Association,* Edmonton, London (18/4/75).

H.L. Gibson, MBE, JP, General Secretary of *The National Union of Hosiery and Knitwear Workers,* Leicester (10/4/75).

N. Grant, Research Officer, *Confederation of Health Service Employees,* (8/4/75).

N.L. Jones, Organising Secretary of the *National Union of Teachers,* (22/4/75).

David Logan, Education Department, *Trades Union Congress,* (27/4/75).

J. Macgoughan, General Secretary, *National Union of Tailors and Garment Workers,* Milton Keynes, (17/4/75).

G.A. Murray, Assistant to the General Secretary of the *Association of Broadcasting Staff,* (11/4/75).

Ben Norris, Assistant Secretary of the *Musicians' Union,* (7/4/75).

Miss C.K. Palfrey, Assistant General Secretary of *The Society of Post Office Executives,* Kingston-upon-Thames, (5/5/75).

Ita Purton, Secretary Assistant to Dr. Hugh Faulkner, Medical Secretary *of the Medical Practitioners' Union,* (30/5/75).

Gareth Richards, Education Department, *Transport and General Workers Union,* (15/4/75).

Peter Rimfield, Education Officer of the *Union of Shop, Distributive and Allied Workers,* (9/4/75).

Alex Ritchie, Head of Organisation and Education Department of the *Civil and Public Services Association,* (16/4/75).

R.I. Rowley, Acting Organising Secretary of the *Union of Post Office Workers,* (9/4/75).

H. Scanlon, President of the *Amalgamated Union of Engineering Workers* (Engineering Section), (30/4/75).

Arnold Stem of the *Inland Revenue Staff Federation,* (9/4/75).

Sidney Weighell, General Secretary of the *National Union of Railwaymen,* (11/4/75).

R.H. Williams, Research Officer of the *Iron and Steel Trade confederation,* (10/4/75).

b   Local Education Authorities

Gordon S. Bessey, CBE, MA, DCL, Director of Education, Cumbria County Council (7/3/75).

A.C. Burns, Senior Adviser for Further Education, Somerset County Council (11/3/75).

R.O. Burton, MA, County Education Officer, Isle of Wight County Council (12/3/75).

Mrs. Patricia Chown, Administrative Assistant, Higher and Further Education, Dorset County Council (10/4/75).

G.V. Cooke, MA, County Education Officer, Lincolnshire County Council (19/3/75).

H.C. Davison, Assistant Director of Education, Durham County Council (12/3/75).

A.D.N. Forgan, Inspector for Adult Education, Surrey County Council (18/3/75).

M.J. Gifford, B.Sc, County Education Officer of the County Council of Hereford and Worcester (13/3/75).

G.V. Gordon, of the Education Department, Kent County Council (11/3/75).

Roy P. Harding, Chief Education Officer, Buckinghamshire County Council (24/4/75).

M.J. Henley, MA, County Education Officer, Northamptonshire County Council (12/3/75).

F.J. Hill, County Education Officer, Suffolk County Council (20/3/75).

A.J.W. Legge, Adult Education Adviser, Royal County of Berkshire (10/3/75).

E.W. Perry, County Adult Education Officer for the County of Avon (20/3/75).

W.T. Reynolds, BSC (Econ), Adviser for In-Service Training in Adult Education for the County of Avon (20/3/75).

M.I. Ridger, MA, County Education Officer, Warwickshire County Council (17/4/75).

A. Riley, BA, Chief Education Officer, Staffordshire County Council (11/4/75).

James A. Stone, MA, Director of Education, Nottinghamshire County Council (20/3/75).

M.H. Trollope, MA, Director of Education, County of Northumberland (13/3/75).

G.B. Yeo, Senior Assistant Education Officer for Further and Higher Education, County of Cleveland (18/3/75).

c   **Voluntary Adult Organisations**

Frances Breeze, Head of Training and Further Education, The Young Women's Christian Association of Great Britain (3/4/75).

G. Ronald Howe, National Council of YMCA (3/4/75).

R.L. Marshall, OBE, MA, Chief Education Officer of the Co-operative Union Ltd. (25/3/75).

K.M. Reinold, General Secretary, The National Federation of Community Associations (2/5/75).

M.A. Erskine-Wyse, National Union of Townswomen's Guilds (11/4/75)

d   **Workers Educational Association**

1.   **Districts Secretaries**

Charles Butler, WEA Berks, Bucks. and Oxon. District, Oxford (21/4/75).

F.D. Connor, West Lancs. and Cheshire, Liverpool (23/4/75).

R.E. Copley, MA, WEA West Midlands District, Birmingham (25/4/75).

W. Long, North Western, Manchester (21/4/75).

Arthur Maddison, South Western, Plymouth (21/4/75).

R.H. Rochell, WEA North Wales District, Bangor (23/4/75).

G.F. Sedgwick, MBE, MA, Yorkshire North District, Leeds (25/4/75).

2.   **WEA Office**

R.J. Jefferies, BA, General Secretary, W.E.A., Temple House, London. (23/4/75).

e   **Mass Media**

Manuel Alvarado, Education Officer, Society for Education in Film and Television (14/2/77).

Stanley Harrison of The Morning Star, London (20/1/75).

Miss Livia Gollancz, Director of Victor Gollancz Ltd., London (7/3/75).

Mrs. Emily Lobo, Commercial Department, The Newspaper Publishers Association (18/11/74).

Lesley D. Robinson, Assistant to the Information Officer, British Federation of Film Societies (22/4/75).

E.I. Savage, UK Sales Manager, Penguin Books Ltd. (6/3/75).

f   **Educational Movements**

A.S. Baxendale, Chief Education Officer, Home Office (12/3/75).

Major D.C.J. Goodban, MA, Ministry of Defence (12/3/75).

Jane Jones, Senior Information Officer, Age Concern, Mitcham, Surrey (16/7/75).

Ray Lamb, Secretary, Educational Centres Association (8/4/75).

A. Sanders, General Secretary of the National Adult School Union (25/3/75).

B   Unpublished Material

Blumer, J.G. *The effects of long-term residential adult education in post-war Britain, with particular reference to Ruskin College, Oxford,* University of Oxford, D Phil thesis, 1961.

Blyth, J.A. *A Comparison of the Development of Liberal Education through the Extra-Mural Departments of the Universities of Leeds, Liverpool and Manchester with that provided by two Ontario Universities 1914-1958,* University of Liverpool, PhD thesis, 1974.

Bonnor, J. *The British Labour Party: a study of Labour cabinet ministers,* University of Liverpool, MA thesis, 1954.

Cleaver, M.J.S. *A century of University Extension on Merseyside 1870-1970,* Dissertation for the Department of Extension Studies, University of Liverpool, 1971, pp.1-50.

Coates, T.H. *The measurement of Adult Interests,* University of London, PhD. thesis, 1950.

Elsley B. *Leisure and Learning in Voluntary Organisations,* University of Liverpool, MA thesis, 1972.

Green, Monica M. *The Leisure Challenge,* Dissertation for the Department of Extension Studies, University of Liverpool, 1971.

Haldane, I.R. *Workers' Education: a psychological survey,* London University PhD thesis, 1962.

Harvey, Peter John *The Working Men's Club Movement and Adult Education – an example of a Lancashire CIU Club,* University of Manchester MEd Degree, 1975.

Hughes, A.M. *Some problems of the short-term adult residential colleges in post-war Britain,* University of Liverpool MA thesis, 1954.

King, Edmund James *The Relationship between Adult Education and Social Attitudes in English Industrial Society,* University of London PhD thesis, 1955.

Linscott, M.P. *The educational work of the Sisters of Notre Dame in Lancashire since 1850,* University of Liverpool MA thesis, 1959.

Moran, James Edward *The Royal Army Educational Corps,* University of Liverpool MEd thesis, 1970.

Moss, Peter D. *Educational Ideas in England in the Second World War, 1938-1948,* University of Durham MEd thesis, 1967.

O'Neill, H.S. *Towards a Theology of Education,* University of Nottingham, PhD thesis, 1954.

Owen, Carol A. *The Content of Newspapers in Relation to Readership and Newspapers,* University of Liverpool MA thesis, 1965.

Parry, Cyril *Socialism in Gwynedd 1900-1920,* University of Wales PhD thesis, 1967.

Pashley, B.W. *Role Definition and Fulfilment in English Adult Education: a study of certain aspects of University and working class adult education, 1900-1950,* University of Liverpool MA thesis, 1966.

Travis, Keith *Adult Education for Polish Immigrants,* Dissertation for the Department of Extension Studies, University of Liverpool, 1971.

Turner, D.M. *A study of the Home Tuition of Asian Women Immigrants in West Yorkshire,* University of Liverpool PhD thesis, 1977.

Whittaker, D.J. *The Slödj System: a Scandinavian contribution to Education with special reference to Britain,* University of Liverpool MA thesis, 1965.

Worthington, G.G. *Clubs for Elderly People,* University of Liverpool MA thesis, 1955.

C Published Material

A Second Chance: Further Education in Multi-Racial Areas, London, Community Relations Commission, March 1976, pp.3-134.

Aberg, F.A. *An Analysis of Extra-Mural Courses in the Leeds University Area, 1961-72,* Leeds University, 1975, pp.1-48.

Abrahart, B.W. "What Was Their Background?" *Adult Education,* XXIV (3), Winter 1951, pp.215-221.

Adam, Sir R. *Problems in Adult Education,* Birbeck College, 1956, pp.1-19.

Adler, Max K. 'The Silent Revolution'. *The Political Quarterly,* XX, 1949, pp.146-153.

Adult Education: a plan for development, Report of a Committee of Enquiry appointed by the Secretary of State for Education and Science under the Chairmanship of Sir Lionel Russell (HMSO) pp.1-310.

Adult Education in Sweden, Stockholm, The Swedish Institute, 1978, pp.1-4.

Advisory Council for Adult and Continuing Education, 1979, Report: *A Strategy for the Basic Education of Adults,* Leicester, pp.1-107.

Aiach, Pierre and Willmott, Peter "Inequality, and education in the East End of Paris", *New Society,* 9 October 1975, pp.79-81.

Albu, Austen "The Member of Parliament, The Executive and Scientific Policy", *Minerva, 2,* 1963-64, pp.1-20.

Alexander, W. Boyd. "England's New Seven. An American View", *The New University* (edited by John Lawler), London, Routledge and Kegan Paul, 1968, pp.27-48.

Allaway, A.J. *Adult Education in England: a brief history,* Vaughan College, Leicester, revised edition 1957, pp.1-46.

Allaway, A.J. *The Educational Centres Movement: a Comprehensive Survey,* NIAE, 1961, pp.1-99.

Allaway, A.J. *Challenge and Response, WEA East Midland District 1919-1969,* Nottingham, WEA East Midland District, 1969, pp.1-131.

Allen, V.L. *Trade Union Leadership: Based on a study of Arthur Deakin,* London, Longmans, Green and Co., 1957, pp.1-336.

Anonymous "The Early Church: What really happened", *Adult Education, 52* (1), May 1979, pp.23-26.

Armstrong, J.R. "Liberal Adult Education in Rural Areas", *Adult Education,* XXV, 1952-3, pp.56-62.

Armytage, W.H.G. *Civic Universities: Aspects of a British Tradition,* London, Ernest Benn Ltd., 1955, pp.11-328.

Attlee, C.R. *The Social Worker,* London, G. Bell & Sons Ltd., 1920, pp.1-286.

Axford, Roger W. *Adult Education: the Open Door,* Scranton, Pennsylvania, International Textbook company, 1969, pp.1-247.

Bailey, J. *The British Co-operative Movement,* London, Hutchinson, 1955, pp.1-178.

Baker, W.P. *The English Village,* London, Oxford University Press, 1953, pp.1-224.

Barker, Edwin "Dr. Basil A. Yeaxlee, 1883-1967" *Adult Education,* 40 (4) November 1967, pp.249-50.

Barker, Rodney "The Labour Party and education for socialism" *International Review of Social History,* XIV, 1969, pp.22-53.

Barker, Rodney *Education and Politics 1900-51: A study of the Labour Party,* Oxford, Clarendon Press, 1972, pp.1-173.

Barr, John "Free Time Britain" *New Society,* 15 April 1965, pp.5-7.

Bartlett, James "Education needs more Showmen" *Adult Education,* XVII (3), March 1945, p.134.

Bayliss, F.J. "The Future of Trade Union Education" *Adult Education,* XXXII (2), Autumn 1959, pp.109-115.

Belson, W.A. *Television and the Family,* London BBC, Audience Research Dept., 1959, pp.1-131.

Bermant, Chaim *Troubled Eden: An Anatomy of British Jewry,* London, Vallentine, Mitchell, 1969, pp.1-274.

Beveridge, W.E. "How Worthwhile is Retirement?" *New Society,* 3 June 1965, pp.14-16.

Blythe, Ronald *Akenfield: Portrait of an English Village,* Harmondsworth, Penguin Books Ltd., 1975 (6th edition), pp.13-336.

Bonacina, Franco "Sociological motivations and cultural prospects of permanent education" *Permanent Education,* Strasbourg, Council of Europe, 1970, pp.433-451.

Bonham-Carter, Victor *The English Village,* Harmondsworth, Penguin Books, 1951, pp.15-249.

Bowen, F. Watson "The Cambridgeshire Village College a Cultural Centre for Rural Life" *Rural Education: Aspects of Education,* 17 (Editor P.W. Warner), The University of Hull Institute of Education, 1973, pp.98-110.

Bragg, Melvyn *Speak for England,* London, Book Club Associates, 1976, pp.1-504.

Brand, Carl F. *The British Labour Party: A Short History,* Stanford, California and London, Stanford University Press, 1965, pp.1-340.

Brech, Ronald *Britain 1984: Unilever's Forecast,* London, Darton, Longman and Todd Ltd., 1963, pp.1-124.

Briggs, A. "The New Society" *Highway,* 48, April 1957, pp.164-168.

Briggs, Asa "W.E.A. Retrenchant" *The Times Educational Supplement,* Friday, 4 April 1958, p.543.

Briggs, Asa *Education for a Changing Society,* London, WEA 1960, pp.3-12.

Briggs, Asa "George Douglas Howard Cole (1889-1959)" *D.N.B. 1951-1960* (Editors: E.T. Williams and Helen M. Palmer), London, Oxford University Press 1971.

Briggs, Asa "Welfare State" *Dictionary of the History of Ideas,* IV (Editor: Philip S. Wiener), New York, Charles Scribner's Sons, 1973, pp.509-515.

Briggs, John "Should the elderly have special educational provisions? — the problem discussed" *Age Concern Education in Retirement* Mitcham, Age Concern, 1974, pp.13-14.

British Broadcasting Corporation *The B.B.C. Looks Ahead,* London, BBC, 1958, pp.1-16.

Broadcasting Committee 1949 Report, London, HMSO, 1951, pp.1-335.

Brogan, D.W. "Gilbert Charles Harding (1907-1960)" *D.N.B. 1951-1960,* (Editors: E.T. Williams and Helen M. Palmer), London, Oxford University Press, 1971, pp.455-456.

Brook, G.L. *The Modern University,* London, André Deutch, 1965, pp.7-192.

Brown, Ivor "The Economics of the Book Trade" *Lloyds Bank Review,* July 1972, 105, pp.34-44.

Brown, Michael Barratt "In Defence of the W.E.A." *Adult Education,* 44 (3), September 1971, pp.151-160.

Brown, Michael Barratt "Adult Education and the Liberal Tradition" *Essays on Socialist Humanism,* (Editor: Ken Coates), Nottingham, Spokesman Books, 1972, pp.139-145.

Bruen, Noel "Oldham — Immigrants' Needs and Experience" *Education for Adult Immigrants* (Edited by A.K. Stock and D. Howell), London, National Institute of Adult Education, 1976, pp.17-31.

Buckland, D.C. "The Education of Travelling Children" *Trends in Education,* 1977, Spring Issue, pp.16-20.

Bullock, a. "The Universities and Adult Education" *Summer Highway,* 44, May — September 1952, pp.1-7.

Burgess, Tyrrell "The Open University" *New Society,* 27 April 1972, pp.176-178.

Burgess, Tyrrell *Education after School,* Harmondsworth, Penguin Books, 1977, pp.11-256.

Burrows, John *University Adult Education in London. A century of Achievement 1876-1976,* University of London, 1976, pp.1-122.

Butler, R.A. "Education: The View of a Conservative" *The Year Book of Education 1952* (Editors: J.A. Lauwerys and R. Hans), London, Evans Brothers Ltd., 1952, pp.42-63.

Cain, John "Recurrent Education and the Mass Media: educational television and radio" *After Fifty Years – the Future,* London, BBC, December 1974, pp.16-28.

Caine, Sir Sydney "Education as a factor of production" *Lloyds Bank Review,* April 1964, 72, pp.1-16.

Cairncross, Sir Alec *Learning to Learn,* Glasgow, University of Glasgow Publications, 1972, pp.5-16.

Cannon, Geoffrey "The Arts in Society: You're sick, daddy" *New Society,* 25 April 1963, p.25.

Carpenter, L.P. *G.D.H. Cole an Intellectual Biography* London, Cambridge University Press, 1973, pp.1-271.

Carter, Charles "Not Enough Higher Education and Too Many Universities?" *The Three Banks Review,* September 1979, 123, pp.3-21.

Cassirer, Henry R. "Adult Education in the era of Modern Technology" *Convergence,* III (2), 1970, pp.37-44.

Cecil, David "Sir Henry Maximilian (Max) Beerbohm (1872-1956)" *D.N.B. 1951-1960* (Editors: E.T. Williams and Helen M. Palmer), London, Oxford University Press, 1971, pp.77-79.

Champion, *Alan Pilgrim's Progress Boston 1945-1975: 30 years of University Adult Education in a Market Town,* Boston, Richard Kay, 1976, pp.11-60.

Charnley, Alan "Education in Retirement" *Age Concern Education in Retirement,* Mitcham, Age Concern, 1974, pp.3-16.

Charnley, A.H. and Jones, H.A. *The Concept of Success in Adult Literacy,* Cambridge, Huntington Publishers Ltd., 1979, pp.1-200.

Citizen Centres for Adult Education (Foreward by Sir Richard Livingstone), London, Educational Settlements Association, 1943, pp.3-24.

Clegg, H.A. and Adams, R. *Trade Union Education,* London, WEA, 1959, pp.1-162.

Clunie, James "N.C.L.C. History" *Plebs,* XLVI, (10), October 1952, p.238.

Clyne, Peter *The Disadvantaged Adult: Educational and Social Needs of Minority Groups,* London, Longman Group Ltd., 1972, pp.3-147.

Cole, G.D.H. "What Workers' Education Means" *Highway,* Volume 44, October 1952, pp.2-11.

Cole, G.D.H. *An Introduction to Trade Unionism,* London, Allen and Unwin, 1953, pp.1-324.

Cooper, Lord (Editor) *Training and Education,* London, General and Municipal Workers' Union, 1966, pp.3-20.

Co-operative Independent Commission Report Manchester, Co-operative Union, Manchester, 1960, pp.1-84.

Cohn, Fannie M. "Why Labour Education?", *Plebs,* LI, (7-9), July — September, 1954, p.177.

Coleman, Francis *Social Action in Television,* London, Independent Broadcasting Authority, 1975, pp.1-77.

Corfield, A.J. *Epoch in Workers' Education,* London, WEA, 1969, pp.1-272.

Cowan, Peter "Communications" *Urban Studies,* Six, (3), 1969, pp.436-446.

Craick, William W. *Central Labour College,* London, Lawrence and Wishart, 1964, pp.9-192.

Cross, K.P. *Beyond the Open Door: New Students to Higher Education,* San Francisco, Jossey-Bass Inc., 1971, pp.1-218.

Cross, K. Patricia and Jones, J. Quentin "Problems of Access" *Explorations in Non-Traditional Society,* San Francisco, Jossey-Bass Inc., 1972, pp.39-63.

Cross, K. Patricia "New forms for New Functions", *Lifelong Learners - A New Clientele for Higher Education* (Editor: Dyckman W. Vermilye), San Francisco, Jossey-Bass Publishers, 1975, pp.86-92.

Culbertson, David J. "Corporate Role in Lifelong Learning" *Lifelong Learners – A New Clientele for Higher Education* (Editor: Dyckman W. Vermilye), San Francisco, Jossey-Bass Publishers, 1975, pp.29-33.

Curtis, S.J. and Boultwood, M.E.A. *An Introductory History of English Education since 1800,* London University Tutorial Press Ltd., 1962 (second edition). pp.1-404.

Davis, Lane "British Socialism and the Perils of Success" *Political Science Quarterly,* 69, 1954, pp.502-516.

317

Dent, H.C. *Growth in English Education 1946-52*, London, Routledge and Kegan Paul, 1954, pp.1-220.

Dickson, H.D. "Education with Social Relevance" *Highway*, 50, March 1959, pp.136-7.

Dobinson, Charles H. "Adult Education in England and Wales" *Education Outlook*, 29 (March 1955), pp.101-110.

Dodd, Peter "Who Goes to Church?" *New Society*, 29 April 1965, p.22.

Doermann, Humphrey *Toward Equal Access*, New York College Entrance Examination Board, 1978, pp.1-143.

Dosanjh, J.S. *Punjabi Immigrant Children: their social and educational problems in adjustment*, University of Nottingham Institute of Education, (n.d.), pp.3-44.

Driver, Christopher *The Exploding University*, London, Hodder and Stoughton, 1971, pp.11-379.

Dudley, D.R. *The Department of Extra-Mural Studies of the University of Birmingham: a Survey of New Developments, 1945-1955*, Nottingham, University of Nottingham, pp.1-26.

Duke, C. and Marriott, S. "Social Science and Adult Education" *Studies in Adult Education*, 1 (2), October 1969, pp.117-139.

Duke, Christopher *Recurrent Education (Policy and Development in OECD Member Countries) Australia*, Paris, Organisation for Economic Co-operation and Development, 1974, pp.7-93.

"Education for Awareness: a talk with Paulo Freire" *Risk*, 6 (4), 1970, pp.6-17.

Edwards, Donald *Local Radio*, London, BBC, 1968, pp.3-14.

Ellwood, Caroline *Adult Learning Today: a New Role for the Universities*, London and Beverly Hills, Sage Publications, 1976.

Elsey, Barry "Voluntary organisations and informal adult education" *Adult Education*, Volume 46, Number 6, March 1974, pp.391-396.

Elvin, H.L. *Education and Contemporary Society*, London, C.A. Watts, 1965, pp.1-144.

Evans, David "Writers' workshops and adult education in the inner city" *International Journal of University Adult Education*, XIII (3), November 1979, pp.41-54.

Everly, Jack C. "The Evaluation of Continuing Education via T.V." *Mass Media and Adult Education* (Editor: John A. Neimi), New Jersey, Educational Technology Publications, 1971, pp.80-94.

Experiments in Dutch Adult Education, Amersfoort, Netherlands Centre for Adult Education and the European Bureau of Adult Education, 1977, pp.1-98.

Ferriman, Annabel "Open University benefits by local collaboration" *Times Higher Education Supplement*, 239, 21 May, 1976.

Field, Frank *Unequal Britain: a report on the cycle of Inequality*, London, Arrow Books, 1973, pp.7-64.

318

Fisher, N.G. "The Brains Trust as a Method of Adult Education" *Adult Education*, XVIII (2), pp.46-57.

Floud, Jean "The Educational Experience of the Adult Population of England and Wales as at July 1949" *Social Mobility in Britain* (edited by D.V. Glass), London, Routledge and Kegan Paul Ltd., 1954, pp.98-140.

Fogarty, Michael P. *Forty to Sixty: How We Waste the Middle Aged.* London, Centre for Studies in Social Policy, 1975, pp.7-250.

Fordham, Paul; Poulton, Geoff; Randle, Lawrence *Learning Networks in Adult Education: Non-formal education on a Housing Estate,* London, Routledge and Kegan Paul, 1979, pp.3-250.

Forster, W. *The Higher Education of Prisoners,* Vaughan Paper 21, Department of Adult Education, University of Leicester (n.d.), pp.1-32.

Francis, Dai "Payments to Tutors" *Plebs,* XLV (2), February 1953, p.45.

Francis, Dai "Dai Dan Evans (1898-1974)" *Llafur,* 1, (3), May 1974, p.3.

Frankena, William K. "Education" *Dictionary of the History of Ideas, Volume II,* (Editor: Philip P. Wiener), New York, Charles Scribner's Sons, 1973, pp.71-85.

Fraser, Sir Robert "Television and Progress" (An address to the Third Advertising Conference of the Indian Society of Advertisers in New Delhi, 30 September 1966) in *Independent Television Authority Notes 10,* October 1966, London ITA, pp.1-11.

Freeson, Reginald "The Right University of the Air" *New Society,* 7 October 1965, pp.20-21.

Freire, Paulo "To the co-ordinator of a 'cultural circle'" *Convergence,* IV (1), 1971, pp.61-62.

Fullick, Leisha "Editorial" *The political papers: an irregular folder of papers concerned with the social and political aspects of adult and community education,* 6, London, City Lit, (1979), pp.1-2.

The Future of Sound Radio and Television (a short version of the Report of the Pilkington Committee), HMSO, 1962, pp.5-48.

Fyrth, Jim "Trade Union Education" *Labour Monthly,* 58 (2), February 1976, pp.82-85.

Gannicott, Ken *Recurrent Education: a preliminary cost-benefit analysis,* Australian Council for Educational Research, 1971, pp.7-21.

Garside, Donald "Short-Term Residential Colleges: Their Origins and Value" *Studies in Adult Education,* 1 (1), April 1969, pp.2-30.

Gillard, Frank "Radio Station in Every City" *The B.B.C. and Local Broadcasting,* January 1964, pp.3-11.

Gilliam, Laurence. "Sir George Reginald Barnes (1904-1960)" *D.N.B. 1951-1960* (Editors: E.T. Williams and Helen M. Palmer), London, Oxford University Press, 1971, pp.67-69.

Gillie, W.B. *A New University: A.D. Lindsay and the Keele Experiment,* London, Chatto and Windus, 1960.

Glass, D.V. (ed.) *Social Mobility in Britain,* London, Routledge and Kegan Paul, 1954, pp.1-420.

Glatter, Ron and Weddell, E.G. with the collaboration of Harris, W.J.A. and Subramanian, S. *Study by Correspondence,* London, Longman Group Ltd., 1971, pp.3-361.

Gould, Samuel B. "Prospects for Non-Traditional Study" *Explorations in Non-Traditional Study,* San Francisco, Jossey-Bass Inc., 1972, pp.1-11.

Green, E. *Adult Education: Why this Apathy?,* London, Allen and Unwin, 1953, pp.1-146.

Green, Ernest "Adult Education — Why this Apathy?" *Fundamental and Adult Education,* VII (1), January 1955, pp.38-43.

Greene, Sir H.C. *The B.B.C. and adult education,* London, BBC, 1961, pp.1-16.

Greene, Sir H.C. *The Third Floor Front: a view of broadcasting in the sixties,* London, Bodley Head, 1969, pp.1-43.

Groombridge, B. "New Objectives for Adult Education" *Adult Education,* XXX, 1957-8, pp.197-215.

Groombridge, B. *Education and Retirement,* London, NIAE, 1960, pp.1-160.

Groombridge, B. "Immigration: First Report to Mr. Foley" *Adult Education,* XXXVIII (6), March 1966, pp.405-12.

Groombridge, Brian "Adult Education and Broadcasting: Open Education" in *The Spirit and the Form: Essays in Adult Education in honour of Professor Harold Wiltshire* (Editor: Alan Rogers), University of Nottingham, Department of Adult Education, 1976, pp.41-46.

Guttsmun, W.L. "The British Political élite and the class structure" *Elites and Power in British Society* (Edited by Philip Stanworth and Anthony Giddens), Cambridge, Cambridge University Press, 1974, pp.22-44.

Haldane, Ian and Groombridge, Brian "Viewer Preferences — Adult Education Television, February 1969" (pp.68-94) in *Needs and Interests of the Adult Community in the United Kingdom,* 1969, BBC Independent Television, pp.1-94.

Haley, Sir W.J. "The Place of Broadcasting" *The B.B.C. Quarterly,* 11 (4), January 1948, pp.193-197.

Haley, William "Politics in the Television Age" *Times Literary Supplement,* 18 March 1977, pp.286-288.

Halloran, J.D. *Mass Communication Research and Adult Education,* University of Leicester, Department of Adult Education, 1969, pp.1-75.

Halsey, A.H. "Higher Education" *Trends in British Society since 1900: a Guide to the Changing Social Structure of Britain* (Editor: A.H. Halsey), London, Macmillan Press, 1972, pp.192-226.

Hanna, Ian "Adult Education Students" *Rewley House Papers, 1965-66,* Oxford, Rewley House, pp.14-43.

Harrington, Fred Harvey *The Future of Adult Education,* San Francisco, Jossey-Bass Publishers, 1977, pp.1-238.

Harris, Dave and Holmes, John "Open to Martha, closed to Mary" *Times Educational Supplement,* 14 February, 1975.

Harris, Sewell "Community Centres in New English Housing Estates" *Fundamental and Adult Education,* VI (1), January 1954, pp.27-31.

Harrison, J.F.C. *A History of the Working Men's College 1854-1954* London, Routledge and Kegan Paul, 1954, pp.1-235.

Harrison, J.F.C. "The W.E.A. in the Welfare State" in *Trends in English Adult Education* (Ed: S.G. Raybould), London, William Heinemann Ltd., 1959, pp.1-29.

Harrison, J.F.C. *Learning and Living 1790-1960,* London, Routledge and Kegan Paul, 1961, pp.3-420.

Hartnett, Rodney T. "Non-Traditional Study: an Overview" in *Explorations in Non-Traditional Study,* San Francisco, Jossey-Bass Inc., 1972, pp.12-38.

Haugh, W.S. "Public Libraries in Crisis" *The Municipal Review,* January 1967, p.21 and p.58.

Haviland, R. Michael "An Introduction to the Writings of Paulo Freire" *Adult Education,* 45(5), January 1973, pp.280-285.

Hawkridge, D.G. "The open university's role in a democracy" *Schriftelijk onderwijs en externe democratisering,* Leiderdorp, de Leidse 'Onderwijsinstellingen, 1974, pp.67-76.

Hazleton, W. *Maes-yr-Haf, 1927-1952,* Trealaw, Maes-yr-Haf Settlement, 1952, pp.1-14.

Hempel, Sandra "Wealthier areas still dominate the Open University" *The Times Higher Educational Supplement,* 4 August 1978, 351, p.28.

Heycock, Wyndham "Summer School in Barry" *Adult Education,* 39 (1), May 1966, pp.21-24.

"George Hicks" *Plebs,* XLVI (8), August 1954, p.197.

Higgins, G.M. and Richardson, J.J. *Political Participation,* Occasional Publications Monograph 3, London, The Politics Association, 1976, pp.3-30.

Hill (Lord) of Luton "Mass Communications and Education" (an address at the Annual Conference of the National Institute of Adult Education at Cambridge, 11th September 1966) in *Independent Television Authority Notes 9, September 1966,* London, ITA, pp.1-7.

Hilton, Anthony "The Economics of the Theatre" *Lloyds Bank Review,* July 1971, 101, pp.26-38.

Hinden, Rita "The N.C.L.C. at Scarborough" *Plebs,* XLVI (7), July 1954, pp.161-166.

Hinden, Rita "Homage to a Socialist" *Plebs,* XLVII (1), January 1955, pp.6-8.

Hoggart, Richard "What Shall the W.E.A. Do?" *Highway,* 44, November 1952, pp.46-53.

Hoggart, Richard *the Uses of Literacy,* London, Chatto and Windus, 1957, pp.1-319.

Hoggart, Richard "The use of Television" *Encounter,* XIV, 1960, pp.38-45.

Hoggart, Richard *After expansion: A time for diversity, the Universities into the 1990's,* Leicester, The Advisory Council for Adult and Continuing Education, 1978, pp.3-12.

Hohenberg, John *Free Press/Free People: The Best Cause,* New York, The Free Press, 1973, pp.1-423.

Hollis, Christopher "William John Brown (1894-1960)" *D.N.B. 1951-1960* (Editors: E.T. Williams and Helen M. Palmer), London, Oxford University Press, 1971, pp.151-152.

Hopper, Earl and Osborn, Marilyn *Adult Students: Education Selection and Social Control,* London, Frances Pinter, 1975, pp.9-187.

Hordley, Irene and Lee, D.J. "The Alternative Route — Social Change and Opportunity in Technical Education" *Sociology,* 4, 1970, pp.23-50.

Horrabin, J.F. and W. *Working-Class Education,* London, Labour Publishing Co., 1924, pp.1-93.

Horwell, G. "The W.E.A. past, present and future" *The Tutors' Bulletin,* Autumn 1950, pp.7-11.

Horwood, T. "A New University College" *Universities Quarterly,* 2, 1947, pp.77-81.

Houghton, Vincent and Richardson, Ken (Editors) *Recurrent Education: a plea for Lifelong Learning,* London, Ward Lock Educational in conjunction with The Association for Recurrent Education, 1974, pp.1-137.

Houle, Cyril, O. *The Inquiring Mind,* Madison, The University of Wisconsin Press, 1961, pp.3-87.

Houle, Cyril O. *The External Degree,* San Francisco, Jossey-Bass Publishers, 1973, pp.1-214.

Hughes, J. Elwyn "Welsh hill farmer" *The Open University Opens* (Edited by Jeremy Tunstall), London, Routledge and Kegan Paul, 1974, pp. xiii + 191.

Hughes, Margaret E. "Educating Women" *Adult Education,* 46 (3), September 1973, pp.166-169.

Hunter, M. "Village College" *Adult Education,* XXX, 1960-1 pp.310-14.

Hutchins, Robert M. *The Learning Society,* London, Pall Mall Press, 1968, pp.3-142.

Hutchinson, Edward "The Reality of Adult Education" *New Society,* 15 September 1966, pp.407-408.

Hutchinson, Enid "Counselling — needs to be met " *Adult Education,* 42 (1), 1969, pp.29-38.

Hutchinson, Enid "Few Women at the Top" *Adult Education,* 1971, 43/44, pp.241-4.

Hutchinson, Enid and Edward *Learning Later: Fresh Horizons in English Adult Education.* London, Routledge and Kegan Paul, 1978, pp.1-200.

Iliffe, A.H. "Are sixth-formers old enough for University?"*The Times Educational Supplement,* July 11th, 1969.

Illich, I. *Deschooling Society,* New York, Harper and Row, 1971, pp.1-116.

Ingle, Stephen J. "The Political Writings of H.G. Wells" *Queen's Quarterly,* 81, 1974, pp.396-411.

Jacks, M.L. *Total Education,* London, Routledge and Kegan Paul, 1946, pp.1-168.

Jacks, M.L. *The Education of Good Men,* London, Gollancz, 1955, pp.1-192.

Jackson, John Archer *The Irish in Britain,* London, Routledge and Kegan Paul, 1963, pp.1-208.

Jackson, J.A. *Neither Fish, Flesh, Fowl nor Good Red Herring*, (New Lecture Series 58), Belfast, The Queen's University, 1971, pp.3-22.

Jamieson, G.H. "Age, Speed and Accuracy: A Study in Industrial Retraining" *Occupational Psychology*, 1946, pp.237-242.

Janne, Henri in collaboration with Roggemans, Marie-Laure *New Trends in Adult Education: Concepts and Recent Empirical Achievements*, Paris, UNESCO, 1972, pp.1-30.

Janne, Henri *Colloquy on the Integration of Adult Education within a Framework of Permanent Education*, Strasbourg, Council of Europe, 1977, pp.1-43.

Jasper, R.C.D. "George Kennedy, Allen Bell (1883-1958)" *Dictionary of National Biography, 1951-1960* (Editors: E.T. Williams and Helen M. Palmer), London, Oxford University Press, 1971, pp.80-82.

Jeffreys-Jones, T.I. "Unearthing hidden talents" *Adult Education*, 40, (1), May 1967, pp.26-9.

Jeffreys, M.V.C. *Glaucon: an Inquiry into the Aims of Education*, London, Pitman, 1950, pp.1-183.

Jenkins, Peter "Unions: What makes the Leaders Tick?" *New Society* (3) 18 October 1962, pp.9-12.

Jennings, Hilda *University Settlement Bristol: Sixty Years of Change 1911-1971*, Bristol, University Settlement Bristol Communicy Association, 1971, pp.5-64.

Jessup, F.W. "Post-war Developments in Adult Education in Kent" *Adult Education*, XXIV (2), Autumn 1951, pp.91-97.

Jessup, F.W. (ed) *Adult Education toward Social and Political Responsibility* Hamburg, UNESCO Institute for Education, 1953, pp.1-144.

Jessup, F.W. "Trends and Resources" *Adult Education*, XXX, 1957-8 pp.167-80.

Jessup, F.W. "Adult Education in England and Wales" *Adult Education in 1961* (Edited by E.M. Hutchinson), London, NIAE, 1961, pp.1-9.

Jessup, F.W. "The Idea of Lifelong Learning" *Lifelong Learning: a Symposium on Continuing Education* (edited by F.W. Jessup), Oxford, Pergamon Press Ltd., 1969, pp.14-31.

Joad, C.E.M. *About Education*, London, Faber, 1945, pp.1-172.

Jocher, Herbert "The future shape of permanent education" *Permanent Education*, Strasbourg Council of Europe, 1970, pp.487-509.

Johnson, Carol "Book Reviews" *The Political Quarterly*, Vol. xvii, 1946, p.126.

Jones, H.A. "Four Terms a Year" *Adult Education*, XXXVII (5), January 1965, pp.245-250.

Jones, H.A. *Education and Disadvantage*, University of Leicester, Department of Adult Education, (Vaughan Paper 22), 1977, pp.1-18.

Jones, H.A., and Glynn, D.R. "Student Wastage", *Adult Education*, 40, (3), September 1967, pp.139-149.

Joselin, A.G. "Pioneering in adult education" *Adult Education,* 42 (4), November 1969, pp.215-225.

Kay, Barbara *Live and Learn: the story of Denman College 1948-1969,* London, National Federation of Women's Institutes, 1970, pp.9-128.

Kelly, T. *Adult Education in Liverpool: a Narrative of Two Hundred Years,* Liverpool University Extra-Mural Department, 1960, pp.1-48.

Kelly, T. *A History of Adult Education in Great Britain,* Liverpool University Press, 1962, pp.1-368.

Kelly, Thomas (ed) *A Select Bibliography of Adult Education in Great Britain,* London, National Institute of Adult Education, 1962 (second edition), pp.1-126.

Kelly, T. "In partibus transmarinis" *Adult Education,* 40 (2), July 1967, pp.115-116.

Kelly, Thomas *Adult Education at the Cross-roads,* Liverpool University Press, 1969, pp.1-20.

Kelly, Thomas (ed) *A European Bibliography of Adult Education,* London, National Institute of Adult Education, 1975, pp.1-67.

Kelly, Thomas and Stephens, Michael D. "Research in Adult Education in Great Britain" *Convergence,* IV (4), 1971, pp.33-38.

Kendall, Michael "Those who failed — the Further Education of Former Students" *Universities Quarterly,* 18 (14), September 1964, pp.398-406.

Kent: *Further Education Scheme,* Maidstone, 1948, pp.1-132.

Kidd, J.R. *How Adults Learn* New York, Association Press, 1959, pp.1-324.

Kidd, J.R. *Learning and Society,* Montreal, Canadian Association for Adult Education, 1963, pp.1-414.

Kidd, J.R. *The implications of continuous learning,* Toronto, Gage, 1966, pp.1-122.

Kidd, J.R. *Education for Perspective,* New Delhi and Toronto, Indian Adult Education Association and Peter Martin Associates Ltd., 1969, pp.3-369.

Knowles, Malcolm *The Adult Learner: a Neglected Species,* Houston, Gulf Publishing Company, 1973, pp.1-198.

Knowles, R.A.S. *The Summer School of English 1904-64,* University of London, Department of Extra-Mural Studies, 1964, pp.3-18.

Kogan, Maurice (ed). *The Politics of Education,* Edward Boyle and Anthony Crosland in conversation with Maurice Kogan, Harmondsworth, Penguin Books, 1971, pp.1-208.

Kojecký, Roger. *T.S. Eliot's Social Criticism,* London, Faber and Faber, 1971, pp.9-255.

Korner, S. "Extra-mural Experiences" *Adult Education,* 41 (4), November 1968, pp.249-252.

Krajne, Ana "The Future of Yugoslav Adult Education depends upon Further Research" *Convergence,* IV (4), pp.55-60.

Kreps, J. *Non-traditional students: the case of Mrs. Smith*, Paper prepared for a meeting of the Commission on Academic Affairs, American Council on Education, Washington, DC, May 16-17, 1971.

Kulich, Jindra *The Role and Training of Adult Educators in Poland*, Center for Continuing Education, The University of British Columbia, Vancouver, Canada, Occasional Papers in Continuing Education, 6, March 1971, pp.3-32.

Kulich, Jindra, Bron-Wojciechowska, Arnieszka *Training of Adult Educators in East Germany*, Department of University Extension, The University of British Columbia, Vancouver, Canada Occasional papers in Continuing Education, 4, December 1969, pp.1-23.

Kulich, Jindra, Bron-Wojciechowska, Agnieszka *The Polish Folk High Schools*, Center for Continuing Education, The University of British Columbia, Vancouver, Canada, Occasional Papers in Continuing Education, 17, December 1978, pp.1-18.

Lambert, R.S. *"New Horizons in Educational Broadcasting" The Political Quarterly*, XVII, 1946, pp.343-353.

Langford, Glenn "The concept of Education" in *New Essays in the Philosophy of Education* (edited by Glenn Langford and D.J. O'Connor), London and Boston, Routledge and Kegan Paul, 1973, pp.3-32.

Laslett, P. "Learning from television" *Twentieth Century*, 172 (1019), Autumn 1963, pp.58-66.

Lawrence, S. "The Pattern of Police Training" *The Municipal Review*, September 1966, p.506.

Lawson, K.H. *Philosophical Concepts and Values in Adult Education*, (Revised Edition) Milton Keynes, The Open University Press, 1979, pp.7-120.

Lee, Terence "Unrealism in Adult Education Centres" *New Society*, 14 April 1966, p.20, based on the article in *The British Journal of Education Psychology*, 36, (1), p.100.

Lees, Dennis (Professor) and Chiplin, Brian "The Economics of Industrial Training" *Lloyds Bank Review*, April 1970, 96, pp.29-41.

Legge, A.J.W. "Katesgrove House — a collective experiment in helping the disadvantaged" *Adult Education*, 46 (6), March 1974, pp.377-382.

Legge, C.D. "Facts and Figures in Further Education — the place of the Responsible Bodies" *Adult Education*, XXVL, 1953-4, pp.269-75.

Legge, C.D. (ed) *Guide to Studies in Adult Education*, annually for the years 1953-60, London, NIAE, 1954-60.

Legge, C.D. "Book Reviews" *Studies in Adult Education*, 1 (1), April 1969, pp.84-87.

Lengrand, Paul "Adult Education" *Fundamental and Adult Education*, X, 1958, pp.91-100.

Lengrand, Paul "Lifelong Education" *International Bulletin of the Leidsche Onderwijsin-stellingen*, Leiderdorp, (Holland), January 1971, p.11.

Lengrand, Paul *An Introduction to Lifelong Education*, London and Paris, Croom Helm and The UNESCO Press, 1975, pp.1-156.

Livingstone, R.W. *Leadership in Education* (Walker Trust Lectures on Leadership X), London, Oxford University Press, 1950, pp.3-25.

Livingstone, R.W. *The Rainbow Bridge and Other Essays on Education,* London, Pall Mall Press, 1959, pp.3-176.

Livingstone, Sir Richard *The Future in Education,* London, Cambridge University Press, 1941, pp.1-127.

Livingstone, Sir Richard *Education for a World Adrift,* London, Cambridge University Press, 1943, pp.1-158.

Livingstone, Sir Richard *Plato and Modern Education* (The Rede Lecture 1944), London, Cambridge University Press, 1944, pp.5-36.

Livingstone, Sir Richard *Some Tasks for Education,* Toronto, Oxford University Press, 1946, pp.3-98.

Livingstone, Sir Richard *Some Thoughts on University Education,* London, National Book League, 1948, pp.7-28.

Livingstone, Sir Richard *On Education,* London, Cambridge University Press, 1954, pp.3-232.

Livingstone, Sir Richard *Thoughts on the Education of Character* (The Second Vaughan Memorial Lecture) Doncaster, Parish Church/Grammar School, 1954, pp.3-13.

Llywelyn-Williams, Alun "Welsh in Adult Education and Life Today" *Adult Education,* XXXII (4), Spring 1960, pp.287-290.

Long, Joyce R. *Universities and the General Public,* University of Birmingham, 1968, pp.9-128.

Lovett, Tom *Adult Education Community Development and the Working Class,* London, Ward Lock Educational, 1975, pp.9-176.

Lowe, John *Adult Education in England and Wales: a Critical Survey,* London, Michael Joseph, 1970, pp.13-356.

Lowe, John "Research priorities in Adult Education in Developing Countries" *Convergence,* IV (4), 1971, pp.78-83.

Lowndes, G.A.N. *The Silent Revolution: an account of the expansion of Public Education in England and Wales, 1895-1935,* London, Oxford University Press, 1937, pp.1-286.

Lund, Ragnar (Ed). *Scandinavian Adult Education,* Copenhagen, Det Danske Forlag, 1949, pp.7-303.

MacArthur, B. "Open University needs ten years to prove itself" *Times,* 22 July 1969, p.9.

Macdonald, Gerard "Why an open college must be different" *Times Higher Education Supplement,* 26 May 1978, p.10.

Mack, Joanna "The Polytechnics' unhappy birthday" *New Society,* 22 January 1976, pp.156-159.

Maclure, S. "Whither Britain's New Universities" *Listener,* 2 February 1967, p.158.

Maddison, J. *New Trends in Educational Technology and Industrial Pedagogy,* Antwerp, (Belgium), International Audio-Visual Technical Centre Foundation, 1971.

Males, Stewart, S. "A Mobile Teaching Unit for Gypsy Children" *Trends in Education,* 1977 Spring Issue, pp.16-20.

Malone, E.W.F. "The W.E.A. — a New Phase" *Adult Education,* XXXIII, 1960-1, pp.78-82, 116-21.

Mansbridge, Albert "Ideals as Facts" *The Way Out* (Edited by Oliver Stanley), London, Oxford University Press, 1923, pp.68-83.

Mansbridge, Albert *The Kingdom of the Mind: Essays and Addresses* (Edited by Leonard Clark), London, J.M. Dent and Sons Ltd., 1944, pp.xix + 200.

Marshall, R.L. *Co-operative Education,* Manchester, Co-operative Union, 1948, pp.1-21.

Marshall, R.L. "Co-operative Education" *Plebs,* XLV (8), August 1953, pp.176-179.

Marwick, Arthur "The Open University" *Listener,* 83, 12 March 1970, pp.329-31.

Matthews, Tony and Cooke, Dan "The Contribution of Educational Broadcasting" in *Education for Adult Immigrants,* (edited by A.K. Stock and D. Howell), London, National Institute of Adult Education, 1976, pp.35-38.

Maud, John (Sir) "The Future of Education",*The Listener,* XLI, 10 February 1949, pp.224-225.

Maurice, Frederick Denison *Learning and Working* (with introduction by W.E. Styler, editor), Oxford University Press for University of Hull, 1960, pp.v + 178.

McIntosh, Naomi E. "Open admission — an open or revolving door" *Universities Quarterly,* 29 (2), Spring 1975, pp.171-181.

McIntosh, Naomi E. "A comprehensive system of education for adults" *World Year Book of Education 1979: Recurrent Education and Lifelong Learning* (Edited by Tom Schuller and Jacquetta Megarry), London and New York, Kogan Page Ltd. and Nichols Publishing Company, 1979, pp.244-256.

McIntosh, Naomi E. and Woodley, A. "The Open University and Second Chance Education — An analysis of the Social and Educational Background of Open University Students" *Paedagogica Europaea,* 9 (2), 1974, pp.85-100.

McLeish, J. "The Philosophical Basis of Adult Education" *The University of Leeds Institute of Education Researches and Studies",* 11, January 1965, pp.65-74.

McLuhan, Marshall *Understanding media – the extensions of man,* London, Routledge and Kegan Paul, 1964, pp.1-359.

McPhee, A. *A Short History of Extra-Mural Work at Liverpool University,* Liverpool, The Department, 1949, pp.1-18.

Mee, Graham and Wiltshire, Harold *Structure and Performance in Adult Education,* London and New York, 1978, pp.1-127.

Metcalfe, George and Houlton, Robert "Popular Culture Courses: A Frontier in Adult Education" *Scottish Journal of Adult Education,* 3 (1), Autumn 1977, pp.15-20.

Michaels, Ruth "New Opportunities for Women Courses" *Adult Education,* 1972, 44/5, p.327.

Millar, J.P.M. "Educational on Three Year Tutorials" *Plebs,* XLIV (1), January 1952, p.5.

Millar, J.P.M. "The N.C.L.C. at Scarborough" *Plebs,* XLIV (8), August 1952, pp.171-174.

Millar J.P.M. "Chaos or Order in Trade Union Education" *Plebs,* XLIV (8), August 1952, p.183.

Millar, J.P.M. "The Truth about Education" *Plebs,* XLIV (11), November 1952, pp.247-248.

Millar, J.P.M. "Some Tips on Literature Selling" *Plebs,* XLV (1), January 1953, p.14.

Millar, J.P.M. "Labour's Poor Vote" *Plebs,* XLV (1), January 1953, p.13.

Millar, J.P.M. "Leeds University and the Giraffe" *Plebs,* XLV (3), March 1953, pp.56-57.

Millar, J.P.M. "Come, Come, Comrade Cole!" *Plebs,* XLV (6), June 1953, pp.138-139.

Millar, J.P.M. "The N.C.L.C. in Conference" *Plebs,* XLV (7), July 1953, pp.153-156.

Millar, J.P.M. "Is the W.E.A. Changing its Policy?" *Plebs,* XLVII (2), February 1954, pp.43-48.

Millar, J.P.M. "Not mentioned" *Plebs,* XLVI (3), March 1954, pp.75-76.

Millar, J.P.M. "News of the Movement" *Plebs,* XLIV, (2), February 1952, p.40; XLIV (3), March 1952, p.64; XLV (2), February 1953, p.47; XLVI (7), July 1954, p.175; XLVI (8), August 1954, pp.197-199; XLVI (12), December 1954, pp.292-295; XLVII (1), January 1955, pp.21-23; XLVII (3), March 1955, pp.67-71; XLVII (6), June 1955, pp.140-143; XLVII (11), November 1955, pp.159-263.

Millar, J.P.M. "The N.C.L.C. Conference at Scarborough" *Plebs,* XLVI (7), July 1954, pp.161-166.

Millar, J.P.M. "Letters" *Plebs,* XLVI (11), November 1954, p.266.

Millar, J.P.M. "Two N.C.L.C. Personalities" *Plebs,* XLVII (1), January 1955, pp.18-19.

Millar J.P.M. "Architect of Victory" *Plebs,* XLVII, (1), January 1955, p.20.

Millar J.P.M. "Life without Pink Forms" *Plebs,* XLVII (5), May 1955, pp.106-107.

Millar, J.P.M. "Notts Miners' School" *Plebs,* XLVII (10), October 1955, p.234.

Millar, J.P.M. "The N.C.L.C. Conference at Scarborough" *Plebs,* XLVII (10), October 1955, pp.228-231.

Millar, J.P.M. and Fyrth, Jim "Correspondence: Trade Union Education" *Labour Monthly,* 58 (5), May 1976, pp.230-231.

Millar J.P.M. "The N.C.L.C. invades Blackpool " *Plebs,* XLVIII (7), July 1956, pp.159-162.

Millar, J.P.M. "British Muddle in Trade Union Education" *Plebs,* XLVIII (8), August 1956, pp.178-179.

Millar, J.P.M. "The Austrian Trade Unionist Pays Up" *Plebs,* XLVIII (9), September 1956, pp.193-196.

Millar, J.P.M. "Hats off to Danish Trade Unionists" *Plebs*, XLIX (4), April 1957, p.84.

Millar, J.P.M. "What's Wrong with Trade Union Education" *Plebs*, XLIX (8), August 1957, pp.170-173.

Millar, J.P.M. *The Labour College Movement*, London, NCLC Publishing Society Ltd., (no date), pp.iv + 301.

Millar, G.W. *Success, Failure and Wastage in Higher Education*, London, Harrap and Co. Ltd., 1970, pp.10-264.

Ministry of Education Pamphlet No 28. Evening Institutes, HMSO, 1956, pp.1-54.

Mobbs, Michael C. *Meeting their Needs: An Account of Language Tuition Schemes for Ethnic Minority Women*, London, Community Relations Commission, April 1977, pp.3-64.

Morris C.R. "The Aims and Content of Adult Education" *Adult Education*, XVIII (2), December 1945, pp.85-92.

Morris, H. *The Village College Being a Memorandum on the Provision of Educational and Social Facilities for the Countryside, with Special Reference to Cambridgeshire*, Cambridge University Press, 1925 (reprint), pp.1-28.

Morris, J. "The development of the Third Programme, its influence on the cultural life of Great Britain and on international cultural exchange" *Cultural Radio Broadcasts*, (Reports and papers on mass communication 23), Paris, UNESCO, 1956, pp.18-21.

Morris, Mary "Voluntary Work Today" *New Society* 25 April 1963, pp.15-17.

Morris P.W. "The Role of the County College of Agriculture in the Rural Community" *Rural Education Aspects of Educatin*, 17 (Editor P.W. Warner), The University of Hull Institute of Education, 1973, pp.98-110.

Morrison, Rt. Hon. Herbert "Commercial Television: The Argument Examined" *Political Quarterly*, XXIV, 1953, pp.338-344.

Musgrave, P.W. *The Sociology of Education*, London, Methuen and Co. Ltd., 1972 (second edition), pp.17-367.

Musgrove, F. "Personal Problems in the Learning Environment" *Educational Research*, 10 (3), 1968, pp.235-238.

Moser, C.A. *Survey Methods in Social Investigation*, London, Heinemann, 1967, (seventh edition), pp.1-352.

National Institute of Adult Education *Social Aspects of Further Education: a survey of Local Education Authority Action*, London, NIAE, 1952, pp.1-59.

Neamtu, Octavian and Topa, Leon "Adult Education in Romania" *Society and Leisure*, V (2), 1973, European Centre for Leisure and Education, pp.81-93.

Newsham, D.B. *The Challenge of Change to the Adult Trainee*, London, HMSO 1969, pp.111 + 39.

Newton, J. *Burton Manor: the First Ten Years*, The College, 1958, pp.1-20.

Nicholson, J.H. "Adult Education" in *Chamber's Encyclopaedia*, 1, Oxford, Pergamon Press, 1967, pp.83-90.

Nilsen, A.B. "They organise their own updating" *Training for Progress*, 9, 1970, Geneva, ILO Office.

Nollen, Stanley 'The Current State of Recurrent Education' *Relating Work and Education: Current Issues in Higher Education 1977* (Edited by Dyckman W. Vermilye), San Francisco, Jossey-Bass Publishers, 1977, pp.65-78.

Normann, E. De. "George Ernest Hicks (1879-1954)" *D.N.B. 1951-1960* (Editors: E.T. Williams and Helen M. Palmer), London, Oxford University Press, 1971, p.474.

Oriel, John "Too Many Learned Societies" *New Scientist*, 7 April 1960, pp.854-856.

Orwin, C.S. "Albert Mansbridge (1876-1952)" *D.N.B. 1951-1960* (Editors: E.T. Williams and Helen M. Palmer), London, Oxford University Press, 1971, pp.686-688.

O'Toole, James *Work Learning and the American Future*, San Francisco, Jossey-Bass Publishers, 1971, pp.1-238.

Page, David "Against Higher Education for Some" *Education for Democracy* (Editors: David Rubinstein and Colin Stoneman), Harmondsworth Penguin Books, 1970, pp.213-214.

Palfrey, C.F. "After a Year" *Adult Education*, 39 (4), November 1966, pp.223-226.

Park, Trevor "Trade Union Education" *Trade Union Register* (edited by Ken Coates, Tony Topham, Michael Barratt Brown), London, The Merlin Press, 1969, pp.96-100.

Parkyn, George W. *Towards a conceptual model of life-long education*, Paris, UNESCO, 1973, pp.3-54.

Pashley, B.W. *University Extension Reconsidered*, Leicester, University of Leicester, Department of Adult Education, 1968, pp.1-71.

Paterson, W. "Education for Social Adjustment" *Adult Education*, 42 (1), May 1969, pp.25-28 and p.38.

Pavitt, L.A., Reed, R.A., Guest, J.T., Marshall, R.L. *Co-operative Education*, Loughborough, Co-operative Union Limited (n.d.) pp.1-242.

Pear, T.H. *English Social Differences*, London, George Allen and Unwin, 1955, pp.1-318.

Peers, R. "Adult Education and the Needs of Democracy" *Adult Education*, X, 1937-8, pp.208-18.

Peers, R. "The Future of Adult Education" *Adult Education*, XXV (2), Autumn 1952, pp.87-95.

Peers, R. *Adult Education: a Comparative Study*, London, Routledge and Kegan Paul, 1958, pp.1-139.

Peers, R. *Fact and Possibility in English Education*, London, Routledge and Kegan Paul, 1963, pp.x + 180.

Penguins Progress 1935-1960, Harmondsworth, Penguin Books, 1960, pp.7-82.

Perry, Sir Walter "Development at the Open University" *Higher Education alternatives* (Edited by Michael D. Stephens and GordonW. Roderick), London and New York, 1978, pp.127-138.

Peterson, A.D.C. *A Hundred Years of Education,* London, Duckworth, 1952, pp.1-272.

Pickering, Sally "The Late Starters" *New Society,* 20 January, 1966, pp.17-19.

Powell, Rachel *Possibilities for Local Radio,* Centre for Contemporary Cultural Studies, Birmingham University, 1965, pp.3-22.

Pratt, John and Burgess, Tyrrell *Polytechnics: a Report,* London, Pitman Publishing, 1974, pp.1-250.

Prosser, Roy "What is Adult Education?" *Mass Education* (Edited by Lars-Olof Edström, Renée Erdos and Roy Prosser), Stockholm, The Dag Hammarskjöld Foundation, 1970, pp.23-47.

Pyke-Lees, Celia and Gardiner, Sue *Elderly Ethnic Minorities,* Mitcham, Age Concern, 1974, pp.3-18.

Quednau, H.W. "Prepare for Change" *Training for Progress,* 9, 1970, Geneva ILO Office, pp.3-7.

Rasmussen, Werner, "The concept of permanent education and its application" *Permanent Education,* Strasbourg, Council of Europe, 1970, pp.419-430.

Raybould, S.G. *The Approach to W.E.A. Teaching,* London, WEA, 1947, pp.1-28.

Raybould, S.G. *University Standards in W.E.A. Work,* London, WEA, 1948, pp.1-34.

Raybould, S.G. *The W.E.A. - The Next Phase,* London, WEA, 1949, pp.1-120.

Raybould, S.G. *The English Universities and Adult Education,* London, WEA, 1951, pp.1-188.

Raybould, S.G. Voluntary Responsible Bodies in English Adult Education. *British Journal of Educational Psychology,* 1, 1952-3, pp.143-53.

Raybould, S.G. "Adult Education in Transition" *Political Quarterly,* XXVIII, 1957, pp.243-53.

Raybould, S.G. (ed) *Trends in English Adult Education,* London, Heinemann, 1959, pp.1-272.

Rees, Christopher and Edmunds, Philip Turnbull "Acacia Avenue and Coronation Street" *Adult Education,* 44 (3), September 1971, pp.161-164.

Rhodes, G. "Labour and the Young Professionals" *Socialist Commentary,* May 1962, p.12.

Richardson, William (Sir) *The C.W.S. in War and Peace, 1938-1976,* Manchester, Co-operative Wholesale Society Ltd., 1977, pp.1-399.

Richmond, W. Kenneth *The Literature of Education: A Critical Bibliography 1945-1970,* London, Methuen & Co. Ltd., 1972, pp.1-206.

Richmond, W. Kenneth "The Concept of Continuous Education" *Scottish Journal of Adult Education,* 3 (1), Autumn 1977, pp.5-9.

Robinson, John (ed) *Educational Television and Radio in Britain: a new phase in Education,* London, British Broadcasting Corporation, 1966, pp.7-292.

Robinson, John "Adult Education and Broadcasting — fifty years of co-operation" *Adult Education,* 47 (4), November 1974, pp.226-231.

Rodgers, Brian "Leisure and Recreation" *Urban Studies,* 6 (3), 1969, pp.368-384.

Rogers, Jennifer *Adults Learning,* Harmondsworth, Penguin Books, 1971, pp.7-222.

Rose, E.J.B. and associates *Colour and Citizenship: a Report on British Race Relations,* London, Oxford University Press, 1969, pp.1-815.

Saunders, J.W. *University of Leeds Adult Education Centre, Middlesbrough, Cleveland, Annual Report 1977/78,* pp.1-7.

Saunders, J.W. *University of Leeds Adult Education Centre, Middlesbrough, Cleveland, Annual Report 1978/79,* pp.1-10.

Saunders, J.W. *University of Leeds Adult Education Centre, Middlesbrough, Cleveland, Annual Report 1979/80,* pp.1-11.

Schwartz, Bertrand "A prospective view of permanent education" *Permanent Education,* Strasbourg, Council of Europe, 1970, pp.47-72.

Scott, Drusilla *A.D. Lindsay, a Biography,* Oxford, Basil Blackwell, 1971, pp.1-437.

Scrimgeour, Cecil *Fifty Years A-Growing: A History of the North Staffordshire District, the Workers' Educational Association 1921-1971,* Hanley, WEA North Staffs, District, 1973, pp.1-130.

Scupham, John "The Media of Mass Communication" *Lifelong Learning: a Symposium on Continuing Education,* Oxford, Pergamon Press Ltd., 1969, pp.91-105.

Selby, David "Should the Elderly have special educational provisions — the problems discussed" *Age Concern Education in Retirement,* Mitcham, Age Concern, 1974, pp.7-10.

Seymour, D. "Re-training for Technological Change" *Personnel Management* (Journal of the Institute of Personnel Management), 48 (378), December 1966, pp.183-190.

Shaw, Roy "The Open University" *Adult Education,* 41, November, 1968, p.213-20.

Shaw Roy, "Universities and the W.E.A.: myths and reality" *Adult Education,* 44 (1), May 1971, pp.7-13.

Silver, Harold "Education and public opinion" *New Society,* 7 December 1978, pp.576-578.

Silvey, Robert and Emmett, Brian "What makes Television Viewers Choose" *New Society,* 24, 14 March 1963, pp.11-14.

Simpson, J.A. "Education for family life" *Adult Education,* 40 (6), March 1968, pp.352-356.

Simpson, J.A. "Permanent Education and Community Development" *Permanent Education,* Strasbourg, Council of Europe, 1970, pp.343-370.

Spencer, F.H. "A Scholar Wasted: a Study of Alfred Williams" *Adult Education,* XVIII (1), September 1945, pp.30-37.

Spoor, Alec *White-Collar Union: Sixty Years of NALGO* London, Heinemann, 1967, pp.1-625.

Sherman, H.C. *Adult Education for Democracy*, London, WEA, 1944, pp.1-95.

Shearman, H.C. *Education – the New Horizon*, London, Nicholson and Watson, 1948, pp.1-128.

Stanford, E.C.D. "The Churches Educate Adults" *Adult Education*, XXXIV, 1961-2, pp.54-7.

Stapleton, G. Brian "Co-operation — a View from the Centre" *Adult Education*, XXXVII (1), May 1964, pp.14-16.

Stead, Peter *Coleg Harlech: The First Fifty Years*, Cardiff University of Wales Press, 1977, pp.1-129.

Stephens, Michael and Roderick, Gordon (eds) *Teaching Techniques in Adult Education*, Newton Abbot, David and Charles, 1971, pp.1-206.

Stephens, Michael and Roderick Gordon "Adult Education and the Communicy University" *Adult Education*, 45 (3), September 1972, pp.138-142.

Stephens, Michael D. and Roderick, Gordon W. (eds) *Universities for a Changing World: the Role of the University in the late Twentieth Century* Newton Abbot, David and Charles, 1975, pp.5-221.

Still, Elizabeth "The Middle Class Takes Over" *New Society*, 7 April 1966, pp.20-21.

Stocks, Mary *The Workers' Educational Association: the First Fifty Years*, London, George Allen and Unwin Ltd., 1953, pp.9-157.

Stocks, Mary *My Commonplace Book*, London, Peter Davies, 1970, pp.1-246.

Styler, W.E. *Who were the Students?*, London, NIAE, 1950, pp.1-28.

Styler, W.E. "Written Work" *Tutor's Bulletin*, Autumn 1950, pp.3-7.

Styler, W.E. *Questions and Discussions*, London, WEA (Study Outline 21), 1952, pp.5-30.

Styler, W.E. "The W.E.A.'s Best" *Adult Education*, XXII, 1959-60, pp.192-6.

Styler, W.E. "Fifty years of Adult Education" *Roscoe Review*, 1975, Department of Extra-Mural Studies, University of Manchester 1974/5, pp.1-13.

Tawney, R.H. "Mr. E.S. Cartwright" *The Highway*, October 1950, pp.13-14.

Taylor, Lord of Mansfield *Uphill all the way: a miner's struggle*, London, Sedgwick and Jackson, 1972, pp.1-193.

Taylor, Richard and Pritchard, Colin "CND twenty years on" *New Society*, 3 July 1980, pp.15-16.

Taylor, Robert "Schooling the Unions" *New Society*, 4 September 1975, pp.521-2.

Technical and Further Education in Australia, April 1974, Vol. 1. The Parliament of the Commonwealth of Australia 1974, Canberra, The Government Printer of Australia, 1975, pp. iii-xlvii + 1-129.

Tenth Annual Report, University of Leeds Extra-Mural Department, (A Review of ten years' work), University Department, 1956, pp.1-32.

Terrill, Ross *R.H. Tawney and His Times: Socialism as a Fellowship*, Cambridge, Massachusetts, Harvard University Press, 1973, pp. 3-373.

Thomas, John "Alfred Zimmern — an Appreciation" *Rewley House Papers*, III (VI), 1957-58, pp.3-6.

"Thomism for Modern Man" *Times Educational Supplement*, Friday, February 7, 1958, p.199.

Thomson, David "Our Changing Universities" *Listener*, XLI (1041), 13 January 1949, pp.45-46.

Thomson, J. Michael "Half Way to a Motorized Society" *Lloyds Bank Review*, 102, October 1971, pp.16-34.

Thompson-McCausland, L.P. "The Working Men's College" *Adult Education*, 45 (6), March 1973, pp.360-363.

Thornton, A.H. "Day-Release for Liberal Studies" *Adult Education*, XXIX, 1956-7, pp.197-204.

Thornton, A.H. "Liberal Studies for Factory Workers" *Adult Education*, XXXIII (1), May 1960, pp.13-15 and p.30.

Tomlinson, George "Debate (July 31, 1947)" *Parliamentary Debates Commons 1946-47*, 441, columns 647-743.

Trade Union Committee *Statement submitted at the Invitations of the Trade Union Congress in connection with consideration of the 1957 Congress Motion calling for a co-ordinated educational policy with affiliated unions and other educational bodies*, 1959, pp.1-23.

Trades Union Congress Annual Reports from 1945 to 1970 (especially Reports for 1954, 1955, 1959-61 and 1978).

Turner, H.A. "The N.C.L.C. the W.E.A., and the Unions: an Enquiry" *Plebs*, XLIV (1) January 1952, pp.16-19.

Tylecote, M. *The Future of Adult Education*, London, Fabian Society, 1960, pp.1-32.

Vaizey, John and Sheehan, John *Resources for Education: an Economic Study of Education in the United Kingdom, 1920-1965*, London, George Allen and Unwin Ltd., 1968, pp.1-176.

Valley, John R. "External Degree Programmes" in *Explorations in Non-Traditional Study*, San Francisco, Jossey-Bass Inc., 1972, pp.95-128.

Venables, Peter "The Open University and the future of continuing education" *Recurrent Education and Lifelong Learning World Year Book of Education 1979*, (edited by Tom Schuller and Jacquetta Megarry). London/New York, Kogan Page and Nichols Publishing Company, 1979, pp.271-284.

Viklund, B. *Trade Union Educational Work*. Stockholm, Swedish Trade Union Confederation 1969, pp.3-38.

Waller, R.D. *Learning to Live*, Art and Educational Publishers, 1946, pp.1-63.

Waller, R.D. *Residential College Origins of the Lamb Guildhouse and Holly Royde*, Manchester, Manchester University Press, 1954, pp.1-59.

Waller R.D. "Challenge and Response in Adult Education: the Established Tradition" *Adult Education*, XXVII (3), Winter 1954, pp.173-181.

Waller R.D. "Teaching Aims in Adult Education" *Adult Education*, XXXI, 1958-9, pp.251-2.

Wand, J.W.C. "College, School and the W.E.A." *The Times Educational Supplement*, Friday, March 7, 1958, p.367.

Watkins, Alan *The Liberal Dilemma*, London, Macgibbon and Kee, 1966, pp.9-158.

"W.E.A. Retrenchant" *The Times Educational Supplement*, Friday, 4 April, 1958, p.543.

Weddell, E.G. "The Next Phase" *Adult Education*, XXXVIII, (3), September 1965, pp.119-123 and p.132.

Weddell, E.G. *Broadcasting and Public Policy*, London, Michael Joseph, 1968, pp.7-370.

Welch, Edwin "The Prehistory of the University Tutorial Class" *History of Education Society Bulletin*, 17, Spring 1976, pp.39-44.

Wilcox, A. "Community Centres — the Consumers' View" *Adult Education*, XXV, 1952-3, pp.101-11.

Williams, C.R. *The South Wales District of the Workers' Educational Association, 1907-1957*, Cardiff, WEA, 1957, pp.1-24.

Williams, J.E. "An Experiment in Trade Union Education" *Adult Education*, XXVII, 1954-5, pp.113-24.

Williams, Shirley *Robbins Plus Twenty - Which Way for Higher Education?* London, Birbeck College, 1977, pp.3-22.

Williams, T.G. "Adult Education as I knew It" *Adult Education*, XXVII (4), Spring 1955, pp.257-272.

Williams, W.E. "Arts Festivals" *Adult Education*, XXVII (1), Summer 1955, pp.63-69.

Williams, W.E. *The Penguin Story*, Harmondsworth, Penguin, 1956, pp.1-124.

Williams, W.E. "Public Patronage of the Arts" *New Society*, 16 May 1963, p.25.

Wilson, Valerie "Escape from the Doll's House? Women and Adult Education" *Scottish Journal of Adult Education*, Autumn 1977, 3 (1), pp.21-27.

Wiltshire, H.C. "Adult Education: Way and Purpose — a Review" *Scottish Journal of Adult Education*, December 1958, 24, pp.5-9.

Wiltshire, H.C. "Giving Adult Education a Home" *Adult Education*, XXXII (2), Autumn 1959, pp.109-115.

Wiltshire, H.C., Brooks, F.R., Dickinson, L., Huckle, F.T., Marsden, J.J., Moore, G.R. "A Profile of Ten Evening Institutes" *Adult Education*, XXXVII (3), September 1964, pp.113-116.

Woodburn, Arthur "From Tory College to Impartial Trust" *Plebs*, XLVI (4), April 1954, pp.84-86.

Workers' Education in Sweden, Stockholm, Arbetarnas, Bildingsförbund (n.d.), pp.1-16.

Workers' Educational Association, Aspects of Adult Education, 1960, pp.1-83.

Wooton, Graham *Pressure Groups in Britain: 1720-1920,* London, Allen Lane, 1970, pp.1-375.

Yeaxlee, B.A. *Lifelong Education,* London, Cassell, 1929, pp.1-168.

Young, M. *The Rise of the Meritocracy,* London, Thomas and Hudson, 1958, pp.1-160.

Zubrzycki, Jerzy *Polish Immigrants in Britain: a study of adjustment,* The Hague, Martinus Nijhoff, 1956, pp.3-219.

Zweig, Ferdynand. *The British Worker.* Harmondsworth, Penguin Books, 1952, pp.7-243.

D   Articles on Adult Education in The Welsh Language from the WEA Magazine 'Lleufer'

Davies, Ruby "Yr Arloeswr: John Davies", *Lleufer,* VII (4), Winter 1954, pp.175-178.

Eames, Aled "Tri Adroddiad ar Addysg", *Lleufer,* XV (4), Winter 1959, pp.185-190.

Evans, David "y Mudiad yn y De", *Lleufer,* 1 (4), Winter 1945, pp.29-31; *Lleufer,* II (1), Spring 1946, pp.31-34.

Guy, D.T. "O'r Swyddfa yng Nghaerdydd", *Lleufer,* X (1), Spring 1954, pp.39-40.

Jones, E.J. "Oedran y Myfyrwyr", *Lleufer,* IX (3), Autumn 1953, pp.129-132.

Lewis, Gwyn Illtyd "Gair o Ddenmarc" *Lleufer,* II (4), Winter 1946, pp.13-137.

Lewis, Gwyn, I. "Y Co-op ac Addysg Pobl Mewn Oed", *Lleufer,* III (4), Winter 1947, pp.133-35.

Lewis, Gwyn I. "Tro i'r Iseldiroedd", *Lleufer,* VI (2), 1950, p.44.

Lloyd, D. Tecwyn "Yr Athro a'i Ddosbarth", *Lleufer,* VI (3), Autumn 1950, pp.141-146.

Owen, T. Jones "Dosbarth Lerpwl", *Lleufer,* III (4), Winter 1947, pp.137-138.

Roberts, T. Lloyd "Bachu Pobl i'r W.E.A.", *Lleufer,* III (3), October 1947, pp.101-102.

Thomas, C.E. "Tudalen y Trefnydd", *Lleufer,* III (3), October 1947, p.103; "Gair o Rhoslas", *Lleufer,* VII (1), Spring 1951, pp.37-38; X (1), Spring 1954, pp.37-38.

Thomas, David "Nodiadau'r Golygydd", *Lleufer,* III (4), Winter 1947, pp.109-110.

Williams, C.R. "Addysg i Gymdeithas sy'n Newid." *Lleufer,* XV (4), Winter 1954, pp.185-190.

Index

Broadcasting

315; by BBC 2, 180; television programmes - *Panorama,* 181, 236; *Nine O'Clock News,* 181, 237; *Nationwide,* 190, 236; *Tonight,* 190, 236; *Mastermind,* 237; BBC Wales - *Heddiw,* 190; Independent Television Programmes - *This Week,* 181; *News at Ten,* 181, 237; *World in Action,* 220, 236; HTV Harlech - *Y Dydd,* 190.

Co-operative Movement, 7, 30, 80, 94-98, 123; Co-operative College (Loughborough), 94-5, 120, 274; consumer education, 95-96; education for leadership, 96; local societies, 96-97; recreational adult education, 96; sectional and national organisation, 97; social and co-operative studies, 96; the adult auxiliaries, 96; the organisation for co-operative education, 96; evaluation of the Co-operative Movement education, 97-98, 317, 327.

348

355

273; Essex, 165, 170, 273; Exeter, 165, 169; Glasgow, 169; Hull, 22, 165; Keele, 11, 133, 165, 168-9, 172, 177, 273; Kent, 165; Lancaster, 170, 273; Leeds, 75, 168-9, 172, 174-5; Leicester, 6, 165, 172-4, 273, 295; Liverpool, 3, 14, 168-9, 172, 174, 259; Loughborough, 166, 273; Manchester, 54, 168-9, 173; Newcastle, 168-9, 172; Nottingham, 165, 168-9, 177, 191; Oxford, 169, 171, 300; Reading, 120, 167; Salford, 166, 274; Sheffield, 294, 300; Southampton, 6, 165; Surrey, 166, 274; Sussex, 165, 169, 170, 177, 273; Warwick, 165, 170, 273; York, 165, 177, 273

University of Wales, 167, 169, 174; Aberystwyth, 174; Swansea, 174

University of the air, 49;

University lectures, 167-170;

Extra Mural Departments of, Birmingham, 98, 318; Bristol, 133; Cambridge, 107, 109; Durham, 98, 133, 155; Hull, 101, 103, 133, 175; Liverpool, 133, 259-61, 307, 312, 327; London, 133-4, 175, 233, 324; Nottingham, 98, 103, 105, 133, 175, 200; Sheffield, 98, 133; Southampton, 133; of Wales, Aberystwyth, 175, 209; Bangor, 133, 209; Cardiff, 135, 231; Swansea, 133, 174;

Extra-Mural Department's teaching, 15, 21-2, 40-1, 53-5, 57, 134-5, 173, 175-8, 191, 225, 259, 281-2, 284, 294, 301

and adult education, 165-178

University of Leeds Adult Education Centre, Middlesbrough, 332

Vaizey, John	294, 334
Valey, John R.	334
Vaughan College, Leicester	131, 173, 314, 323
Venables, Peter	49, 276, 334
Vermilye, Dyckman W.	317, 330
Vienna	79
Vietnam	261
Viklund, B.	334
Village Colleges	205-7
Vocational training	59-60, 176
Vrooman, Walter	71
Wakefield	173
Walbottle	147
Wales	279
Walker, A.P.	165
Wallasey	264
Waller, R.D.	54, 72, 334-5
Walton, G.E.	77
Walton (Liverpool)	263
Wand, J.W.C.	20, 335
Warbey, William	74
Ward, J.	109
Ward, Sheila	vii
Warner, P.W.	315
Waterloo (Merseyside)	264
Watkins, Alan	335
Watson, Sam	74, 82
Waugh, Evelyn	45
Webb, Beatrice	100 .
Webster, Rev. Mary	221-2
Weddell, E.G.	40, 67, 290, 292, 303, 309, 320, 335
Week-end Schools	77-8, 88, 107, 110, 113-4, 117, 121, 123-5, 132
Weighell, Sidney	310
Welch, Edwin	99, 335

358